1634399

S0-BIW-290

BREVARD COMMUNITY COLLEGE
MELBOURNE CAMPUS LIBRARY
3865 N. WICKHAM ROAD
MELBOURNE, FL 32935

Mysticism in Judaism, Christianity, and Islam

DATE DUE

JAN 0 5 2009

GAYLORD   PRINTED IN U.S.A

Mysticism in Judaism, Christianity, and Islam

Searching for Oneness

Ori Z. Soltes

ROWMAN & LITTLEFIELD PUBLISHERS, INC.
Lanham • Boulder • New York • Toronto • Plymouth, UK

ROWMAN & LITTLEFIELD PUBLISHERS, INC.

Published in the United States of America
by Rowman & Littlefield Publishers, Inc.
A wholly owned subsidiary of The Rowman & Littlefield Publishing Group, Inc.
4501 Forbes Boulevard, Suite 200, Lanham, Maryland 20706
www.rowmanlittlefield.com

Estover Road
Plymouth PL6 7PY
United Kingdom

Copyright © 2008 by Rowman & Littlefield Publishers, Inc.
First paperback edition 2009

All rights reserved. No part of this publication may be reproduced, stored
in a retrieval system, or transmitted in any form or by any means, electronic,
mechanical, photocopying, recording, or otherwise, without the prior permission
of the publisher.

British Library Cataloguing in Publication Information Available

Library of Congress Cataloging-in-Publication Data

Soltes, Ori Z.
  Mysticism in Judaism, Christianity, and Islam : searching for oneness / Ori Z. Soltes.
    p. cm.
  Includes bibliographical references and index.
  1. Mysticism. 2. Mysticism—Islam. 3. Mysticism—Judaism. I. Title.
  BL625.S63 2008
  204'.22—dc22   2008007145

  ISBN-13: 978-0-7425-6276-9 (cloth : alk. paper)
  ISBN-13: 978-0-7425-6277-6 (pbk. : alk. paper)
  ISBN-13: 978-0-7425-6588-3 (electronic)

Printed in the United States of America

©™ The paper used in this publication meets the minimum requirements of American
National Standard for Information Sciences—Permanence of Paper for Printed Library
Materials, ANSI/NISO Z39.48-1992.

For my brothers, Eyton Shalom and Marnin Judah,
and my sisters, Dafna Gina Rahel and Michal Rena:
each, differently, has taught me about the *mysterion*.

Contents

Preface and Acknowledgments

My intention in writing this book is not to presume to deepen the supply of insightful scholarship on any one of the three primary modes—Jewish, Christian, and Muslim—of mysticism in what might be called the Abrahamic traditions. My intention, rather, is threefold. The primary intention has been to offer a discussion that juxtaposes the mystical expressions of all three traditions in a coherent and accessible, yet fairly detailed, manner. Thus, an astute reader can appreciate how these three mystical traditions derive from both general and specific shared sources, as well as where and why they diverge from each other. The literature of discussion and analysis in each of the three is large; the literature of comparison between any two of them is much sparser; that which offers all three in a straightforward chronological and conceptual manner is virtually nonexistent.

So, one might say that I hope to introduce my readers to the aesthetics of a trifocal conceptual viewpoint, and I am counting on them to dig deeper in each direction by way of the bibliography, which is also intended to offer stepping-off points and not completeness. My second intention has been to offer a basis for understanding the mystical intention and process offered in any number of times and places with a slightly different twist. I have been at pains, as the reader will see within the first few pages of the introduction, to expose the problematic of language, among other ways, by turning from the standard vocabulary pair, "sacred" and "profane," to their Latin antecedents, *sacer* and *profanus*. I do this both because those antecedents have different nuances from their English descendants, and it is the earlier nuances that are essential to religion in general and to mysticism in particular, and because the unfamiliarity with those antecedents should force the reader to pause for a moment every time those terms are used, where she or he would more likely glide too easily past or through the English terms.

Thus, the use and lengthy discussion of *sacer* and *profanus* is intended to underscore both the problematic of language and, by emphasizing the ambiguities of the *sacer* even in the Abrahamic context, to underscore the paradoxical and problematic nature of the mystical quest. My third intention is to argue that that quest not only assumes varied specific forms across history, both within each of the Abrahamic traditions and across and beyond them all, but that what drives that quest never dies out. Thus, even in a modern, "secular" age, we find the mystical inquiry manifest and variously expressed. This is so not only in overt modes of continuing to develop aspects of the Abrahamic mystical traditions from past to present. It is so in various indirect modes, from rearticulating the mystical sensibility in apparently nonreligious—and yet spiritual—terms, to utilizing issues and ideas from the Abraham traditions in various literary, visual, or cinematic forms.

But one can only appreciate these last-named sorts of efforts if one is familiar with some of the rudiments of the traditions from which works in these different artistic forms draw their content. Thus, the brief push in these directions at the end of my narrative grows out of my overriding intention to suggest links both in the vertical sense, from the beginnings of mystical thinking in the Abrahamic traditions to the present day, and in the horizontal sense, across these traditions and across a range of disciplines in which, in the contemporary world, one may discern the imprint of the mystical impulse and the proof of an ongoing need to connect to the hiddenmost recesses of the One assumed by all three traditions to have created us.

This book is the result of four distinct, yet interwoven, experiences. I was first asked to teach a course on Jewish mysticism at Siegal College in Cleveland, Ohio (at that time known as the Cleveland College of Jewish Studies). I thank both presidents under whom I served, Meir Ben-Horin and David S. Ariel, for offering me the opportunity to spread my intellectual wings in such an intriguing direction. Similarly, the Theology Department at Georgetown University has, over the past several years, encouraged the teaching of such a course, in which I began to expand the subject territory to encompass the rudiments of Christian and Muslim mysticism. I thank Tony Tambasco, then chairman of the department, who first encouraged a course perceived in many quarters to be somewhat off the undergraduate beaten track. Many of the questions that I have had to think about and which thinking has fed directly into this text have come from my students in my classes in both of these schools; they have helped me to expand my perceptions both within each of these traditions and across them.

I owe a debt, too, to the Smithsonian Institution and to both the 92nd Street YMHA and the American Institute for Mental Imagery, both in New York

City, under whose auspices I have been privileged to teach a number of seminars in a range of formats that have focused on mysticism in all three Abrahamic traditions. These were the seminars that truly pushed me to broaden and deepen my understanding in a trifocal direction in order to present the three traditions in tandem, along parallel and crisscrossing lines. Finally, my seven years as the director and curator of the B'nai B'rith Klutznick National Jewish Museum offered a number of opportunities to consider some of the ways in which contemporary artists have turned to the mystical tradition as a source of inspiration and visual energy. For those opportunities, I am grateful in particular to Janice Rothschild Blumberg, former chair of the museum board, who supported my efforts and pushed others to recognize that "Jewish" expression is often at its richest when its connection to other traditions, mystical and otherwise, is made manifest.

I thank Brian Romer, farseeing acquisitions editor at Rowman & Littlefield, for his interest in and strong support of this project; Sarah Stanton, associate editor, for her kind and careful attention to every detail from cover to cover; Elaine McGarraugh, production editor, for her meticulous oversight of so many copyediting issues; and my good friend Allison Archambault for her careful reading and insightful comments on the manuscript.

Most of all, I am indebted to Leslie, Brahm, and Nadav for never allowing me to stray so far into thinking about the *mysterion* within the *sacer* that I cannot find my way back to the *profanus*, with so many exquisite aspects of its own—of which they are three of the most wondrous.

Introduction

What Is Mysticism?

INTO THE REALM OF PARADOX: *SACER, PROFANUS,* AND *RELIGIO*

One might begin the inquiry into mysticism by noting the first problem that hampers the *process* of inquiry. For the instrument with which we inquire—that preeminent human instrument with which we engage so many aspects of the world around and beyond us—is *language*. And language is a paradox of sorts with regard to its usefulness as an instrument. It extends humans beyond other species in the complexity of ideational representation that it makes possible, but at the same time it is profoundly limited and limiting. No quantity or quality of words can perfectly capture the exquisite beauty of a sunset, which is why poets continue to write poems about sunsets down through the ages: If the perfect poetic portrait were ever painted, there would be little point in continuing to write about them. How much the more so do words fall short in expressing the love of a parent for his or her child: Love in general, and certainly parental love in particular, defies words, even as one wordsmith after another seeks to describe it.

These are two examples of aspects of our own world in the description and discussion of which words prove insufficient. How much the more so in the engagement of God, that is beyond our world and, in the Abrahamic traditions at least, understood to have engendered everything within it: How does one—how *can* one—describe and discuss God? How does one find God with words, when anything and everything one might say about or to God is necessarily said with a vocabulary drawn from our own limited human experience—however expansive both that vocabulary and that experience compared with whomever and whatever else resides within our world? How can one understand God, who resides in a fundamental way *outside* human experience—for God's is *divine* experience, and what is the vocabulary that God uses, derived from divine experience? The very notion of "vocabulary," the idea of "words," even if they are understood not to be human, in being referred to as "vocabulary" and "words," are notions and ideas derived from *us*. Does God *have* a vocabulary? Does God *use* words? Does God *speak*? With what physiological mechanism? Lips and tongue, pharynx and larynx?

In short, even in normative, mainstream religious thought, if and when we stop and think about it, the discussion of God and God's "speaking" to us, or speaking to us by "speaking" to and through prophets like Moses or Muhammad, is inherently problematic. The idea that we can describe God and therefore prescribe means of coming closer to God is informed by paradox. Can you come closer to that which is all around you and therefore already as close to you as your own breath—even as it is more distant than the most distant star? Yet that is what the mystic seeks to accomplish, and more. Our goal is to understand the goal of the mystics in the evolving Abrahamic traditions— what they seek to accomplish and how—and to explore what those we term "mystics" in those traditions have actually achieved with respect to those goals.

If the preceding three paragraphs should suggest that mysticism is a complex subject, the rest of this discussion will demonstrate that it is nonetheless an accessible one. To begin with—having accepted the problematic of language and temporarily put it aside, to be returned to again and again later on—an understanding of mysticism requires a grasp of the broad purposes of religion. Religion presupposes an opposition between the life of the everyday—the safely circumscribed, the familiar and knowable, the human—and a realm beyond the human, unknown and ultimately, in a most fundamental sense, unknowable, fraught with both hope and fear, with both positive and negative possibilities. That realm, so rigorously separated from the realm of the day-to-day, is referred to in English as the "sacred."

It is the province and purpose of religion not only to *address* that realm beyond the everyday but also to define how we should *understand* it. The word "religion" is a simple development of the Latin word *religio*, the root of which, *-lig-*, means a "binding" (one finds that root in "lig-aments," which bind muscle to bone, and "lig-atures," which bind up wounds, for example). *Religio* binds a community together with regard to its sense of the sacred. More precisely, since "re-" means "back" or "again," religion binds a community *back again* to the sacred realm that it assumes *created* it.

As we shall see as this discussion proceeds, an understanding of the opposition between the sacred and profane is better served by reference to the Latin antecedents of these terms: *sacer* and *profanus*. Whereas "sacred" and "profane" tend, particularly when juxtaposed with each other, to offer positive and negative connotations, respectively, it is critical to the understanding of religion in general and mysticism in particular to recognize the *intrinsic neutrality* of these terms and the concepts that they represented as they were originally used in Western vocabulary.[1] The Romans used the term *profanus,* meaning simply "before (i.e., outside) the temple/sanctuary," to refer to the realm of the *known* and the *safely circumscribed* in all its aspects: the community, daytime, awakeness, life—the realm, in time and space where things happen according to what we might term normal patterns of expectation. The *profanus* is that realm in which one o'clock is reliably followed by two o'clock, which is followed by three o'clock; where the distance between Cleveland and New York is different from that between Los Angeles and Paris, and the amount of time it takes to go between these two pairs of places differs predictably.

Conversely, the *sacer* realm is the *unknown* and *not safely circumscribed* in all its aspects. It is that which falls beyond the edge of the community— wilderness, forest, desert, ocean; it is nighttime, sleep and dreams; it is before birth and after death; it is the realm of divinity. It is the realm that operates unpredictably for us in both time and space, according to its *own* patterns. In dreams, for instance, normative patterns of time and space disappear: One can be in Cleveland one instant and in Paris the next; one can converse with people not only thousands of miles away as if they were beside one but also with those who have died and thus moved altogether beyond normal (*profanus*) reach.

The realm of the *sacer* is inherently neutral but potentially and unpredictably (since it operates according to its own terms) positive or negative in its interface with us. When I sleep, I may have (or at least remember) no dreams, or I may have dreams that are sweet (that instantaneous visit to Paris, perhaps!) or horrific (the nightmare that I am stopped for speeding as I hurry to the airport to catch my plane from Cleveland Hopkins Airport to Paris— and miss my plane). When I go out into the forest, nothing unusual may happen—or I may be torn apart by wolves, or my fairy godmother may tap me on the shoulder and offer to fulfill three wonderful wishes of my choice. When I make offerings or prayers to the gods for rain, there may be no response, or the gods may respond with a deluge that drowns half the community or with precisely the right amount of rain so that our crops flourish and we survive another year.

The term *sacer* can also apply to an individual, in which case it also implies being apart from the community, the familiar, the everyday: So (in the positive sense) a prophet or priest is one separate from the community, particularly, in the case of a priest, in the enactment of rituals. Such a figure, in turn, guides the community (the *profanus*) in its relationship with the *sacer*;

hence that figure is termed, in Latin, *sacerdos*—"one who gives the *sacer* [to us]" (and "one who gives us to the *sacer*").[2] So, too (in the negative sense), one who has transgressed a *boundary* between *profanus* and *sacer* space becomes, as we shall see, *sacer*.

We can best understand this last notion—and, ultimately, the importance of the concept of *sacer* for religion and for mysticism—by considering the origin of the term. *Sacer* (actually an earlier form of the word) appears on an eighth-to-seventh-century BCE inscription on the black stone—*lapis niger*—in the old Roman Forum. The stone marked a boundary between the small community in general and a grove sacred to the goddess who in the later classical era would be called Diana. The inscription warns that one who upsets the stone and thus disturbs the boundary will, together with his cattle (a common form of wealth in that time and place), be *sacer*. *Sacer*, then, in this early context, is a far cry from the positive connotation of its descendant, "sacred." The one foolish or unfortunate enough to upset the boundary marked by the stone would be the recipient of a *curse*. More precisely, that individual would become estranged from the community (the *profanus*), no longer protected by that which ties the community together (*leg-es*, or "laws," and *re-lig-io*),[3] and forced out into the realm beyond its familiar bounds: The one *labeled sacer* must go *out into* the *sacer*.

Why does such a curse of estrangement attach itself to the boundary marker that is the *lapis niger*? Because of the perceived analogy[4] between the *sacer-profanus* boundary that the stone marks and the ultimate boundary between the safely circumscribed, predictable, known *profanus* and the potentially dangerous, boundless, unpredictable, unknowable *sacer*—the realm of gods and daimons who can be as malignant as they can be beneficent in their interaction with the *profanus*. Thus, to disturb *any* boundary—but particularly one such as that marked by the *lapis niger*, between the community at large and a grove hallowed by the goddess's protection—may *potentially* disturb that ultimate boundary, bringing catastrophe upon the community from a goddess (*sacer*) turned angry.

Consider Oedipus (to switch from Roman to Greek culture for a moment), who unwittingly offended the gods and the natural order of things that they have engendered by killing his father and sleeping with his mother. His actions, unintentional as they may have been, wrought havoc: They brought plague onto the city of Thebes. Oedipus was necessarily cast out of Thebes, carrying the curse with him and relieving the city of its malady. Similarly, to avoid potential disaster to the community, the one who has engendered that potential for disaster by disturbing the *lapis niger* and the boundary that it marks departs, like Oedipus, carrying whatever malignancy from the *sacer* with him- or herself.[5] This is why the transgressor of a *sacer/profanus* boundary *must* become *sacer*, must leave the *profanus* to protect the community.

But in such a situation, how might the offending one return from apartness, estrangement, curse, *sacerness* back to the *profanus*, back to the community? He or she may do so by offering a gift of expiation to the offended powers. More precisely, the offender offers a surrogate—a lamb, a goat, a cow, an ox, a bouquet of flowers, a bowl of fruit—upon which his *sacer*-inducing sin is deemed to rest, to the *sacer*. That is, he or she makes something *sacer* in his or her stead. In Roman culture, this sort of action must have been common enough (there could be many reasons for wishing to make such an offering) that the Latin word *facere* ("make") and the term *sacer* were ultimately combined in a one-word configuration: *sacrificare*—"to sacrifice."

Yet, while in English the word "sacrifice" is derived from *sacrificare* and its linguistic siblings, the latter does not necessary imply slitting the surrogate's throat (although it certainly can), reminding us that the Latin term, like the term *sacer* itself, has a broader meaning than the reflex that we use possesses. Nor, of course, is this principle unique to Roman religion. It is precisely what occurred at the Israelite-Judaean temple at the annual time of expiation called *Yom Kippur* (Day of Atonement or Expiation): The high priest (*sacerdos*), bearing a year's worth of sins from the community (*profanus*) on his shoulders, would in turn, by placing his hands on a goat (the *scapegoat*), transfer that pollution onto the animal, which, cursed (*sacer*) by bearing the sins, was thereafter cast out into the wilderness (*sacer*)—sent to its death (*sacer*).

Two paradoxes are inherent in this sensibility. First, the *sacer* is an intrinsically neutral and potentially positive or negative concept, as we have noted: One doesn't know, going into the wilderness, whether nothing will occur, or whether one will be torn apart by wild animals or brigands, or whether one's fairy godmother will appear, granting three wishes that transform and elevate one's life. One doesn't know, when one goes to sleep, whether nothing, nightmares, or sweet dreams will occur. One doesn't know whether, at death, nothing or hell or heaven follows. One doesn't know—and this is the most profound aspect of this dichotomy—when one addresses the gods whether they will respond negatively, positively, or not at all.

Each religion assumes that the divine-aspected powers of the *sacer* are, on the whole, beneficent (that assumption is present, both for Roman polytheism and for the evolving Israelite-Judean monotheism that is contemporary with it). So to be *sacer*—to be what the gods are, to be with the gods—must mean to be *blessed*. Thus, for example, in dying, one may come to reside with the gods— a blessed state of being concerning which there is ample discussion in Greco-Roman and other mythologies. Yet, in the case of a *scapegoat*, that animal, *sacer*, is clearly understood to be *cursed*. The bilateral, contradictory nature of the *sacer*, then, is clear—and it is essential to Western religious history. For Christianity, Jesus in earthly death is *sacer*. He who bears humanity's sins on his shoulders is, one might say, as cursed as one can be; he who returns to the realm of God the Father is as blessed as one can be.

The second paradox pertains to the space-time quality of the *sacer*. It is boundless; yet, in addressing it, we do so in carefully circumscribed places, at carefully circumscribed times, by way of carefully prescribed ritual—as if, in defining precise boundaries about the aspects of relationship to the *sacer*, we can render its unfathomability accessible, its intrinsic unpredictable chaos ordered to our limited understanding of it. Thus, the offender, the one who has upset the boundary marked by the *lapis niger*, performs his sacrifice not just anywhere, anytime, in any way he or she wishes. He or she does so in a carefully circumscribed space—in a temple, at an altar (in other traditions, in a ziggurat, a synagogue, a church, a mosque), at a carefully prescribed time (almost invariably a *border* time: sunset, sunrise, high noon, midnight), according to carefully prescribed procedures. And how will he or she know what time, place, and procedure to observe? The *sacerdos*, to whom the *sacer* has revealed this information, will guide him or her.

But these aspects of precision will apply not only to the case of an individual who has inappropriately transgressed the boundary between *profanus* and *sacer* or offended the powers of the *sacer*. Every *religio* will prescribe precise times within precise spaces for the precise rituals, which, on a periodic basis—be it daily, weekly, monthly, or annually—define the relationship between the *profanus* of each such *religio* and its sense of the *sacer*. Thus, for example, in the Jewish tradition, *Shabbat* (the Sabbath) begins *precisely* at sunset—as do all Jewish *sacer* times, set off from the amorphous *profanus* of the rest of the week or the rest of the year—and ends precisely when, after sunset, three stars appear in the sky. One enters and exits this *sacer* time (celebrated within *sacer* space—the synagogue or the home conceived as a *sacer* space, as a "synagogue away from the synagogue")—by means of precisely prescribed rituals: candle lighting, the blessing and consumption of wine and bread of a special sort.[6]

The *sacer* spaces into which one enters to celebrate religious rituals are, moreover, analogs of an ultimate centering point for the cosmos. The far-flung *profanus* of diasporatic Judaism centers on synagogues as surrogates of the destroyed Temple in Jerusalem. When that edifice still stood and the community of Israel-Judah was still geographically circumscribed, the *sacer* space of the Temple was the bounded and prescribed center of that community, its architecture carefully articulated, from its three exterior courtyards to its threefold interior. Access to each of these six spatial elements was carefully prescribed as well: from the access to the outermost courtyard granted to the entire Judaean community—both pagan Judaeans and adherents to the God of Israel—to the Holy of Holies in the inner depths of the edifice to which only the high priest had access, and even he only once a year, on the Day of Atonement.

Such a fixed centering point is part of the *sacer* paradox of every religious tradition. A centering space within the bounded and yet amorphous *profanus* is understood to be connected (by analogy) to the centering point assumed (by further paradox) to be found within the boundless *sacer*. So, the Holy of Holies in the Temple in Jerusalem; so the stone known as the *omphalos* at Delphi (and so-called because of the belief that it marked the umbilical connection between heaven and earth).[7] Different traditions offer a variety of accounts of time *before* our own time and space, *centered* around a tree in a garden as Sumerian Dilmun or biblical Eden, or as the tree, *Isdril*, at the center of the Norse conception of the universe, or as a mountain such as Indra's mountain at the center of the Indic cosmos.

All of this is so—to return to the beginning of this discussion—because religion, which presupposes the dichotomy between *sacer* and *profanus*, addresses itself most particularly to that aspect of the *sacer* called "divinity." That aspect of the *sacer* is by far its most disturbing one because of the assumption made by religion that it has the power to determine the extent and patterns of our lives. The assumption that the *sacer* created the *profanus* carries with it the corollary assumption that it can destroy us. It can help or harm, further or hinder, bless or curse us, and it is the purpose and province of religion and its leadership to assure that the positive side of these possibilities is visited upon the *profanus*. The boundless *sacer*, in its aspect as divinity, may, in most religious traditions, assume myriad shapes (or none at all): gods and goddesses, daimons and spirits, sometimes benevolent and sometimes malicious, unpredictable and intrinsically inaccessible to the modes of access— the five senses and the intellect—with which humans ordinarily address the world around them.

The *sacer* realm offers both fear and hope, both nightmare and sweet dream; it is therefore intrinsically neutral, potentially positive or negative. Thus, we must address ourselves carefully, in particular, to that aspect of the *sacer*—divinity—that can make or break our world. It is the purpose and province of religion to do so, in order to actualize its positive potential in relating to the *profanus*. Religion prescribes the times and spaces within which, addressing the *sacer*, we make it more accessible to our aspirations. Religious rite and ritual govern the boundaries between ourselves and the *sacer*, regulating their traversal when appropriate, structuring the process with minutely detailed care in order to ensure as much as possible a positive response from that realm toward our own realm. *Sacerdotes* are those who, in every religious tradition, are believed to possess the peculiar knowledge (granted to them in revelation from the *sacer*) of what rituals and rites to prescribe and of how properly to accomplish them. So, we have in their respective traditions Abraham, Moses, Jesus, Muhammad, Buddha, the Baha'ullah and the priests in the Israelite temple, in the Sumerian Great Ziggurat, and in the Temple of Jupiter Capitolinus in Rome.

RELIGIO, THE *MYSTERION,* AND THEIR GOALS

Thus, religion is based on a complex of ideas, asserting the existence of a multilayered and doubly aspected *sacer*. As a construct, its reason for being is to offer a means of relationship between the *sacer* and the *profanus*. Religion does this by prescribing precisely defined spaces and times where and when the *sacer* may most efficaciously be addressed, as by prescribing precise methods—rites, rituals, ceremonies—of interaction with that realm (including those for entering circumscribed *sacer* times and spaces—Sabbaths and holy days—within the *profanus*) and individuals to act as guides and intermediators in such interaction.

Mysticism may be understood as a particularly intense aspect of religious experience, as a particular means of traversing the boundary into relationship with the *sacer*. The term *mysticism*, related to the term *mystery*, derives from the Latin *mysterium*, which in turn derives from the Greek *mysterion*. This term, in turn, comes from the Greek verb *mystein*, meaning "to close" or "to hide": The *mysterion* is the *closed*, the *hidden* center of the *sacer*, which the mystic seeks to enter and the mystical method seeks to uncover.

That method (for whichever mystical system) is itself intrinsically hidden: The mystic hopes to travel hidden paths, to absorb hidden knowledge of interpreting and understanding the world by transcending its bounds into communion with the *sacer* that engendered our world. Mysticism presupposes that, within the heart of the *sacer*, deeply centered in its recesses, the hiddenness is the ultimate essence of the *sacer*—the ultimate goal of ultimate hope of merging the mystic's *profanus* self with the *sacer*. That ultimate unknown is the wholly transcendent, wholly unintelligible, which is beyond normative religious ritual, to be sought by carefully and precisely prescribed methods inaccessible to "normative" religious method and sensibility.

Mysticism, moreover, implies a *personalized* communion with the *sacer*—as opposed to "normative" religious experience, with its strong communal emphasis, involving a *group* defined by its *religio* and its particular relationship to the *sacer*.[8] Mystics who succeed, achieve ecstasy—*ek-stasis* in Greek, meaning "out of [where one ordinarily] stands": They stand outside their normal, *profanus* state of being, in bursting the bounds of themselves via a method that carries them beyond normative patterns of logic and intuition. By further paradox, at least within the Abrahamic traditions, that *ek-stasis* may also be understood as *en-stasis*, since to find the hidden innermost recess of God one might dig into the innermost recesses of one's own soul, which is that element of God *within* all of us. Of course, when one deals with the *sacer*, one does not deal with the linear sort of space with which we are familiar in the *profanus*, so looking inward as a means of looking outward has its own *sacer* "spatial" logic.

The mystic must, if he or she would merge with the center of the *sacer*, be in perfect equilibrium within him- or herself—centered, as the cosmos is, a pivot that spins without wobbling—so that, traveling beyond (or deeply within) his or her *profanus* self, he or she is able to return to that self without being harmed by the experience. Indeed, as we shall see, one of the distinguishing features of Jewish mysticism (less emphatically, Christian and Muslim mysticism) is the obligation of the mystic to *return* to the *profanus* and to benefit the community of which he or she remains a part, with whatever insights have been gained through communion with the innermost recesses of the unknown. So the *real* goal is not to enter the hiddenmost recesses of the *sacer* but to get there and *return* to the heart of the *profanus*, changed, bettered, and in a position to change and improve the world of which the mystic is part.

NOTES

1. I am therefore suggesting that Mircea Eliade's brilliant discussion in his seminal *Sacred and Profane* requires further neutralizing broadening.

2. A slightly different theory derives *sacerdos* from *sacer* plus a putative Indo-European root, **dhe−*, meaning "do," thus, "do, make *sacer*."

3. In this particular linguistic context, it is the consonants that count; thus, the Latin root for "binding" is properly "l-vowel-g." It is variously expressed as "lig-" or as "leg-," since vocalic alternation is not uncommon, for various reasons under various conditions, but that discussion is well beyond the scope of this one.

4. As the *profanus* and *sacer* are both realms with a large number of analogic aspects or subcategories, so the notion of analogs that is endemic to religious sensibility and is observable across the panoply of human cultures applies here: All boundaries are analogs of each other and of the ultimate *profanus-sacer* boundary, and thus all boundary crossings are potentially dangerous or propitious.

5. Note that Oedipus saved Thebes from the plague of the sphinx when he met her and solved her riddle at a *crossroads* (where two paths meet and cross: a *boundary*

zone) and met and killed the one he did not know was his father at a second cross-roads.

6. Go to any American city with a reasonably sized Jewish community and the local Jewish newspaper will come out on Thursday, and on the top or bottom of the front page the precise time to kindle the Sabbath lights will be indicated. Because of the preciousness of the Sabbath and the reluctance to leave it behind and get back to the *profanus* of the workweek, its endpoint offers a paradoxical exception to the rule of precision: The appearance of three stars is a precise formulation, but seeing precisely three stars is virtually impossible as by then there are many more than three that are visible. So in waiting for three stars, one is waiting for *more* than three and therefore waiting for a moment that is actually imprecise but in any case well beyond sunset and the end of the Sabbath day.

7. *Omphalos* is the Greek form of the Latin *umbilicus*.

8. This is so in a particular way in the Jewish tradition, wherein some prayers or words and phrases within prayer sequences are not recited without at least three participants and many without a minimum of ten participants—the group of ten referred to in Hebrew as a *minyan*.

Chapter One

The Birth and Development of the Abrahamic Faiths

Judaism, Christianity, and Islam share the conviction that Abraham brought about the beginnings of a revolution in thinking about the *sacer* some two thousand years before the time of Christ. In contrast to his contemporaries across the Middle East and eastern Mediterranean, from Mesopotamia and Anatolia to Canaan and Egypt to the Aegean basin, all of whom worshipped many gods assumed to offer human or animal or combined human and animal forms, Abraham is understood to have begun to direct himself to a single God, one with no tangible form at all. Abraham is referred to in the Hebrew Bible as a Hebrew, a term that refers neither to his ethnicity nor to his religion but to his socioeconomic place in the world around him: He was an itinerant, a keeper of flocks who moved from place to place to graze them rather than owning his own land. This is why it was necessary for him to negotiate with Ephron the Hittite in Genesis 23 to purchase the Cave of Makhpelah as a burial site for Sarah.[1]

In one of the most famous wrestling matches in history, Abraham's grandson, Jacob, contended with an angel, a divine messenger, all night long at the time of his (Jacob's) return from Haran to Canaan after a twenty-year absence. The upshot of that encounter was that Jacob was gifted with a new name, *Israel*, meaning "one who has striven with God," and as a consequence, his sons and their descendants are referred to as children of Israel, or simply as Israelites. Jacob-Israel's actual children go down into Egypt during a time of severe famine and end up settling there, in the border territory of Goshen. Their Israelite descendants end up enslaved by the pharaoh, and the descendants of their descendants are led forth from Egypt by Moses. Moses leads the Israelites to the middle of the wilderness (the *sacer*) at the foot of Mount Sinai, where they embrace the covenant with God articulated in the Ten Commandments; eventually, after forty years in the wilderness, they arrive back in the Canaan whence their ancestors had departed so many generations earlier.

A close look at the usage of the term *Israelite* throughout the narrative that encompasses these events suggests that, while it is ostensibly an ethnic, genealogical term referring to those who are connected by bloodline to the lineage of Abraham, Isaac, Jacob-Israel, and their wives, it comes more fully to refer to the *religio* of those who have embraced the covenant with the God of Israel. Consider, for example, the father-in-law of Moses, Jethro, a Midianite—the descendant of that group to whom Moses's ancestor, Jacob's son Joseph, was sold by his brothers. The Midianites had in turn sold Joseph to an Egyptian, which event—to make a long story short—eventually led to the arrival of Jacob-Israel and his family in Egypt. Exodus 18:1–12 observes that when Jethro saw all the extraordinary things that the God of Israel accomplished for Moses and the Israelites, he embraced that god. That is, Jethro, the ethnic Midianite, became a spiritual Israelite, just as his daughter, Moses's wife Tzipporah, had earlier in the narrative.

Nonetheless, the Israelites were essentially organized along genealogical lines, as a series of tribes descended from Jacob's sons and grandsons. Led by Moses and Joshua in perhaps the fifteenth and fourteenth centuries before Christ, eventually they would be organized as a united kingdom by Saul, David, and Solomon in turn. Each of these kings was understood to have been chosen by God; the first two were anointed—*mashiah* in Hebrew; *christos* in Greek—by the *sacerdos*, Samuel. The third of these kings would build the Temple in Jerusalem in around 960 BCE. At the heart of Solomon's temple was the Holy of Holies, where the Tablets of the Law, inscribed with the Ten Commandments, were stored. The prayer with which Solomon dedicated the Temple (recorded in 1 Kings 8:12–53) is an interesting one. It suggests that the Israelite king's hope is that God will be particularly focused on this site dedicated to the bond between Israel and God, as opposed to the expectation that God will be circumscribed by this dwelling. One may recognize a subtle tension between a strong ethnocentric, localized sense of "the God of Israel"—parallel to the gods of the Canaanites or the gods of the Egyptians—and the beginnings of a sense of God's universal quality and ubiquitous presence.

History loves irony. So it must have exulted in the fact that Solomon both built the structure that was intended to unify the faith of Israel by offering a permanent, concrete focus for its faith and sowed the seeds for the divisiveness among the Israelites that would follow almost immediately after his death. For Solomon negotiated with Hiram of Tyre to build the temple and to expand David's palace substantially. This meant two things: 1 Kings 5:15–26 suggests that Solomon paid Hiram a premium for the project rather than negotiating astutely for a better price, and since the two projects took twenty years to complete—seven for the Temple and thirteen for Solomon's palace—that meant that, for a generation, the royal precinct in the Jerusalem capital was largely inhabited by Tyrians, who surely brought with them their own *religio*, their god images, and their rites and ceremonies. Moreover, as he aged, Solomon began to build temples to the gods of his non-Israelite wives. And Solomon's building projects—including other royal cities, such as Hatzor, Megiddo, and Gezer—taxed the Israelites heavily.

It would be surprising if the Israelites had not been confused by these developments: a temple to the imageless God festooned with Tyrian-style images; other temples to other gods (1 Kings 11:1–8) built at the command of the king who had been anointed by the Israelite God; increasing tax burdens in terms not only of olives and grains but also of sons and daughters to serve the king; and a king who, dwelling in a royal precinct surrounded by walls in which the Temple and palace complexes were both contained, was literally cut off from the people. It is also not surprising that, after Solomon's death, representatives of the people approached his son, Rehoboam, and begged for a remission of that tax burden. Nor is it surprising that the new king—counseled by young advisers who, like him, had grown up apart from the people and convinced that to yield an inch would be to give a mile to the people and lose his royal prerogatives—should respond that "my little finger is thicker than my father's thigh . . . my father chastised you with whips, but I shall chastise you with scorpions" (1 Kings 12:10–11). In the end, the result (about 925 BCE) was revolution on the part of the ten northern tribes and division of the kingdom. Thereafter, the northern tribes, led initially by Jeroboam, would be called Israel, and the south, consisting of the tribes of Judah and Benjamin and led by Rehoboam, would be referred to as Judah.

Two hundred years later, the northern kingdom was swallowed up by the juggernaut of Assyrian political-military power that extended from northern Mesopotamia to the Mediterranean. In 722–721 BCE, the northern capital of Samaria was sacked, and the northern tribes disappeared from history. The combination of a gradual weakening of faith, aided by having been largely cut off from Jerusalem and its Temple for two hundred years and the breaking up of families and communities by the Assyrians (as a strategy to prevent the easy organization of revolts against their authority), led to the loss of their sense of connection to the Hebrew-Israelite continuum. Judah remained, maintaining its identity and independence by the skin of its teeth. The southernmost area of Assyrian-controlled Israel, overlapping into northern Judah, was called Samaria, after the destroyed Israelite capital city. There the inhabitants seem to have been an ethnospiritual combination of

Israelite remnants, pagans brought by the Assyrians from elsewhere, and the occasional Judaean.

By the end of the next century, the Assyrians had fallen to the Chaldaean Babylonians, and this time the Judaeans would not escape. In 586 BCE, the Temple would be destroyed, and anyone of use or threat to the regime of Nebuchadnezzar II would be carried off into exile. The poor and the powerless remained behind or fled, led by the prophet Jeremiah, down into Egypt from which they would trickle back over the decades that followed. No doubt those who were not exiled continued to bring modest offerings to the site of the Temple. After all, it is a principle of the history of religion that once a site has been recognized as propitious for *sacer-profanus* contact, it never ceases to be sacerdotally propitious, regardless of who controls it politically.[2]

For those in exile, however, a most important development may be observed. Had they followed the conventions of the world around them, the Judaeans would have abandoned worship of a God that could not protect them or the temple to that God. Instead, they interpreted the debacle as an act engineered *by* God to punish them for their failure to live up to the Covenant. They recognized that Nebuchadnezzar had been a chastising rod in God's hand and not the willful victor over God through his own gods; that the God of Israel had far-reaching presence and power; that God could be addressed anywhere Judaeans gathered together to pray and read from God's word; and that if they returned to God in full faith, they would be redeemed from exile. When the Babylonians fell to the Achaemenid Medo-Persians barely fifty years later (538 BCE) and the Medo-Persian king, Cyrus II, invited the Judaeans to return to Judah and rebuild their temple, such convictions were confirmed.

The evolving dynamic tension between ethnocentric and universal senses of God may be observed in two different ways. One is the reference to Cyrus in 2 Chronicles as *mashiah*—"anointed [by God]"—as if the universally active God is yet focused largely on Israel-Judah, and international events such as Cyrus's coming to power are effected by that God but largely for Israelite-Judaean benefit. The second way, and more to the point, is that the rebuilding of the Temple took twenty-three years. Divisions within the community were rampant between those who had been in exile and those who had not; between the rich and the poor; more importantly, between those who perceived God as universal and those who perceived God as ethnocentric; and between those who believed that the leadership of the community should be religious—focused on the high priest in the Temple, who must be a descendant of Tzadok, the high priest in Solomon's temple, who was a descendant of Aaron, brother of Moses—and those who felt that the leader should be a descendant of David and Solomon, a political *mashiah*.

The Judaean world of the next six hundred years was characterized by a number of features, two of which are of particular significance for our purposes. Externally, Judah was caught in the historical currents that swept the Achaemenid Persian Empire into the conquering path of Alexander the Great; saw Alexander's early death in 323 BCE, followed by division of his empire among his oldest friends and best generals so that Judah was caught between the Seleucids to the north mainly in Syria and the Ptolemies to the south mainly in Egypt; and eventually saw both of these kingdoms swallowed up by the Roman Empire during the last pre-Christian century. Along the way, one of the Seleucids, Antiochus IV, attempted to subvert the Judaean religion, which led to a revolt against his authority. That Hasmonean (a.k.a. Maccabean)-led revolt ended in a Judaean victory in 165 BCE and to effective political independence for Judaea within the twenty years that followed. The Hasmoneans shortly made themselves kings over Judah and high priests in the Temple, although they were descendants neither of King David nor of Tzadok. In 37 BCE, the last of them was extirpated with Roman help by Herod the Idumaean, ruler of a polity to the south of Judea (as "Judah" was now commonly called in the Greek and Roman languages). Part of what made this last political development so interesting and problematic is that the Idumaeans had been defeated by the Hasmonean-led Judaeans at the end of the second century and force-converted to Judaeanism. So, on his father's side, Herod was a Judaean by faith but an Idumaean by ethnicity—and, in any case, on his mother's side, he was a Nabataean by ethnicity and thus presumably a pagan as well.

All of these issues lead to the second feature of primary significance during this era: In the nearly six hundred years between the completion of the Second Temple in 515 BCE and its destruction by the Romans in 70 CE, division was at least as common as unity within the Judaean community. For our purposes, what is most noteworthy is a pair of schismatic moments that occurred relatively late in this history. The first took place perhaps a century or so before the time of Christ. In the aftermath of the successful Hasmonean (so-called Maccabean) revolt against Antiochus IV, the arrogation of high priesthood and then kingship to the Hasmoneans, and the various political and spiritual divisions in the leadership of the Judaean community—the primary terms of reference for these divisions are "Sadducees" and "Pharisees"—at least one group withdrew altogether from the mainstream of that community and took refuge in the wilderness. The group or groups that established themselves along the northwestern shore of the Dead Sea at Qumran (as the site would later be called in Arabic) took to writing a series of texts that have survived and from which we can deduce a good deal about their ideology. Conventional scholarship has tended to associate this group with a group otherwise known as the Essenes.[3]

They were a mystical community both in being apart from the Judaean community and the world at large as they lived their ascetic, precisely regulated lives and in claiming possession of secret knowledge that provided them with potential contact with the innermost recesses of the *sacer*. They saw themselves as the only Judaeans living lives true to the covenant. They saw the world as caught in a titanic struggle between good and evil, light and darkness—in which thinking they were no doubt influenced by the Zoroastrian religion of Persia. This influence would have been picked up in exile or in the continuous contact with Persia that would have been natural not only in general socioeconomic terms but also, more specifically, because many Judaeans had chosen not to return from Perso-Babylonia, and the resultant primary pair of Judaean communities maintained contact with each other. The Qumran sect saw the end of the world as we know it as imminent in a conflagration in which the powers of good, led by the Good Teacher and ultimately by God, would eventually defeat the powers of evil, led by the Wicked Priest and those who oppose God. They saw themselves as the sole survivors of the aftermath of that conflagration, when a new, divinely guided reality would shift into place.

The second schism would come from within the mainstream community about a century and a half later. This is the schism that would lead Judaeanism to become Judaism and Christianity. Between about 30 and 130 CE, as those two *religiones* were taking the kind of shape that would be recognizable today, an array of issues came to divide them. The nature of God became the most fundamental of these. For Judaism, God is unequivocally inaccessible to the senses, invisible, intangible, even beyond intellect; God never would or could assume human form. For Christianity, God could and did assume human form as Jesus of Nazareth for the sake of the salvation of humankind. For Christianity, salvation is directed to the *sacer* realm of death and the achievement of heaven rather than hell. It is necessary—and divine intervention is needed to achieve it—due to the egregiousness of Adam and Eve's disobedience to God in eating fruit from the Tree of Knowledge. That sin, called "original sin," was a unique problem and therefore required the unique solution not only of God's assuming human form but also the accomplishment of this transformation through the unprecedented process of a virgin birth. For Judaism, Adam and Eve sinned egregiously, but not so egregiously that the sin imprinted itself on all of subsequent humanity; there is no clear doctrine of heaven and hell and an afterlife; and thus salvation pertains more to the end of a homeless, diasporatic existence and a return to *Eretz Yisrael* (the Land of Israel) than to an otherworldly, *sacer* condition.

These differences of interpreting the *sacer* and the *sacer-profanus* relationship derive from and lead back to differences not only in interpreting the texts that Judaism and Christianity share in common but also in determining *which* texts should be read and understood as divinely inspired. Thus, it is not only a matter of how words or phrases in the prophetic books are read by

Christians to point toward Jesus and not read by Jews to point that way. For Judaism, God is understood to have ceased speaking to the Judaeans through prophetic figures—*sacerdotes*—within a century of the return from Perso-Babylonian exile. Specifically, Ezra the Scribe is credited with redacting the Torah in 444 BCE—organizing, editing, and finalizing the five books of Moses in their current form. Thereafter, God ceased to communicate as It had through Moses and other prophets, leaving the written-down words of God as the guide for a covenantal life.

The leadership of the Judaean-Jewish community in the centuries that follow is comprised of scribes and scholars who can interpret God's word—and determine which writings (minimally those understood to have been written down before 444) may be construed as containing God's word so that they might end up in the canon of the Hebrew Bible. For Christianity, God did not cease direct, prophetic communication in the time of Ezra. On the contrary, not only did that sort of contact continue for hundreds of years but also with the emergence half a millennium later of Jesus—God become human—the writings that focus on him supplanted in importance those of the earlier Israelite-Judaean era. A new Covenant, articulated in a New Testament, reduced the old Covenant and its Old Testament to a forerunner text, albeit an important forerunner.

Concomitant with these essential differences was an array of subsidiary ones. On the one hand, there was a schism with regard to the celebration of the Sabbath and the host of holidays throughout the year. On the other, there was divergence with regard to life cycle events, from birth to death, most obviously with regard to the circumcision ceremony that, for Jews, marks the entrance of males into the covenantal community on the eighth day after birth but was eliminated in Christianity, for which the new Covenant had replaced the old. Over time, separate but equally vast bodies of interpretive literatures would develop: the Talmud and Midrash, or *Halakhic* (legalistic) and *Aggadic* (legend-bound) literature in Judaism; the patristic literature in Christianity. Both bodies of literature have in common the struggle to understand how to be a good Jew or a good Christian—how to live within the bounds of the sort of life that will please, not offend, God. They share a sense of the problematic of determining how and when to effect the transition from a condition of divine revelation to and through prophetic *sacerdotes* to that of interpretation of the revelation into intelligibility and relevance to the *profanus* of the here and now.

I have belabored this account of how history carries us from Hebrew-Israelite-Judaeanism to Judaism and Christianity for two reasons. One is because many of the issues raised in the two thousand years between the time of Abraham and the aftermath of Jesus will play important roles in aspects of

Jewish or Christian mysticism or of both. The other is to underscore the often misunderstood relationship between Judaism and Christianity as *siblings*, children of the same Hebrew-Israelite-Judaean parent, each seeing itself as the legitimate child of that parent and the other as the bastard child, each seeing itself as fulfilling the prescriptions of the *sacer-profanus* relationship and the other as misconstruing those prescriptions and thus endangering that relationship for the community. Related to these two issues, as we shall shortly see, is the nature of the diverse literary sources that stream into what will become Jewish and Christian mysticism and effect their respective early developments.

Nor, before turning to those sources, can we forget that the question of which of the two faiths most legitimately fulfills God's word and wishes does not end here—in two different ways. First, the theological conflict between nascent Judaism and Christianity did not occur in a political vacuum. As they competed with each other spiritually, they also competed for legitimacy within the pagan Roman world. The political and legal system of that world distinguished between *religio licita*—in this context the word *religio* means a form of faith acceptable to the regime—and *superstitio*, meaning a form of faith regarded as politically subversive. Judaeanism had been treated as *religio* since the time when Pompey first led Roman forces into Judaea in the 60s BCE. Even while the suppression of the *politically* motivated Judaean revolt was in process (65–70 CE), Judaeanism as a *religion* operated freely. In the decades that followed, as Judaeanism bifurcated into Judaism and Christianity, Judaism inherited that *religio* status, and Christianity was viewed as a *superstitio* (with one brief exception: the three years immediately following the Bar Kokhba Revolt of 132 to 135, during which Judaism was proscribed, but that proscription ended with the death of the Emperor Hadrian and the advent of his successor, Antoninus Pius, in 138 CE). This meant that it was illegal and dangerous to practice Christianity until Constantine's Edict of Milan in 313 granted *religio* status to it. The Emperor Theodosius, in around 390, declared Christianity the official *religio* of the empire. Thus, Judaism and Christianity reversed political conditions vis-à-vis each other between the early second and late fourth centuries. This process of reversal would affect the next seventeen centuries of their relationship with each other.

The second way in which the matter of faith-legitimacy conflict continues forward is that in the seventh century Islam would step onto the stage of history. Islam asserts that the ultimate successor to the prophetic writings through which God speaks to the *profanus* was transmitted through the ultimate prophet, Muhammad, that the versions of God's word being read by Jews and Christians as the Torah and the Gospels became corrupted over time (either through political intention or through scribal error), and that the recitations of the Prophet, contained within the Qur'an, provide the definitive version of God's word and thus the ultimate guide for living a covenantal life.[4] Beyond the Qur'an as a textual source, Islam offers a body of literature called *hadith* ("statement"), which offers primarily passages ascribed to or about the prophet Muhammad. The hadith tradition is complex; not all of the hadiths are universally accepted by all Muslims; nor do all of them carry equal weight.[5]

All three Abrahamic faiths further their exploration of the relationship between *sacer* and *profanus* with deep and wide oceans of interpretive literature directed to the material that they regard as divinely revealed. Thus, the early Jewish rabbinic literature, the Midrash and Talmud, will continue as a wealth of medieval and postmedieval commentary; the Christian patristic literatures, East and West, will continue as a rich body of medieval scholastic and postmedieval commentary; the Shi'ite and Sunni branches of Islam will each yield major schools of theological perspective that carry from the medieval toward the modern world.[6]

Islam offers parallels to Judaism and Christianity with respect to the sense of God (as in Judaism, unequivocally nonphysical, inaccessible to the senses and intellect) and to a singular text that connects God to the *profanus*, as well as a deep ocean of interpretive texts and commentaries that evolve over the centuries that follow the founding of the faith.[7] It divides the do's and don't's of living within a meaningful relationship with the *sacer* in terms of the obligatory (e.g., prayer), the desirable or recommended (e.g., the *hajj*—pilgrimage to Makka once in one's life), the indifferent or not precisely prescribed (e.g., relations with non-Muslims), the objectionable (e.g., too many wives), and the forbidden (e.g., eating pork, gambling, usury). We recognize certain parallels between these categories and aspects of Judaism as well as Christianity. Islam's sense of original sin and of heaven and hell fall short of the profound detail that evolves within Christian literature, but it is more specific and focused than that found in Jewish literature.[8] It offers celebrations that parallel those in Judaism and Christianity. Most importantly for subsequent history, it shares with Christianity (and with Judaism at its beginnings but decreasingly since the end of the fourth century) the desire to reach out and convince or compel others to see the light of God through its eyes. Where Judaism became increasingly *exclusive*, Christianity and Islam remained emphatically *inclusive*—for better and for worse in all three cases.

This last issue has meant, in practical terms, that for much of the past fourteen centuries the Middle Eastern, Mediterranean, and European worlds have been battlegrounds between Christian and Muslim ideology, with Judaism often sandwiched between the two. It has also meant, however, that constant contact among the three Abrahamic faiths has led to an array of influences and counterinfluences on each other. While one might state this in general terms, there have been particular times and places—such as in Spain between the early eighth and late fourteenth (or perhaps late fifteenth) centuries or Sicily between the early ninth and late eleventh centuries—where that cultural interchange was particularly rich. Given the intentions and goals of mysticism, we might expect and will find both differences and parallels among the mystical traditions of the three Abrahamic traditions, in general and in particular times and places.

NOTES

1. In the Hebrew language, Abraham is called an *eevree*. The triconsonantal root for this word, *-v-r*, means "to pass." He owned no property but was not by any means necessarily without means. Consider that Abraham raised a small army of four hundred men from within his own household to go out and rescue his nephew Lot and the Sodomites and Gomorrans from the Kings of the Plain in Genesis 14. But he grazed his flocks in an itinerant manner; he passed from place to place (in negotiating with Ephron, he refers to himself as a *ger vitoshav*: "a stranger and sojourner"), as did Isaac and Jacob. So the term *Hebrew* refers to his itinerant niche in the world of the Hurrians and others in which he grew up and flourished.

2. My favorite example of this principle is this: in digging beneath the crypt beneath the altar in the Cathedral of Notre Dame in Paris in the 1980s, excavators found not only the remains of a pagan Roman temple but also, beneath it, the remains of a pagan Gallic (druidic) temple. Once a *sacer* space always a *sacer* space—and few conquerors wish to risk eschewing something so numinous.

3. Our sources—the *Books of the Maccabees*, the writings of Philo and of Josephus—variously refer to this group (or these groups) as *Hosiotes* (meaning "holy ones" in Greek), as *hassidim* (meaning "pious ones" in Hebrew), or as *Essaioi* or *Assidaioi* (apparent Greek versions or Aramaic or Hebrew terms). *Essaioi* would yield the English designation "Essenes."

4. The basic building blocks of Muslim belief are never laid out in some systematic manner as, say, the Ten Commandments are in the Torah, but they are elaborated early on as the Five Pillars: *Shahada* (belief in the One God and Muhammad as his ultimate messenger, together with a series of other beliefs, in prior prophets, in angels and demons, in the predisposition of humans to good and evil, in heaven and hell, in final judgment), *salat* (formal prayer, five times a day; *du'a*, or informal prayer may take place anytime), *zakat* (charity, ultimately in a prescribed percentage of one's wealth), *som* (fasting, during the month of Ramadan, from sunrise to sunset), and *hajj* (pilgrimage, ideally once during one's lifetime, to Makka and Madina).

5. The degree of their acceptance is based on *sanad* ("backing"): the degree of solidity of their chain of authority (this is similar to the rabbinic tradition of relative degrees of authoritative precedence regarding certain issues). The most widely accepted are asserted to derive from the companions—the first generation of seven followers

of the Prophet. The second generation is that of "followers-on," and the third is that of "followers of the followers." They are thus classified as *sahih* ("sound"), meaning that the *hadith* can be reliably traced back to the original seven companions of the Prophet; *hasan* ("good"), meaning that there is one weak link in what is, through other confirmation sources, an otherwise strong chain of historical reliability; and *da'if* ("weak"). The first authoritative compendium was that organized into eight volumes by Ibn Said (d. 844). Shortly thereafter, other compendia followed, notably that containing 7,300 *hadiths* by al-Bukkhiri (d. 870) and that of Muslim (d. 875).

6. Thus, the *Sunnis* ("orthodox"—the term *sunna* means "tradition" and is similar in original usage to the Latin term *mos* and the Hebrew term *masoret*) yielded four major schools by the ninth century—*Hanafi*, *Maliki*, *Shafi'i*, and *Hanbali*—and the *Shi'ites* ("absolutists" or "sectarians"—the term *shi'a* actually means "followers"; thus, *shi'at Ali* means "followers of Ali" but connotes following the true path set forth by Muhammad) yielded the *Zaidis*, *Imamis*, and *Isma'ilis*. These terms, like the terms *rabbinic* and *patristic-scholastic*, offer the tip of a much more detailed and complex iceberg.

7. The Arabic-language word *God* is *'Allah*—the result of a linguistic process, particularly common in Arabic, called *crasis*, whereby *'al-Illah* is pushed together to form *'Allah* and a cognate with the Hebrew words *'El* and *'Eloheem*. Since Arabic is the primary language of Islam (as Hebrew is of Judaism), it would not be inappropriate to use the term *'Allah* in discussing Islam. But in my experience, we don't tend to do that when discussing Judaism (when writing in a language other than Hebrew), and when we *do* do that in discussing Islam, non-Muslims tend too easily to see a sea of difference between their own sense of God and that within Islam, so I prefer to use the word *God* to underscore the parallelism with the Jewish concept and the identical-to-Judaism contrast with the triunity of the Christian concept.

8. More precisely, the Qur'an is fiercer in its descriptions of hell than the New Testament is, but Christian commentary comes to elaborate a far more detailed and terrifying vision than does Muslim commentary. In the Hebrew Bible and the Jewish tradition, there is not actually even a word that is the equivalent of "hell," but there evolves a sense that the righteous and the unrighteous end up at two separate postmortem destinations.

Chapter Two

The Roots of Jewish and Christian Mysticism

BIBLICAL ROOTS

Judaism and Christianity are edifices built on the same foundations, those of the Hebrew Bible, but each has used those foundations differently, which is why they are two different edifices. Thus, both traditions in general, and particularly with regard to the development of Jewish and Christian mysticism, might be expected to have the Hebrew Bible as a starting point. The underlying principle that governs the Hebrew Bible for both Jews and Christians is that it contains material revealed to a series of individuals, prophets, by God itself. The prophetic experience offers itself as a natural starting point for Jewish and Christian mystical thinking in that the prophet experiences a form of the intimacy with God that the mystic hopes to achieve.

The most obvious difference is that prophets are generally represented in the Hebrew Bible as having been chosen by God (Jeremiah 1:4–5 offers the most direct case in point: He reports that God said to him, "Before I formed thee in the belly I knew thee and before thou camest forth out of the womb I sanctified[1] thee; I have appointed thee a prophet unto the nations"). The prophet of prophets, Moses, in fact expresses enormous reluctance to be a prophet—the word for prophet, *navi*, as it is used in Exodus 4:16,[2] means "mouthpiece"—requiring a good deal of arm-twisting from God before he agrees to take on the task. By contrast, the mystic is made, not born, and desperately *seeks* the contact that he or she hopes will come about with sufficient discipline, focus, and preparation.

Within the Hebrew Bible, amid the range of prophetic experiences that might prove inspirational to a would-be mystic, are several that stand out as even more intense than the prophetic "norm." Thus, for example, Moses's initial direct contact with God takes shape in Exodus 3. Shepherding the flocks of his father-in-law, the future prophet goes out to the "farthest end of the wilderness" (Ex 3:1)—the *sacer*, in our terms. The first thing a student of mysticism might note is the way in which the place where Moses ends up is expressed: What is the *farthest end* of the wilderness? Is it the center or the edge of the *sacer*? Wouldn't the end of the wilderness, if one thought in conventional *profanus* terms, be in precise proximity to another *profanus* at the opposite end of the *profanus* from which Moses has come? Or is that other *profanus*, by virtue of being unfamiliar to him, a *sacer* realm? So wouldn't the "farthest end" have to be the dead center of the *sacer*, equidistant from any and all forms of the *profanus*? But can there be either a center or an edge to a space that is amorphous, functionally spaceless? So, in a sense, Moses's encounter takes place nowhere—or at least nowhere that can be pointed to using *profanus* thinking.

It takes place on "the mountain of God, Horeb," where not God but "an angel of the Lord appeared unto him in a flame of fire out of the midst of a bush" (Ex 3:1–2). So even as God speaks to Moses, it is a circumlocutionary process, accomplished by an intermediating messenger.[3] Then there is the experience itself: A bush is burning yet is not consumed; a "voice" speaks out to the prophet from within the bush. Moses is instructed to remove his footwear because he is entering *sacer* space. And it is within this spaceless space within the spaceless space of the *sacer* wilderness that he is called upon to return to the *profanus*—not merely the *profanus* where he tends his flocks beyond Midian, or that of Midian beyond Egypt, but that of Egypt—to save his people. Moses has been led to the center within the center of the *sacer* to intimate contact with God—or with the "voice" of God from within the paradoxical burning bush—and is transformed from keeper of flocks to savior of Israel.

The story of Moses includes at least two other experiences that a would-be Jewish or Christian mystic might study in order to emulate them. The most obvious, that at Sinai, where the prophet receives the instructions for a covenantal life that he transmits to the people of Israel, is mostly hidden in an absence of detail (Ex 19–32). The biblical narrative is more focused on the principles of faith being outlined on the mountaintop and the problems of faith for the Israelites waiting at the foot of the mountain than on the details of Moses's experience up in the fog of the *sacer*. More fascinating and fraught with paradox is the passage that follows, in Exodus 33–34, when Moses, having smashed the pair of Tablets of the Law in his frustration with Israelite weakness of faith, returns to the mountaintop to hew out a second pair of stone tablets and reinscribe the words of God on them. Moses asks to see God's glory—not *God*, but God's *glory* (Ex 33:18). Observing that to see God's glory would result, even for Moses, in the death of the viewer, God says that "while My glory passeth by, I will put thee in a cleft of the rock, and will cover thee with my hand until I have passed by. And I will take away My hand, and thou shalt see My back; but my face shall not be seen" (Ex 33:22–23).

Three issues arise from these passages. The first is that even Moses can get only so close, and yet Moses gets *so* close! So he is a model to emulate, even as the mystic recognizes that absolute proximity to God may be impossible: He or she seeks intimate contact with God, as Moses had (Ex 33:11: "And the Lord spoke unto Moses face to face, as a man speaketh unto his friend"), while recognizing that if even Moses's contact was limited, so will the mystic's be. The second is that the description of God is paradoxical: This is a God with no physical description, but the text uses terms that suggest physicality, such as face and hand; yet, what Moses "sees" is God's glory, not God. Is this because God is invisible or because seeing God would be too intense an experience, even for Moses? Are these terms metaphors, the result of the limits on our own vocabulary, or, if intended to be understood in some literal way, what exactly do they mean?

What of the notion of God's *back*? It not only offers another "physiological" aspect of the divinity but also implies a spatial aspect in which God turns one way rather than another way. It also offers potential implications for the supreme question of Abrahamic monotheism: Why do good things sometimes happen to bad people, and bad things to good people, in a world made by a God understood to be both all-good and all-powerful? Is it because God sometimes turns Its back on us? Is the blinding "face" of God's glory present (merely turned away from our sight) even when things apparently go darker than dark? How does the mystical tradition parse the ratio of divine to human participation in the process of morally perfecting the world? The third issue is that the results of Moses's experience are—literally—written across his countenance. When he returns from the mountaintop with the new Tablets of the Law in his grasp, "Moses knew not that the skin of his face sent forth rays" (Ex 34:29).[4] So his face glows with the kind of light otherwise associated with God's glory, and so, too, the mystical model of transformation— the "me" who returns from the *mysterion* is not the same "me" who sought it out, as we shall subsequently see—is also encompassed by this account of Moses's experience.

Other Hebrew biblical passages drawn from prophetic narratives will potentially function as focus points for Jewish and Christian mystics, offering models to emulate. Isaiah, in the midst of his ongoing series of encounters with God and God's voice, also has one experience that stands out from others as particularly *sacer*-intense. At the beginning of Isaiah 6, the prophet reports having seen "the Lord sitting upon a throne high and lifted up, and His train filled the Temple. Above Him stood the seraphim; each one had six wings; with two he covered his face, and with two he covered his feet, and with two he did fly. And one called unto another, and said: "Holy, holy, holy, is the Lord of hosts; the whole earth is full of his glory." His response to this vision is awe as well as fear: "Woe is me! For I am undone; Because I am a man of unclean lips; and I dwell in the midst of a people of unclean lips; For mine eyes have seen the King, the Lord of Hosts" (Is 6:1–3).

So this passage underscores the double manner in which the prophet serves as a model for the mystic—to experience the kind of divine proximity that is related in the text and not to forget that he or she is part of a people to whom whatever messages are gained through that proximity must be brought back from the *sacer*. At the same time, it underscores the double danger of attempting to achieve that proximity. First, if even Isaiah feels himself unworthy, how much more so must *I* be? And given that unworthiness, how great is the danger that, instead of being purified as the prophet is, with a coal taken from the altar and touched to his lips by a seraph, I will be burned up. Second, there is the danger that my mind will be boggled by the imagery that this passage offers: Is the throne real? Is it within or hovering above the temple? (The Temple in Jerusalem or a heavenly temple?) What are "seraphim," beyond the simple details regarding their wings? How does one hear the "voice of the Lord" that speaks to Isaiah in verse 8? If my mind is centered enough, then meditating on these matters may lead me beyond my mind to where I wish to get—but insufficiently centered, my mind may simply be torn apart.

Let us consider one more biblical passage, the most extensive of those that lend themselves to particularly strong mystical contemplation: Ezekiel 1. This extraordinary chapter presents the prophet as asserting that he was "among the captives by the river Chebar, [when] the heavens were opened, and I saw visions of God" (Ex 1:1). The extensive description that follows strains to convert imagery that defies *profanus* grasp into terms that a *profanus* reader can apprehend. From within a "stormy wind from the north, a great cloud, with a fire flashing up, so that brightness was round about it" (Ez 1:4), there emerges something with the color of electrum out of the midst of the fire, and out of the midst of that midst, "the likeness of four living creatures," each with the likeness of a man, but with four faces and four wings—and "as for the likeness of their faces, they had the face of a man; and the four had the face of a lion on the right side; and the four had the face of an ox on the left side; the four had also the face of an eagle" (Ez 1:10). These "living creatures" had an "appearance like coals of fire, burning like the appearance of torches; it flashed up and down among the living creatures; and there was brightness to the fire, and out of the fire went forth lightning" (Ez 1:13).

This configuration is in turn supported by wheels the color of beryl and made of eyes, "and their appearance and their work was as it were a wheel within a wheel" (Ez 1:16). The wheels of eyes and living creatures are entirely interconnected, so that if the creatures move, the wheels do, and if the creatures are still, the wheels are. "And over the heads of the living creatures there was the likeness of a firmament, like the color of the terrible ice" (Ez 1:22), and when the whole contrivance "went, I heard the noise of their wings like the noise of great waters, like the voice of the Almighty, a noise of tumult like the noise of a host" (Ez 1:24). "And above the firmament that was over their heads was the likeness of a throne, as the appearance of a sapphire stone; and on the likeness of the throne was a likeness as the appearance of a man upon it above" (Ez 1:26).

The culmination of the vision then describes this being as "the color of electrum, as the appearance of fire round about enclosing it, from the appearance of his loins and upward; and from the appearance of his loins and downward I saw *as it were* the appearance of fire, and there was brightness round about him. As the appearance of the bow that is in the cloud in the day of rain, so was the appearance of the brightness round about. This was the appearance of the likeness of the glory of the Lord" (Ez 1:27–28, emphasis added).

One comes away from this extraordinary description of what comes, in summary, to be referred to as the *merkavah*—a word whose translation falls between "throne" and "chariot"—with a threefold sense of wonder. First, it is easy to recognize that the first challenge that Ezekiel is attempting to address is that of the indescribability—the ineffability—of what he has "seen." To have a vision of elements beyond the *profanus* is one thing; to have a vision of the imageless God is another. Second—and this is part of how he attempts to solve the first problem—there is the paradox, contradiction, and ambiguity shooting through the description. The four creatures seem to move without moving. The color of the eyes/wheels is, in Hebrew, *eyn tarshish*, which may be translated as "beryl" but also as "topaz" (*tarshish* more generally in biblical Hebrew refers to a site where there are mines and the smelting of metals); beryl is variously colorless or a range of colors, so the description can be construed both to be that of colorless color and of some specific, albeit translucent, color. The figure on the throne above the firmament (and what exactly is a firmament, although the word appears at the beginning of Genesis as a separator of the waters below from the waters above?) is described as lightning or electrum in its upper-body coloration and surrounded by fire, but its lower parts, spoken of as if the appearance were different from the upper parts, also offers the appearance of fire—but surrounded by a brightness that is likened to the rainbow.

Dominating both the matter of ineffability and that of paradox and contradiction is a steady state of circumlocution, as if to underscore both the paradox inherent in seeing what cannot be seen and the near impossibility of attempting to describe it. Thus, the four *hayyot* have the *likeness* of four living creatures, with the *likeness* of a man, and all of their details are referred to by way of "appearance" or "likeness." As for the *ophanim* of eyes, "their appearance and their work was *as it were* a wheel within a wheel." Above these "was the *likeness* of a firmament," above which "was the *likeness* of a throne, as the *appearance* of a sapphire stone; and upon the *likeness* of the throne was a *likeness* as the *appearance* of a man upon it above." One "as it were," "appearance," or "likeness" would hardly merit comment, but the repetition of such qualifiers underscores how untranslatable into *profanus* terms the entire visual experience of the prophet is—particularly when the entire vision culminates with the triple circumlocution: "this was the *appearance* of the *likeness* of the *glory* of the Lord" (Ez 1:28).

Ezekiel has not seen God; he has not even seen what Moses did, the back of the glory of God (and we are reminded that the Hebrew word translated as "glory"—*kavod*—is built from the same root as the word *kaved*, meaning "heavy," suggesting a paradoxical concreteness to this otherwise abstract concept). Nor has he seen the likeness of the glory of God. He has seen the appearance of the likeness of the glory of God. Thus, Ezekiel's vision might serve and will serve the Jewish or Christian mystic—particularly the Jewish mystic, for reasons that will be explored below—as a model, in antithetical yet connected ways. The prophet has the sort of vision to which a mystic might aspire, but at the same time the mystic studying this vision is reminded that the experience will—must—fall short of a vision of the God who (for Judaism, not for Christianity) may not be seen and (for mystics of both religions) that the accessible Godhead always has an inaccessibility to it. Even should the mystic reach the hiddenmost center, he will be—even if only infinitesimally—off center.

JUDAEAN PRELUDES TO A FORMAL
MYSTICAL DOCTRINE

In theory, one might assume that when one moves beyond the Hebrew Bible, one moves away from legitimate source material for Jewish mysticism and toward legitimate source material for Christianity.[5] But the history of Jewish and Christian mysticism weaves as much outside as within the mainstreams of both traditions. Thus, as we shall see, not only is the Hebrew Bible as significant a direct source of inspiration for Christian early mystics as the New Testament is, but also, more surprisingly, there are various postbiblical sources of inspiration for Jewish mysticism that include not only rabbinic material but also material based on, but carrying beyond, the Hebrew Bible and rejected as canonical even by mainstream Christians, as well as certain pagan material.

Thus, as we have observed, Judaism understands direct divine inspiration of the prophetic sort to have ended by the time Ezra was redacting the Torah. And all Christian groups agree that the Hebrew Bible serves as a prelude—the Old Testament of an old covenant—to what emerged as the New Testament of a new covenant articulated through the presence of God itself on earth in the form of Jesus of Nazareth. But in the course of the sixteenth century and the Protestant Reformation taking form in the West, a handful of books already rejected by Judaism as noncanonical were similarly rejected by the growing array of Protestant denominations. Thus, books such as 1 and 2 Maccabees, Judith, and The Wisdom of Ben Sirah, which both the Catholic and the Eastern denominations embrace as part of the intertestamental literature that comes between the Old and New Testaments, are treated by Jews and Protestants alike as Apocrypha.

The term "apocrypha" means "hidden away," presumably because the Jewish (and later the Protestant) leadership felt it essential that such works be hidden from unsuspecting Jews (and later, Protestants) who, if they were to read them and imagine them to be divinely inspired as the Hebrew Bible is (and as the New Testament is for Christians), would be led spiritually astray. Beyond those works considered intertestamental by Catholics and Orthodox Christians but apocryphal by Jews and Protestants are others that are regarded as noncanonical by all Christian and Jewish groups. They are appropriately called Pseudepigrapha: "false (*pseud-*) after (*epi-*) writings (*grapha*)." Among this large body of texts is one—or a series—associated with Enoch, father of Methusaleh.

Enoch, whose Hebrew name (*Hanoch*) means "education/teaching," is mentioned only briefly, in Genesis 5, in the genealogy that leads from Adam to Noah. But the nature of how he is mentioned is deemed significant by those for whom no word or nuance found in the text of God's word can be without significance. For every other individual in the list of descendants of Adam the text reads, "[So-and-so] lived [so-many years] and begot [so-and-so]. And [so-and-so] lived [so many years] after he begot [so-and-so] and begot sons and daughters. And all the days of [so-and-so] were [so-many]; and he died." Enoch, however, is said to have "lived sixty and five years and begot Methusaleh. And Enoch *walked with God* after he begot Methusaleh three hundred years, and begot sons and daughters. And all the days of Enoch were 365 years. And Enoch *walked with God, and he was not; for God took him*" (Gen 5:21–24, emphasis added).

This strange series of shifted references—from "died" to "walked with God, and he was not; for God took him"—could not fail to focus the attention of those studying the text of the Torah carefully. For Judaeans for whom the Torah was the ultimate guide to a covenantal life—and to the branch of their spiritual descendants called Jews—the passages could not be without peculiar significance. It is not surprising, then, that not one but three variant versions of what purportedly happened to Enoch appeared in that part of the world between the last few centuries BCE and the first few centuries CE. One version is in Ethiopic (perhaps based on an Aramaic original), one is in Old Church Slavonic (no doubt based on a Greek original), and one is in Hebrew. Since neither mainstream Jews nor mainstream Christians regard these works as canonical—as directly inspired by God—they are all relegated to the pseudepigrapha.

But for the Jewish *mystic*, who, like other traditional Jews, views every word of the Torah as laden with hidden secrets, the account of Enoch's transcendence into the *sacer*, return to the *profanus*, and final ascent into the *sacer* offers an unraveling of some of those secrets. The experience recorded in the books of Enoch offers another, postbiblical model, beyond the Israelite prophets, for the mystic to emulate. The location of the books of Enoch within the foundations of what will become formal Jewish and Christian mystical doctrine is based on the assumption made by parts of both traditions that, at the least, there are hidden truths to be garnered from a study of Enoch's autobiographical narrative. At the very most, the account has the weight of an inspired, "God's truth" narrative.

The books of Enoch offer variants of the following story. The prophet (for that is how Enoch is viewed by those who accept the books as legitimately God inspired and God true) has lain down to nap when two angelic beings appear at the foot of his bed. After coming toward the frightened hero, they conduct him up through seven heavens, each guarded by a different sort of angel and each offering its own wonders or secrets. At the seventh heaven, Enoch's angelic guides inform him that they can go no further; instead, the archangel Michael leads him further, through the eighth, ninth, and tenth heavens. In the first of these, the planets reside, and in the second, the stars and constellations. In the tenth heaven, he sees before him the throne of God, a vision reminiscent in part of the vision in Isaiah 6 and in part of the vision in Ezekiel 1.

Before the throne of God, Enoch learns why he has been carried on this spectacular journey. He will hear and see and learn and record about the beginning and the end of time—creation and destruction—so that he may return to his children and inform them of all that he has learned, so that they in turn may train themselves and their children to act in a more God-fearing manner and thus be spared destruction when the end of the world as we know it arrives. The narrative then offers a description of some of this, and the reader is to understand that what he or she is reading has been passed down through esoteric channels from the time of Enoch, through his son Methusaleh and through subsequent generations, to the present time.

From the point of view of emerging Jewish and Christian—particularly Jewish—mysticism, the Enoch literature offers four particular points of interest. First, it becomes part of that emergence in spite of not being part of the Hebrew Bible or New Testament, much less the Torah or Gospels. Second, its legitimacy for the mystic is tied to the perception that it offers information extracted from deep beneath the surface of the Torah's text. Third, it offers a vision of the *sacer* that is divided into ten realms, and both the general principal of a paradoxical subdivision of the indivisible *sacer* and the specific notion of "ten-ness" will offer further food for mystical thought.

Fourth, and perhaps most significant, is the manner in which Enoch himself is transformed by the experience he describes. He is, as it were, reborn as a messenger who had been nobody in particular before. In the Hebrew version of the narrative, the principle of transformation is carried in an extraordinary direction. As he is ascending toward the upper heavens, Enoch's flesh-and-blood body changes into pure flame—so he literally and physically ceases to be what he was and becomes something reminiscent of the figure on the *merkavah* of Ezekiel 1.

Moreover, that change is signified by the change of name to which he is subject in the course of his time before the divine presence. He is now called Metatron. It is not only that he becomes someone "else," someone "other"—and thus emulates Jacob, who in his encounter with the *sacer* in the nightlong wrestling match with a *mal'akh/angelos/angelus*/angel, after twenty years away from home, is transformed into Israel—but also that the name change, as with Jacob-Israel, offers great potential significance. For it comes to be associated with his stepping even beyond the uppermost angels in his proximity to God.[6]

Thus, Enoch-become-Metatron offers a powerful experiential model for the mystic to emulate: to be transformed in ascending into intimate contact with God and returning to benefit the community from that experience. His experience also offers a powerful warning: If one were to attempt the mystical enterprise without being properly prepared and properly centered within one's self, and if one began the journey through partial preparation, one might be burned to a crisp. To be transformed into pure fire can be spectacularly uplifting or utterly destructive.

It is the concern for the destructive potential of the *sacer* as it would be manifested upon someone seeking mystical contact with God that would have most preoccupied the Judaean-Jewish and Christian leadership along at least three different but parallel lines. First, the individual would be destroyed. Second, if everyone in the community began to seek oneness with the One on his own, then spiritual anarchy would ensue and the *community* would self-destruct—or an angry God would destroy the community. Third, those designated to lead the community through their wisdom and their knowledge of the Torah or Gospels would lose their position of leadership. Thus, politics and ego are intertwined with spiritual welfare concerns for the individual and the community.

NOTES

1. The English word derives from the Latin *sanctificare*, which, like *sacrificare*, means "to make *sacer*."
2. The word *navi* refers in fact to Aaron as the one who will speak for Moses, who will speak for God.
3. The Hebrew word that is conventionally translated as "angel"—*mal'akh*—means a "messenger," but the term refers only to a divine messenger. The ordinary Hebrew word for an ordinary, *profanus* messenger is *shaliach*.
4. This passage has been subject to two primary interpretations. Judaism understands the Hebrew word *k-r-n* to mean "rays (of light)." Christianity—in part, perhaps because of the association made by the medieval church between Moses and Jews (as opposed to that between Jesus and Christians) and, in turn, between Jews and the Antichrist (who, as the son of Satan by a Judaean harlot, is pictured with horns)—has interpreted *k-r-n* to mean "horn." *K-r-n* means both.
5. This is so since the Hebrew Bible is the totality of divinely inspired scripture according to the Jewish tradition, but according to the Christian tradition, minimally the New Testament and maximally the intertestamental/apocryphal (the label depending upon whether the one referring to it is Catholic, Orthodox, or Protestant) literature, as well as the New Testament, are divinely inspired.
6. Several different interpretations of the name Metatron have been offered over time. One asserts that the name derives from the Greek phrase *meta ton thronon*, or "beyond the throne" (suggesting that Enoch transformed is even closer to God than the throne upon which God paradoxically is said to sit). A second connects the name to the Old Persian/Avestan name *Mithra*—referring to the avatar of Ahura Mazda in Zoroastrianism, who sacrifices his own son to atone for the world's sins and overcome evil. A third theory connects the name to the Latin *mater* or *matrona*, by way of Aramaic *matronita*, referring to the caretaking quality for humanity of Metatron. A fourth suggests that the name comes from the Latin *metator*, meaning "measurer," since, in a sense, he measures the universe in his end-to-end examination of it. Finally, there is the theory that suggests that the name is derived from the Hebrew root *natar*, meaning "to watch, observe," a reference to the manner in which the prophet is offered an oversight of all of reality from the perspective of the uppermost heaven.

Chapter Three

The Emergence of Jewish Mystical Thought

EVOLVING PRELUDES

Since the God of Israel, the *sacer* of Judaism, is by definition seamless, singular, indivisible, then Jewish mysticism *engenders* a paradox in supposing that there is a center within the *sacer* with which the mystic aspires to merge; it hovers at the edge of doctrines that suggest *parts* to the *sacer*. Not surprisingly, the literature of the rabbis—the second postbiblical thread in the tapestry of premystical Jewish literature—contains passages that directly warn the reader away from mystical speculation. The most famous passage in the Talmud, in this respect, is that found in the Tosefta, *Hagiga* 14b:

> Four entered the *Pardes* ("garden/orchard"[1]): Ben 'Azzai, Ben Zoma, Aher, and Rabbi Akiva. Ben 'Azzai glimpsed and died. . . . Ben Zoma glimpsed and went mad. . . . Aher glimpsed and cut the shoots.[2] . . . Only Rabbi Akiva entered in peace and went out in peace.

Thus, the dangers of mystical speculation—of being burnt to a crisp, in Enoch-Metatron terms—are threefold in nature. One might die, go mad, or apostatize—which last, in the world of early Jewish-Christian relations, was considered as dangerous to the individual and to the community as madness or death. And if three very prominent rabbinic figures were not well-enough equipped to survive the experience—if only one in four, the great Akiva, managed it—then what of the rest of us?

There are other references to mystical thought, such as the injunction in tractate *Hagiga* 2:1 not to discuss sexual regulations with three persons, not to discuss the process of the creation of the universe with two persons, and not to discuss the workings of the *merkavah*, the throne-chariot of Ezekiel's vision, with even one.

On the other hand, it is the rabbinic tradition itself that offers occasional glimpses into the mystical enterprise in which those very venerated rabbis who warn us away from that enterprise are sometimes engaged. Thus, we read in chapter 18 of the greater *heikhalot* literature of Rabbi Nehuniah ben HaKana's technique for approaching the throne of God. He achieves a deep trance by means of awe, love, yearning, and utmost concentration, in which he trembles and shakes, chanting as loudly as he can a succession of terms descriptive of God's indescribable qualities. These are repeated in a threefold Hebrew alphabetic series—so that the meaningless alphabetic elements themselves merge with the sense of God that is "meaningless" (i.e., beyond ordinary *profanus* "meaning").

Thus, God is a *noble* king, *powerful* king, *commanding* king, with each descriptive beginning with the first letter of the Hebrew alphabet; then, God is a *blessed* king, *chosen* king, *blinding* king, with each descriptive beginning with the second letter of the Hebrew alphabet, and so on, to the end of the alphabet.[3] He chants these with an ever-increasing speed so that the words cease to make sense as *profanus* words—so that he is uttering nonsense at an increasing pace in order to *transcend* sense.

Suddenly, he finds himself before the throne of glory. (He *suddenly finds himself there* because he has suddenly reached that moment when God reaches toward the properly prepared mystic—he who is in perfect equilibrium—and pulls him over the border into the heart of the *sacer*.) The danger for one who follows this method is that, in losing a sense of *profanus* reality, he will not be able to get it back. And the obligation for the Jewish mystic to return and benefit those around him or her is unequivocal.

Similarly, there is a passage in a *heikhalot* tract in which Rabbi Akiva relates to Rabbi Ishmael the conditions through which he apprehended the divine name. He tells him how first he was *hassid* ("pious"), then "I was *tahor* ('pure')," then "I was *yashar* ('straight, proper')," then "I was *tameem* ('perfect, perfectly simple [in my faith]')," then "I was *m'koodash* ('sanctified')," then "I was *m'daber k'dooshah* ('speaking sanctities, or reciting the prayer known as the *kedooshah*')," then finally he was filled with *yara oopahad* ("fear and trembling"), and suddenly "I grasped the *Shem haM'forash* ('the expounded Name of God')."[4]

The difficulty for the one who would seek to be like Akiva is that he cannot ascend purely through the progression of these attributes. He cannot sufficiently abandon his sense of self (in order to merge with God's "self") so that he may be characterized by these phases or stages without their being statements of self, of narcissistic self-praise, and then be able regain the self that had been abandoned in order to return to the *profanus*. He cannot completely and unequivocally focus on merging with God not for the sake of merging with God, but for the sake of returning to the *profanus* from that mysterious mergence in order to benefit the community for whose sake (rather than for his own) he undertook the journey in the first place. For the goal was not to experience the mysterious mergence but to return from that experience able to benefit the community.

The danger is that he will glimpse and die, go mad, or apostatize as he makes it there, that the ineffability of the experience, which even Akiva cannot fully describe, will be so beyond description that the "returning" mystic will be useless to himself and the community. And what does it mean to grasp God's expounded *name*? It is to traverse that almost absolute distance to God itself: for to grasp someone's name is to grasp that individual's essence and thus, in *some* sense (note the equivocation), to grasp that individual. But the name is not the same as the individual; to pronounce Abraham Lincoln's name is not the same as if Abraham Lincoln, made of flesh and blood, were to enter the room.

And God is not made (in Jewish or Muslim thought) of flesh and blood. But neither is God's name graspable the way a human being's name might be, because as every name is a descriptive, yet God is beyond description, and, moreover, every descriptive term one might use for God is drawn from our *profanus* vocabulary and our *profanus* experience, which we use to attempt to describe what we cannot. So to grasp God's name is to grasp our own terms for God. We get some sense of this from Moses's experience at the burning bush, when he asks God what he should reply to the children of Israel when they ask, "What is His Name? What shall I say unto them?" God's response is both coy and straightforward: "I am that I am" (Ex 3:13–14). It is coy in that at first this seems no response at all, certainly less sensible than the words that follow—"Thus shalt thou say unto the children of Israel: The Lord, the God of your fathers, the God of Abraham, the God of Isaac, the God of Jacob, hath sent me unto you; this is my Name for ever" (Ex 3:15)—which explain who God is in the *profanus* terms of genealogy: the One who led your ancestors and therefore has an interest in and a relationship with you.

But "I am that I am" is more difficult to grasp, yet closer to the truth of who and what God *is*. God is pure being—pure "is-ness"—and has no predication (I am a man; you are tall; she is a teacher; he is smart): *what* God is, is simply *that* God is. Thus, if a name captures the essence of its bearer, "I am" captures the essence of God, who *is* pure essence. The ultimate root letter of the Hebrew verb "to be," found in the word *ehyeh* translated as "I am"—the "h"—centers the Hebrew name of God, the Tetragrammaton, *YHVH*, just as it centers the phrase in Genesis 1:1 that refers to the nature of reality before the creative process begins—*tohu vavohu*. So God has actually responded to Moses's question straightforwardly: My name, which is my essence, is that I am. More to the point, "I am and will [always] be that I am and will [always] be," since the Hebrew verb "to be" does not distinguish the present from future tenses. Past perfect (in the grammatical sense of *perfectus*—"completely done") is one condition, and the other is present-future, imperfect: not done. God is eternal, not done, ongoingness itself, and that is how God has responded to Moses's inquiry.

But what other means does Akiva possess to express what he experienced than merely to refer to God's name? He says that he grasped God's *expounded, expanded, precise* name. The *Shem haM'forash* is both the precise and correct articulation of the Tetragrammaton (known only to the high priest in the Temple in Jerusalem and, since its destruction, to nobody else in the *profanus* realm) and the expanded deconstruction of God's ineffable name by way of permutations and combinations of numerology and phrases from the Torah. Thus, for example—in perhaps its most frequent form—if one examines the Tetragrammaton from a numerological viewpoint, its four letters "add up" to 26 (Y = 10; H = 5; V = 6; H = 5). If one then systematically deconstructs the name, by successively removing the last letter (H, leaving YHV), the last two letters (VH, leaving YH), and finally the last three letters (HVH, leaving Y), the remaining three sequences of letters "add up" to 21, 15, and 10, respectively. If one then adds all four iterations of the Divine Name and its parts together by way of this process—known in the pagan Greek Pythagorean circles that may have exerted an influence on early Jewish mysticism as *klima*—one arrives at 72. And thus, there is a secret, hidden correspondence between that number and God's hidden, inner essence.

That this is the *Shem haM'forash*—the expounded, expanded, precise name of God—is "confirmed" by the fact that the number 72 figures so significantly into a central passage in the Hebrew Bible. That passage comes in the book of Exodus at the critical moment when the Israelites are about to pass safely from the *profanus* of Egypt into the *sacer* of the wilderness across the boundary of the Sea of Reeds. This is both a passage in which God acts as a dramatic savior—parting the waves through which they pass and stopping their Egyptian pursuers, literally, dead in their tracks so that the Israelites may move forward—and the beginning of the transformation of the Israelites as a priestly people, defined as such by the moment at Sinai, in the heart of the *sacer*, when they embrace the covenant. In the moment leading to their salvation and the passage into transformation,

> the angel of God, who went before the camp of Israel, removed and went behind them; and the pillar of cloud removed from before them, and stood behind them;

and it came between the camp of Egypt and the camp of Israel; and there was the cloud and the darkness here, yet it gave light by night there; and the one came not near the other the entire night. And Moses stretched forth his hand over the sea; and the Lord caused the sea to go back by a strong east wind all the night, and made the sea dry land, and the waters divided. (Ex 14:19–21)

Each of the three verses of the text consists of precisely seventy-two letters. Since it is a given to the Jewish mystic that not a single letter of the Torah, which is God's word, can be spoken or written in error or by accident or without significance, the repetition of seventy-two at this crucial moment must be a hint at something important: a key to an understanding of God's soteriological essence. That essence is conveyed not on the surface of a name made up of four letters but hidden beneath the surface of that name and accessible only by the appropriate deconstruction of it—and by the connection of it to the central soteriological passage in the Torah. For by laying out the three verses from Exodus side by side and continually shifting them against each other, one obtains an exponentially expanded series of permutational "names" for God. *That* is the name and the essence that Akiva grasped.[5]

In the general terms that lead to the specifics of this sort of numerological discussion of the name(s) of God, we also recognize not only that the Jewish mystical tradition has part of its own roots in the rabbinic tradition but also that the goal and methodology of Jewish mysticism is a furthering, an intensification, of the midrashic tradition. Specifically, the term *midrash* is based on a Hebrew root meaning "to dig." Midrash seeks to dig beneath the surface of the Torah's text for answers to God-related and other questions that are not apparent on the surface, for the ultimate bridge between God and Israel *is* the Torah, the five books of Moses. All matters regarding the prescribed patterns of behavior for a community that wishes to exist in a covenantal relationship with the *sacer*, to *be* a *sacer profanus*, will be found there, according to the Jewish tradition. So also will the answer to the ultimate question, the initial paradox of macrocosmic reality in its relationship to the *sacer*: How is it that an invisible, intangible, singular, seamless, inaccessible, transcendent, all-good God engendered a reality—our world—which is visible, tangible, multifarious, seamed, accessible, immanent, and a mixture of good and evil?

The long and varied history of Jewish mysticism is the history of an intense and varied response to this ultimate paradox as it is the history of an intense superrational inquiry into the *sacer* as it is understood in Judaism. It is, in a fundamental sense, an ongoing exploration of the Torah, which holds the key to the door out of the paradox. The Torah, after all, *offers* us the answer to the question: Genesis tells us, "In the beginning, God created . . . and God said, 'Let there be . . . ' and there was." Yet that hardly answers the question, even as it answers the question, because it doesn't indicate *how* God created or God said. Stated otherwise, the text offers only the surface, and much digging is required to find the fuller answer hidden in the center of the centerless/centered *sacer*—beneath the surface of that which, in its absolute amorphousness, has no "surface" and no "beneath."[6]

There are particular *midrashim* that might be called mystical because of the intensity with which they dig, because of the method that they suggest for understanding moments in the text of the Torah that address God and God's creative act, and because of the presupposition they offer that there *is* a hiddenmost recess of God to which their digging can bring us. So a midrash that focuses on the opening word of the Torah, *berayshit*—in English, it becomes a phrase, "in the beginning"—in order to understand an aspect of that equiprimordial process, is addressed by juxtaposing that phrase with a passage in Psalm 111. At the beginning of the last verse of the psalm, *rayshit* ("beginning") and *hokhmah* ("wisdom") are juxtaposed. The passage is normally rendered as "the beginning of wisdom" (which phrase is followed by "is fear/ awe of the Lord"). But digging beneath the surface of the text yields to the midrashic interpreter the idea that *hokhmah* and *rayshit* are intended to be treated as equivalents; therefore, to impose that understanding on Genesis 1:1 yields the phrase "With wisdom God created the heavens and the earth" as the opening phrase of the Torah.

That such a rendering is both legitimate and self-declared to be mystical—*hidden* from everyday view—is confirmed for the mystic by the fact that Psalm 111 begins with the words, "I shall give thanks to the Lord with all my heart, [and] with the council of the upright and in the congregation," for the word rendered here conventionally as "council" (*sod*) may also be rendered as "secret"; thus, "in [both] the secret [realm] of the upright [and] in the congregation" (i.e., both in secret and publicly, I shall give thanks). The use of the term *sod,* among the several that could have served here if the intention were merely to say "council," cannot, to the mystic, be accidental. It is used by God (the psalms, after all, are God's words filtered through the ultimate anointed king over Israel, David) to inform the deconstructionist mystic that the juxtaposition at the end of the psalm is also intentional. And the notion of wisdom—*hokhmah* in Hebrew and *sophia* in Greek—as an instrument in God's creative process will have repercussions for Jewish mysticism, from its early stages in which Greek (more precisely, Stoic) thinking is an influence on it, to its later developments.[7]

Moreover, just as other scriptural passages, such as Proverbs 8 and Job 28, point the mystic toward divine wisdom as the instrument with which God creates the universe, for some of those mystical thinkers, wisdom is understood to be equated with the Torah itself: The text that describes creation is understood to embody and encompass divine wisdom as that wisdom has been dispensed to us, which means that it (the Torah) predates the creative process it describes, just as divine wisdom naturally (or, rather, supernaturally) does.[8] Further, since the Torah is the word of God, then "word" itself will come to be perceived, in some circles, as an intermediating instrument of God's creative acts. For not only do the words of the Torah repeatedly offer, "and God said, 'Let there be . . . ' and there was" (so that God's words yielded *profanus* reality), but also the biblical word for "word"—*davar*—is also the word for "thing." Thus, words as abstract effluences from God inherently (mysteriously, one might say) *are*—or *represent*—every abstract and concrete aspect of *profanus* reality that God calls into being, from light to humans.

Similarly, the question is asked, where does the light declared into creation in Genesis 1:3 come from? The *Midrash Rabba* (*Great Midrash*) asserts that God wrapped itself in light as in a robe and irradiated the whole world thereby—suggesting the notion of a substance (i.e., light) emanating from pure being, which substance, while making it possible for us to see the world is itself neither visible nor touchable—and the midrash observes that this tale is told "in a whisper," as if a secret, as if it is part of the mass of secret doctrines that are the basis for mysticism. This is one instance, then, in which the midrash self-reflexively claims to be part of a hidden body of knowledge available only to a select group of initiates.

A particular group of late–Second Temple–period initiates with their own literature exemplified the notion of a fringe community within the late Judaean time frame. The Dead Sea texts of the Qumran community included one that is popularly called the "Battle Scroll" in which the forces of good, led by the Good Teacher, will confront the forces of evil, led by the Wicked Priest, in an apocalyptic battle at the end of time as we know it. More to the point, the forces of good, led by God, pour forth the sort of hosts—armies— of angelic beings that, in retrospect, *must* (from the viewpoint of a Qumran interpreter) have been meant by the phrase in Isaiah 6, "Lord of hosts." Those forces are described with respect to two noteworthy kinds of detail. One is numerological: They are inevitably arrayed in groups of seven or in forces organized along lines that emphasize the number seven ("on the seventh occasion the great hand of God shall finally subdue [the army of Belial]"). Thus, the scroll offers broad allusion to that symbol of perfection and completion in the ancient pagan Middle Eastern cultural and religious tradition (tied to the number of the *planetes* viewable with the naked eye)[9] and its specific reference to conclusion and perfection in the Hebrew-Israelite-Judaean tradition that connects the completion of the physical universe in Genesis 1–2 to the twice-stated commandment to keep the seventh day *sacer*, in Exodus 20 and Deuteronomy 5.

The second noteworthy detail is that the hosts of the Lord are described as bearing banners into that final battle on which are inscribed key soteriological passages echoing that aspect of Torah-based thinking that represents God in a warrior aspect (as, for example, in the battle of the Israelites in the wilderness against the Amalekites), such as "[t]he Wrath of God will burn against Belial"[10] and against men "whose loss is with him until none survives," or "[t]he Place of the Power of Evil Men shall cease through the might of God," or "Truth of God, Righteousness of God, Glory of God, Judgment of God"—which last is notably a four-part statement of God's powerful presence in the conflict about to unfold, corresponding in numerologically symbolic terms to the four letters in the Tetragrammaton. The trumpets that lead the Sons of Light into battle will also be marked by mottos, such as "God smites all the Children of Darkness; may His Anger not subside until they are destroyed."

It should not surprise us if the thinking reflected in the Qumran material were also to offer a thread that will be woven into the Jewish (and Christian) mystical tapestry as that tapestry is taking form during the first centuries CE. Moreover, other sources that fall even farther outside the mainstream than the books of Enoch or the Dead Sea texts—or certainly outside what the mainstream leadership views as legitimate reading for Jews—feed into nascent Jewish mysticism. Some of these texts derive from concerns that would seem to fall outside the highly esoterically charged, deepest, hiddenmost, God-focused concerns of mysticism altogether. Thus, Greco-Roman pagan material may be seen to have filtered into what is developing as Jewish and Christian mysticism, ranging from the numerology of Pythagoreanism to magical papyrae to philosophical writings by Hellenized Judaeans such as Philo of Alexandria.

Pythagoras (ca. 569–475 BCE) was widely known for having founded a community in Croton, in southern Italy, which combined scientific and religious thinking and followed a code of secrecy. His group was ascetic, vegetarian, and asserted that, in its deepest recesses, reality is mathematical in nature; that the soul can merge, under the proper conditions, with the divine; and that certain symbols carry hidden—mystical—meanings. His circle was arguably the first in Western civilization to wrestle with the concept of pure number and mathematical figures like the triangle as a means of grappling with the abstract principles of mathematics and using abstract ideas to formulate mathematical proofs. Thus, "twoness" and "fiveness" as concepts, rather than, say, "two books" or "five fingers," were his focus, and he believed that reality could be reduced to numerical relations. Moreover, he ascribed to each number a "personality," or identity, including masculine or feminine, complete or incomplete, beautiful or ugly. The perfect number is, according to his thinking, ten. It is contained within the first four numbers—$1 + 2 + 3 + 4 = 10$—and these four integers, written in dot notation, form a perfect triangle. (Pythagoras is best known today for the various theorems that associate his name with the geometric and algebraic identities of triangles.)

Philo's discussion of *logos*—a term which, in the late Hellenistic Greek of Philo's time (ca. 50 BCE to 50 CE), may be roughly translated as "word"—addresses the issue of God *saying*, "Let there be light," "Let there be a firmament," and so on. As we have observed above, if God *said*, then the *word* of God may be understood to *intermediate* between God itself and the universe that God creates through the *word*, the *saying*. For Philo, *logos* is quasiconcretized as the eldest among the angels, as he treats God's words (*d'varim*, *logoi*) as *malakhim* (angels). So it is that Jacob, in wrestling with an angel, is transformed and reborn as Israel (one who has wrestled with God by wrestling with God's word). So it is that *d'varim-logoi* is the process of transforming God—pure form, substanceless essence—into the universe of matter and substance. In this, Philo is drawing upon the Platonic philosophical tradition (in which pure form is found in the realm of the forms or ideas) to aid him in understanding the biblical text. And this concatenation of thought patterns will feed into early Jewish and Christian mysticism.

Conventional thinking would suggest that, from the passages within the Torah and the Hebrew Bible, to the dangerous texts of Enoch, to passages within early rabbinic literature, to material from Qumran, to that from the pagan world of Pythagoras and the Hellenized Jewish world of Philo, one should have exhausted the source material for the beginnings of Jewish mysticism. More broadly, the goals of early Jewish mysticism seem to be set: to gain an impossible proximity to the awesome, transcendent, inaccessible God and to return to the community spiritually enriched by that experience and capable of spiritually enriching the community in a world fraught both with a sense of the ubiquity of the *sacer* and, for Christians and Jews in particular, with a concern that the wrong approach to the *sacer* will yield disastrous results for the *profanus*. But there is still more.

The notion of "magical" texts raises an obvious issue: religion addresses the *sacer*; the point and purpose of religious systems is to engage the *sacer*, in its guise as divinity, to assure the survival of the *profanus* by receiving blessing and not curse from the *sacer*. Mysticism offers both the assumption that there is a hiddenness within the *sacer* that ordinary religious rite and ritual do not and cannot access and the method to access it. Magic also addresses itself to the *sacer* in order to affect some positive (or negative) result in the *profanus*. There are at least two different ways of understanding the distinction between magic and religion. The broadest and most common is that "what is mine is religion; what is yours is magic"—by which I mean that the *sacerdos* who either understands the *sacer* to be different from what I think it is or who seeks to engage it by a method that I don't recognize as legitimate is labeled by me a magician rather than a priest. Thus, the priests of the pharaoh, when they are shown in competition with Moses and Aaron, are referred to by the biblical text as *magicians*, not *priests* as the pharaoh would have called them. Indeed, the term "magic" itself, derived from the Latin word *magus*, is itself ultimately a derivative of a Persian word meaning "priest," but in the competition with Zoroastrianism, the early church reduced its (Zoroastrianism's) misguided *sacerdotes* in conception. The legacy of that reduction is the nuance that attached itself, and still does, in the various European languages, to the Persian, Zoroastrian-derived terms *magus* or "magician."

This sort of process, of distinguishing mine from yours, is the same that leads to the labels "superstition" and "myth." What's mine is a God's-truth account, say, of the creation, which is the basis of my religion; yours—Hesiod's Greek account or the Mesopotamian Enuma Elish—is mythology. My legitimate and real sense of how to engage the *sacer* is religion; yours, false and misguided, is superstition. Of course, that distinction is also rooted in the legal-political usage of these last two terms by the Romans, who distinguished *religio licita* (a legitimate belief system) from *superstitio* (an illegitimate, illegal, political subversion, the spiritual particulars of which are almost beside the point), as we have seen. In the centuries during which the pagan Roman world was subject to the spread in popularity of Judaeanism and its progeny, as those progeny became increasingly distinct from each other, Christianity was treated as a *superstitio* until Constantine's famous Edict of Milan (313 CE) legitimized it; Judaism was treated, with a few exceptions (e.g., the 135–138 CE aftermath of the 132–135 CE Bar Kokhba Revolt), as a *religio*. By circa 390, under Theodosius, Christianity had become the only *religio* of the empire, and Judaism, Zoroastrianism, and all of the pagan forms of faith came to be called and understood as *superstitiones*.

But the magical texts to which I refer fall into a more complicated category than that labeled "magical" due to a connection with the wrong tradition. On the contrary, what often marks them is the degree to which one may discern elements that are both pagan and either Jewish, Christian, or both. Works like the so-called *Greek Magical Papyrae* are understood to be essentially pagan texts; yet, they possess a wealth of vocabulary and imagery that may be recognized as Jewish or Christian, such as references to the *sacer*, which use names for God which derive, for instance, from the phraseology of Isaiah 6: *Adonai Tzva'ot* ("Lord of Hosts")—but usually corrupted to *Adonai Sabbaoth*, as the words *shabbat* and *tzva'ot* ("hosts, armies") have been confused and synthesized. If confusion and synthesis correctly account for this verbal corruption, then that would suggest a non-Jewish practitioner, but one who covers his spiritual bases by including the names of the Jewish God among the elements of the *sacer* that he addresses. Similarly, a range of angelic names is found in these texts, suggesting both a connection to or influence from the Judaeans associated with Qumran or, later, the Christian community and its extended angelology.

Another biblical figure who is significant in what are primarily pagan texts is Moses, for it turns out that pagans of the late Roman period were very aware of that Israelite *sacerdos* par excellence and, based on the stories that they had heard, also saw him as a preeminent practitioner of magic. He who with his staff could guide the transformation of Aaron's staff into a serpent that devoured the serpent-staffs of the pharaoh's magician-priests; who could part the seas and cause them to return to unity; who could bring forth water from a rock and edible food from the empty skies—such an individual must truly be a most powerful *sacerdos*.[11]

Nor was the importance of Moses as a magician limited to the pagan population. Any number of apparently Jewish texts—they are written in Hebrew—look to Moses either as the model to emulate in seeking to establish a connection with God or present him as a guide for that connection. *The Sword of Moses*, for example, is a compendium of magical formulae that make use of "secret" divine names that have as their goal to effect results in the *profanus* by setting in motion elements in the *sacer* through the manipulation of those names. The "sword" of the book's title is in fact devised of God's ineffable and expounded, expanded names: Moses, master of the names, possesses the "sword" with which he can accomplish virtually anything; the practitioner petitions him to put that power to use on behalf of the petitioner.

A similar text, albeit not one that focuses through Moses, is the *Sepher HaRazim*, the *Book of Secrets*.[12] Like *The Sword of Moses* and the *Greek Magical Papyrae*, it dates from the second or third century CE and, for the most part, has as its purpose to effect immediate and limited results in the *profanus*. The text opens with the following words:

This is one of the books of mysteries that were given to Noah, the son of Lamech, the son of Jared, the son of Methuselah, the son of Enoch [and so on, back to Adam]. It was given to him by Razi-El, the angel, at the time when he [Noah] came to the ark but before his entrance [into it]. And he [Noah] inscribed it on a sapphire stone very clearly. He learned from it the doing of wondrous deeds, secrets of knowledge, hierarchies of understanding, conceptions of humility, and ideas of wisdom. [He learned] how to ascend toward searching the heights of heaven, to gaze into the destinies of the stars, to examine the course of the sun, to explain the phases of the moon and to know the paths of the Great Bear, Orion and the Pleiades. He learned how to reveal the names of the overseers of each and every firmament, and their kingdoms, and how they will be appropriate for each thing and the names of their attendants, and what is a [proper] libation for [each of] them, and what is the proper time to hearken to them, so that one may accomplish in purity each and every offering for them.

We recognize, first of all, that Noah, referred to in Genesis 6 as *tzadik beDoro*—"righteous within his generation"—and builder of the great ark that enabled him, his family, and a carefully prescribed percentage of the animal world to survive the great deluge, is also perceived as a great *sacerdos*. In the case of this text, he is offered as the intermediary between the *sacer* and the *profanus* for the practitioner; the secrets found within the text that follows this introduction were revealed to him by a higher intermediator, an emissary of the *sacer*, whose very Hebrew name, Razi-El, means "secret(s) of God." This text purports to have been handed down, generation by generation, until it arrived into the hands of the writer of the introduction, and it claims to offer an amazing range of kinds of esoteric knowledge. This includes some of the very sorts of knowledge (such as the workings of the heavens) that Job lacks when God inquires of his loyal and long-suffering acolyte in the divine response out of the whirlwind (Job 38ff); it also includes the implied knowledge of how to ascend toward the throne of Heaven through the sort of passageways through which Enoch traveled.

The text goes on to note that Noah learned from it how to understand good and evil and to know "the time to give birth and the time to die"—this last a reference to the biblical book of Ecclesiastes. But following the introductory material, the *Book of Secrets* turns to very practical information, such as how to cause someone to fall in love with you. Thus,

[i]f you desire to speak with the moon or the stars concerning any matter, take a white rooster and fine flour, slaughter the rooster so that its blood is caught in fresh water. Mix the flour with the water and the blood and make three cakes and place them in the sun and write upon them in blood the name of the overseer and then place the three of them upon a table of myrtle wood and stand facing the sun and say:

I adjure you, that you bring the planet of X and his/her star near to the star and planet of Y so that the love of him/her will be tied to the heart of Y son of Z. Place fire from your fire in the heart of this man/woman so that s/he will abandon his/her father's and mother's house because of his/her love for Y, son/daughter of Z.

Then take two of the cakes and put them with the rooster[13] in a new flask, seal its mouth with wax and hide the flask in a place where there is no sunlight. (lines 160–69)

And it continues from there. What we may immediately recognize is that such a "magical" text has, as its goal, to provide its user with decidedly localized, *personal* results. This connects at most in methodological configuration to the pattern of "mystical" texts. The latter are by definition—must be, if they are to be efficacious—focused on improving the spiritual lot of the community at large. The practitioner must be humble and selfless—by definition, since his or her goal is to be filled with God (and that can only happen if the self is emptied of "self") and to return from the experience of being thusly filled spiritually enriched and functional as a source of enrichment for the *profanus*. Having as a goal to make someone love you, or "if you desire that deeds of kindness [be done] to you" (line 170), then your invocation of the *sacer*, with its much more limited and selfish scope, cannot be called mystical. What distinguishes these texts from mystical texts—even as they are part of the rich threading that will become the double tapestry of Jewish and Christian mysticism—is the nature of what it is that they seek in seeking an engagement with the *sacer*.

There are other texts that feed into early Jewish mysticism and present difficulties to the purist—certainly the Jewish (as opposed to Christian) purist. The *She'ur Komah*—the *Measure of Stature*—which offers a gargantuan metaphor of God's greatness by presenting the enormous measurement of God's body, is by definition anathema to the Jewish view of an unequivocally nonphysical God. The work may be understood as allegorical, as one that uses aspects of human experience—words, numbers, and the various concepts of size—as a means of underscoring how beyond the scope of human experience and understanding God truly is, how much more unfathomable than the unfathomable description before the student of this text. In which case, the awesome distance from God—the impossible transcendence of a God who is completely inaccessible and yet whom, by paradox, the mystic seeks and whom the mystic believes he or she can access—is underscored. That sensibility will feed directly into *merkavah* mysticism, as we shall shortly see. But such a text also underscores the danger to the unprepared inquirer: To mistake the discussion in the *She'ur Komah* as anything but allegorical would be to risk apostasy or madness.

THE BEGINNINGS OF FORMAL JEWISH MYSTICISM

But the earliest systematic treatment that might be called mystical turns to the problem to which mystical thought, like religious thought in general, always returns—the problem of creation, of how it is and why it is that a singular

God created an endlessly multifarious universe (and additionally, from a Jewish or Muslim viewpoint, being inaccessible to the senses, created a universe that is so largely defined by the senses). That first treatment is credited by tradition to none other than Rabbi Akiva and called the *Sepher Yetzirah*. A later tradition suggests that the book was revealed to Abraham, who passed it on to Isaac, who in turn passed it on to Jacob, and so it was passed down all the way to Akiva, who wrote it down. This is a short work, only six chapters long, written in a rhythmical style not atypical of Near Eastern wisdom literature, with key terminology that is borrowed from Greek. There are legends within rabbinic literature itself that, with the help of the *Sepher Yetzirah*, Rabbi Osaiah and Rabbi Haninah created a three-year-old calf (*Sanhedrin* 65b, 67b) and that Rabbi Joshua ben Hananyah created deer and fawns from cucumbers and pumpkins (*Sanhedrin* VII, 154).

Two issues should immediately occur to us. First, the rabbinic references to its usage in this manner once again raise the question as to where the line between mysticism and its goals and magic should be drawn. Both of these legends suggest effecting material, not spiritual, results in the *profanus*, with no clear intention regarding how the community will be morally or otherwise improved by the success of the practitioners' *sacer* contacts. Second, the very name of the book implies the humility of its author (whoever he or she may have been), who, in spite of writing a treatise about how God created the universe, dared not use the term *bri'ah*, which is used in Genesis to refer to God's creation *ex nihilo*—and is only used for such *divine* creative acts—as if that would be presumptuous. The word *yetzirah* means "formation" or "shaping"—such as a potter or sculptor does with the clay or stone that becomes a bowl or a sculpture or such as a carpenter does in transforming a block of wood into a table or statue. Thus, the *Sepher Yetzirah*, in explaining *bri'ah*, refers to it as *yetzirah*, as if there is still something further, still more hidden, beyond the point at which the book begins.

We might expect the *Sepher* to be an exposition of the Torah, since that text is the ultimate access panel to the *sacer* and therefore to its *mysterion* in the Jewish tradition. As the direct word of God, the Torah would be expected to contain all the ultimate secrets that might exist for making contact with the *mysterion*, and we have observed that any number of passages in the early rabbinic tradition that we term mystical are deconstructive explorations of words or phrases in the Torah, digging beneath the surface of the text in order to dig beneath the surface of the *sacer* source of that text. But a systematic exposition will come later. The *Sepher Yetzirah*, beginning where the Torah does, with the problematic of creation, might be called a commentary on the first chapter of Genesis, but only by implication. For the *Sepher* asserts,

With 32 miraculous paths of Wisdom engraved *Yah* the Lord of Hosts the God of Israel the living God and King of the Universe *El Shaddai*, Merciful and Gracious High and Exalted Dwelling in Eternity and Whose Name is Holy—He is lofty and holy—and created His universe with three books: with text and number and telling.

In this first sentence, we might note at least three issues of interest. First, the process of creation (and the verb to which the text arrives toward the end of the sentence *is* the sibling of the noun *bri'ah*) is one of engraving along the paths that we shall shortly recognize as those of the twenty-two letters of the Hebrew alphabet and the ten numbers. Put otherwise, the question of how a singular God, invisible, intangible, inaccessible to the senses, created a universe that seems to be the opposite of itself—for our world is endlessly multifarious; it is visible, tangible, and accessed in large part by the senses—is answered by means of elements that fall, in parallel ways, between sense and concreteness on the one hand and absolute senseless abstraction on the other.

The letters—and the intention is to suggest both the sounds signified by the letters and their written forms, but not necessarily their written forms, per se[14]—are themselves abstract, both visually and phonically. One cannot put one's finger on "b-ness" or "d-ness" or the sounds signified by those letters (or rather, their Hebrew equivalents, *bet* and *dalet*), but the quintessential instrument with which humans engage the world, language, is a compendium of such sounds (and in its written form, of such letters) that, organized in specified groupings (as words and phrases), are our uniquely human means of accessing the world around us, of addressing and describing it. One could argue that we don't really grasp the world's concrete *elementa* until we have labeled them with the terms that, comprised of sound-letters, comprise language. That the *Sepher Yetzirah* assumes that the most fundamental of sound-letters are those of Hebrew reflects the emerging importance given in the Jewish mystical tradition to that language: If the Torah was originally written in Hebrew, and the Torah is the ultimate exemplum of God's word, then God's preferred language must be Hebrew. Analogously, the numbers are themselves abstract: One cannot put one's finger on "oneness" or "fiveness." (We should recognize the echo of Pythagoras in this issue.) But they are fundamental to how humans live in the world: We not only understand simply enough the difference between one finger or book and five fingers or books, but in the *profanus* reality of the marketplace, understanding how numbers work is essential for survival.

The second issue is that most of the sentence is occupied with varied name references to God. This preoccupation offers two aspects of interest. First, the range of names underscores the impossibility of "labeling" God by means of a name—and the same is at least as true with respect to adjectives used to describe God. Second, at the same time, there are particular significances to the names. Thus, what I have not translated—*Yah*—cannot be easily rendered into English; it might be translated as "is-ness." But the name that follows, for which I have followed the convention of translating it as "Lord" (of Hosts), is built on the same Hebrew root and could also be translated as "is-ness." It is with this in mind that we think back—and the *Sepher Yetzirah* thinks back—to the passage in Exodus 3 in which God responds to Moses's question as to who it is that sends him (Moses) by stating "I am/will be that I am/will be"; in other words, God's response is to assert that God is is-ness itself (see above, pp. 35–36). Similarly, I have not translated *El Shaddai*. The first part, *El*, might easily enough be rendered as "Lord" or even as "God," but *Shaddai* brooks no translation, but rather interpretation: It is the name used to refer to God's power-protective aspect.[15]

The point in this simple and complex exercise in the ineffability of God's name—unspeakable, ultimately unknowable except by the sort of *sacerdos* that Moses or Isaiah were, or that the high priest in the temple was, or that the Messiah might be—intersects the notion of how sound-letters function in the human access of both the *profanus* and the *sacer*. That is, language is a particularly rich and far-reaching instrument, but ultimately language falls short of being an effective instrument, even in aspects of engaging the *profanus*, and the more so in *engaging* the *sacer*. Words can hardly succeed in expressing the beauty of a sunset or the love a parent for his or her child; how can they possibly afford an effective means of labeling or describing God, as we observed at the beginning of this discussion?

The third issue of interest, which interweaves with the first two, is the way in which the sentence ends. The word that I have translated as "books" (*sepharim*) and the three words that follow are all contrived from precisely the same consonantal roots: "text" is *sepher*, "number" is *sephar*, and "telling" is *sippur*. Since, in Hebrew, vowels are of virtual insignificance with respect to how a word conveys the essence of the entity to which it is attached, even though the three terms are vocally different from each other, they are all the same term, for they are comprised of the same elements.[16] The connection between numbers and counting on the one hand and telling and texts on the other will offer a wide range of issues that will be picked up in the subsequent layers of Jewish mystical thought. Further, the notion of a *triune* concept that is linguistically suggested in the *Sepher Yetzirah*'s first sentence will help contribute to the concern that mainstream Jewish leadership will periodically voice regarding mystical speculation, since one of the dangers that leadership will see is that of apostasy, and the Christian concept of God as triune could be perceived as legitimized by that sentence.

The second sentence of the book elaborates, both on the *s-p(h)-r* root, which it now uses to construct yet another word, *sephirot* ("countings" or possibly "spheres," in which second case, the word would be a borrowing from Greek[17]), and so,

> ten *sephirot* of nothingness

and also on the sound-letters:

> and twenty-two foundation letters: three mothers, seven doubles, and twelve elementals.

Thus, the twenty-two sound-letters are themselves subdivided into three types. The first type corresponds in its number (three) to the number of elements beyond the earth (water, air, and fire), but also to the number of components of the Jewish people for ritual purposes: *kohayn, levi, yisrael*[18]. The second corresponds to the number of planets (seven), but also to the number of branches of the temple menorah. The third corresponds to the number of zodiacal zones into which the Greco-Roman world habitually divided the sphere of fixed stars (twelve), but this is also the number of Israelite tribes.

Part of this interpretation needs to be inferred from later commentators, since the *Sepher* merely refers to the three categories of sound-letters, without specifying which are which. But it becomes fairly simple to accept the deduction: the "doubles"—*bet, gimmel, dalet, kaf, peh, resh*, and *tav*—were all originally phonemic pairs (some still are, in contemporary Hebrew), the sound value of which shifted depending whether a *dagesh* (dot) was associated with the spelling.[19] The "mothers" derive their identity from the phonemic association with the words for the three trans-*profanus* elements: *aleph* would be the first letter of the word for air, *aveer*; *mem* would be the first letter of the word for water, *mayim*; and *shin* would be the first letter of the word for heaven (in Greek terms, the *aither*: the "blazing" and thus "fire"), *shamayim*. This leaves the twelve letters that are otherwise unaccounted for. We recognize in this discussion the intention of underscoring that these sound-letters are ultimately connectors between the Creator and the macrocosm in its transcendental aspects, as well as between the Creator and the people Israel.

But it is the *sephirot*, not the sound-letters, that preoccupies most of the *Sepher*[20]; in the third sentence, that preoccupation forges a connection between the Creator and the human microcosm. Thus,

> Ten *Sephirot* of nothingness in the number of fingers. Five opposite five.

which alludes, perhaps, to the passage in Psalms 8:4 that refers to the heavens as "the work of Your fingers." Later commentators have asserted that the number of bones in the five fingers is fourteen, which corresponds to the numerology for the Hebrew word for "hand" (*YaD*), but this is nowhere stated in the *Sepher* itself. The fourth verse, however, which repeats the mantra "Ten *Sephirot* of nothingness," follows it with the words "ten and not nine, ten and not eleven," underscoring the important principle of precision, endemic to religion and its rites of engagement with the *sacer*. So, too, the fifth verse (after repeating the same mantra) continues

> Their measure is ten, which have no end, a depth of beginning a depth of end, a depth of good a depth of evil, a depth of above a depth of below, a depth of east a depth of west, a depth of north a depth of south, the singular Master God, faithful King rules them all from His holy dwelling until eternity of eternities.

Thus, space and time, in their infinite, unfathomable natures, are engaged: Opposed spatial and moral concepts are juxtaposed to suggest their nonoppositional coexistence—all of reality in all of its aspects and directions is contained in the *Sephirot* that are both precisely ten and infinite (and "ten-ness" itself possesses no end, of course!)—and the One God who encompasses them all is itself beyond time. Even "eternity" is insufficient as a term to characterize God's timelessness; the text generates a beyond-the-beyond, timeless time turn of phrase: "eternity of eternities."

That the *Sepher Yetzirah* looks both backward and forward becomes obvious in the sixth verse, where the "ten *Sephirot* of nothingness" have their vision likened to "the appearance of lightning," and God's word in them is "running and returning." One might recognize the sort of imagery found in Ezekiel 1 and its vision of the *merkavah*—although the Hebrew terminology is not identical. The word that I have rendered as "vision" is *Tzafiyah*, which term, in biblical Hebrew, is one of the words used of a prophetic vision and appears in the *heikhalot* literature (to which we shall shortly turn) within the phrase "vision of the *Merkavah*." It is the *merkavah* literature that is in the process of being born with the *Sepher Yetzirah*, and in both the emphasis on the ten *Sephirot* and this particular turn of phrase, we have entered the first period of formal mysticism in the Jewish tradition.

That phase, *merkavah* mysticism, derives its designation from the emphasis it puts on the vision of Ezekiel as a mystical starting point. Five issues might be immediately noted in considering the shape of that starting point. First, whereas the *Sepher Yetzirah* in an indirect sense derives its inspiration from the Torah in discussing the process of creation that is presented in Genesis, *merkavah* mysticism's starting point is a text within the Hebrew Bible (the book of Ezekiel) but outside the Torah. Second, whereas the *Sepher Yet-zirah* presents a discussion of the process of creation, the *merkavah* literature offers visions of the *sacer* whence that creative process was initiated, not of the process. Third, in turning to the book that bears his name, the *merkavah* tradition presents the prophet Ezekiel as an individual worthy of particular focus as a model to emulate, as someone whose vision carried him into intimate contact with the otherwise hidden *sacer*. Fourth, the vision of the *merkavah*, as a focus of mediation and concentration, is an exceedingly complex one fraught with paradox and contradiction. Fifth, the culmination of the vision underscores both that complexity and paradox and the nature of the prophet's experience: As intimate as his contact with the hiddenmost *sacer* is, beyond the lower aspects of the *merkavah*—the *hayyot* and the *ophanim*—toward the fiery, icy being that hovers above/within the throne and the firmament, that contact is, in the end, thrice removed from absolute. He "arrives" at what is "merely" the "*appearance* of the *likeness* of the *glory* of God," as we recall, and not, as it were, at God itself.

Thus, the *merkavah*-envisioning experience of Ezekiel underscores the emphasis in *merkavah* mysticism on the absolute transcendence—the ultimate inaccessibility—of God, even as it offers a model of access into the transcendent, inaccessible realm of God. That inaccessibility is underscored by the various references to the *pargod*: the "curtain" or "veil" that separates the enthroned God both from the other parts of the *merkavah* and from the mystic. The *pargod*, on which are embroidered the archetypes of all of creation, is infinitesimally, inconceivably thin, yet decidedly present as a separator; however intimately close to the *mysterion* one gets, one never quite achieves absolute contact. As the *merkavah* doctrines evolved, by way of often anonymous tracts or teachings ascribed to a particular array of teachers prominent within early rabbinic literature (such as Yohanan ben Zakkai, Eliezer ben Hyrkanos, Ishmael, and, of course, Akiva), certain basic ideas take definitive form. Thus, for example, the notion of "ten-ness" that is so important to the *Sepher Yetzirah* (and which may have Pythagorean thinking among its ancestors), wedded, as it were, to the account in the Enoch literature of an ascent through ten heavens, yields the notion, by the fifth and sixth centuries, of the ten *heikhalot*.

This last term, which might be translated as "halls," "chambers," or "palaces," is used to describe the configuration of the *sacer* realm, the throne/chariot world beyond ours.[21] There are ten *heikhalot* (singular, *heikhal*) through which the mystic strives to move; the seventh possesses the throne or chariot itself. Yet, that *heikhal* is merely the uppermost of the lower *heikhalot*, for the *merkavah* mystics come to perceive a separation between the seven lower—*zutratai*—and three upper—*rabbatai*—*heikhalot*, a division

reminiscent of, and perhaps ultimately inspired by, that regional division
within the Enoch literature. The idea of seven *heikhalot zutratai* might also
be seen to have derived inspiration from the passage, earlier quoted, in which
Rabbi Akiva, returned from the *pardes*, describes to Rabbi Ishmael the sevenfold transformation that culminated in his sudden apprehension of the hidden and precise name of God—the *Shem haM'forash*. In that context, the
"seventy-two" of the name was arrived at through the process called *klima*
("incline") in the Greek terminology of the Pythagoreans: Like the four integers that, added up, become ten in combination and offer a triangular configuration in dot matrix, the Tetragrammaton, in being focused upon with four,
three, two, and one letters, yields both a triangular configuration and the numerical value $26 + 21 + 15 + 10 = 72$, as we have also noted earlier.[22] In
one of the *heikhalot zutratai* texts that has survived,[23] we read that the mystic seeks to get beyond the sphere of the angels to the place where "God is beyond sight . . . hidden [even] from the angels . . . and revealed [only] to
Akiva."

And he is the ultimate model of how to move beyond the *heikhalot zutratai*
to the unbearable *heikhalot rabbatai*:

> When a man wishes to descend to the *Merkavah*, the angel 'Anafiel opens the
> gates to the seventh *heikhal*, and that man enters and stands upon the threshold
> of the gate of the seventh *heikhal*; and the Holy Creatures (*hayyot*) lift their five
> hundred and twelve eyes against him . . . their eyes are like bolts of lightning:
> darting from the eyes of the Cherubim (*keruvim*) of the Mighty One and the
> Wheels of Eyes (*ophanim*) of the Divine Presence; they are like torches of light
> and burning embers.
>
> That man trembles and shakes, is awestruck and terrified, and is faint, and
> falls. But 'Anafiel and the sixty-three guards of the seventh *heikhal* support him,
> and all of them assist him and say: Do not fear, beloved mortal! Enter and see
> the King in His Beauty, and you will not be burned!"

The sum total of *merkavah* sensibility is to emphasize the awesome, distant, transcendent qualities of God. God's inaccessibility, underscored by the
labyrinth of names that, even as they connect the mystic to God, disconnect
and distance God from the mystic, is only arrived at through a process that,
after all, culminates, in Akiva's own self-description, with fear and trembling.
Yet, on the other hand, both Enoch—turned to flame as Metatron but not consumed—and Akiva transcended the seventh realm and, assisted by the ultimate emissaries of the Lord, arrived at their destination, which is the same
destination sought by the mystic.

Among the more fascinating and paradoxical aspects of *merkavah* mysticism is the turn of phrase that emerges to refer to its practitioners: *yordei*

merkavah, meaning "descenders of the *merkavah*." Those who call themselves by this phrase, who assert that they can attain or have attained a vision of the *merkavah* after a rigorous course of moral and ascetic preparation, would appear to be suggesting by the term "descent/descender" their complete self-effacement: to be filled with such a vision, one must be emptied of one's self; thus, what might under other conditions be assumed to be an ascent is termed a descent. *Ek-stasis* means "self-oblivion." Or perhaps the turn of phrase is to underscore how, at the last moment, the vision is achieved only if God descends and lifts the mystic up: for he is the Holy King who emerges from unknown worlds and descends "through 955 heavens to the Throne of Glory."

There is a third possibility—and we must keep in mind that none of these explanations is exclusive of the others—which is that we are being reminded that, when entering into communion with the *sacer*, *profanus* concepts of time and space must be left completely behind. Thus, concepts such as "up" and "down" and "ascent" and "descent," as well as "inward" and "outward," which are spatially relevant in the *profanus*, have no place in the *sacer*, and certainly not in the hiddenmost innermost recesses of the *sacer* to which the *merkavah* mystic seeks access. *Ek-stasis* and *en-stasis*, as well as ascent and descent, can be the same experience and process simply because, in the *sacer*, "outside of" and "within" and "up" and "down" are not the opposites that they are in the *profanus*.

And so, the *merkavah* mystic who succeeds arrives at an extraordinary vision, of a realm in which

> [God's] throne radiates before Him and His palace is full of splendor
> His majesty is becoming and His Glory is an adornment for Him
> His servants sing before Him and proclaim the might of His wonders
> as King of all kings and Master of all masters,
> encircled by rows of crowns,
> surrounded by the ranks of the princes of His splendor.
> With a gleam of His ray He encompasses the sky
> and His splendor radiates from the heights.
> Abysses flame from His mouth and firmaments sparkle from His body.

This passage from the literature of the *heikhalot rabbatai* emphasizes the great, glorious grandeur of God and, in so doing, accentuates his distance from us, as well as treads very close to the border of what mainstream Judaism would view as sacrilege, or at least as dangerous. Imagery that is so physical—that speaks of his *body*—at least might misguide an everyday Jew with respect to God's nonphysicality. At worst, it might lead such a Jew to apostatize (if the paradox of such descriptive material did not drive him mad first). One might also note of this description that it is grounded in a very human vocabulary, thus underscoring the problematic with which religion and particularly mysticism of any sort—but particularly those kinds of religion and mysticism that understand the *sacer* to be absolutely without physical attributes—wrestles: how to describe the indescribable, when the terms of description, human language, are by definition drawn from human, *profanus* experience. That complication will continue to haunt Jewish mysticism as it moves forward in history and shifts its geographic centers.

NOTES

1. This is presumably the "garden/orchard" of mystical speculation. This is not only the standard metaphoric understanding of the term in this context but also the word itself comes to be used in kabbalistic thought as an acronym for modes of interpreting the Torah (see chapter 6, p. 128).

2. "Cut the shoots" is understood as a metaphor for apostatizing—probably, by the way, as a Gnostic and not as a Christian. Aher is a pseudonym for Alisha ben Abuya, a well-known second-century rabbi whose renown was mostly derived from the fact that he apostatized. Thereafter, he was known by the sobriquet Aher, meaning "other," or, in this context, "estranged one."

3. "[God is an] *Abir* (noble) King, *Adir* (powerful) King, *Adon* (commanding) King; *Baruch* (blessed) King, *Bahor* (chosen) King, *Barak* (blinding) King; *Gadol* (great) King, *Gibor* (heroic) King, *G'avah* (majestic) King"—continuing through the entire Hebrew alphabet.

4. The tract is Oxford MS 1531 f. 52a.

5. The obsessive significance of the *Shem haM'forash* may be still more fully grasped by the myriad other ways, which are arrived at by myriad methodologies, in which that phrase has been taken. These extend from within the midrash (Exodus Midrash Rabbah 3:6), suggesting that God revealed to Moses seven different names that relate to the statement "I am that I am," to the reference to God's "12-lettered name" (perhaps derived from the twelve results effected by all the possible transpositions of the letters of the Tetragrammaton) and God's "42-lettered name," in the Talmud (*Kiddushin* 71a)—in a context that speaks of God's true name as hidden and revealed by the sages to their pupils only once (or others say twice) every seven years. For a concise discussion of the "42-lettered name" and the post-Talmudic "discovery of names of 8, 10, 14, 16, 18, 21, 22, 32, and 60 letters or syllables," see Joshua Trachtenberg, *Jewish Magic and Superstition: A Study in Folk Religion* (New York: Athenaeum, 1979), 90–100. Trachtenberg's seminal work offers very concrete evidence of how thin or blurred the line can be between what we call "religion" and what we call "superstition," as between "mysticism" and "magic."

6. The search, the exploration, the inquiry, the response to the paradox is not an idle one. Since the assumption that underlies religious—and therefore mystical—thinking is that the *sacer*, which has created the *profanus* and can destroy it, has en-

gendered it with a purpose and maintains an interventional relationship with it, then the problem-paradox and its solution are connected both to our *survival* and to the *meaning* of our existence.

7. See below, p. 98.

8. Later on, in kabbalistic thinking, this notion will be reaffirmed in part due to the fact that both "wisdom" and "Torah" are grammatically feminine, thus associatable not only with each other but also with God's Presence, the *Shekhinah* (which is also grammatically feminine). See chapter 6.

9. The term comes from the Greek verb *planeo*, meaning "to wander," since they are wanderers across the heavens, against the backdrop of the sphere of "fixed stars." And they are associated with gods, hence the connotation of perfection and completion. They are thus the planets Mercury, Venus, Mars, Jupiter, and Saturn, as well as the sun and the moon.

10. One notes that this name, like others that refer to the Satan as a leader of opposition against God, reflects back toward influence from Persian Zoroastrianism in its sense of reality as divided between light and darkness, good and evil; and forward toward the development of Satan as a character in Christian thought (more so than in Jewish thought) who carries the flag of evil against the Power of the All-good God.

11. See John Gager, *Moses in Greco-Roman Paganism* (Nashville: Abingdon Press, 1972) for a fuller discussion of this issue.

12. It is also known as the *Sepher Razi-El*, for the angel who gave it to Noah.

13. So the text reads. In having some difficulty imagining the stuffing of the dead rooster into a flask, I am thinking that either the text means us to understand certain parts of the rooster or means a bigger container—a pot of some sort—rather than a flask.

14. Later on, the shapes of the letters will become an important focus of Jewish mysticism, beginning with the *Sepher Bahir* and the advent of systematic kabbalistic thought, as we shall see.

15. In other words, when God is invoked or discussed in the context of offering protection—whether it is the story of the Israelites being rescued from the Egyptians by the passage through the Sea of Reeds (a.k.a. "Red Sea") or the protection of my house by "writ[ing] it upon the doorposts (*mezuzot*) of [my] house," as prescribed in Deuteronomy 6:9—the form of God's name that serves as a reference point is *Shaddai*. The container with the passages from Deuteronomy 6 that includes these words and that is placed on the doorposts—the *mezuzah* (which term actually means "doorpost")—is often marked by the Hebrew letter "shin," which is the first letter of the word/name *Shaddai*. So, God as *Shaddai* protects my house by the "writing" of the first letter of that name on my doorposts, as well as by my fulfilling God's commandment by marking my doorposts with the text of that commandment.

16. All share the same triliteral root, "*s-p-r*." For reasons discussed in note 19, the "p" becomes a "ph" under certain circumstances.

17. The Greek word *sphairon* (from which the English "sphere" derives) would be the source from which *sephirah* would have been borrowed. But the *s-p(h)-r* root in Hebrew, which might simply be the source, is a root leading both in the direction of number (*mispar*) and counting (*sapar*) and in the direction of book (*sepher*) and

telling (*seepair*), so it is, in any case, a truly pregnant root, which is part of why and how the *Sepher Yetzirah* runs with it in three simultaneous directions.

18. That is, those understood to be descended from the high priestly family, those from the priestly tribe, and everyone else.

19. Thus, the "p" of "*s-p-r*," as we have noted in note 16, alternates, depending upon the surrounding phonemic conditions, between "p" (with a *dagesh* within it) and "ph" (without a *dagesh*). This is why it is one of the "doubles."

20. It might be noted that in "mainstream" rabbinic Judaism there is an early association between "ten" and the divine creation process: The Talmudic Pirkei Avot 5:1 refers to "ten sayings" by which the world was created.

21. In everyday biblical Hebrew, the word used to refer to the Temple as "the house (*heikhal*) of God." Thus, when Jeremiah rails against the conduct of the priesthood and the Judaean populace in the Temple precincts, he bellows, *Heikhal Adonai henah!* ("This is the House of the Lord!"). That specialized use of the term has been adopted and been further rarified within *merkavah* mysticism and its *heikhalot* literature.

22. See above, p. 36.

23. In this case, Oxford MS 1531 f. 456.

Chapter Four

Early Christian Mysticism

The issue raised at the very end of the previous chapter—how to describe, using human terms of physical description, a God perceived to be without physicality and beyond human grasp—which issue applies so obviously to Jewish mysticism, would seem, at first glance, not to apply (at least not in the same way) to Christian mysticism. After all, Christianity posits a God that not only is triune but also, in one of its aspects, assumes a fully human form and experiences the range of the human condition, from birth and childhood to growing up and death. If for Jewish mysticism the primary access panel into the *sacer*, both generally and where its innermost hidden recesses are concerned, is the Torah—God's word cast into a particular written form conveyed by ink on parchment, the latter material rolled into a double scroll—then for Christianity, the primary access panel is the figure of Jesus: God assumed human form. Jesus is the ultimate articulation of the paradox of a God—that is, by definition utterly other than what we are, but who must somehow yet be like us, since if Godness is within us, then in some sense we must be like God, and therefore God must in some sense be like us. Jesus concretizes that abstract notion within his being; moreover, he endures the human experience to an extreme felt by few humans: He is tortured and dies an agonizing death—and he does this both as one of us and as the God who does this *for* all of us.

Christianity, one might argue, is inherently mystical in ways in which Judaism is not. After all, the building blocks of Christian belief include not only God-become-human in a literal, incarnate sense, as well as a Godhead that is accordingly, by absolute paradox, simultaneously threefold and singular, as well as fully divine and fully human, but also the miracle of the Virgin Birth. That is, the process according to which God assumes human form is an emanation of itself as the Holy Spirit, directly into the womb of Mary, where that spark of Godness begins to evolve as a human embryo. That evolution then follows a more or less "normal" human course of events until the moment of postmortem resurrection. The very term typically used to refer to these building blocks of Christian faith—"mysteries"—underscores the manner in which even the mainstream believer must transcend *profanus* reason in order to embrace that which offers itself to that embrace: the hidden, mysterious triune God, both transcendent, awesome, and ultimately inaccessible as the "Father" and immanent, loving, and intimately available as the "Son"—which latter aspect of God is understood to be still more accessible through the accompanying presence of the "Mother/Spouse."

The Christian mystic's starting point will be the figure of Jesus as a focus of meditation, contemplation, and concentration. But that, too, offers a paradox of sorts. For, in order to contemplate Jesus, a Christian mystic of, say, the third century, must do so through the primary texts that reveal what the Christ *is*. Thus, the text of the Gospels (which term, in Middle English, literally means "God's word") will be the logical starting point, offering a parallel to the manner in which the Jewish mystic focuses on the text of the Torah as a starting point. These are parallel, but not identical, paths. It is not only that the two texts are different, that they date from different times and offer different historical and conceptual material. Whereas the text of the Torah is analyzed with respect to what it may hide beneath its surface regarding God, the process of creation, and the sacerdotal meeting between God and ourselves, the Gospels are analyzed with respect to what they may hide beneath their surface—or even with regard to what is on their surface—regarding Jesus. And what they tell, in telling the story of his birth, life, and *profanus* death, is how he suffered on our account: how he self-sacrificed.

There is thus an obvious direction for early Christian mysticism that is not evident in early Jewish mysticism, a focus on emulating Jesus in order to mind-meld with God, and that emulation means an attachment to martyrdom. This is conceived not only in an abstract metaphysical sense but also in concrete physical terms: The God that assumes physical form offers an intense connectability to it by means of the physical access panel of itself that can be emulated. When we recall that for the first two centuries of its existence, Christianity was deemed a *superstitio* by the pagan Roman authorities—making it illegal to practice the faith, as a political subversion, on pain of death by crucifixion (the preferred Roman method of executing political criminals)—then we realize how relatively easy it could be to emulate Jesus's martyrdom in very literal terms. If, as far as we know, there were relatively few early Christians who chose such an extreme path of witnessing their faith (the Greek word *martyros* means "witness"), the ones who are recorded as having done so in the hagiography that began to be organized and written down in the late sixth and early seventh century by Pope Gregory I ("The Great") achieved sainthood. One might suppose that those whose martyrdom is not recorded, and who are therefore not counted among the saints (a term which, through French, evolves from the Latin *sacer*),[1] were nonetheless equally intense emulators of both Christ and those saints, with a goal of union with the innermost hidden recess of God. In short, they were mystics.

Such mystics and their successors throughout the centuries could focus not only upon the figure of Jesus himself but also on the encounters between Jesus and the disciples—both when he was alive in the *profanus* sense and when he walked the earth in the *sacer*, postmortem, risen sense. Thus, the accounts—*mythoi*—of encounters, such as that with the pilgrims on the road to and at Emmaus or that with St. Paul on the road to Damascus, could and did present themselves to early Christian mystics as paradigms of the transformative "meeting" with God that is the mystic's goal. In Galations 2:20, St. Paul, in fact, reminds the devotee that, in achieving a sense of union with God, "it is not longer I who live, but it is Christ who lives in me." If the mystic wishes to emulate and imitate Christ, he or she also wishes to emulate and imitate those who were intimate with Christ since to do that, by definition, is to be intimate with God. That all of us have the potential to become one with God is underscored even in the mainstream Christian tradition by the recognition of the indwelling of the Holy Spirit within us all: It is a matter, merely, of locating it—of achieving *en-stasis*.[2]

It should not surprise us that among the early Christian thinkers considered part of the mystical tradition are those who wrote commentaries on texts that led toward new ways of thinking regarding Jesus, the disciples, early saints and martyrs, and monastic models. We recall that the Christian view of God's word is different from the Jewish view in three primary ways. One, the same passages from various prophetic books in the Hebrew Bible are interpreted differently: Most fundamentally, for Christians these passages point to Jesus as the *Mashiah/Christos*; for Jews they do not. Two, the two sibling faiths differ as to what constitutes God's word through prophetic beings. For Jews that form of text disappears by 444 BCE with Ezra's redaction of the Torah; for Christians it continues for hundreds of years forward—at least until the time of Jesus and the Apostles. Thus, even though the Jewish and Christian bibles are canonized within half a century of each other, the former encompasses texts all of which are traditionally believed to have been written six centuries prior to canonization, whereas the latter encompasses texts traditionally understood to have been written virtually up to the time of canonization. Three, the linguistic perspective of the two traditions is different. For Judaism, Hebrew is the essential language in which God spoke to the prophets. For Christianity, specificity of language is of less consequence; as Christianity reaches out to the gentiles, it prefers to render God's word in languages that make the text accessible to them, rather than pushing them to meet God in a particular language. Moreover, while internally the canon of the New Testament is built upon the foundation of the Gospels, there are four somewhat variant versions of these.

Thus, Christian mystical approaches to divinely inspired texts are far less obsessed with linguistic issues and nuances, deconstructions, and numerological passageways than are their Jewish counterparts, and the texts upon which such commentaries focus are not the same. It is not only the case that, say, the Gospels rather than the Torah are a primary focus. Certain texts from the Hebrew Bible are often an object of intense interest. Thus, Origen (b. 185) on the one hand wrote *Exhortation to Martyrdom* in the mid-third century, possibly during the time of the persecutions of Christians effected by the Emperor Decius (in 250–251, when Origen was arrested and tortured but not executed. But the *Exhortation* was directed to two friends who suffered apparently toward the outset of the earlier persecutions effected by the Emperor Maximinus (ca. 235). The point is that Origen's *Exhortation* noted, in examining Matthew 16:24–25[3] as a source of inspiration, that the contemplation of and concentration on the act of Christ's martyrdom would transform the mystic's *nous* ("mind") in the image of God, that the perfect imitation of Christ's suffering would yield perfection of wisdom. Origen also writes about the mystical life as presenting a full efflorescence by means of the union between Christ and the soul of the mystic effected through baptism. He speaks of the mystical ascent in which the mystic senses a tension between the inward affliction of *profanus* temptations and the consolation that he or she feels by viewing the glory of Christ. (We recognize a parallel to *merkavah* thinking in this last aspect of his thinking: his reference to the *glory* of God.)

Origen writes that the mystic's goal is to be transfigured—as Jesus was—to be overwhelmed by the unveiled light of Christ and the unveiled voice of the Father. We recognize in this last element in his description of the mystical experience a parallel to the early Jewish mystical notion both that God remains always beyond a veil, a *pargod*, however infinitesimally thin that veil becomes for the successful mystic, and that what is unveiled, when it is unveiled, is not *God* but God's *glory*, God's *light*, God's *voice*. God is both achieved and yet not achieved.[4] We recognize, moreover, that the distinction between the light of the Son and the voice of the Father both is and is not a true distinction, analogous to the way in which, in line 14 of John's Gospel, the concept that "the Word (*logos*) became flesh" represents both a transformation and yet no change at all: The phrase offers in the incarnate Son an entity that ultimately cannot be distinguished either from the word emanating from the Father as the Holy Spirit or from the Father Itself.

These issues are raised by Origen, on the other hand, in extensive commentaries on the Song of Songs—where he most specifically addresses the notion of the union between Christ and the mystic's soul, which he couches in terms of a mystical marriage. He elaborates on the stages that lead through purgation to illumination and union with God.[5] Origen also writes on Proverbs and Ecclesiastes as guides for morality and the contemplation of nature, but because of its love imagery, he treats Song of Songs as offering the highest form of contemplation. And this, as he points out in his commentary, marks a reversal of the Christian mainstream viewpoint, which places Proverbs first, Ecclesiastes second, and Song of Songs third in importance of the books ascribed to King Solomon. It is, he asserts, the study of such a text as this last that can lead to the ecstatic union of the soul with God and not some other nontext-focused path to ecstasy.

Yet, other texts that we might expect to be of particular interest to the mystical enterprise, based on our discussion of early Jewish mysticism, are not of interest to him; nor are they generally of interest to early Christian mystics. Where early Jewish mystics direct themselves intensely to passages such as that in Exodus 3, Isaiah 6, or Ezekiel 1—the Jewish mystic wants to be like Moses, Isaiah, and Ezekiel—the early Christian mystics look elsewhere. As the Hebrew Bible qua Old Testament is the text of an old covenant that has been supplanted by the new covenant and its New Testament, so the kind of figures to emulate are Peter, John, and Paul, rather than Moses, Isaiah, and Ezekiel.

Thus, it is, as we might expect, not the Torah and the Prophets but the Gospels and the Acts that are perceived to offer the most important information regarding the most direct way to commune with God. And beyond the New Testament there are the intertestamental texts, primary among them those that mainstream Christianity, like mainstream Judaism, emphatically rejects as canonical, such as the books of Enoch. These play a role in early Christian mysticism as they do in early Jewish mysticism—albeit, ironically enough, a more limited one.

Even before Christianity achieved acceptance as a *religio* under Constantine (in 313) and hegemony in the Roman world as the *only religio* of the empire under Theodosius (ca. 390), a second mode of seeking communion with God presented itself to Christian mystics. This alternative to emulating Christ by means of martyrdom sought to emulate him by denying the most basic of physical human needs: eating, drinking, sleeping, and human fellowship accompanied by words and physical contact. Monasticism as an idea and as an ideal, as a means of *ek-stasis*—disconnection from the *profanus* world as we know it and withdrawal into the *sacer* of the wilderness—is apparently already present in the second and third centuries in the person of individuals like St. Anthony and his followers. As Christianity became more acceptable and then mainstream, monasticism as a means of intensified connection to God developed further and spread.

In retrospect, the monastic idea surely owes its conceptual origin to the community at Qumran—and possibly to other similar contemporary communities that may have existed but remain unknown to us—that emerged in the late Second Temple (late Judaean) period. If some of the texts of that group offer one of the lines that feeds into early Jewish mysticism, and if, arguably, the ideology of those texts (most obviously, the so-called Battle Scroll) feeds into the ideology of Christianity,[6] then the notion of a community apart from the mainstream that believes that its apartness can help it connect more directly and firmly to God than is possible for the mainstream would feed very naturally into early Christian mysticism.

The Desert Fathers, such as St. Anthony, emulated figures such as Elijah, as well as John the Baptist and Jesus, all of whom are associated with long stretches of time spent in the *sacer* (wilderness), during which their relationship with the *sacer* (God) was deepened. There the individual could find solitude and quiet in which to meditate, contemplate, and concentrate on God. Formal Christian meditation began during this period by way of the monastic practice of reading the Bible at an extremely slow pace in order to dwell on the meaning of each verse as one read it. Such a process is called "divine reading" (*lectio divina*). One of the passages ascribed to an anonymous figure among the Desert Fathers gives a sense of the context in which the monastic focuses himself, asserting,

> Fish, if they tarry on dry land, die. So monks who tarry outside their cell or abide with men of the world, fall away from their vows . . . as fish must return to the sea, so we must return to our cells, lest it befall us that by tarrying without, we forget the watch within.

If sometimes a monk found himself spontaneously praying as a consequence of scriptural meditation, which led to a simple, wordless love for God called "contemplation," monastic isolation also offered a different sort of temptation from that of the outside world and those he left behind in the *profanus*: the temptation to lose one's concentration through *acedia* ("boredom"), particularly at the height of the long day. What pagan Mediterranean antiquity long referred to as being carried "away" by the "Noonday Demon," and which is associated with what we would call sunstroke, becomes here something more subtly dangerous, not to the dehydrated body but to the unfocused mind of the monk. Thus, Evagrius Ponticus (b. 345) writes in his *Praktikos*—his guide for the would-be monastic mystic—regarding *acedia*, that the Noonday Demon "makes it seem as if the sun barely moves, if at all, and that the day is fifty hours long . . . he instills hatred for the place [of isolated meditation], for his [the monastic's] very life."

Evagrius recommends the study of texts, vigils, and prayer to battle *acedia* and to gain control over thought. As the monk observes his own thoughts—"their intensity, their period of decline, and [as he] follow[s] them as they rise and fall"—he is by definition in the first stages of *ek-stasis*, in being outside himself and his own thoughts. That condition will yield what the monk seeks, *apatheia,* or "unsuffering," and thus perfect health[7]—for his soul. *Apatheia* will in turn lead him to *agape* (a Greek word referring to perfect spiritual love, in this case, of God), an intertwining of his own soul with God's soul or a filling of his own soul with Godness.

That concept of *agape* is found in the evolving mainstream thought of the early church, most particularly in the vocabulary of St. Augustine of Hippo (354–430), who calls to mind Rabbis Akiva, Shimeon bar Yochai, and Ishmael in the early Jewish tradition in being both a pillar of the mainstream leadership of the community and of its legalistic (in the Christian context, patristic) thinking and at the same time an important figure in the shaping of the mystical tradition. The son of a pagan father and a Christian mother, Augustine led an essentially pagan life until, at the age of thirty-two, he was baptized by St. Ambrose, bishop of Milan. Inspired by the stories of St. Anthony, he set off for North Africa (where he had been born) with the intention of establishing a monastic community on the model of those Egyptian ascetic monastic communities associated with Anthony, but the death of his mother seems to have turned him further inward, and in returning to his birth place, Thagaste, Algeria, he lived a more isolated than communal monastic life. He was convinced, however, to return to the world to become the assistant to Bishop Valerius of Hippo in 391, and after the latter's death a few years later, he became the bishop of Hippo. In the thirty-five years that followed, he published a steady stream of writings.

Augustine is the first Church Father to wrestle extensively with the paradox of the Trinity and to seek a means of rationalizing the miracle of the Virgin Birth. It is he who completes the shaping of the doctrine of original sin that may be seen to have its beginnings in the teachings of Paul. Augustine argues that the egregiousness of the act of disobedience by Adam and Eve, who abused the gift of free will and thus allowed evil into the world, is so profound that all of the descendants of the primordial pair are marked by that sin, since we are all born through the procreative act that became known (and acted upon) by Adam and Eve after they ate from the Tree of Knowledge. But he further suggests that it is God's inestimable merciful love for us that yields the decision to *become* one of us and thus to atone as a human for the ultimate human sin. That divine love is called *agape* in Greek.

But in his *Enchiridion (Handbook) on Faith, Hope and Love*, Augustine offers a further transformation of the concept conveyed by the term *agape* (spiritual love, as opposed to *eros* as physical love or lust) toward that conveyed by the Latin term *caritas* (which contrasts with the Latin translation of *eros*, *amor*). With this discussion, he does more than merely translate Greek terms into Latin; he reshapes them. He also crosses over from the legalistic bases for the mainstream directions of Christian thought of which he is a progenitor toward the sort of mystical thinking that marked his earlier Christian years and which resurfaced in his writing sporadically throughout his years as bishop.

The *Enchiridion* links three essential concepts, but for our purposes, the key one is *caritas*, which can be translated as both "love" and as "charity," of which latter word it is the obvious, direct ancestor. It is also a cognate derivative of the Greek word *charis*, meaning "grace" or "favor." Thus, when the favor of the gods rest on a hero—as for example, the favor of Athena consistently rests on Odysseus, making possible his survival under extreme conditions—then one might say of that hero that he possesses *charis*ma or that he is *charis*matic. The reason that both "charity" and "charisma" derive from the same term becomes clear through Augustine's discussion of *caritas*. To possess *caritas* is to possess the kind of love for others that is purely spiritual, in being rooted in recognizing the God that resides within them. Thus, the ideal of *caritas* is that one feels equal love for one's child and for the beggar on the street, because in both cases it is the God within them that one recognizes and loves. But the ability to truly possess that kind of love is only achievable if God favors us, graces us with that ability. But God will do that only if we strive for it. If we submit to purity of faith, we can genuinely hope for the grace to feel the kind of love that causes us to offer charity not out of obligation or a sense of guilt, not with contempt, but out of pure spiritual love.

If we may recognize this circular articulation as an important goal that is endemic to the general tenets of Christian thought of which Augustine's teachings are a cornerstone, we may also recognize how particular the described process is to Christian *mystical* thinking—and how it parallels what we have seen of Jewish mystical thought: The mystic reaches out to God through whatever means (faith, prayers, study, the deconstructive digging within and beneath the surface of texts, abstinence, and so forth) and manages to achieve a degree of transcendent *ek-stasis* that is completed when God reaches in and pulls the mystic into a final state of communion. That communion yields *caritas*, which is more than mere *agape*—or perhaps its activation in the *profanus* world in which we live.

Thus, the *Enchiridion* may also be seen, in part, as a handbook for the Christian mystic. But Augustine also evinces the sort of imagery that becomes endemic to mystical thought in works like his commentary on Psalm 42:2,[8] in which, in an act of midrashic dexterity, he connects this biblical passage to a second one in order to synthesize the ideas of a fountain of waters and light, and then presents that synthesis as a hiddenness within ourselves, located by those who strive—mystics who actively seek that hiddenness—through the *ek-stasis* of *en-stasis*.

> Come, my brethren . . . share with me in this my longing: let us both love, let us both be influenced by this thirst, let us both hasten to the well of understanding. . . . For His is both the Fountain and the Light; for it is 'In Thy Light that we shall see light.' . . . There is, then, a certain light within, not possessed by those who understand not. . . . 'With God is the fountain of Life' . . . a certain fountain, a certain light, such as the bodily eyes know not . . . to see which the inner eye must be prepared.

Augustine's slightly older contemporary, the Cappodocian father Gregory of Nyssa (334/35[?]–385/86[?])—influenced directly by Origen's writings and also, it appears, by Philo and the Greek Neoplatonist, Plotinus—wrote a commentary on the Song of Songs in which he charts a course toward the inaccessible, unknowable hiddenness of God's innermost being. If part of the context of his writing is the spiritual conflict among Christianity, Judaism, and paganism, another part is the concern regarding heresy—*misbelief* on the part of a professed *believer*, as opposed to the *wrong* belief of an *infidel* (i.e., nonbeliever)—within the increasingly dominant church. Specifically, the struggle between Athanasian and Arian understandings of God—as absolutely triune or as a Father separate from and superior to the Son and Holy Spirit—had dominated the expanding Christian world between the Council of Nicaea at which Constantine presided in 325 and that council in which Gregory himself played a role in 381. Thus, those in darkness may be understood to be infidels and heretics, as well as those in the mainstream who cannot see past the outer carapace of God toward God's inner recesses.

> Our initial withdrawal from wrong and erroneous ideas of God is a transition from darkness to light. Next comes a closer awareness of *hidden things*, and by this the soul is guided through sense phenomena to the world of the invisible. And this awareness is a kind of cloud which overshadows all appearances, and slowly guides and accustoms the soul to look toward what is hidden. Next the soul . . . leaves behind all that human nature can attain, she enters within the secret chamber of divine knowledge. . . . Now she leaves outside all that can be grasped by sense or by reason. (emphasis added)

We may recognize the imagery of the cloud that guides as not only a metaphor for the obscuring of intellective and rational processes of thinking but also as an allusion to the form that God's guidance of the Israelites through the wilderness took by day—and recall that Gregory's masterwork was his study of Moses. One notes the staged journey of a soul that is spoken of in the feminine form. In part this may be merely an accident of grammar— in Hebrew (*nefesh*, *n'shamah*, or *ruah*), Greek (*psyche*), and Latin (*anima*), the word that is here translated as "soul" is feminine in grammatical gender— or it may be that Gregory is thinking in terms of the allegory of love spelled out in the Song of Songs. There God is spoken of as the bridegroom and there-fore thought of in masculine terms (which terms are more natural to Chris-tianity with its sense of God the Father and God the Son than to Judaism with its at least theoretical sense of a genderless God), and the Bride is already an allegory that represents Israel in Jewish terms; Gregory will have transformed that allegory into a further allegory as the Christian soul. The union of the mystical Christian soul and God is filled with spiritual bride-and-groom love that transcends—and indeed cannot be understood by—reason.

The monastic idea was carried from the Middle East and North Africa up into western Europe by St. Benedict in the early sixth century. His code, worked out in 529, lays out the formula for a life lived outside the mainstream world but within a community of like-minded aspirants to a closer relation-ship with God. Its essential dictates divide the monastic calling into equal commitments to poverty, humility, and chastity and divide the day into times of individualized prayer and serving God and times of serving the community through working, cooking, and communion. The Benedictine model offers the community as an enlarged family and its leader as a *paterfamilias*, desig-nated by the Aramaic term for father, *abbas*, which ultimately yields the Eng-lish-language term "abbot." The Benedictine order would, over the course of time, spread and yield various offspring, and from within its ranks, some of the most important of the Christian mystics emerged.

Certainly none of these is more singular than Hildegard of Bingen (1098–1179). Hildegard was dedicated by her family to the church at birth. She began to have visions of luminous objects sometime between the ages of three and five and, at the age of eight, was entrusted to learn with Jutta, a beautiful noblewoman (her brother was a count whom Hildegard's father had served as a knight) who had decided to dedicate her life to God. Jutta was an anchorite living in a cell cut off from the world—as an anchorite, she cele-brated a funeral ceremony to mark her death from the *profanus* world prior to entering the condition of confinement in the anchorage and spent most of her time in prayer, contemplation, and solitary hand-working activities—near the Benedictine monastery of St. Disibod (also known as Disibodenberg). Even-tually, Jutta's renown brought her enough acolytes so that her anchorage grew into a Benedictine monastery parallel to that for male monastics where the anchorage was located. Jutta became the prioress, and after her death in 1136, Hildegard succeeded her in that role. By the end of the 1140s, Hildegard had established a new monastery, dedicated to St. Rupert, at Bingen, about twenty miles further north along the Rhine River.

Meanwhile, she had begun to become famous. The visions about which, for many years, she confided only to her confessors presented two turning points for her. The first was that, in 1141, she experienced a vision of God that left her in possession of instant understanding of religious texts that had not been clear to her before.

> The heavens opened up and a blinding light of exceptional brilliance flowed through my entire brain. It so enflamed my entire heart and my entire breast—not with a burning, but a warming flame, like the sun warming anything its rays touch—and immediately I understood the meaning of the expositions of the Psalms, the Gospels and the other books of the Old and New Testaments.

Although God itself seemed to be commanding her to write these visions down, she remained uncertain—"because of doubt and a low opinion of myself . . . I refused for a long time to write, not out of stubbornness but out of humility"—until, as she continues, "I fell onto a bed of illness."

By 1147 she had written to St. Bernard of Clairvaux—and this is the second turning point in her life—to ask his opinion on the matter. He in turn brought the question of whether she should continue to write down the visions she was continuing to experience before fellow Cistercian Pope Eugenius, who insisted that she continue. Thus, her first visionary work, *Scivias* (*Know* [the Ways of the Lord]) was published by 1152, by which time her fame was spreading steadily. Included in *Scivias* are passages that recall Ezekiel I but subsume that similarity into an attempt to articulate the Trinity in words:

> Then I saw a bright light, and in this light the figure of a man the color of a sapphire, which was all blazing with a gentle glowing fire. And that bright light bathed the entirety of the glowing fire, and the glowing fire bathed the bright light; and the bright light and the glowing fire poured over the entire figure, so that the three were one light.

Other writings that stemmed from her visions were gathered into her *Liber vitae meritorum* (*Book of Life's Merits*) between circa 1158 and 1163 and her *Liber divinorum operum* (*Book of Divine Works*) in 1163, but it is noteworthy that one of the most significant areas of Hildegard's productivity recalls the limitations offered by words in addressing and describing the hidden revelations of the *sacer*. Her seventy-seven songs gathered together as a *Symphonia*

armoniae celestium revelationum harness the "harmony of celestial revelations" to the wordless realm of melody, harmony, and the insistent, rhythmic
pattern of twelfth-century music in her desire to extend her ability beyond
where words can follow to capture the essence of her experiences in the *mysterion*.

Hildegard's contemporary and the beginning point of her decision to write
publicly, St. Bernard (1090–1153), like a number of his predecessors, produced a commentary on the Song of Songs that uses the allegory of a love relationship to encapsulate the goal of the mystic with regard to his soul.
Bernard twists the imagery another turn, though, in asserting that the relationship between the divine word and the soul is, when the one merges with
the other, a spiritual marriage, like that between the heavenly bridegroom and
a human bride. We recognize the parallel aspects of this comment. The word
of God, as Jews understand it, is to be found most purely in the Torah; in
Christian understanding, it is to be found most purely in the Gospels and most
descriptively in the opening lines of John, where that word becomes flesh.
The Greek word used in John for "word," *logos*, that Bernard has most specifically in mind is grammatically masculine (the bridegroom), and both the
Greek and Latin words for soul are grammatically feminine, as we have seen
(the bride).

The very act of contemplating this pattern of thought offers to the devotee
a foretaste of heaven, he maintains in Sermon 52. That act turns one out of
the world of the here and now (the *profanus*), bringing about a kind of sleep—
a dying, an *ek-stasis* from the *profanus*—made possible by God (as God is
"contained" within the word of God—which containment yields, further, the
transformation of that word into flesh):

> Let me explain if I can what this sleep is which the Bridegroom wishes his
> beloved to enjoy. . . . It is a slumber which is vital and watchful, which enlight-
> ens the heart, drives away death and communicates eternal life. For it is a gen-
> uine sleep that does not supply the mind but transports it. . . . It is not absurd for
> me to call the bride's ecstasy a death. . . . How good the death that does not take
> away life but makes it better.

Thus, we recognize the essence of Christianity's assertion that through Christ
one can achieve a pleasurable and eternal life—that the death of the body is
not the death of the soul. That verity is understood to be concentrated into a
process for the mystic that he or she achieves at any number of times in the
course of earthly, *profanus* life: the death that is a pleasurable and eternal life
of the soul within the *sacer* and that can also make it possible for the soul
reawakened/reborn after the experience of ecstatic sleep/death to experience
a richer life within the *profanus*. That is, what all Christians anticipate after

death, the Christian mystic expects any number of times while still alive. There is more, for paradoxical sleep/death that is a living awakeness is a slumber marked by acute watchfulness—an ability to see beyond the *profanus* reminiscent of that watchfulness described of Enoch in the literature that bears his name.

⳥ⳤ

In retrospect, we may recognize three key differences between the Jewish and Christian mystical traditions up to this point. The first, purely formal difference is that Jewish mysticism comes to be organized in a type or ideology— almost a "movement," to be succeeded, as we shall shortly see, by other types, ideologies, or "movements," and often there are no specific individuals we can definitively name as founders of such "movements," although there is a group of names that typically surface as associated with them. Christian mysticism, on the other hand, moves through a succession of individuals whose work we recognize as theirs and thus associate with their names and who may or may not have followers whose presence would cause us to label their work as the centerpiece of a type, ideology, or "movement."

The second difference is this: Whereas early Jewish mysticism—at least as far as we know—like the study of Torah in the mainstream community, is reserved fairly exclusively for men, the Christian mystical world presents an impressive array of women mystics. There is a layered logic to this difference. First, Christianity, with its growing veneration of the Virgin Mother (for reasons beyond the scope of this discussion) presents an inherent psychological condition in which to associate women with accessing the *sacer*. Second, the development of monasticism in Christianity, along both male and female lines—and the status accorded to celibacy from the time of Pope Gregory I (590–605) as superior to earthbound marriage—presents a wide-open door of opportunity for fulfillment, particularly for women of the upper classes, beyond that derived from serving their fathers, brothers, and husbands. Where for Christians the New Testament had supplanted the Old in primacy, for Jews the Hebrew Bible and within it the Torah remained the supreme connector to God—and in Genesis the commandment to "be fruitful and multiply" would have eliminated most female inclinations toward celibacy and its concomitants for Jews.

There is an important and obvious consequence of this practical difference. While early Jewish mysticism—*merkavah* mysticism—emphasizes the awesome, transcendent, ultimately inaccessible nature of God's inner recesses, early Christian mysticism, particularly as it pushes toward the beginning of the second millennium, with the advent of a growing number of women mystics, more naturally emphasizes the loving, immanent, touchable nature of God's inner recesses. This is not only due to the importance of Mary as an accepted intercessor even in mainstream Christianity (or at least, in important branches of the church, such as Catholicism), which would help generate a natural comfort with and acceptance of female participation in intense and personal contact with the *sacer*, as we have just noted. But the physicality of the Christian God and his consequently more distinct maleness would present an access to the *mysterion* toward which the female mystic could more obviously direct herself by means of the language and imagery of sensual—even sexual—love than could or would a male mystic. Thus, Origen or Augustine may use love imagery that is emphatically spiritual, but Hildegard, and after her others, can and do use love imagery that is far more sensual in tone.[9]

Thus, the third, more content-based distinction between early Jewish and early Christian mysticism is twofold. Early (and later) Jewish mysticism is primarily preoccupied with the question of the process of creation and then with a delineation of a multiaspected *sacer*, and the process of gaining access to its hidden recesses is described or implied, but no method is prescribed for how to get there (there will be more prescription later on, as we shall see). Early Christian mysticism is more focused on how to gain access—through emulating Jesus and others, martyrdom, asceticism, meditation, and monastic concentration—and less preoccupied with either the question of creation or the description of the *sacer* (more of *that* will come later). The formal aspects of Christian meditation that are evolving during the first millennium of its development are first delineated by Guigo II, a Carthusian monk and prior of the Grande Chartreuse in the twelfth century. He refers to four rungs on the ladder of monastic, mystical prayer as *lectio* (Bible reading), *meditatio* (meditation on the verses that are being read slowly to facilitate meditation upon them), *oratio* (prayer, calling out to God), and *contemplatio* (achieving silent, simple loving regard for God).

Early Christian mysticism also emphasizes the *physicality* of its processes where early Jewish mysticism does not. There is an obvious logic to this double distinction cognate with the logic to the imagery just mentioned: The *sacer* as understood by Christians assumes tangible, physical, human form; as understood by Jews, it does not. So Christian access to the *sacer*, even to its hidden recesses, through physical processes—which, by paradox, ultimately cause the mystic to transcend physicality in *ek-stasis*—is as appropriate as the Jewish access through unfleshed words, which the mystic ultimately transcends. Moreover, the Jewish sense of the uniqueness of Hebrew as God's preferred language makes the notion of focus on words and their letters and the letters' numerical values and other aspects of word deconstruction logical, as the Christian sense of the uniqueness of Christ as word-become-flesh makes the Christian notion of focus on flesh logical.

Issues of comparison, parallel, and difference will continue as the two traditions continue to evolve side by side—and as they are both joined by a third branch of Abrahamic mystical focus, that within Islam—over the centuries that follow.

NOTES

1. For reasons that fall beyond this discussion, the intervocalic velar found in any number of Latin words drops out in their French equivalent. Thus, not only *sacer* > *saint* but *facere* > *faire*, to offer one further example.

2. This notion of indwelling—and the notion of the mystery whereby the Holy Spirit and Christ are ultimately one and the same, with each other as with the Father— is expressed in Jesus's own words at the Last Supper, as reported in John 6:48–58: "I am that living bread which has come down from heaven: if anyone eats from this bread he shall live forever. Moreover, the bread which I will give is my own flesh. . . . Whoever eats my flesh and drinks my blood dwells continually in me and I dwell in him." These words are literalized in a manner that transcends that particular moment in history (that merely involved the Apostles) to encompass all even merely mainstream Christians in the Eucharist.

3. "If any one would come after me, let him deny himself and take up his cross and follow me. For whoever would save his soul would lose it and whoever loses his soul for my sake will save it."

4. See chapter 3, p. 51.

5. In the late first-century emergent mainstream Jewish tradition, Song of Songs was one of the last books to be accepted into the canon of the Hebrew Bible because it was perceived as almost pornographic in a literal reading. (I recall a student whom I observed when I was an exchange student in an Israeli high school secretly reading the Song of Songs under his desk as if it were pornographic writing!) Rabbi Akiva is credited with convincing his fellow rabbis that the book should be read as an allegory of the love relationship between God and Israel.

6. I am referring to the development of a Manichean view of reality, wherein the sons of lightness (angels) and the sons of darkness (demons) are in contention with each other, led respectively by the Opposer (Satan) and God, and wherein an apocalyptic battle between good and evil at the end of time as we know it is anticipated.

7. *Pathos* is the Greek word for "enduring" or "suffering," and the prefixed letter "a-" corresponds to the English "un-".

8. "As the deer pants after the water brooks, so my soul pants after Thee, O God."

9. See chapter 7 for two powerful examples in the writings of Hadewijch of Antwerp and Teresa of Avila.

Chapter Five

A Third Player on the Stage

Muslim Mysticism from the
Qur'an to Ibn 'Arabi[1]

FROM FEAR TO LOVE: THE BEGINNINGS OF SUFISM

The term commonly used to refer to Muslim mysticism is Sufism. The Arabic word *suf* means "wool" and the designation *al-sufiya*, referring to someone who wears a simple woolen garment, may first have been used by Ibn Sirin (d. 729)[2] in criticizing those who prefer wool to cotton as the material for a simple garment.[3] But the wearers of simple brown woolen garments who are the beginning and backbone of the Muslim mystical tradition use the self-referential term to underscore both the simple purity of their approach to the *sacer* and the completeness with which they have pushed aside material concerns in a manner that anticipates by five centuries the sartorial symbolism of Christian mendicant-monastic-mystics like St. Francis of Assisi.[4]

For if Islam joins Judaism and Christianity more than half a millennium after they have begun to diverge from each other and become clear as separate faiths, its mystical side arrived into history within a century of Muhammad's death. That side may be generalized along two conceptual lines. One, while the term *Sufism* suggests the ascetic side of Muslim mysticism's beginning point, the mystic's goal grows from mere asceticism and an emphasis on fear or awe of God to the sense of this as a starting point on the path that leads to fuller love of God—*mahabba*. We may recognize in this a parallel to the general contours of Jewish mysticism, which (as we shall shortly see), in shifting from its *merkavah* to its Kabbalah phases, shifts its emphasis from awe to love with regard to God. Two, the sources of inspiration and emulation are, in the first place, Muhammad himself, the ultimate prophet intimate with God—thus, the source for grasping Muhammad is the Qur'an—but also the hadith and also the *auliya* (singular: *wali*). These last are the companions, both of

Muhammad and, over time, God. They are similar to what saints are in the Christian tradition.[5]

The nutshell summary of crucial moments in the life of the Prophet might be said to begin with the first revelation that he experiences in the year 610, at age forty, in a cave on Mount Hira outside Makka; follow to his flight (*hijra*) from Makka to Yathrib (later called *al'Madina*—"The City") in 622; culminate with his triumphant return to and conquest of Makka in 627–628; and end with his death in 632. The quintessential experience within the narrative of his life that inspires the Muslim mystical tradition is found not in the Qur'an, in fact, but in a hadith.[6] This is the hadith that tells the extraordinary tale of the Prophet's miraculous night ride—the '*isra*—which took him in one night from Makka to al'Kuds (the Holy, i.e., Jerusalem) and back, carried on a winged steed called Buraq (lightning). That journey culminated with the ascent—*mir'aj*—from the Rock to the seventh heaven and the throne (the "Near Presence") of God and the return to that rock. This is the Rock where, in the late seventh century, the Umayyad caliph Abdul'Malik would build the great dome to commemorate the *mir'aj*. This is the rock where, according to the Jewish and Christian traditions, Abraham offered Isaac to God (as described in Genesis 22) and where, according to part of the Muslim tradition, Abraham offered Isaac to God, although in part of the Muslim tradition it was Ismael who was offered (and in most of that part of the tradition, the location of the offering was near Makka and not in Jerusalem at all).[7]

This hadith offers an important focus for Muslim mystics, since in an obvious way it presents the ultimate model of arriving at an intimate connection with God for the mystic to emulate. Moreover, one can recognize elements of it that are precise parallels to elements in the Jewish and Christian traditions. Like Enoch, the Prophet is accompanied by angels—in this case, the angel Gabriel is the particular angel who accompanies Muhammad until the last part of the journey, when he is on his own. As in Isaiah and Ezekiel and the subsequent Jewish tradition, the Prophet ascends to God, yet does not see God itself, but the Near Presence of God. The most obvious divergence from familiar patterns is what we might expect, given the contention among the three Abrahamic faiths as to who offers the most perfect version of it to the world: Muhammad passes earlier prophets during his ascent, all of whom acknowledge his preeminence. God's voice asserts to him that "I will make the universe thy deputy, that all its atoms may praise Me in thy name."[8]

On the other hand, there are dozens of *auliya* whose examples one might follow. Eventually, there would be mystics who recorded their own experiences for others to emulate. Thus, Muslim mysticism looks to a series of figures and texts for inspiration, as we have observed Jewish and Christian mysticism to do. In the second and third centuries after the *hijra* (which marks the beginning year of the Muslim calendar), as mystical doctrines begin to shift more formally into place, the first shaping of monastic groups, dwelling in isolated cells and gathering for discussions of the Qur'an and hadith, may be observed, and with reading aloud from these texts, the idea of the *dhikr* begins to achieve prominence. While the term is generally rendered to mean recitations from the Qur'an and hadith to shape a rhythmic liturgy, the term comes from the Arabic root meaning "remember." Thus, we recognize that its underlying principle is to use the slow, careful, and repetitive recitation as an instrument to help the mystic keep God and the Prophet always before him. We recognize parallels to Christian mystical "recollection" as part of the contemplative process and to the early Jewish mystical method of repetition to the point of mindlessness. The emphasis on sound as a means to accomplish *dhikr*, since, as in Judaism, visual imagery might be more problematic, is suggested by the development of the *dhikr* into *sama'*, or "spiritual concerts," from the root of the Arabic word meaning "hear."

Muslims are reminded by Muhammad in the Qur'an, sura 3:33, to "love God," and it is that commandment that, from early in its formal shape, Sufism seeks to fulfill. The goal of the Muslim mystic may be articulated within the parameters of a trio of terms—love, lover, and loved one—and the notion that they describe a circle. Thus, love binds the lover (the mystic) to the beloved (God), but when the goal of perfect spiritual love, which is perfect spiritual union, has been achieved, then the beloved becomes the lover and the lover becomes the beloved—or rather, they are both *both*, and the overarching love (*mahabba*) that unifies them cannot be distinguished from either of them any more than they can be distinguished from each *other*. The process of moving from separation to union is a spiritual pilgrimage through what, over time, various Sufi mystics will delineate as a series of stages (*maqamat*; singular, *maqam*) and states (*ahwal*; singular, *hal*), which, continuously marked by *dhikr*, when marked by *karamat* ("graces"), define that special relationship with God articulated as *baqa* ("eternal continuance"), *tawakkul* ("sincere trust"), *fana'* ("passing away of one's self"), and intense *rida* ("satisfaction"). This series of four aspects of where and how the mystic arrives at perfect union with God is itself circular: *baqa* leads to *tawakkul*, which leads to *fana'* and to *rida*; *rida* leads to *fana'*, *tawakkul*, and *baqa*.

Among the most significant of early Muslim mystics, and particularly significant in turning away from the fear and awe of God articulated by the previous few generations of Muslim ascetics toward the notion of achieving closeness to God through love, is Rabi'a al-Adawiya (d. 801). She was a renowned mystic from Basra, whose hand in marriage was sought by many men but who turned them all down, asserting that marriage was for those with a worldly existence and "for me there is none, for I have ceased to exist, having

passed out of [my]self. I exist in God and am all together His." It is she who began to formalize the concept of *dhikr* as an ecstatic process cum center of seeking closeness with God's inner recesses, in which the gender of the mystic is irrelevant—as an alternative to the mainstream *masjid*, the male-dominated
mosque as a house of prayer and of study. "Love of God," she wrote, "has so
completely absorbed me," and further,

> I love you with two loves,
> love of my [own] happiness [i.e., selfishly],
> and perfect love: to love You as is Your due.
> . . . that purest love, which is Your due
> is that the veils which hide you fall, and I gaze, adoringly, on You.

Rabi'a's articulation of the concept of selfless *mahabba* that would come to
dominate Sufism over the next several centuries also carried with it at least two
socioeconomic consequences. The first is that—perhaps influenced by Christianity and its monastic and mystical communities—there emerged from the
ninth through eleventh centuries an increasing number of Sufis who remained
unmarried, preserving their marital love for God. Thus, "the best and most distinguished Sufis are the unmarried ones, if their hearts are unstained and their
minds free from sin and lust." This would rub against the mainstream understanding of what God wants of us, based on the line in Qur'an 24:32 prescribing
that "ye who are unmarried shall marry." The second socioeconomic consequence of Rabi'a's teachings is that the domination of the sacerdotal relationship
with God by the *'ulama* and Orthodox teachers could and did feel increasingly
challenged by a doctrine that made it possible for craftspeople and the middle—
and even lower—classes to assert their intense connection to the *sacer*.

Moreover, such nonorthodox leaders, called *shaikhs*, were venerated by
their disciples in a manner very reminiscent of the veneration of saints by
Christians and (as we shall see below, in chapter 9) of *tzadikim* by their
Hassidic constituents in late Jewish mysticism. The intensity of connection to
God, achieved by a *shaikh* through and defined as *ma'rifa*—a direct, personal experience of God (rather than through "second-hand knowledge," which is how
'ilm was viewed by the mystics) provided by the traditional legalist leaders—
opened a new set of spiritual possibilities, but also of threats to the mainstream leadership. It is not surprising, perhaps, that conflicts grew over the
next two centuries—or that the mystic Mansur al-Hallaj, a wool carder who
identified himself with God, was executed as a heretic in 922. That is, from
the outside, his pronouncements were emphatically sacrilegious. From the
perspective of a Sufi adherent, his assertions merely underscored the fact that
he had successfully emptied himself of *self* and become so filled with God

that God was within the otherwise empty vessel of himself, rather than that he qua himself was *godlike*, much less God itself.

✧

We have earlier distinguished between the mode in which one conceives Jewish mysticism—along lines that divide its history into periods and "styles"—and that for conceiving Christian mysticism: beyond an early distinction between modes of Christ emulation (from martyrdom to monasticism and extreme asceticism) toward a progression of key individuals whose writings elaborate familiar prescriptions and descriptions. Muslim mysticism begins as both a progression of names and a shifting of modes—from emphasis on asceticism to emphasis on *mahabba*—to further elaborating modes of expression and eventually (as we shall see in chapter 8) proliferating into a range of stylistically and geographically distinct schools.

It is noteworthy that few of the Muslim mystics thus far discussed and about to be discussed originated where Islam itself did, on the Arabian Peninsula, but rather in Syria, Mesopotamia (Iraq), and Persia (Iran). There is a certain logic to this: As Islam spread up out of the *'Arav*, its political center shifted northward rather quickly. By 650 (less than a generation after the death of the Prophet), the dominating Umayyad dynasty ruled from Damascus, Syria; by 720 the Abbassid caliphate had supplanted the Umayyads in hegemony, and the new political capital was Baghdad—and would remain so for several centuries. Each of these cities and others within their political ambit also became religious and cultural centers,[9] and so the growth and spread of Sufism within and around them is not surprising.

Al'Harith Ibn Asad al-Muhasibi (b. 781, Basra; d. 837, Baghdad) may be considered the first individual whose writings assume substantial weight in Sufi history. The bulk of his works, growing out of responses to inquiries directed to him by his students and organized into treatises, such as *Al-Ri'aya lihuquq Allah* and *Kitab al-Wasaya*, focus on the issues of self-discipline and self-examination—for which the Arabic word, *muhasaba*, yields his epithet: al-Muhasibi ("the self-examiner"). In the *Kitab al-Wasaya* he explains how

with all my heart I sought for the path of salvation; and I found, through the consensus of believers regarding the revealed Book of God [i.e., the Qur'an], that the path of salvation consists in laying hold of the fear of God, and performing His ordinances, abstaining from what He has made lawful and unlawful alike and following all that He has prescribed, sincere obedience to God, and the imitation of His Prophet. So I sought to inform myself of God's Ordinances, and the Prophet's practices as well as the pious conduct of the saints. . . . Then the Merciful One gave me to know a people in whom I found my god-fearing guides, models of piety, that preferred the world to come above this world. . . .

These men have elaborated the nature of religious conduct, and have prescribed rules for piety, which are past my power to follow. . . . Then God opened unto me a knowledge in which both proof was clear and decision shone, and I had hopes that whoever should draw near to this knowledge and adopt it for his own would be saved. I therefore saw that it was necessary for me to adopt this knowledge, and to practice its ordinances; I believed in it in my heart and embraced it in my mind and made it the foundation of my faith.

Most of his writings, then, build on the ascetic and awestruck early side of Sufism—in his *Kitab al-Tawahhum* he offers a detailed picture of the terrors of death and final judgment—but al-Muhasibi's most original work, his *Fasl fi l'Mahabba* (which is known to us only through later sources), turns toward love, furthering the tradition begun by Rabi'a. The renowned eleventh-century historian of early Sufism, Abu Nu'aim al-Isfahani, quotes him as asserting that the original form of love (the "original love"—this stated as if in response to the Christian notion and doctrine of original sin) is

the love of Faith. God has testified to the love of the faithful, saying 'and those who believe do love God the stronger' (Qur 2:160). The light of yearning (*shauq*) is the light of love (*mahabba*); its superabundance is of the light of fondness (*widad*). Yearning is stirred up in the heart by the light of fondness. When God kindles that lamp in the heart of his servant, it burns fiercely in the crevices of his heart until he is lighted by it, and that lamp is never extinguished except when a man regards his actions with the eye of complacency.

And he continues (in Abu Nu'aim's reporting):

[L]ove is yearning, because one does not yearn except for a beloved. There is no distinction between love and yearning, when yearning is a branch of the original love.

The starting point of al-Muhasibi's discourse is, not surprisingly, a passage from the Qur'an, from which he builds his comments. Thus, he is represented as producing a kind of midrash, as we have seen (and shall see) Jewish and Christian mystics do with respect to texts from the Torah, Gospels, and elsewhere within the Hebrew Bible and New Testament. The importance of the imagery of light also parallels the same imagery in the Jewish and Christian traditions. But "light" is specifically, and uniquely, connected to *yearning*, and it is through that connection that light is connected to love, for yearning is connected to love. Or rather, in the dissolution of the yearner into the One into whom he yearns to be dissolved, yearner and yearned-for not only become one but also that process achieves "success" because the One yearned for—God—kindles the light of yearning.[10]

We recognize a parallel to the discussion of *caritas* in Augustine's *Enchiridion*, in which one seeking to experience true *caritas* is said to inspire God to extend the favor or grace (*charis*) necessary for one to feel true *caritas* (in part because true *caritas* is to feel love for everyone, including the beggar, through perceiving and loving the Godness within everyone). The mystic seeks God, which causes or inspires God to seek the mystic; God engenders yearning in the mystic because the mystic already truly yearns for God—and that true yearning is true love for God ("original love"), which, as God reciprocates, dissolves the boundary between lover and love, love and beloved, lover and beloved.

There are modes of losing one's self into God so that that boundary dissolves. Abu Yazid (Bayazid) of Bistan, Persia (d. 875), is commonly referred to as the first of the "intoxicated" Sufis. He would be so filled with the "wine" of God's presence within him that he would become transported and cry out in ecstasy, with words like, "Glory to me! How great is my majesty!" Such ecstatic utterances (*shathiyat*) naturally scandalized the orthodox. We recognize the extremity of a mode of experience that was first discussed in the context of Rabbi Akiva's report to Rabbi Ishmael on the stages he (Akiva) went through before grasping the cloak of God's names: in another context, one would view the description or the utterance as hopelessly and sacrilegiously bloated by ego, but the mystic recognizes that Bayazid or Akiva is speaking entirely without ego, describing, rather, an emptying out—so complete in Bayazid's case that the very voice that speaks through his mouth is the voice of the God that has filled him. We recognize, too, how this emulates the prophetic way of being—the mystic is, as the prophets were, a conduit through which the word of God pours out—and how, by definition, the assertion of that mode of being would scandalize the orthodox.

Bayazid was also the first of the Sufis to fasten most specifically on the *mir'aj* as a source of emulation and a means of expressing his mystical experience. But he writes of the experience as if outside himself (in *ek-stasis*), watching what is happening to his soul:

I saw that my spirit was borne up to the heavens. . . . Then I became a bird, whose body was of Oneness and whose wings were Everlastingness, and I continued to fly within the air of the Absolute, until I passed into the sphere of Purification and looked upon the field of Eternity and beheld there the Tree of Oneness . . . [and] I cried out: 'O Lord, with my ego [intact] I cannot attain to Thee, and I cannot escape my selfness. What should I do?' [And God spoke:] 'O Abu Yazid, you must gain release from your you-ness by following my Beloved [i.e., Muhammad]. Smear your eyes with the dust of his feet and follow him continually.'

Thus, he explicitly addresses both issues that the orthodox could not grasp: that his success at union with God is predicated on a complete absence of ego and that, although both the *mir'aj* of the spirit that he describes echoes the *mir'aj* of the Prophet and his utterances may take on the form of prophetic utterances, he recognizes by a simple paradox that he has not yet achieved his goal of access even to the mere dust on the Prophet's feet. He is intimate with God, yet nowhere near God—not yet arrived at the dust on the feet of the one who excelled all previous prophets with regard to intimacy with God.

Bayazid exemplifies the condition of *fana'*—"passing [completely] away" within God—which hereafter will be stated as a central doctrine or goal of the Sufis. There is a sense in which this doctrine continues a direct developmental line from the ascetic focus of the first Muslim mystics: from a conviction that the material world ought to disappear in its insignificance before the omnisignificance of God, we have arrived at a completed statement regarding the insignificance of the self and the desirability of eradicating it in passing completely into the omnisignificant God. The individual who articulated this most distinctly as a coherent doctrine was al-Muhasibi's pupil al-Junaid al-Baghdadi ("the Baghdadi"; d. 910). "The *Shaikh* of the Order," as he was later called, sought to organize the Sufi tradition as it had thus far developed into a clear statement and to define the concept of *tawhid*—"divine unity"—that could legitimize Sufism in the eyes of orthodoxy by demonstrating how the two aspects of the Muslim tradition are connected to each other.

Thus, *tawhid* is "the eternal separation of the Eternal from that which was originated in time." One may recognize the unending challenge to Abrahamic mysticism and orthodoxy alike that is being addressed in this statement: to articulate the relationship between God and the universe (or more immediately, between God and humanity). For God's unity is indistinguishable from God's eternity, and, in turn, God, having created the universe, is utterly Other than the universe that it created, since the latter is time bound (not only because no part of it will last forever but also because it was created and thus has a beginning point in time) and also since that time-bound quality is by implication also connected to the universe's multifariousness of parts. History within Abrahamic spirituality—and the history of religion in general and certainly of Abrahamic mysticism in particular—may be understood as the human quest to fulfill the tenets of the covenant between humans and God. That covenant is understood by al-Junaid to be "pre-eternal"—an understanding that mirrors the Jewish mystical understanding of the Torah and its covenantal tenets as having predated the beginning of humanity and thus predated the moment when history arrives at Sinai and the *giving* of the Torah to the Israelites.

Humanity spends its history catching up to the preexistent Torah, to which it arrives at Sinai, and thereafter trying to live up to the tenets laid out in the

Torah. Al-Junaid's focus on Qur'an 7:166–68, and his interpretation of the passage, are the Sufi equivalent of this sensibility, finding in those words the notion of covenantal tenets and the history of wrestling with them. Thus,

> We cut them up in the earth into nations. Of them that are righteous and of them that are the reverse of that; we have tried them with good things and with bad things; happily they may return. But there succeeded them successors who inherited the Book! . . . But those who hold fast by the Book and are steadfast in prayer—verily we will not waste the hire of those who do right.

The tenets were set forth in the book that preexisted all peoples (all nations), that was handed to Moses and other prophets (see Qur 4:161–64); as the *Tawrat*—the Torah—as the *Injil*—the Gospels—and eventually, in its consummate form, as the Qur'an, to Muhammad. It is with the words of this last book that the mystic wrestles, holding fast to them, so that he or she may understand them correctly and be returned to a oneness with the One and be fulfilled.

That fulfillment will yield a "return to the state in which [humanity] was before s/he was." Thus, it is not only the case that the Qur'an predates, in God's "mind," the Qur'an as it is passed on to us through Muhammad, but also humanity predates humanity as it stepped onto the stage of history in the form of Adam and Eve. That preexistence was one in which humanity existed only in God's "mind"—in human terms, humans existed *in potentia* ("they [only] existed in Him. . . . It is a type of existence of which only God knows and of which only He is aware") but were not yet actualized, until the moment of creation when that potential existence was transformed into actuality.[11] If on the one hand God's will led to the existence of humans as individuals, separate from each other and from God, on the other God desires to "overcome" human existence by the ongoing outpouring of its own being into reality—not only at the outset of the creation but also in the millennia since that moment. Sufism is thus defined as a condition in which "God causes one to die from one's self and to live in Him": the mystic experiences *fana'* and a continuous life within God called *baqa* ("continuance"). At the same time, full union is elusive, the Beloved (God) remains hidden behind a veil from the lover (the mystic), but the suffering engendered by this sense of separation is at the same time spiritually joyful, for the condition of recognizing that condition is part of the condition of melting into and being filled by God's eternal being.

If we may recognize parallels to the impossible distance interwoven with the supreme accessibility principle expressed in Jewish and Christian mysticism and the distinct love terminology of both Christian and earlier Muslim mysticism, we also recognize the condition of danger to which the mystical experience exposes the practitioner that we have seen expressed in particular in the early Jewish tradition: that one may not wish to return, that losing one's self in the embrace of the *sacer* may mean death, madness, or apostasy with regard to the *profanus*. But we see this by reverse implication, for al-Junaid understands that whatever union is achieved will be temporary, for after the mystic's union with God, "He separates them from Himself; He makes them absent [from the *profanus*] when they are in union with Him, and makes them present [in the *profanus*] when He has separated them from Himself." If the implication is that the mystic is obligated—by God itself—to return to the world, it is also that the mystic will be reluctant to return (for who would wish to return to the imperfect world from the perfect realm of God?), and thus God is the one who not only "makes them absent" from the *profanus* but also returns them to the *profanus*. Blessed by the experience, the mystic is cursed by the impossibility of finding anything in the *profanus* that can come close to providing the bliss experienced in the *mysterion* of the *sacer*.

Moreover, while al-Junaid struggled to articulate the Sufi tradition in a manner that would not be found threatening to the mainstream Muslim leadership, the fate of his younger contemporary, Mansur al-Hallaj, reminds us that this was not necessarily an easily accomplished task. For al-Hallaj was crucified as a heretic in 922. His interpretation of the intoxicated Sufi teachings of al-Junaid not only encompassed the idea of ecstatic utterances indicative of the emptying of the self and the filling of the self, instead, with God. He also taught that *any* mystic can achieve that sort of godhood—and most interestingly, he focused not on Muhammad as his model but on Jesus. That is, he recognized in Jesus not the unique God-Man of Christian thought but an outstanding model of self-perishing (*fana'*) for the mystic to emulate.

As such, the mystic, like Jesus, could become one with God and, as it were, *be* God (without him*self* being *God*). From the perspective of mainstream Muslim thinkers, he appeared blasphemous. They saw him as the embodiment of the third of the threefold dangers attending the would-be mystic that are referred to in the Jewish rabbinic literature: apostasy. When in his *Kitab al-Tawasin* (*The Book of the Dialogue*—between God and the Satan) he asserted that "I am the Truth (*ana 'al-haqq*), because through the Truth I am a truth eternally," the mainstream leadership, rather than perceiving that statement as one of complete absorption into God and accession to God's will, saw it meriting his execution.[12]

Al-Hallaj seems to have reveled in the idea of his own martyrdom in a manner reminiscent of early Christian martyr-saints and mystics, and parts of his *Kitab al-Tawasin* seem perilously close to apostasy, even to the sympathetic reader, for he asserts that "Iblis [i.e., the Satan] and the pharaoh are my friends and teachers. Iblis was threatened with the fires of hell, yet he did not recant. The pharaoh was drowned in the sea, yet he did not recant, for he would not acknowledge anything *between* him and God. And I, though I were to be killed and crucified, and though my hands and feet be cut off, do not recant" (emphasis added). Thus, if on the one hand we may recognize simply the claim to have eliminated any obstruction whatsoever between himself and God and to be holding firm to that unobstructed relationship (and in both those senses sharing common ground with both Iblis and the pharaoh), on the other, the models to which he likens himself are both figures associated with *opposition* to God.

But if we consider the implications of his being an "intoxicated" Sufi, and if we think, along less dire parallel lines, of the *yordei merkavah* in Jewish mysticism for whom down is up and up is down, since *profanus* spatial relations are inapplicable in the *sacer* realm and the less so within the *mysterion*, then perhaps the obvious paradox of likening one's self to opposers to God in order to offer extreme examples of refusal to abandon one's God-adhering viewpoint has a perfectly paradoxical logic to it. If, from the perspective of the mainstream leadership, he was an apostate, from the perspective of his followers his Christ-like demise and his references to Iblis and the pharaoh are aspects of his universalistic recognition that the single *mysterion* may be approached from any number of directions.

By the mid- to late tenth century, not only was Sufism continuing to spread further afield but also there began to emerge writers of systematic accounts of the movement and its exponents. Thus, Abu Nasr al-Sarraj, for example (d. 988), authored the *Kitab al-Luma'* (*The Book of Flashes*), the earliest surviving general history of Sufism, in which he parses the expanding range of specialized vocabulary while laying out the development of doctrines and practices. Al-Sarraj delineated seven stages (*maqamat*) of spiritual preparation for achieving oneness with God, and ten states (*ahlal*) that, once God has begun to embrace the mystic, define the condition of his soul.[13]

So, too, Abu Talib al-Makki (d. 996), in his *Qut al-Qulub* (*The Nourishment of Hearts*) offers the earliest attempt to systemize Sufi doctrine as its own orthodoxy. That is, he analyzes the customs and rituals of mainstream Islam in detail in order to demonstrate their accord with the mystical perspective that he offers to them. Al-Makki's text insists that Sufism is an authentic mode of Muslim life, part of Muhammad's teaching that has been transmitted, like hadiths, down through the centuries. Indeed, in a manner reminiscent of the broader divide within the Muslim world between Sunnis and Shi'ites, he argues that, in his own era,

compilations of scholasticism (*kalam*) have begun to appear in which the scholastic theologians have begun to write according to opinion, reason and by analogy. But gone [in that mainstream] are the [long transmitted, true] instruction (*'ilm*) of the pious, vanished is the intuitive knowledge (*ma'rifa*) of the firm of faith. . . . Now the scholastics are called "learned" (*'ulama*), mere romancers are labeled "gnostics" (*'arifin*), the narrators and informants [are considered] learned, although they possess no true grounding in religious lore nor the perceptions that come from faith.

Thus, those who claim to "know" do not, for true knowledge, which is knowledge of God, comes through an entirely different channel from the one upon which they rely for their information. Those declared outside the acceptable pattern of being are within the very center of God-preferred patterns.

What places them at that center is the specific sort of intuitive, hidden knowledge of God to which they have access—the term for which knowledge is *ma'rifa*: Gnosis (which term I am capitalizing and italicizing in translation to underscore that the term is used in the sense in which the Gnostics used it, to refer to specialized, hidden, esoteric knowledge regarding the *true* workings of the universe, as opposed to mere knowledge of the ultimately false workings of the world around us understood by mainstream believers). This word will be used with increasing frequency hereafter in Sufi vocabulary. One might see it as both the centerpiece of Islamic mysticism and, as a concept, a key connective to Jewish and Christian mysticism. All three traditions share the sense that the successful mystics possess a kind of knowledge *beyond* normative knowledge that, like the knowledge possessed by the prophets, connects them to the innermost, hidden recess of God, as we have seen and shall continue to see.

THE SHAPING OF A CLASSIC SYSTEM: AL-QUSHAIRI

Other works, other authors, and variant movements mark this period—including the development of the *Malamatiya* sect, an extreme variant of the "intoxicated" Sufi movement, whose adherents maintained that true worship of God is expressed by behaving in a manner repugnant to one's fellow humans (including ignoring Islam's most basic precepts and living a debauched life): the greater the contempt others have for the Sufi, thus the more distant from them he is, the closer to God's *mysterion* he becomes. On the other hand, by the eleventh century, the first classical period of Sufism was taking shape around the spectacular *Risala ila al-Sufiya* (*Letter to the Sufis*) of Abu l'Qasim al-Qushairi (d. 1072/74).[14] Al-Qushairi was already well established and highly regarded as the very kind of scholastic-jurist of whom al-Makki would not have approved when he (al-Qushairi) began to search for a deeper spiritual connection to the very traditions of which he was an analyst, interpreter, and exponent. A collector of the different versions that developed over time regarding Muhammad's *mir'aj*, he blossomed as a Sufi, and his *Risala* (ca. 1046) on the theory and practice of Sufism is largely regarded as the most important Sufi treatise. In it, he asserts that Sufi doctrine in no way contradicts orthodoxy (this in particular after the period of the *Malamatiya*, which so severely impressed itself on the popular imagination as a summary presentation of Sufism overall), beginning his work with a series of biographies of key Sufi thinkers and discussions of their thought.

Thus, his discussion of al-Hallaj, for example, reviews the latter's discussion of the divine attributes. The elaboration is introduced in a manner that parallels discussions in rabbinic literature and obliquely echoes the assertion of al-Makki that the Sufi tradition has a long and venerable (and thus legitimate) heritage. Thus,

> Shaikh Abu 'Abd al-Rahman al-Sulami—God have mercy on him!—told us: I heard Muhammad ibn Muhammad ibn Ghalib say: I heard Abu Nasr Ahmad ibn Sa'id al-Isfanjani say: al-Husain ibn Mansur said:

Then the opening statement that has been passed down is offered: "You must categorically consider all to be contingent, for pre-existence belongs to Him [alone]." What follows, then, is a series of statements, such as, "All that appears though the body is necessarily an accident (*'arad*)"; "No 'above' shades Him—Exalted be He!—nor does any 'below' carry Him"; "No 'all' gathered Him"; "His description: He has none"; and "If you ask 'When?'—His being is before Time. . . . And if you say 'Where?'—His existence precedes Place. . . . His existence is the affirmation of Him; Gnosis (*ma'rifa*) of him is the upholding of His Oneness; and his Oneness (*tawhid*) is to distinguish Him clearly from His creatures. Whatever you imagine in your imaginings, He is different from that."

Thus, the very discussion of divine attributes is intentionally futile; it is an exercise in the exercise of seeking to reach the unreachable and grasp the ungraspable. The exercise in reaching leads one to that grasp—almost. Al-Qushairi's review of al-Hallaj recalls the sensibility expressed at the end of Ezekiel 1, wherein the prophet has seen "the likeness of the appearance of the Glory of the Lord" (that in turn feeds into *merkavah* mysticism): He is there and yet he is not there, if *there* means before the God before whom one cannot stand, since that very verb implies a place and an entity with which one can engage in a prepositional—before, behind, above, below—relationship.

From this discussion of earlier Sufis, the *Risala* moves to the discussion of technical terminology that has emerged in Sufi literature, such as the terms that distinguish *maqam* ("stage") from *hal* ("state"). The distinction is fundamentally between the point (*maqam*) to which one arrives through one's own effort and that to which one arrives through the reaching "down" of God: Each *maqam* "is an earning"; each *hal* is a "gift," the *Risala* states, as it then delineates forty-three stages and states of mystical transcendence.[15] Thus, the first stage al-Qushairi identifies—which we can recognize from earlier Sufi writers—is *tauba*, or "conversion" (in the Latinate sense of "intensely turning one's self" away from a focus on worldly things and toward a life fully devoted to the service of God). This was in fact the course followed by al-Qushairi himself in a very specific way. The second stage is *mujahada*, meaning "struggle" or "striving" toward an intense spiritual—a mystical—life.[16] In the third stage, "solitariness and withdrawal" (*khalwa wa-'uzla*), we recognize a parallel to the monastic emphasis in Christian mysticism: It is in isolation and withdrawal from the community that the beginner will succeed in his *mujahada* to achieve the fourth stage, *taqwa,* in which a full sense of awe of God furthers the mystic's resolve (since that sense of awe will help the mystic keep in mind the divine chastisement that his newly chosen way of life will permit him to escape).

By the time the mystic has arrived at the sixteenth stage of his development as a transforming spiritual being, he has arrived at contentment (*qana'a*), and in the seventeenth stage, complete *tawakkul* ("trust in God"): He has become like the prophetic figures, Abraham, Isaac, and Ishmael, who in the moment of Abraham's offering, exhibited absolute trust and therefore were able to offer a son or be offered by a father without a scintilla of question, much less protest, to God's commandment to do so.[17] By stage twenty-one, the mystic is endowed with *muraqaba*, or constant awareness of God's presence, and by stage twenty-two, he is enveloped in *rida*, or complete satisfaction. This "stage" is also regarded as the point of transition to "states" and is thus both the final *maqam* and the first *hal*, based on the Qur'anic verse, "God was well-pleased with them and they were well-pleased with God" (Qur 5:119). The sense of reciprocity expressed in this verse may be understood in at least two ways in al-Qushairi's interpretive context. The first is that humans arrive at satisfaction (*rida*) with God as and when God is satisfied with us—so the emphasis on reciprocity that we have observed elsewhere, both within the Sufi and within the Jewish and Christian traditions, is apparent in the association of this Qur'anic verse with this *maqam/hal*. The second is that the understanding of *rida* as both *maqam* and *hal* offers a *structural* mirror of that sense of reciprocity: *maqam* becomes *hal*, and *hal* becomes *maqam*, when and as *rida* is felt from both the human and the divine sides of the relationship—and *rida* is the particular term among the forty-three stages and states delineated by al-Qushairi in which that reciprocity is most specifically articulated.[18]

What "follows" (my quotation marks are intended to underscore the fact that the progression should not be understood in simple linear terms) is a series of twenty-one states through which the mystic "progresses," beginning with *'ubudiya* ("servanthood"), a sense of complete subjection to the will of God. This *hal* should not be mistaken for an imperative to serve one's fellow humans, although that will follow immediately, as *irada* ("desire")—the desire to abandon one's own desires and to fulfill only that which God desires— and a progression of five further states will lead to *hurriya* ("magnanimity"; number twenty-nine on the list of forty-three principles; it is both numbers seven and eight—given *rida* as both *maqam* and *hal*—of the list of twenty-one states). This last shapes the mystic as a *hurr*, a "freeman" no longer enslaved to worldly needs and desires and therefore fully capable and ecstatically happy to put the needs, interests, and desires of others before his or her own. Similarly, *jud* and *sakha'* ("generosity" and "givingness," together comprising number thirty-four of the forty-three principles) reflect thought and action toward others, inspired by the word of the Prophet in asserting that "the giving man is near to God, near to men, near to Paradise, far from Hell." Thus, to be truly embedded within God is to turn toward, not away from, one's fellows, but in a newly shaped, purer, realer, truer manner.

Du'a (informal prayer—as opposed to the formal prayer offered five times daily in mainstream Islam, called *salat*), number thirty-seven of al-Qushairi's principles, suggests more distinctly, perhaps, then any of the other forty-three principles in the *Risala*, both the connectedness between Sufism and mainstream Islam and the difference between the two. Since the Five Pillars of Islam, while not including *du'a*, do include the prescription that one may certainly pray, and is encouraged to pray, at times other than those prescribed for *salat* (sunrise, noon, mid-afternoon, sunset, and evening), then the emphasis on *du'a* connects the mystical mode with the nonmystical mode of Islam. This is reinforced by the fact that the basis for the principle is the Qur'anic verse, "pray to me and I will answer you" (Qur 40:62). On the other hand, it is precisely the fact of emphasizing *du'a*, of suggesting a constant state of supplancy before God and address of God, that separates Sufi doctrine as outlined by al-Qushairi from mainstream conduct. This is followed by *faqr* ("poverty"), which we can recognize as a constant element in Sufism from its beginnings. And *tasauwuf* ("purity"), which follows *faqr*, is, interestingly, derived for al-Qushairi from the trilateral Arabic root *sfw* (to be pure), rather than from *suf* (wool). Nonetheless, the dual possibility for derivation provides an effective play on words. After all, the wearing of a plain woolen garment is connected with a rejection of worldly goods, so that it connotes poverty as much as purity.

The *Risala* carries the would-be mystic to the culminating *ahlal* of *ma'rifa*, *mahabba*, and *shauq*. These last three interweave each other: The achievement of hidden knowledge comes into the heart, not the head, and enters when the heart is perfectly still (as if the mystic were dead).[19] That knowledge is indistinguishable from intense, perfect, real love in which the lover, beloved, and love itself are one and the same—in which the mystic, God, and the love of the one for the Other and the Other (who is the *One*) for the one cannot be distinguished. The resultant condition, of having achieved God, is that one yearns never to be parted from God. The dangers are apparent: that one dies, that one goes mad—for one *cannot* return from the intimate recesses of the *sacer*—or, differently, where *mahabba* is concerned, that one apostatizes in the same way that the Jewish mystic might be feared to apostatize.

The layered notion of multiplicity with indistinguishable elements that are therefore part of unity might drive the mystic over the precipice toward Christianity. If I embrace the notion that lover, love, and beloved are one, might I not embrace Father, Son, and Holy Spirit as one? Both Judaism and Islam share the concern that the Christian view of the *sacer* is not purely monotheistic; but both Jewish and Muslim mysticism, having embraced the notion of a *mysterion*, have accepted the paradox of unity that is yet somehow divisible between its inner and outer aspects (or more aspects than merely these two). Thus, from a mainstream perspective, mystics run the danger of taking the one further step, which would be to accept not only the idea of a triune God but also the notion that one of the aspects of the indivisible, unaspected God is human in form.[20]

Al-Qushairi's delineation of these forty-three principles often blurs the line between *maqamat* and *ahlal*—or rather, appears to, to the student who is merely a student and not a would-be initiate. As a practical matter, his breakdown differs both from the more simplified breakdown articulated by al-Sarraj (see note 13) and also from that offered by subsequent theorists. But the *Risala* is not only an obvious watershed in the history of Sufi theory because of its complexity and apparent contradictions. As a guide for the would-be Sufi, it is a text that invites years of careful study, in part *because* of its contradictions, the embrace of which would be part of the shaping of a Sufi's spirituality (and which parallels the shaping of Jewish and Christian mystical spirituality as an embrace of complexity, paradox, and contradiction).

EXTENDING THE SYSTEM: AL-GHAZALI

Abu Hamid Muhammad Ibn Muhammad al-Ghazali (1059–1111) must be considered the next of the outstanding articulators of Sufism. Like al-Qushairi, his early development was as a scholar of Muslim jurisprudence, although, in retrospect, a believer in the ultimately logical workings of the *sacer* within the *profanus* might suppose that it was just a matter of time until he experienced the "turn," the "conversion" (*tauba*), toward a Sufi way of engaging God and God's engagement of humanity. He was born and grew up in the Persian province of Khorasan, which had nurtured an array of earlier Sufis. Trained, however, as an orthodox theologian and legalist, al-Ghazali was regarded as the most outstanding Sunni scholar of his era by the time he was appointed as professor of divinity at the renowned Nazamiya Madrasa in Baghdad in 1091. Like al-Qushairi, he soon thereafter found the intellectual life that he led lacking in something essential, particularly in the application of a merely intellectual approach to religious matters. In 1095, a mere four years after his appointment, he resigned his teaching position and spent the next ten years in retirement and isolation, seeking a more intimate relationship with God. He wrote about his conversion in his autobiographical *Al-Munqidh min al-dalal*:

> I remained, torn asunder by the opposite forces of earthly passions and religious aspirations, for about six months from the month Rajab of the year AD 1096. At the close of that time my will yielded and I gave myself up to destiny. God caused an impediment to chain my tongue and prevented me from lecturing. . . .
>
> . . . Then I turned my attention to the Path of the Sufis. I knew that it could not be traversed to the end without both theory and practice, and that the theory, in brief, consists of overcoming the appetites of the flesh and ridding one's self of the evil dispositions and vile aspects [of the flesh], so that the heart may be cleared of everything but God; and that the means of clearing the heart is *dhikr Allah* [the litany of constantly keeping God in one's mind] and concentrating every thought on God. . . . But [eventually] I saw clearly that what is unique to them [the Sufis] cannot be learned [through theory and the study of doctrines] but only by immediate experience and ecstasy and inward transformation. . . . [But in examining myself I saw that] worldly interests surrounded me on every side. Even my work as a teacher—the most significant activity in which I was engaged—seemed unimportant and useless in view of the life in the hereafter. When I considered the intention of my teaching, I recognized that instead of doing it for God's sake alone I had no motive other than glory and reputation. . . . Having surrendered my will entirely, I took refuge with God. . . . God answered my prayer and made it easy for me to turn my back on reputation and wealth and [even] wife and children and friends.

From his scholastic labors, which he had come to regard as mere ego-bound verbiage,[21] he had been led to living contact with the word that filled him, passing into every nook and cranny of the self in which beforehand ego or attachment not only to material goods and political glory but also to earthbound love had resided.

The remaining years of al-Ghazali's life were marked by a singular devotion to God. He lived a simple life, engaged in study and the writing of
a series of books in which he explored aspects of the moral and metaphysical system of Sufism, which he sought to reconcile with orthodoxy. The
culmination of his efforts to demonstrate that the fullest means whereby a
Muslim may live a life of devotion to God is through Sufism is the *Ihya'
'ulum al-Din* (*The Rebirth of Religious Knowledge*).[22] This work is arguably the ultimate masterpiece of Muslim religious writing and not only
of Sufi doctrine. In it, al-Ghazali broadly solidified the position of Sufism
within Islam and, more specifically, reintroduced the notion of fear that
had dominated the beginnings of Muslim mysticism, albeit from a different angle. He reminded the devotee of the horrors of hell, while validating
the position of the *shaikh* (in Persian, *pir*) as a guide—one is reminded in
his discussion of the Indic concept of the *guru*—the veneration of whom is
based on his significance for the achievement of enlightenment by his
pupils: "the disciple (*murid*) must of necessity have recourse to a mentor
(*shaikh*) to guide him right. For the Path of the faith is obscure, but Iblis's
ways are many and potent, and he who has no *shaikh* to guide him will be
led by Iblis into his ways."

Al-Ghazali's *Ihya* divides the process of following the path and achieving
enlightened oneness with God into four aspects, each with its own elements.
These four aspects are worship, personal behavior, the deadly sins, and the
way to salvation. In an obvious sense, the first three areas of focus could easily apply to mainstream Islam without a mystical turn, except that parts of
each suggest that turn. The fourth area of discussion will be recognizable in
all ten of its elements to connect to the specifically Sufi writings of al-
Qushairi, al-Sarraj, and other Sufi thinkers back to and beyond Rabi'a. Thus,
the first six parts of his discussion of worship are devoted first (in parts one
and two) to the differences and connections between knowledge (as that
term—'*ilm*—is traditionally used in Islam, and not as al-Makki uses it dis-
paragingly) and belief ('*iman*). These two areas in essence offer al-Ghazali's
exploration of Islamic epistemology (which includes the influence of Aristotle to which that thinking was subject, over the centuries) and theology. Next,
there follow four sections that focus on ritual and canon law as they are expressed in and impinge upon purification rites, prayer, charity, and pilgrimage—thus, in effect, addressing three of the Five Pillars of Islam. But his discussion of them seeks out their inner meanings; thus, while he presents
nothing with which a mainstream Muslim could be uncomfortable, his intention is to begin to transform a mainstream believer for whom the fulfillment
of the pillars has perhaps become too perfunctory into one who is more intensely engaged in that fulfillment.

That intention leads directly into the last three foci of al-Ghazali's discussion of prayer. The devotional acts of reciting the Qur'an, recollections (*dhikr*, expressed as litanies) and prayers, and the recitation of hymns at set times (a kind of synthesis of the idea of *salat* and that of *dhikr*) all offer further material that could be comfortably received by the mainstream, but open themselves to a Sufi perspective in furthering the agenda set out throughout his discussion of intense, genuine worship of God that has as its goal neither personal gain (in terms of what God might give the worshipper) nor outward glory (in terms of the impressiveness with which one demonstrates to others the properness of one's praying), but a deeper, fuller closeness with God.

One might see the entire second major area of al-Ghazali's discussion, personal behavior, as important for a mainstream Muslim, and certainly the first four aspects of the discussion—eating, drinking, earning, and "lawful and unlawful things"—are directly out of the general theological focus of Islam.[23] But the remaining seven aspects of this discussion—companionship, character, solitude, travel, listening to poetry and music as a vehicle for achieving spiritual ecstasy, good counseling (of *shaikh* to *murid*), and truly God-connected living and prophetship—while they could apply broadly, are clearly intended as discussion points for the training of the would-be mystic. Similarly, all ten aspects of his third area of discussion, the deadly sins, could easily apply to Muslims (those who "commit" and "submit" themselves to God) in general, although they have an even more emphatic role in shaping a Sufi way of being. They may certainly be understood as part of al-Ghazali's ongoing discussion of spiritual discipline, and the absorption of his teachings about them can be understood as prerequisite to *tauba* ("conversion"): the wonderful nature of the heart; self-discipline; gluttony and sensuality; vices in speaking; anger, malice, and envy; worldly goods; wealth and avarice; high rank and hypocrisy; arrogance and conceit; and pride. These issues move between elements of being that ought to be embraced (such as self-discipline, or the recognition of the potential of the heart for goodness) and those from which one should turn away in turning to God (such as anger, malice, and envy, worldly goods, and pride).

The discussion of all of these issues and ideas may ultimately be viewed as an extended prelude to the path laid out in the fourth section of al-Ghazali's *Ihya*. He highlights many of the *maqamat* and *ahlal* discussed in al-Qushairi's *Risala* but adds elements of his own. Thus, among the first eight of these, we recognize *tauba* ("conversion") as a starting point, but al-Ghazali then moves to *sabr* ("fortitude") and *shukr* ("gratitude") before discussing fear (*khauf*) and hope (*raja'*). Sections four, five, and six expand upon familiar ideas—poverty (*faqr*) and self-denial (*zuhd*), belief in God's unity (*tawhid*) and trust in God (*tawakkul*), love (*mahabba*), yearning (*shauq*), intimacy (*uns*), and satisfaction (*rida*)—but seven and eight offer new areas of contemplation, even if the general principles that they suggest are familiar: *niya* ("resolve"), *sidq* ("truthfulness; righteousness") and sincerity (*ihlas*), contemplation (*muraqaba*), and self-scrutiny (*muhasaba*). The final two stages of the path are meditation (*tafakkur*) and the recollection of death (*dhikr*), which brings the devotee full circle back to the notion of recollection (*dhikr*) as it applies to the awareness of God's eternal presence and the litany that reinforces that awareness.

We may all aspire to and arrive at the full awareness of God, that true knowledge of God hidden from those who do not pursue it assiduously:

> When the human being can elevate himself above the world of [relying on nothing but physical] sense, toward the age of seven, he receives the faculty of discrimination. . . . He then passes to another phase and receives reason, by which he discerns things necessary, possible and impossible; in a word, all the notions which he could not combine in the former stages of his existence. But beyond reason and at a higher level a new faculty of vision is bestowed upon him, by which he perceives invisible things, the secrets of the future and other concepts as inaccessible to reason as the concepts of reason are inaccessible to mere discrimination and what is perceived by discrimination to the senses.

Moreover, God is eager to offer us a sense of where our transrational faculties can take us, if we allow them to do so, for "God, wishing to render intelligible to men the idea of inspiration [i.e., being *inspirited* with God], has given them a kind of glimpse of it in sleep." But in order to carry the sort of experience that is glimpsed by the sleeping unconscious mind, one must be free of doubts, which is not that difficult, for

> [t]o believe in the prophet is to admit that there is above intelligence a sphere in which are revealed to the inner vision truths beyond the grasp of intelligence, just as things seen are not apprehended by the sense of hearing, nor things understood by that of touch.

In the end, the intense proximity to God assures that the Sufi is a true Muslim (i.e., one who truly submits and commits to the will of God), for "true knowledge . . . inspires in him who is initiated in it more fear and more reverence, and raises a barrier of defense between him and sin. He may slip and stumble, it is true, as is inevitable with one encompassed by human infirmity, but these slips and stumbles will not weaken his faith."

The centrality of al-Ghazali not only to the codification of Sufi thought but also to the assertion of its legitimacy within the broader world of Islam is incomparable. His impact on the middle development of Islam has often been compared to that of St. Augustine on the early development of Christianity. Both thinkers share the characteristic of having both articulated significant principles that became part of the legalistic or conceptual mainstream of their respective faith traditions and of having then been able, due to the weight of their positions within that mainstream, to contribute powerfully to the embrace of their respective mystical traditions as valid modes of spiritual expression by most of the mainstream within Christianity and Islam, respectively.

CULMINATION AND REDIRECTION: IBN 'ARABI

The thirteenth and fourteenth centuries, so rich in general and mystical writing within the Jewish and Christian worlds, were no less important in the world of Islam in general and Sufism in particular. Among the most significant Muslim figures of this era the Spaniard, Muhammad Ibn 'Ali al'Arabi, stands out. Born in Murcia in 1165, Ibn 'Arabi also came to be known and commonly referred to as Muhyi id-Din—"Reviver of the Religion"—a symptom of how significant a figure he was in the expansion of Muslim thought.[24] Ibn 'Arabi was prolific: He authored over 300 works, of which about 110 have survived in manuscript form, perhaps 18 of these in Ibn 'Arabi's own hand. In these works he demonstrates a rich synthesis of intellectual acuity with intuitive, visionary thinking and of legalistic and scientific learning with experiential awareness. His mystical interpretations of Islamic doctrine are understood by his vast array of followers to have been revealed to him as the "seal of the saints."[25]

After spending the first thirty-five years of his life in southern Spain and the Maghrib (northwestern Africa), Ibn 'Arabi traveled as a pilgrim to Makka, where he ended up spending three years, and was inspired by the aura of the region and his experiences within it to write his great work, the *Makka Illuminations (al-Futuhat al-Makkiyya)*. Thereafter, he moved about for a time in Syro-Palestine and Anatolia (Turkey), finally settling in Damascus for the remainder of his life. It was during this last, post-Makkan period that he married, raised a family, gathered an ever-growing circle of disciples, came to include key political rulers among those who sought his advice, and authored a steady stream of important works. These included *Bezels of Wisdom (Fusus al-Hikam*, which is often regarded as his greatest work, though others regard the thirty-seven-volume *Makkan Illuminations* as his greatest work), *The Contemplation of the [Holy] Mysteries (Mashadid al-Asrar)*, and *The Book of Annihilation through Contemplation (Ktab al-Fana' fi'l-Mushahada*, a short treatise on the meaning of *fana'*, or the annihilation of the self within the hiddenness of God).[26]

One may recognize in Ibn 'Arabi's thought the first clear articulation within Sufism of panhenotheism, the conviction that the one (*heno*) God (*theos*) can be found in everything (*pan*); since all of reality is the work of God, and since it is a given that a creator is embedded, in one way or another, in that which he or she creates ("I see him in his painting"; "I hear her in her music"), then God must be embedded in its creation. God is unequivocally One, yet the points of access to God are as infinite as the elements of our reality: One must merely understand how to use them as access portals. For, Ibn 'Arabi points out, the Qur'an itself notes that "wherever one turns, there is the Face of God"[27]; thus, to assert, "The Universe is God's form. . . . [The aspects of] the Universe are manifest reality"—God is what the universe makes manifest, and "is also the inner essence [of those aspects] Who is Himself the unmanifest"[28]—makes logical sense. Yet, "He is Being itself; the Essence of Being," and thus impossibly beyond our grasp (who cannot grasp pure being).[29] Thus, God is simultaneously immanent within the world around us and yet more transcendent than the most distant star.

We cannot *see* God or in any sense *perceive* God or *know* God—because God is by definition beyond our senses, our sense of meaning, our knowing, our understanding: "None sees Him except Himself. None perceives Him except Himself. By Himself He sees Himself and by Himself He knows Himself."[30] He is inaccessibly hidden from us, but uniquely so: The veil that hides him is not only part of him, but also indistinguishably, "His Veil is part of his Oneness."[31] The very terms, therefore—"veil" and "oneness"—defy our understanding, as we cannot conceive of a veil that is indistinguishable from that which it hides and cannot imagine a veil concealing something so completely that it is inalterably inaccessible to the senses or even the intellect. Yet, it is the goal of the mystic—which goal is somehow achievable—to pierce, peer through, push aside that veil that is not a veil behind which something is concealed (for it is indistinguishable from the oneness of which it is part) and cannot, by paradox, be pierced, peered through, or pushed aside. One also recognizes the parallels between the imagery of a veil here in Ibn 'Arabi and that same image in the Jewish mystical tradition extending back as far as the *merkavah* era: As close as the mystic may get to God's innermost core, it remains a *mysterion* because there always remains a veil, however infinitesimally thin, that separates even the most profoundly successful devotee from it.[32]

The paradox is simple in its perfect impossibility: Since "He is the Observer in the observer and the Observed in the observed,"[33] and since ultimately "thou art not thou; thou are He" and "thou are not what *is* beside God,"[34] then it is a matter of finding one's self, finding God within one's self, and finding one's self within God—and the instruments of discovery are all around us in all the elements of the creation. Achieving the goal of merging with God is made possible by recognizing that one can achieve that goal, by recognizing the availability of instrumentation, which means rising beyond the everyday manner in which we look at the elements of the universe around us, emptying the mind of its *profanus* relationship to reality, and seeking simultaneously within and without (and understanding that these "directionalities" are one and the same). Ultimately, "he who knows himself understands that his existence is not his own existence, but his existence is the Existence of God."[35] That individual becomes the complete, perfect man (*al-Insan al-kamil*).

Those who find God and verify their success at having found God (he calls these individuals *al-muhaqqiqun*, "the Verifiers") remove the veils that prevent them from recognizing the God within themselves—from recognizing the fact of their *being* God. They are the People of Unveiling and Finding—*ahl al-kashf wa'l-wujud*—who have moved beyond the veils separating us from God. They have found what is always there, within themselves, falling first, in the discovery, into bewilderment (*hayra*). For this requires a different mode of thinking and feeling and sensing from those that we use in the *profanus* of the everyday; indeed, it means to have arrived at finding and knowing God and at not-finding and not-knowing God at the same time (for how can anyone *find* or *know*, with respect to God, in any sense in which we would use those verbs?). But the *muhaqqiqun* are fully cognizant of the impossible paradox of their situation. It is not merely, then, that the One God is completely *other* than and yet *within* everything within the *profanus*, but, as we find/don't find and come to know/not know, then we can say, *huwa/la huwa*—"He is/He is not"—in any way that we speak of "is" in the *profanus* and the language that is used in the *profanus*.

The dangers to the practitioner are obvious. Should his or her mind be insufficiently prepared, then the paradox of achievability-impossibility, of God's inaccessibility/presence in and around us, of God's very being/not being, might lead to madness. The paradox of absolute oneness—wherein the veil that cannot be distinguished from God might still be understood as *between* the One and the devotee—might lead to apostasy. We recognize this second issue as parallel to that within Jewish mysticism in particular (more so than for Christian mysticism), where the concern for apostatizing in a Christianate direction (toward embracing the notion of a triune God) is constant. On the other hand, understanding God and one's self to be one and the same might be misunderstood by those outside the Sufi circle as heretical and lead to one's death. We have seen how, in the past, this in fact transpired as some Muslim mystics were executed for just such a reason.[36]

One can observe these themes throughout Ibn 'Arabi's work. From the absoluteness of God, in whom being and existence are indistinguishable (*that*

God is—God's existence—is *what* God is—God's essence, God's being; and *what* God is is *that* God is), the universe derives; the universe, by contrast, is comprised of relative being. But it is not that simple: to the extent that all of reality is already and always present in God's "mind" and God's "knowledge" (the quotation marks are necessary given the inherent problematic of using terms that we are wont to understand from our own limited human, *profanus* perspective), it is eternal; yet, in being external to God, in having had an actual beginning and facing an actual end, it is temporal and both was and will be (at some point) nonexistent.

Nor is God's absoluteness a simple matter, in that God is both transcendent and immanent: "The Reality (*Haqq*—referring to God) of which transcendence is asserted [by us humans] is the same as the Creation (*Khalq*) of which immanence is asserted, although logically the Creator is distinguished from the created."[37] By definition, I and my painting, she and her poem are not one and the same; my painting resides in a gallery in Paris, and I am here in Washington; her poem is being read by someone else in Moscow, while she is asleep in New York City. But the point is precisely that one must *abandon* the *profanus* logic that applies legitimately enough to the *profanus* if one is to grasp the inner recesses of the *sacer*. This does not render God any less than fully absolute; it renders God's absoluteness more complicated.

All that is—from Being itself to all that exists—exists due to God's will. And in what one recognizes as parallel to the thinking within Jewish mysticism, God's agents for bringing that which exists into being are the Divine Names. Thus, one might imagine a process of emanation from the singular absolute God, through the multiplicity of names that are and are not the same as God itself, out into the realm of universal concepts and thence further "out"—into the temporal universe being shaped in time and space, but eternally extant in God's mind. But, of course, the names—the words *we use and refer to* as divine names—are not the Names (as God would "know" them) but merely the "names of the Name" (*asma' al-asma'*), which God has revealed through the Qur'an and the hadith to those who are intimately connected to God: "the Divine Names which we have are the names of the Divine Names (*asma' al-asma'*). God names Himself by them in respect to the fact that He is the One-who-reveals-by-means-of-His-speaking (*al-Mutakallim*)." More to the point:

God says [in Qur'an 17:110], to "call upon God [Allah] or call upon the All-Merciful; Whichever you call upon, to Him belong the most beautiful of Names."[38] Here God makes the most beautiful Names belong equally to both "Allah" and "All-Merciful." But notice this subtle point: Every Name has a meaning [*ma'na*] and a form [*sura*]. "Allah" is called by the Name's meaning, while "All-Merciful" is called by the Name's form. This is because the Breath [*nafas*] is ascribed to the All-Merciful, and through the Breath the divine words become manifest within the various levels of the Void, which is where the universe becomes manifest. So we only call upon God by means of the form of the Name.

There is thus a play on "breath" (*nafas*). God "says"—with whatever the divine equivalent of "breath" actually *is*—the entities that thereby come into existence. (God *says* the universe into existence: "let there be. . ."[39]) It is the breath of God that *besouls* beings, thus making them live and thus populating the universe with an endless array of them—the universe is both reified and animated[40] by God's breath. And it is with our breath that we say the things or words that we say, including the names of God. Thus, further,

> every name has two forms. One form is with us in our breaths and in the letters we combine. These are the Names by which we call upon Him. They are the "names of the Divine Names" and are like robes upon the Names. Through the forms of these names in our breaths we express the Divine Names. Then the Divine Names have another kind of form within the Breath of the All-Merciful, with respect to the fact that God is the Speaker [*al-ka'il*] and is described by speech [*al-kalam*]. . . . The forms of the divine Names though which God mentions Himself in His speech are their existence within the All-Merciful.

In Ibn 'Arabi's notion of universal concepts (expressed and shaped by the names), one may also discern a debt to Platonic thought and its discussion of the forms. This is further suggested by his discussion of the manner in which the elements of the *profanus* world, prior to coming into existence, were already present in God's mind as *a'yan thabita*—"fixed prototypes." What obviously distinguishes these "prototypes" from Plato's forms is that they intermediate between God and the phenomenal world, rather than being the end or beginning point from which and to which all discussion of reality is ultimately directed.

Further, in Plato's understanding of reality, there is a hierarchy of relationship to absolute reality: Not only is the painting of a chair or a description of piety further from "chairness" or "piety" than a chair or a pious act is (and thus not even worthy of study, due to their distance from the reality of their forms), but "chairness" and "piety" themselves as forms are lower than the ultimate form, "the Good." We might assume that, in Ibn 'Arabi's doctrines, there would be a hierarchy of names, as there appears to be in the emanation like process of creation referred to above. But since there is no hierarchy within the unified God, then "there can be no ranking in degrees the Divine things, since a thing cannot be considered superior to itself," and therefore,

> [t]here can be no ranking in degrees among the Divine Names, for two reasons: First, the relationship of the Names to the Essence is one relationship, so there

is no ranking of degrees in this relationship . . . [otherwise] there would be superiority among the Names of God. . . . Second, the Divine Names go back to
His Essence, and the Essence is One. But ranking in degrees demands many-
ness. And a [unified] thing cannot be considered superior to itself.

Moreover, given the paradox of everything in the *profanus* already existing
in God's mind and of God's being manifest in all of reality, then the goal of
the mystic is not to achieve *unity* with God but rather to achieve full,
transcognitive *awareness* of *already* being one with the One. As with all of
Muslim mysticism, the models for such a process are prophets—except that
Ibn 'Arabi uses terminology that one may recognize as part of the continuum
shared by all three Abrahamic disciplines with later Greek and Roman
(specifically Stoic) thought. Thus, each prophet is a *Logos* of God, a material
manifestation of God's word, as each is a physical conduit through which
God's word is articulated to humanity. The ultimate model—the *Logos* of *logoi*[41]—is the prophet Muhammad; all other *logoi* (all individual previous
prophets) are united within the reality of the seal of the prophets.

That reality is referred to as *al-Haqiqat al-Muhammadiya*—"the reality (or
idea, or truth) of Muhammad"—or *al-Haqiqat al-haqa'iq*—"the reality of realities." These phrases associate the Prophet with the ultimate creative and
animating principle of the universe; they assert the Prophet's very being as
the first stage of divine intellection that, through the divine word, initiates the
process of creation, of emanation from eternal unity into temporality in its
myriad aspects. In playing that role in the shaping of reality, Muhammad is
also synonymous with the complete and full manifestation of realized human
perfectibility: the perfect man, or *al-Insan al-kamil*. The perfect man is the ultimate microcosm of idealized reality: He reflects all of the perfect aspects of
the universe. (Again, one may recognize a parallel to the notion that the kabbalistic *sephirot* can, in part, offer a pattern of an idealized human physical
and spiritual configuration superimposed against the macrocosm; this is, in
turn, a parallel to the notion of Vitruvian man. See chapter 6.)

The reality of Muhammad is spoken of as the creative principle and the
perfect man as the cause of the universe—but they are one and the same, just
as by analogy God and God's veil are one and the same and God and God's
names are one and the same—and are not one and the same.[42] The creative
principle sets the universe in motion; the perfect man is the epiphany of God's
will and desire to be known. The perfect man—and he alone among humans—fully knows God and loves God and is loved in turn by God: For his
sake, the world was made and is maintained.[43] The mystic who emulates
Muhammad hopes to gain that knowledge and love by achieving that perfection—which perfection will be the full recognition of being one with God, of

loving and being loved by the awesome, transcendent God of infinite inaccessibility.

All of this leads our discussion in two interwoven directions. First, in his discussions, Ibn 'Arabi makes frequent use of the language of earthly love in his attempts to describe the condition of *ek-stasis/en-stasis* (not only because to leap out of one's self is to dive into one's self but also because to embed one's self successfully into God's hiddenmost inner recess is merely to embed one's self deeply enough into one's selfless *self*, in the spaceless center of which God is found) toward complete merging with the divine. The matter of recognizing what was true all along—that God is all around us and within us and that we are within God—which is true *fana'*, is to experience on an exponentially greater scale (and by means of a spiritual, rather than a physical, process, yet with a profound sense of physical consequence) the simultaneous death and (re)birth that those perfectly in love experience.

In the imagery of earthly love, one may recognize an obvious parallel to that aspect of Christian mysticism that is particularly evident in the writings of women mystics such as St. Catherine of Siena and St. Teresa of Avila.[44] On the other hand, one is struck by the dissimilarity between both these traditions and that of Jewish mysticism, which, on the one hand, introduces the paradigm of male-female love into its imagery but, on the other, typically directs that imagery in the opposite direction from that found in both Muslim and Christian mysticism. Thus, the *Shekhinah* is the term used to refer to the "female" aspect of God,[45] which is then further referred to as a bride or as a queen, with rarely any emphasis on earthly love imagery to describe the meeting between mystic and Godhead. (As we shall see, the beginning of exceptions to this emphasis will arise in the seventeenth century with the false messianic figure Shabbetai Tzvi.[46])

Second, in Ibn 'Arabi's excursus, prophets and saints (*auliya*) who achieve this experience are one and the same.[47] This is as it should be: They are *both* aspects of sacerdotal intermediation between *profanus* and *sacer*, but he is more overt and emphatic about the association than others before him in the Muslim mystical tradition. And all prophets, by definition, precede the time of the seal of the prophets. Yet, between the time of Muhammad and our own time, others can have achieved sainthood (and, in fact, the mystic hopes to accomplish precisely this, a condition that is prophet and saintlike, in order to achieve full awareness of oneness with God), and—in Ibn 'Arabi's thought—the prophets are more fully saints than prophets. In any case, all prophets and saints are manifestations of Muhammad's prophetship, of the reality of Muhammad (*al Haqiqat al-Muhammadiya*). Moreover, Ibn 'Arabi asserts that there is also a seal of the saints (*Khatim al-auliya'*) who, in the time between Muhammad and Ibn 'Arabi's own time, offers a perfect manifestation of the reality of Muhammad (who is the perfect man): He was "born in our time. I have met him and seen the mark of the Seal which he had upon him."

This is the context in which Ibn 'Arabi himself is referred to by that very designation: the seal of the saints, to whom the mystical (hidden) interpretations of Muslim doctrines have been revealed. Indeed, he himself asserts, "I am the Seal of the saints, no doubt, [the Seal of] the heritage of the Hashemite [i.e., Muhammad] and the Messiah [the one anointed by God as the ultimate intermediary between God and humanity]."[48] In some other context, this would have to strike one as a profound statement of misguided egotism and a recipe for disaster for himself and any who followed him, but in the context of Ibn 'Arabi's larger corpus of work, such a statement is, rather, reminiscent of Rabbi Akiva's recounting of the stages through which he went in finding himself before the throne of God: completely, purely, perfectly devoid of ego and of all of the ego-trappings that confine one to the *profanus*. By definition, to be the seal of saintship is to be so filled with God, so perfectly aware of one's being embedded within God, that there is no "space" for ego.

As a practical matter, no Muslim mystic after the time of Ibn 'Arabi was independent of his enormous influence. If, on the one hand, the ideas summarized in the previous pages would, not surprisingly, have led to strong attacks from the orthodox mainstream who perceived them as heretical, on the other hand, Ibn 'Arabi's work exerted a profound impact not only on subsequent Muslim mysticism—most significantly in the realm of Sufi poetry, as we shall see in chapter 8—but also on medieval Christian mysticism. Moreover, there is an obvious parallel in many of his discussions, especially that of the names of God, to that same discussion in Kabbalah, as we shall see in the chapter that follows this.

NOTES

1. One finds the abbreviated version of Ibn 'Arabi's name also given as Ibn al'Arabi.

2. The Muslim calendar begins with the *hijra*—the migration of Muhammad and his followers from Makka to Yathrib (Madina) in 622. Moreover, because the calendar is lunar, the Muslim year is 355 days long, and it thus obviously completes itself approximately 10 days more quickly than the Gregorian year. Thus, on the one hand, the Muslim months move through the Gregorian year approximately ten days earlier, year by year; and on the other, the comparison of year numbers is not accomplished simply by deducting 622. Thus, for example, the year 1182 on the Gregorian calendar is the year 577 on the Muslim calendar; the year 1234 is the year 632, and so on. For simplicity's sake—because I assume that the vast majority of my readership is

likely to be more familiar with the Gregorian calendar—I will use Gregorian dates throughout this narrative.

3. Ibn Sirin accused them of trying to emulate Jesus in wearing wool, whereas, he asserted, the Prophet dressed in cotton. Thus, it appears that in the early eighth century there was a group of ascetics in Kufa (a city in Iraq where the Arabic calligraphic writing style *kufic* developed) called *al-Sufiya*. Two hundred years later, woolen garments had become the standard sartorial mode of Muslim ascetics throughout Mesopotamia, and the term *Sufi* was being applied to all Muslim mystics.

4. In a fascinating, if tendentious, book of recent advent, Moustafa Gadalla argues that Sufism predated Islam (and Judaism and Christianity) by thousands of years and originated in Egypt (convention associates the first Sufi leaders with Persia). Gadalla also claims that the word *Sufi* is actually of Ancient Egyptian origin. *Seph/Soph* was often a component of common Egyptian names—meaning "wisdom, purity" (among many other meanings). "See Moustafa Gadalla, *Egyptian Mystics: Seekers of the Way* (Greensboro, NC: Tehuti Foundation, 2003), 23; also see chapter 11, p. 289.

5. It is a (Western) convention to render *wali* as "saint," just as it is a convention to render *rajul* as "prophet," but perhaps a more accurate rendering of the first term would be "friend," just as the second is better rendered as "messenger."

6. It is first recorded in the compendium of the scholar, Muslim (ca. 850–875).

7. See the extensive discussion of this in Reuven Firestone's *Journeys in Holy Lands: The Evolution of the Abraham-Ishmael Legends in Islamic Exegesis* (Albany: State University of New York Press, 1990), especially chapter 8.

8. This is quoted in Kalabadhi's *al-Ta'arruf*, 26–27. The translation is from A. J. Arberry, *Sufism: An Account of the Mystics of Islam* (New York: Harper Torchbooks, 1970), 29.

9. We recall that it was in the context of this early shift north that Abdul 'Malik built the Dome of the Rock in Jerusalem (ca. 691), which both offered support to and received support from the hadith regarding the *'isra* and the *mir'aj*, marking the ascent/descent from/to that very rock; and helped cement the spiritual significance of Jerusalem as *al-Kuds*—"the Holy", thus providing the Umayyad caliphate with a sacred city much closer to Damascus than are Makka and Madina.

10. Moreover, light as a symbol of God is part of mainstream Muslim thinking. Most obviously, the placement of a lamp in the *mihrab* (the niche within the wall of the mosque that faces toward Makka) is typically explained by reference to Qur 24:35: "The world is a niche and God is a light within [the niche]."

11. Not so surprisingly, the articulation of this idea echoes the terminology of Aristotle, in whose *Nicomachaean Ethics* the distinction is offered between something that exists potentially and the same entity actualized. The interest in Aristotle on the part of Muslim theologians was deep and broad—here the Greek thinker may arguably have influenced al-Junaid—and incidentally helped to preserve Aristotle's writings and eventually to transmit them toward the postmedieval Christian world both directly and through Jewish scholars.

12. *Haqq* might also be rendered as "reality," underscoring the sense that the speaker has become completely identified with a reality that is other than that of his

auditors—but it is the Reality of God, therefore the Reality that they all, in theory, seek, but which he claims to have found: the *real, true* Reality. It should also be noted as a minor point that in writing, the distinction between "Truth" and "truth"—the first with a majuscule, the second with a miniscule—cannot be made in Arabic and Persian. Thus, an unsympathetic reader would have an easier time being offended than a reader in, say, English, who could more immediately recognize the implications of becoming "a truth" when filled with and by "the Truth."

13. The seven stages are conversion, abstinence, renunciation, poverty, patience, trust in God, and satisfaction; the ten states are constant meditation, nearness (to God), love, fear, hope, longing, intimacy, tranquility, contemplation, and certainty.

14. His full name is Zayn al-Islam Abu al-Qasim 'Abd al-Karim ibn Hawzan ibn 'Abd al-Malik ibn Talha ibn Muhammad al-Qushairi al-Naysaburi al-Istiwa'i al-Shafi'i al-Ah'ari. He is called by the Sufi poet al-Farisi "the absolute Imam, jurist, *mutakallim*, scholar of Principles, Qur'anic commentator, man of letters, grammarian, writer and poet, the spokesman of his time, leader among his contemporaries, the secret of God in His creation, the Shaikh of Shaikhs, the Teacher of the Congregation and most advanced one of the Fold [i.e., the Sufi fold], the goal of those who tread the Path, the ensign of Truth, wellspring of Felicity, pole of Leadership, and grace personified."

15. Some readings of the *Risala* count up forty-five. See note 19 below.

16. The term is derived from the same root found in the word *jihad*, which in the vocabulary of everyday Islam refers to the struggle to perfect one's self as a Muslim (which term, we recall, means "one who submits/is committed" to God's will), to perfect the *Dar al-Islam*, and to perfect the world by causing it to recognize the Truth of Islam.

17. We must keep in mind that whereas in Judaism and Christianity, it is a given that Isaac was the son who was offered, as described in Genesis 22, in Islam the Qur'an merely refers to "a gentle son" without specifying which one, and Muslim commentators debated which son it was for centuries. See Qur 37:100ff: "When he reached the age to work with him, he [Abraham] said, 'Oh my boy! Verily I have seen in a dream that I should sacrifice you; what then do you see [that is] right?' Said he [Isaac/Ishmael]: 'Oh my sire! Do what you are bidden; you will find me, if it please God, one of the patient!' So together they submitted [to God's will]." And see, for example, the discussion by the tenth-century scholar Ath-Tha'labi in his *Stories of the Prophets* of the question of which son it was. He observes that Ali and Umar had both asserted that it was Isaac, while others have asserted that it was Ishmael.

18. There is also a more banal, historical-technical aspect of this discussion. Al-Qushairi explains that the Khorasanian School (in Iran) maintained that *rida* is a *maqam* that develops directly out of *tawakkul*, whereas the Iraqi school argued that *rida* is a *hal*. So his stance, he points out, is an intermediate one, in which the beginning of the experience of *rida* for the mystic is as a *maqam*, but the culmination of the experience is as a *hal*.

19. Some readers (such as A. J. Arberry in his *Sufism: An Account of the Mystics of Islam*) read the number of Principles as 45, not 43. Arberry fails to recognize *hasad* (envy) and *ghiba* (slander) as individual principles (14 and 15), but then regards *safar* (travel), *subhad* (companionship, *tauhid* ([unequivocal belief in the] oneness [of

God]), and *fana'* ("noble dying"), which Al-Qushairi discusses between *adab* (40) and *ma'rifa* (41) as additional principles. *Tauhid* and *fana'* are part of an ultimate, underlying condition to which the Sufi arrives, so that they are not counted as part of the ladder of *maqamat* and *ahlal*. *Safar* and *subhad* are part of the larger discussion, but are neither *maqamat* nor *ahlal*, whereas *hasad* and *ghiba* (or rather the elimination of these qualities) are part of the ladder of *maqamat* that Al-Qushairi sets before his reader.

20. As a practical historical, political matter, this danger would arguably be more present for the Jewish mystic than for the Muslim mystic, since the condition of Jewish life within the world of the past fifteen centuries has been more tenuous than that of Muslim life, and thus becoming Christian would offer a practical attraction for a Jew that it would not for a Muslim. On the other hand, this last consideration should be fundamentally irrelevant, since the mystic eschews concerns for physical and psychological comfort, by definition. If, as a mystic, I dedicate myself to turning toward and seeking union with God, and thus turn myself away from the world, then my worldly condition should not affect my spiritual condition and my religious choices.

21. See chapter 9 for the Jewish equivalent and the Hebrew-language term *pilpul*.

22. If one were to seek parallels within the Jewish and Christian traditions, they would surely be *The Guide for the Perplexed* (*Moreh N'vookheem*) by Maimonides and the *Summa Theologica* by St. Thomas Aquinas. Interestingly, both of these works fall strictly within the mainstream of Jewish and Christian religious thought and outside their respective mystical traditions. While within those mystical traditions there are important works—such as the masterful *Zohar* in Jewish mysticism (see chapter 6) or any number of works within the Christian mystical canon—none of them offers an overall impact comparable to that of al-Ghazali's *Ihya*.

23. Thus, for example, there is a five-rung scale of do's and don't's that moves from absolute don't's to absolute do's, in which the consumption (or, rather, prohibition against consuming) certain foods and liquids, such as pork and alcohol, is included.

24. Ibn 'Arabi contributed broadly to Muslim thought, but he is primarily known for his role as a teacher of Sufism; his name is often confused with that of a second Ibn al-Arabi, also from Andalusia, who was a scholar of al-Maliki jurisprudence.

25. This is a play, of course, on the phrase referring to Muhammad as the Seal of the Prophets.

26. See above, pp. 75, 80, 81, 82.

27. Qur'an II.115.

28. Ibn Al'Arabi, *The Bezels of Wisdom* (Mahwah, NJ: Paulist Press, 1980), 92, 135.

29. The quote is from Ibn Al'Arabi, *Bezels*, 135. The issue of God as pure being is precisely parallel to that around which Jewish mysticism not only centers but also focuses with respect to God's name, *YHVH*, in Hebrew, the root of which word is "to be" (see chapter 3, pp. 35–36). For Sufism the issue does not focus on the linguistic issue of the name of God since the name/word "Allah" is not built from an Arabic language root that means "to be."

30. From *The Treatise on Being*, W. H. Weir, transl. (London: Beshara Publications, 1975), 9.

31. Ibn Al'Arabi, *The Treatise on Being*, 9.

32. See chapter 3, p. 51. The imagery of God's "veil" will appear and reappear subsequently in all three traditions, as we shall see.

33. Ibn Al'Arabi, *Bezels*, 184.

34. Ibn Al'Arabi, *The Treatise on Being*, p. 10.

35. Ibn Al'Arabi, *The Treatise on Being*, p. 10.

36. See above, p. 76.

37. Ibn Al'Arabi, *Bezels,* p. 106.

38. One recognizes this kind of statement as an outgrowth of the broader Abrahamic concept of God's ubiquity: In general, God may be found anywhere and everywhere; here, more specifically, God may be addressed by any number of appellations.

39. One not only recognizes the identity with Jewish and Christian thinking regarding divine animation/besoulment of beings as part of the creation process recounted in Genesis 1 but also the precise cognate between the Arabic *nafas* and the Hebrew *nefesh* as one of the words used to refer to the breath that God breathes into the clod of earth (*adamah*, in Hebrew) to yield the first human being (Adam).

40. From the Latin *anima*, meaning "breath" and also meaning "soul."

41. Properly put, in Greek: *ho Logos ton Logon*.

42. See above, p. 35: To say God's name and thus make God present is and is not the same as if God were actually present, just as to say Bill Clinton's name and to discuss him is in some sense to bring him into the room, but not in the same way as if he were actually to walk into the room.

43. See chapter 11, pp. 290–91, with regard to the Jewish mystical notion of the *lamed-vav*, for whose sake the universe is maintained.

44. See chapter 7, 143ff and 151ff.

45. See chapter 6, pp. 114, 120–24.

46. See chapter 9, pp. 206–10.

47. See note 5 regarding the translation of *auliya*.

48. See chapter 1, pp. 1, 12, 14, and chapter 4, p. 59. "Anointed" means neither the descendant of David and God-become-Man (of Christianity) nor the descendant of David and a vague idea (of Judaism), but the continuation of sacerdotal intermediation of which Muhammad is the culmination and of which Ibn 'Arabi is, so to speak, the culmination of the emulation.

Chapter Six

Medieval Jewish Mysticism
From Merkavah *to* Kabbalah

Merkavah mysticism, as we have seen, is geographically centered in the Middle East, primarily in Palestine—more broadly, from Egypt to Mesopotamia— and its tone emphasizes the awesome greatness and indescribable, unfathomable inaccessibility of God. But by the time Islam, having entered onto the stage of history, has begun to dominate the Middle East politically and to expand its presence from Spain to India and as the *Dar al-Islam* has begun to push up against the borders of Christendom (during the eighth though eleventh centuries), Jewish mysticism has begun to shift both its geographic center and its nuance. Kabbalah will evolve away from the Middle East, its birth and development carrying it from the Balkans to Spain, and it will emphasize the loving closeness of God to us, in spite of that unfathomable inaccessibility. To *merkavah*'s insistence on God's transcendent *apartness from* us, Kabbalah offers a focus on God's immanent being *a part of* us. As much as God is self-concealing, Kabbalah asserts, God is self-revealing—to those who understand how to look.

In the broad sense, Kabbalah as a mystical perspective pushes the devotee toward the apprehension of God and of the creation, both of whose most intrinsic elements are beyond the grasp of the intellect, although the intellect is rarely belittled or rejected; rather, it is understood to be an important instrument for grasping the *beginnings* of deeper truths, which require transintellectual, *unnatural* (*super-natural*, in the Latinate sense meaning "beyond nature") processes. These processes are centered on contemplation and the achievement of illumination, receiving the transmission of a primeval revelation concerning the nature of the Torah (the ultimate guide to God and God's initial and ongoing relationship with created reality) and related spiritual matters. In the narrower sense, Kabbalah expresses the profound yearning for direct human communion with God achieved through the annihilation of the individual's own personality—*Bittul ha-Yesh* (literally, "annihilation or cancellation of the what-there-is [of myself])." In this latter sense, we recognize the danger to all but the few who can manage self-annihilation and mergence into the One that yet leads to a return to the self—and also have the ability to improve the condition of their community (*profanus*) based on the experience of *Bittul ha-Yesh*.

The term *Kabbalah* refers to a series of different Jewish mystical systems developed in different times and places, but all of which assert a strong connection to Jewish traditions. The term means "acceptance/that which has been accepted," "that which has been received," "tradition." As such, its early practitioners see themselves as functioning very much within the confines of Jewish tradition and not outside its legitimate boundaries. It's just that the kabbalists believe that Judaism in all of its aspects, both historical and spiritual, presents a system of mystical (i.e., hidden) symbols that reflect the mystery (hiddenness) of God and God's relationship to the universe, and they (the kabbalists) seek the keys (whether discovering them or inventing them) to these symbols. In other words, they understand the universe, and within it, more particularly, the Jewish tradition, from the Torah's text to the rituals associated with the holidays, to present elements that *stand for* Godness. The inaccessible is made accessible by parsing the symbols, or "elements that stand for," Godness.[1]

The term *Kabbalah* first appears in the writing of the eleventh-century Spanish poet, Solomon Ibn Gabirol, who refers to *hokhmat haKabbalah* ("the wisdom of the Kabbalah") in his work *Tikkun Midot haNefesh* (*Repairing the Dimensions of the Soul*); he seems to mean by this those "secret" doctrines handed down through the so-called Essenes and the *yordei merkavah* and others. The term is first used in the narrow and more specific sense of referring to specific mystical doctrines and to the doctrine of *Bittul ha-Yesh* by Isaac the Blind around 1200. Yet, the teachings ultimately encompassed by the term in its narrow sense have a history that begins earlier and elsewhere, and the term referring to them does not come into general usage until the fourteenth century.

Those teachings are first associated with the Kalonymides family, which, from its name, may have originated in northern Greece. But by the time the family name is connected to early Kabbalah, Samuel the Hassid, as he is known, was in Germany. His primary disciple and head of a small Jewish mystical community was his son, Judah the Hassid. The term *hassid* used for both father and son is a general term meaning "pious," and the *hassidim* of twelfth- and thirteen-century Germany constituted a group that cultivated deep inner piety and approached the prayers offered to God by all Jews with an intensity that set them apart from others. They practiced asceticism and penitence—recalling *merkavah* mysticism—with the goal of both detaching the God-seeking soul from physical preoccupations and of being ever aware of how much ethical improvement is necessary if one is to approach and hope to cling to the all-good God. Moreover, they are said to have focused in particular on the letters and sounds of God's name, turning prayer into meditation and concentration of a deconstructive sort that we can recognize as continuing an aspect of Jewish mystical emphasis begun, in part, with the *Sepher Yetzirah*—and which we also recognize as offering a parallel to part of Ibn 'Arabi's writing.

The German *hassidim* asserted as a goal a state of spirit in which a constant sense of God's presence around and among them would dominate. The term they coined to refer to both the pursuit and the achievement of that goal, *d'vekut*—from the Hebrew root *d-v-k*, meaning "to stick" or "glue"—suggests a state of total interpenetration between God and the devotee, wherein the connectedness between the one and the other is so total that it becomes almost impossible to separate them from each other. Judah the Hassid penned a work called *Sepher HaHassidim* (*Book of the Pious*) in which these issues are addressed. In turn, his disciple, Eliezer ben Yehudah—literally, Eliezer the son of Judah; thus, he saw Judah as his spiritual father[2]—authored a well-respected commentary on the *Sepher Yetzirah* and also an important work called *Rokeah* (*Apothecary*). The title of this last-named work is intended to suggest both an extensive compendium and a kind of esoteric mixture of means of thinking beyond the norms of rabbinic intellect toward a deeper closeness—an intense *d'vekut* and *yihud* (intuitive grasping of divine unity, for *yihud* means "unity") with God.[3]

Eliezer is also credited with a work called *Ma'asechet Atzilut* (*The Tractate of Emanation*). This work is essentially a midrash that arrives at hidden knowledge by deconstructing and juxtaposing certain biblical passages with key word connections to each other. Thus, the first half of Psalm 25:14, which reads, "The *secret counsel* of the Lord is with those who *fear/are in awe of* Him," is connected to Psalm 111:10: "The *fear/awe* of the Lord is the beginning of *wisdom*." The repetition of the word that translates into English as "awe" or "fear" offers several paths to hidden wisdom. One is to conclude that in fearing the Lord, there is nothing else to fear, since nothing is as fearsome as God, which also therefore means that an intense and secret connection to God offers protection from anything else that one might fear—so a God fearer becomes fearless in the *profanus*. The second is to connect "wisdom" to "secret" by means of a chiastic parallel between the two passages. A third is to thereby understand that the kind of wisdom—*hokhmah*—intended by this divinely revealed text is *hochmat haKabbalah*, "the wisdom of the Kabbalah." A fourth is to equate *hokhmah* with "Torah" since both terms are grammatically feminine—a notion that will bear fruit in the central kabbalistic text, the *Zohar* (as we shall see).[4] Of course, none of these understandings excludes the others.

Eliezer ben Yehudah's disciple was Abraham of Cologne, whose son and disciple, Isaac of Cologne, was known as Isaac the Blind and also as the "Father of Kabbalah." Isaac's other epithet was *Sagi Nahor*, meaning "very clear-sighted." While on the one hand this is a euphemism for "blind," on the other it is intended to suggest that his outer blindness was balanced (chiastically, one might say) by an inner sight that connected him to the center of the *sacer*, even as his outer blindness disconnected him in obvious ways from the workings of the *profanus*. It is he who not only put emphasis on *Bittul ha-Yesh* but also introduced the notion of the transmigration of souls—another idea that will bear significant fruit in later Kabbalah (specifically that of Isaac Luria, as we shall see). Isaac seems to have transmitted an interest in Kabbalah from Germany to France, and in turn his disciple, Azriel ben Solomon, is credited with transmitting the study of Kabbalah from France to Spain, where an increase in the intellective and philosophical range of mystical intensity may be seen emerging through the thirteenth and fourteenth centuries.

It is in southern France—Provence, properly speaking—however, that the next major Jewish mystical text emerged toward the end of the twelfth century. The *Sepher Bahir* (*Book of Brightness*) might be called the earliest work of formal kabbalistic literature, offering a structure that emphasizes the symbolic thinking endemic to kabbalistic teachings. It is the *Sepher Bahir*, in fact, that first offers the use of the term *Kabbalah* as "acceptance," meaning that those teachings are accepted by God as a legitimate means of seeking intimacy with God. The phrase *m'koobaleem lifney haShem* ("accepted/acceptable before the Name")—that is, the Name of God, "the Name" being the double circumlocution for the name that is ineffable of the God who can only be grasped by way of grasping its ineffable Name—is used in the *Bahir* to refer to the practitioners of Kabbalah. Thus, one might say that "tradition" and "acceptance" as descriptives of the kabbalistic tradition meet in the *Bahir*.

The name of the book is derived from Job 37:21: "And now men do not see the bright (*bahir*) light that is in the clouds." This is the passage announcing God's imminent appearance out of the whirlwind to respond to Job's long-suffering inquiry, and it offers the only appearance of the word *bahir* in the Hebrew Bible. Given the culminating words of the chapter, which refer to the fear of God on the part of men and God's inaccessibility even to the wise of heart—and given that, immediately following these words, God directly addresses Job with an answer full of questions and ultimately without answer— there is a singular appropriateness to the use of this word as a title to the book.

For the *Sepher Bahir* is a guide to accessing the inaccessible God, a source of answers that are hardly *answers* to questions without answers. Authored all but anonymously, the *Sepher Bahir* is a midrash in form, presenting brief statements attributed to various *tana'im* and *amor'aim* (i.e., the authors of the Mishnah and the Gemara, which two works comprise the basic texts of the Talmud, the preeminent rabbinic guide for living a proper Jewish life guided by God's instruction as offered in the Hebrew Bible). I say "all but anonymously" because tradition ascribes the book to Rabbi Nehuniah ben HaKana, who is cited in the very first line, in which the quote from Job 37:21 appears, together with two other biblical quotes. The first two are presented as contradicting each other and the third as resolving the contradiction, in Nehuniah's analysis:

> Rabbi Nehuniah ben HaKana said: One verse states, "And now they do not see the *bahir* in the skies." . . . Another verse, however (Psalm 18:12), states: "He made darkness His hiding place." It is also written (Psalm 97:2), "Cloud and gloom surround him." This is an apparent contradiction. A third verse comes and reconciles the two. It is written (Psalm 139:12), "even darkness is not dark to You. Night shines like day—light and darkness are the same."

No statement could be more conducive to the sensibility of mysticism in any case, as we have seen—darkness and light are not opposed in the *sacer* as they are in the *profanus*. After all, where Kabbalah is concerned, Isaac the Blind, the "Father of Kabbalah," can be bursting with enlightened perception regarding the *mysterion* while being completely in the dark regarding the *profanus* world, so this is a perfect issue with which to begin the exposition of the book of brightness. And as for Nehuniah, albeit the putative author, he is never mentioned again in the text of the *Bahir*. After that first verse, a succession of midrashic analyses—at the outset, largely focused on the description of the creation offered in Genesis—is associated with a range of interpreters, some with well-known names and others with names found only within the pages of the *Bahir*.

These analyses are strung together without a clear order, some of them reflecting back on passages in the *Sepher Yetzirah*. Certainly, the discussion of the forms of certain Hebrew letters may be seen as a furtherance of the focus on those letters first offered in the *Sepher Yetzirah*. One of the areas in which order, rather than an apparent haphazardness, prevails in the discussion is in the focus on numbers, by way of a listing of the *sephirot* (the ten "countings" or "numbers" discussed in the *Sepher Yetzirah*) that are, as a compendium, associated with the letter *yud*, the tenth letter in the Hebrew alphabet. The *Bahir*, however, refers to them as *ma'amarot*—"sayings" or "statements," perhaps to be understood the way *logoi* ("words" or "statements") would be understood in Greek—as symbolic expressions of, or ten aspects of, the creation, as much as it refers to them as *sephirot*.

That is, if in Genesis 1:3, "God *said*, 'Let there be light,' and there was light," then one might conclude (as the *Bahir* does) that the words themselves "spoken" or "uttered" or "said" by God intermediate between God and the consequences of the utterance (the coming into being of light, in this case— or of the firmament or of animals and birds in subsequent verses in the same creation cycle). The ten utterances, words, sayings are emanations from God. For how does God create? By *saying, uttering*. But how does God "say" or "utter"? If that question cannot be easily answered (for God possesses—at least in the Jewish tradition—no mouth or tongue or teeth or cheeks or lungs with which to articulate sounds as we humans do), then we may try to grasp the creation process by understanding it as one of emanation in which the closest element to God is the series of words that initiate the actualizing process that had begun *in potentia* in God's decision to create the world.

The main importance of the *Bahir* in terms of kabbalistic history is the extent of its symbolic language. It offers the earliest source that deals at some length with the realm of the *sephirot*, and in speaking of them as a continuum extending from the Creator through the process of creation to the created universe, it pursues that line of thought regarding creation that is at the heart of Eliezer ben Yehudah's *Ma'asechet Atzilut*: that the universe is the consequence of a process of *emanation* out of the One God.[5]

To the extent that, as aspects of creation, the *sephirot* are also presented as *attributes* of God or *powers*, or aspects, of the equiprimordial light that initiated creation, the discussion in the *Bahir* gives symbolic names to the divine attributes for the first time. The work asserts that each of these is found in allusions offered either in the Bible or in the rabbinic writings. It conceives of those attributes as a "secret tree" from which human souls "blossom forth." Its emphasis is on the "thought" of God, rather than the "will" of God, on the why of the creation rather than the how, even if the discussion of the ten *ma'amarot* impinges on the matter of how.[6]

⟨◇⟩

The carrying of Kabbalah from France into Spain with which Azriel ben Solomon is associated, where it would reach the peak of its "classic" efflorescence, was marked by an increasingly esoteric and philosophical bent and by the emergence of a number of important figures and their writings, most notably the "sister" text of the *Sepher Bahir*, the *Zohar*. Spain had begun its five-hundred year reign as the cultural, intellectual, and spiritual center of the Jewish world, and as an extraordinary center of Jewish-Christian-Muslim interface, by the beginning of the tenth century.[7] There the writings, both poetical and philosophical, of key Jewish figures, such as Samuel HaNagid, Solomon Ibn Gabirol, Moses and Abraham Ibn Ezra, and, above all, Yehuda HaLevy—to say nothing of Maimonides and Nachmanides (although by the time Maimonides was writing his great works, he had left Spain and was living in North Africa, first in Morocco and then in Egypt)—meant that writers of kabbalistic texts could hardly avoid being influenced to think along profound intellectual lines, even if the whole point of thinking along kabbalistic lines was to think beyond intellect.

Certainly, these writers evinced awareness of the Jewish mystical tradition. Yehudah HaLevy discusses and interprets the *Sepher Yetzirah* in section 4 of his *Kuzari* (ca. 1080), for example, and Abraham Ibn Ezra (ca. 1089–1164) applies what he terms a mystical number and letter analysis to the name of God. He also often includes in the marginalia of his commentary on the Torah the phrase *hameyveen yaveen*—"the initiate [literally, 'the one who understands'] will understand"—in the context of particularly obscure passages and obscure explanations (ca. 1125). Maimonides mentions the *sotrei Torah* ("secrets of the Torah") in his *Guide for the Perplexed*, chapter 71, which secrets, he says, "are transmitted only by a chosen few to a chosen few." Thus, the atmosphere seems to have been rife with interface between legalistic, intellectual, philosophical thinking on the one hand and intense spiritual feeling on the other, while at the same time, in a manner somewhat reminiscent of the interwoven pagan-Jewish-Christian atmosphere of Roman-era Palestine, the atmosphere of tenth through fourteenth-century Spain was intense with Jewish-Christian-Muslim intercommunication. This in turn also meant that varied forms of interface with classical pagan thought, as expressed in diverse forms of Neoplatonism, were also available to affect developing Kabbalah.

The kabbalistic text par excellence that grew out of this extraordinary atmosphere is associated with Moses de Leon (1240–1305) from northern central Christian Spain (Leon was an important city along the pilgrims' route to Santiago de Compostela from France; its thirteenth-century, Gothic-styled cathedral is marked by the most astonishing stained glass windows in all of Spain). That text is called the *Zohar* and is generally considered the ultimate exponent and primary work of classical Kabbalah. The title, like that of the *Sepher Bahir*, is derived from a rarely appearing term in the Hebrew Bible, in this case, in Daniel 12:3: "and they that be wise [affect wisdom] shall shine as the brightness [*zohar*] of the firmament." The word *zohar* appears one other time in the Hebrew Bible, in Ezekiel 8:2. There the prophet begins the report of his second vision by describing a figure with the likeness of the appearance of fire, the features of which recall those of the likeness of the appearance of a man upon the throne described in Ezekiel 1. In other words, the title of the kabbalistic work forges a direct link both with the culminating words from God to the prophet who walked through fire unscathed and to that paradoxical biblical text which is the basis for *merkavah* mysticism.

The *Zohar* was published after Moses de Leon's death by his widow. It is not clear who—whether it was she or, while he lived, he—asserted that its author was Shimeon bar Yochai, a second-century contemporary of Rabbi Akiva and the other key "hero" of the Jewish mystical tradition after Akiva. The claim that Shimeon bar Yochai authored the text, and that it was transmitted generation by generation down to Moses de Leon, was a means of elevating the seriousness with which it would be taken by its audience; that it is written in Aramaic rather than Arabic, Hebrew, or Latin suggested a second-century provenance to them. A century later, the Spanish Jewish thinker Abraham Zacuto asserted this unequivocally, adding the following provenance narrative: that Rabbi Isaac of Acre (on the northern Mediterranean coast of Palestine) asserted that Moses ben Nachman [Nachmanides] found a manuscript, authored by Shimeon bar Yochai and sent it to Catalonia (in northeastern Spain) from where it was transmitted west into Aragon and thence to Castille, where it came into the possession of Moses de Leon. Shortly after Moses de Leon died, two wealthy men came to his widow asking to see the manuscript but she claimed it did not exist; rather that the manuscript in her possession was his (Moses de Leon's) own work.

But the fact that the Aramaic that purports to be second-century in dialect style is so awkward suggests rather—as has been well argued in the last century[8]—that Moses de Leon gathered and edited and even authored most or all of the text. It is filled with anachronisms, such as references to the Crusades and to the domination of Islam, as well as to Hebrew vowel signs (which were not in use until the eighth century); and there are interpretations of religious customs that may be traced to medieval authorities. Moreover, there are phrases and passages that are identical to those within another work written by Moses de Leon, *Sepher haNefesh haHakhamah* (*The Book of the Wise Soul*). It seems in any case singularly appropriate that the most prominent text in classic Kabbalah—of parsing the hidden mysteries of the *sacer* in its relationship to the *profanus*—should offer such a mystery with regard to its own creation.

The *Zohar* is an extensive work. It is largely a midrash in form, offering an extensive series of anecdotes and commentaries focused on the Torah (so that we may regard it as the first Jewish mystical text that somewhat systematically deconstructs the Torah) spiced up by an eclectic array of kabbalistic issues, subjects, and beliefs. In these discussions, the main speaker is generally Shimeon bar Yochai, but the narrative presents him in the third person, speaking about different issues in different dramatic contexts (as we shall shortly see). Interspersed with this are "inserts" drawn from small older works, such as the *'Idra* (or *Hadra*) *Rabba* ("Greater Assembly"), the *'Idra* (or *Hadra*) *Zutra* ("Lesser Assembly"), and *Sifra* (or *Saphra*) *de Tzneuta* ("Book of Secrecy").[9] In the first of these, the reader encounters Rabbi Shimeon for the first time; he offers an allegorical description of God's organs, equating these details with the image of primordial man (*adam kadmon*). The second of these offers a description of the death of Rabbi Shimeon, and the third offers secrets regarding the divine nature, with a strong emphasis on letter mysticism (i.e., deducing secrets from the combined numerological values and sounds of the Hebrew letters in particular words).

There are further elements, such as a text that focuses on the figure of Moses (the ultimate, prophet-magician-mystic), called *Ra'ayah M'hameynah* ("Faithful Shepherd"), and the *Sitrei Torah* ("Secrets of the Torah"), another book of secrets, as well as material on the *heikhalot* (forging a direct link back to *merkavah* mysticism) and what are taken by most students of the *Zohar* to be the final elements to have been included, the *Tikkunei haZohar* ("Corrections of the *Zohar*") and the *Zohar Hadash* ("New *Zohar*"). The first of these two later additions consists of seventy chapters on the word *breshit* ("in the beginning"—the very first word/phrase of the Torah—in Hebrew it takes the form of a single word, whereas in English it constitutes a phrase). The second is a series of chapters of commentary on the book of Ruth and the *Song of Songs*. These two biblical books have in common the theme of love. Ruth is the story of the love of the Moabite heroine for her husband, which translates, at his death, into love for her mother-in-law and her embrace of the Israelite people and, in turn, to her love and marriage to her husband's kinsman, Boaz, the denouement of which is that the union between Ruth and Boaz leads, two generations later, to the birth of the ultimate Israelite king and *Mashiah*, David.[10] The Song of Songs is pure love poetry, of the sort traditionally exchanged, in the Middle East, between a bride and groom. It was one of the last of the books to be accepted into the Jewish canon because it was perceived as too profane, but Rabbi Akiva is said to have convinced his fellow religious leaders that it is an allegory of the love relationship between God and the people Israel, and so it was ultimately embraced by the canon.

Thus, both Ruth and the Song of Songs share an appropriateness for commentary within a text that has as an important part of its emphasis the immanent accessibility of a loving God (as opposed to the transcendent inaccessibility of an awesome God). They are model biblical narratives upon which a Jewish (or Christian) mystic might logically focus in his search for the mental and transmental means of spiritual union with God's inner depths. Moreover, the central figures of the first are women, and the focus of the second is at least half female (the putative narrator of the poems focused on the male beloved and the object of the poems regarding the female beloved). Indeed, if we analyze what are arguably the two most important ideas or doctrines that emerge within the *Zohar*, we can get a sense of the strong dynamic tension between the sense of God as eternally inaccessibly transcendent, apart from us, and yet, by paradox, forever accessibly immanent, a part of us—more distant than the most distant star and yet closer to us than our own breathing. While this paradox is a consistent leitmotif in mainstream Judaism, it is an intense attribute of classic Kabbalah, and the form it takes in the *Zohar* and other texts is to articulate a "female" aspect of God.

These two doctrines, developed out of previous references and discussions that, to a certain extent are already found in early Jewish mysticism, but which in any case take shape in early Kabbalah—in the *Sepher Bahir*, for example—are those of the *sephirot* (as we have seen) and of the *Shekhinah* (which we have not yet discussed). In a sense, the one complements the other, the first offering a means of access to the deepest, hiddenmost God that remains inaccessible in spite of the means, and the other suggesting the consistent immanence of God among and within us. The first may derive, as a term, from the passage in Exodus 24:10, as Moses and the elders ascend the mountain below which the Israelites stand and see the invisible God beneath whose feet there was "the like of a paved work of sapphire stone, and the like of the very heaven for clearness." The word *sephirah* may be related to "sapphire" as it appears in that verse. Seven verses later, as Moses alone ascends the upper mountain into a cloud hiding its summit, "the appearance of the Glory of the Lord was like devouring fire on the top of the mount in the eyes of Israel." (Certainly, the imagery of ascent to a vision of the visionless God anticipates other passages in the Hebrew Bible that feed into Jewish mysticism, particularly Isaiah 6 and Ezekiel 1). There, Moses would disappear for forty days and nights.

The concept of the *Shekhinah*, as we shall shortly see, emphasizes God's love for humankind and the possibility for the mystic to become one with God, whereas the concept of the *sephirot* accentuates the unbridgeable distance between God and us—while simultaneously suggesting God's accessibility due to the following paradox: The nine lowest of the *sephirot*, from *malkhut* to *hokhmah* ("wisdom"), are still within our realm; one does not exit our reality toward divine reality until one has exited *keter*. Yet, as soon as one has entered *malkhut*, one has *already* exited our reality and begun an ascent through aspects of the aspectless divine realm. Of course, the very understanding of "aspects" of divine, *sacer* reality are based on and derive from our understanding of human, *profanus* reality: If the Creator may be perceived in the creation, then one might suppose it possible to infer the Creator from the creation—but we are still caught in the problematic web of our language of description. It is *profanus* based, and using it to describe the *sacer*—the more so the *mysterion* within the deepest recesses of the *sacer*—is tricky, to say the least.

Moreover, the *sephirot* are imaged as a series of ascending/descending triads, with central, left, and right "columns"; the left is treated as male and active, and the right as female and passive—except that there is no left and right, male and female, active and passive in Godness, so one must recognize that imaging the *spherot* in a static medium, flat on the page, fails to offer what *should* be the image. One must imagine the entire "tree" as spinning on its axis, as it were, so that the one "side" instantly becomes the other. Thus, active, male, left becomes passive, female, right and vice versa, so quickly that they cease to be the opposed categories that they would be in the *profanus*. Nor must one simply imagine these as "aspects" of God—inferred from their being aspects of ourselves and our reality— since they may also be understood as articulating the *process of creation*. The process emanates down from *keter* to *malkhut*, achieving increasing concreteness and clarity as it moves downward.[11] And therefore, in grasping the *sephirot*, the mystic is recapitulating that process in reverse, carrying him or her "back" to the Creator.

If such thinking suggests the shaping of a vocabulary of connectedness between human and divine, at the same time the doctrine is one of distancing us from the God who made us and is yet utterly Other than what we are. This is further accentuated by the notion that,

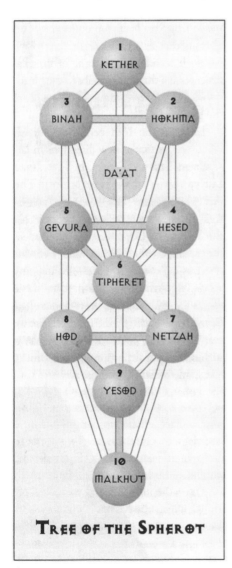

TREE OF THE SPHEROT

Figure 6.1.

beyond the uppermost *sephirah* (*keter*) (and the term "uppermost" is, by definition, misleading: It underscores that sense of the *sephirot* as entirely part
of the relative universe of directions in which we humans customarily dwell),
one moves simultaneously into and out to the absolute universe beyond (in toward the hiddenmost center; out toward the hiddenmost periphery of spaceless space). One emerges through *keter* into (out to) the *'eyn sof or* (the "endless light"; the primordial, cosmic light articulated in Genesis 1:2). From the
'eyn sof or, the mystic moves deeper in (further out) to the *'eyn sof* ("endless;
infinite") and finally to the absolute *'eyn* ("nothingness"). Here, within the
realm of pure no-thing-ness—even pre- or non-*is*-ness, at least in the *profanus* sense of "being"—the mystic is as close as possible to the inaccessible
God of pure no-thing-ness.

There is more: The *sephirot* are understood in a variety of different ways
simultaneously—their paradoxical differences appropriate to a concept that,
after all, has as its goal to draw us closer to the innermost *mysterion* of the
sacer, and must do so, to repeat, by means of the only language available to
us, that of the *profanus*. Thus, corresponding to "male" and "female" is the
sense of the two "sides" of the tree of the *sephirot* as active and passive (e.g.,
hokhmah as outer intellect and *binah* as inner intellect; *gevurah* as outer emotion and *hesed* as inner emotion; *hod* as voluntary processes and *netzah* as in-
voluntary processes). This mode of understanding them is part of the pattern
of considering the "tree" of the *sephirot* as a schematic delineation of the ultimate product of the creation process, the human being, and, as such, the
macrocosmic image that connects earth to heaven in extending from roots to
branches is simultaneously the human microcosm. But the individual over
whom the *sephirot* may be imposed as an image, a kabbalistic "Vitruvian
man," is an idealized, perfect human; Adam not as the male Adam, where Eve
is female, but Adam in the etymological sense in Genesis 1 that refers to the
first human being, made of earth (*adamah*), into which God breathes the soul
of its own breath.

The two "sides" are both within the same individual, accentuating the falseness of mistaking either vertical triad as a true "side" separated by the central
column from the other triadic "side." The image is, one must not forget, not to
be imagined as stagnant or stationery. So in the idealized individual—the
Adam-like mystic, for that is the practical reality of what and who the individual thusly delineated *is*—who is in harmony with the universe and with the Creator of himself and the universe, left/right, male/female, and active/passive
don't really exist as concepts in those moments of perfect harmony. Then, like
a top spinning on its central axis, the rhythms of the mystic's accord with *sacer*
and *profanus* reality offer the illusion of being absolutely stationery, when in reality the mystic is spinning at a breathtaking rate.

The image may be applied to the heavenly bodies that reside between earth and heaven, to the zodiacal layout of the sphere of fixed stars, and beyond them all, to the prime mover. Thus, in such a conception, *malkhut* is the earth and its elements; *yesod* is the moon; *tipheret* is the sun; *hod* corresponds to Mercury, *netzah* to Venus, *gevurah* to Mars, and *hesed* to Jupiter, *binah* to Saturn and *hokhmah* to the sphere of fixed stars—sub-schematicized as the zodiac—and *keter* is the *primum mobile*: the first mover. Such a vocabulary implies the absorption into kabbalistic, Zoharic thinking of the pagan tradition derived from the Greeks and Romans in that tradition's understanding of transmundane reality. And thus, the presentation of the *sephirot* presents itself as dangerous to those who might confuse the presence of such thinking with ignorance of what lies beyond the imagery: the *'eyn sof or*, *'eyn sof*, and ultimately the *'eyn* in the depths of which the true God may be found. Understood thusly, the *sephirot* suggest—reinforce the notion of—the macrocosm in its purely physical aspects, as connected both to the microcosm in its physical and spiritual aspects and to the *process* by which the physical universe was engendered by the metaphysical God.

Thus, to repeat, the idea of the *sephirot* functions to both access God for us and distance God from us. Moreover, the notion of possessing, and yet not possessing, distinguishable left/right and related matrices means that the doctrine also has implications for the Zohar's understanding of ethics and the problem of evil.[12] For if in "normative" symbolic thinking, good is associated with the right side and evil is associated with the left side,[13] then, on the one hand, the left side of the tree of the *sephirot* should carry that negative side of reality, human and otherwise. But actually, as we have observed, the never-stationery tree has no real left and right sides, since its spinning prevents such a simple lateral distinction. Of course, evil is in any case an entity without substance: The all-good, all-powerful God created a universe and, within it, humans, who must therefore (reflecting the all-good God who created us) be all-good at the beginning of reality. Evil appears into our reality when the first humans exercise the gift of free will in a manner that abrogates God's command regarding a certain tree and its fruit: The failure to adhere to God's commandment represents a failure to do good, not an act of *being* evil. Evil is therefore not a creation in and of itself but an arrival made possible by human failure to be good. The paradox of evil's nonreality—paradoxical, since it nonetheless exists—is articulated in the *Zohar* by the left side in opposition to the right; since there really is no left, it doesn't really exist. But it exists just as left and right exist, except not straightforwardly as "left" and "right."

These are only a few of the complex interweaves of the diverse handlings of the ten *sephirot* in which the Zoharic literature engages in thinking up and down on the two "sides" of the "tree." That literature also thinks in an interesting series of combinations of up-down, left-right directions when it refers to the "Four Worlds" located along the tree of the *sephirot*—more correctly labeled, four modes of creation. In this context, the *sephirot* are "divided" vertically in accordance, in part, with a passage in the book of Isaiah (God's words filtered through this particular prophetic conduit: "that which is called by my Name, I have *created* it, I have *formed* it, and I have *made* it" [Is 43:7]). The emphasis, not surprisingly, is on the name of God, that consistent mode of expressing God itself without expressing what cannot ultimately be expressed effectively by humans—twice removed, indeed, since it is not a specific named name but merely "my Name." The three verbs are those which, in common Hebrew parlance, as we have earlier seen (p. 46), convey, respectively, uniquely divine *creatio* ex nihilo (*bri'ah*), creative reshaping of chaotic material into identifiable and ordered shape (*yetzirah*), and broad and generalized "making" or "doing" (*'asiyah*). The trio of terms implicitly returns the issue back to the beginnings of Jewish mysticism and the creation question answered in some fashion in the *Sepher Yetzirah*—and yet neither answered nor answerable. In fact, to further intensify matters, one wends one's way up through *'asiyah* to *yetzirah* to *bri'ah* and thence to a fourth realm—the uppermost realm—*'atzilut* ("emanation").

Thus, the bottommost realm, as far as the image of the *sephirot* is typically configured—bounded by the bottom triad of *hod*, *netzah*, and *malkhut*, with *yesod* centering the configuration, is *'asiyah* ("making/doing"). This last term is both the broadest and most generic of Hebrew terms for human acts of shaping both physical and metaphysical reality, as we have noted, and, in this context, a reference to the world of action in all of its aspects. It is the realm in which we all live and function, work and play, think and pray, help and harm, and hinder and further each other and the world around us. It is the realm in which we choose to further or obstruct the process of ordering begun by God. At its best, it is the realm of *tikkun*, or moral and ethical repairing of the world; at its worst, it is continuing and expanding the process begun by Adam and Eve of abrogating God's commandment to use our gifts in the right way. Its *sacer* aspects are connoted by the wheels made of eyes—the *ophanim*—in Ezekiel's vision (thus continuing the extending of overt threads of continuity between *merkavah* and Kabbalah), and by angels who deal with the prayers of humans—as well as those in contact with *Sama-el*, associated with the shaping of evil in the *profanus*.

The next realm "up," *yetzirah* ("formation") is encompassed by *gevurah* and *hesed* above and *netzah* and *hod* below; *tipheret* anchors it as its center. This is the realm in which physical and perhaps spiritual reality are shaped from pre-existent matter. It is the realm signified by the four creatures (with their human, leonine, avian, and bovine visages) of Ezekiel's vision. It is the realm in which humans emulate God by our creativity: the transformation of clay into pottery, stone into statuary, wood into furniture and homes. It is the realm in which the artist is operative as a *sacerdos*, perceiving the chair in the tree, the vase in the clump of clay, the human figure in the rough-shaped rock, and intermediating between the material and the shape the artist imposes on it. *Yetzirah*, we recall, moreover, is the term used in that earliest of Jewish mystical texts to refer to the divine creative process with humility: While speculatively describing the process of divine creation, the author recognizes that his description can only be accomplished with parallel and circumlocutionary terms, which recognition is signified by the choice of *yetzirah* (human creative experience, transformation of matter) rather than *bri'ah* (fully divine creative experience, *creatio ex nihilo*) as the term to summarize the description of creation.

The realm encompassed by *hokhmah, binah, gevurah*, and *hesed*, the world of *bri'ah* "[divine] creation," is the beginning of the process of physical creation ex nihilo—through which God molds no-thing-ness into the myriad reified ("thingified") aspects of reality that define the world as it is articulated in Genesis 1—from light and the firmament separating waters above from those below to all of the creatures, including human beings, that are engendered by God's mere saying "let there be . . ." This is that aspect of creation spoken into existence. This is the most singular of the processes referred to in Isaiah 43:7, leading us back to the surface of Genesis 1:1.

But the mystic, as we keep recalling, needs to explore deep beneath the surface. The *Zohar*'s descriptive terms for articulating creation go—must go—beyond *bri'ah*. Thus, the uppermost triad of the *sephirot* (*keter, hokhmah*, and *binah*) is referred to as the world, realm, reality of *'atzilut*. This is that "world" of pure radiation, self-mirroring, and self-reproducing from which God emanates itself outward into the spaceless space, beyond the physical universe, that encompasses the Torah and the Sabbath, that it is creating at that moment outside time (that moment of timeless time before time as we know it and *bri'ah* which initiates it) of spaceless self-expansion (before even *tohu vavohu* exist) into space. This realm is articulated in the story of creation as "the Spirit of the Lord" (that "swooped over the face of the deep" in Genesis 1:2, but this is, of course, before the deep existed and before, therefore, the Spirit swooped over it); it is referred to with the references to God's glory (*kavod*) and is associated with what Enoch becomes when transformed into Metatron—who travels beyond the highest of the angels, perhaps even beyond the throne of God to become the "Officer of the Visage"—*Sar Ha-Panim*.[14] This is the realm associated with the three uppermost *heikhalot* of *merkavah* literature. Above all, it is referred to as the "dwelling" of God's *Shekhinah* "aspect"—that aspect of Godness that dwells among us even as God is so ungraspably beyond us.

It is obvious that each of these "worlds" feeds into the next without inter-
ruption. The *Zohar*'s sense is of a continuum that expresses our relationship
with God. To understand the *sephirot* from the perspective of this fourfold
framework is to begin the process of working one's way back up to the emanation process with which creation begins, in order to return and find one's
ability to commit actions that are filled with *tikkun* ("fixing" or "repairing"
the *profanus*). That there are *four* "worlds" that comprise the *sephirot* is also
not mere happenstance where the issue of connection to God is concerned.
The number four is inherently important, since the primary Hebrew name for
God, *YHVH* (variously vocalized as *Yahweh*, *Yehovah*, and so forth) is comprised of four letters—thus that name is referred to as the Tetragrammaton—
and there are four directions to created reality. Thus, "fourness" carries with
it part of the secret meaning of God carried within God's name and accessed
by deconstructing the name in terms not only of its letters and their numerical values but also of the numerical "value" of the name arrived at by the
number of letters that comprise it. That hidden meaning is carried, further, by
the linkage (God's name and the world's directions) between Creator and creation offered by that number.

So both the "ten-ness" and the "fourness" of the *sephirot* are linked aspects
of accessing the hidden *mysterion* within God. Multiplied together, they offer
a number, forty, that further connects God to us through the ultimate *sacerdos*, Moses, forty years old when he first encountered God through the burning bush, in the *sacer*, twice forty when he led the Israelites out into the *sacer*,
and thrice forty when he left them at the gateway to the promised land—the
terra sacra—to which they arrived after forty years as a sacerdotal people in
the making.[15] The central moment within that passage through the wilderness
was, of course, the covenantal experience at the foot of Mount Sinai. There,
the Ten Commandments were offered to the Israelites, the fourth of which enjoined them to keep the Sabbath day as a *sacer* day apart from the *profanus*
of the week. The Sabbath, conceived as a grammatical feminine, is directly
connected, we are reminded, to the Torah as a grammatical feminine (in
which divinely inspired text the Ten Commandments are the heart) and in turn
to the concept of the *Shekhinah*. We have thus come full circle to move forward with the discussion of that essential term.

Paradox and difficulty of access are at the heart of the term *sephirah* and
its underlying meaning, as it is at the heart of the *Zohar* in general. Perhaps
inspired by continuous contact with both Christianity and Islam—as Judaism
is either enveloped as a series of islands within these two large seas, or functions as a religious and political intermediary between the two, in Spain in
particular—Kabbalah articulates an understanding of God that offers a female
emphasis through the idea of the *Shekhinah*. The term itself is built on the

same Hebrew root that engenders the word *mishkan* ("tabernacle"): that structure devised to house the Tablets of the Law brought down from the mountain by Moses, as the Israelites wandered through the wilderness. Over the tabernacle hovered a pillar of cloud by day and of fire by night, thus signifying to the far-flung tribes the presence—*shekhinah*, in straightfoward Hebrew—of God among them.

The *presence* of God is manifest in the center of their encampment when they rest and at the head of it when they move. It is made manifest both by the tent and within it the structure that houses the stone tablets that bear God's words and by the smoke and fire pillars hovering above it. These immanent, visible, tangible elements connote the presence within and among the people of the transcendent, invisible, intangible God. But the mystic sees more in *shekhinah* than its common-parlance meaning and the fact that it is cognate with *mishkan*, intimately sharing with that term the conveyance of the paradox of an immanent presence that is part of, yet somehow distinct from, the singular, transcendent God.

For the grammatical gender of the term *shekhinah* is feminine, whereas the grammatical gender of the usual words in Hebrew for God—*El, Elohim, Adonai, YHVH, Shaddai*—is masculine. Thus, kabbalistic thinking imputes to that aspect of the aspectless, genderless God that is present among us a certain femaleness, whereas the aspect of its distance is, as it were, masculine. We observe this paradox discussed quite matter-of-factly in a passage from the *Zohar*, as Rabbi Shimeon is depicted telling an educative tale to four other rabbis as they all pause to rest while on their journey to Tiberias (*Zohar* 1: 49b). His discussion has to do with proper behavior towards one's wife before one leaves on a journey, while one travels, and after one has returned home.

The starting point of his discussion is, as one might expect (given the essentially midrashic form of the *Zohar*), a passage from the Torah, referring to a journey undertaken by Abraham (Genesis 13:3). But there is what a nonmystic or even a nontraditionalist would label a scribal error: The word *journey* is rendered as *journeys*. For a traditionalist, there can simply be no textual errors in God's word or its transcription; and even more so for the mystic, nothing can have been placed there in error or without deliberate *intention*. So, Rabbi Shimeon explains that the doubling of the term is intended to signify that the *Shekhinah* is with Abraham when he travels (*he* is doubled, as it were): "we read 'journeys,' which is intended to mean that on the journey with him was the Divine Presence." He goes on to explain that the *Shekhinah* is present with all those who treat their wives properly, particularly before a journey, for it is through the wife that the husband acquires that connection to God's presence. In other words, the *Shekhinah* is inherently present with and within women, by virtue of its femaleness, but its inherence is achieved for males only through contact with females:

> How with the man who makes a journey, and away from his wife, ceases to be "male and female"? Such a one, before starting, and while he is still "male and female," must pray to God, to draw unto himself the Presence of his Master. . . . . The whole time of his traveling a man should heed well his actions, lest the holy union break off, and he should be left imperfect, deprived of the union with the female. . . . Moreover, it is his duty, once back home, to give his wife pleasure, inasmuch as it was she who obtained for him the heavenly union.

Sex is then not something to be shunned but to be enjoyed. And sexual relations with one's wife upon returning home after a journey not only rejoices her but also rejoices God in God's "capacity" as the *Shekhinah*. Moreover, not only are "females" not limited to human wives, but it encompasses the *Shekhinah* through its *grammatical* gender. Since the Hebrew word *Torah* is also *grammatically* feminine, then the scholar who spends all day long engaged in spiritual and intellectual intercourse with the Torah is encompassed by God's presence. And the Sabbath, properly welcomed, as a queen and as a bride—for the Hebrew word *shabbat* is also grammatically feminine—also encompasses all of those within the community.[16]

> Hence a man should be as zealous to enjoy this joy [sexual relations with his wife] as to enjoy the joy of the Sabbath, at which time the union of the sages with their wives is consummated . . . the Presence accompanies you and sojourns in your house, and for this reason "thou shall visit thy habitation and not sin,"[17] in gladly carrying out the religious duty to have conjugal intercourse before the Presence.

And so Rabbi Shimeon's discourse continues with reminders that "the wife is the foundation of a man's house, for it is by virtue of her that the Presence does not leave the house" and with references to the Torah and other biblical passages that he is therefore connecting and elucidating. We realize how much this is midrashic in style, both with regard to the connecting of disparate scriptural passages and by connecting esoteric interpretation to practical, down-to-earth, *profanus* matters: These are, after all, five men on a business trip, who, it might be supposed, may be inclined while away from home to allow their minds, eyes, and even certain body parts to wander from the path of proper wife-remembering behavior.

Moreover, we discern other issues. The "sages"—an almost generic term (it encompasses but is not limited to prophets, since it also refers to the earliest Talmudic figures) for all of those who, as part of past generations, are viewed as closer to God—are the model that "we" wish to emulate, in our everyday behavior that contributes to our ability to get closer to God as much as in our specific *mysterion*-seeking behavior, which contributes to our ability to be better in our everyday lives. Every action, from intense Torah study to sex, is imbued with a *sacer*-connected significance. As much as the text is created by and directed to a male audience, it is unusual within the normative Abrahamic narrative for the importance it accords to women; as important as women are as explained in the text, the latter is limited, with regard to its intended audience, to males.

We may choose to see this as a function of the "feminine" presence of God: The fact that in its "feminineness" it is inherently located within women means that they don't *need* to be mystics; or we may see this as a backhanded compliment on the part of the Jewish mystical tradition, the backhandedness of which still discourages (or forbids) women from engaging in mystical activity. And from a modernist perspective, we may understand this as no compliment at all, backhanded or otherwise: Women are perceived as not emotionally and intellectually equipped to study Kabbalah. They are insufficiently stable. In this case, the adulation of femaleness found in the *Zohar* is itself paradoxical. And the understanding of femaleness as expressed by the concept of the *Shekhinah* as embodying not only God's immanence but also God's loving and empathetic relationship to humanity furthers that sense of paradox.

For when God exiles Adam and Eve from the Garden of Eden, that act is performed by God as *YHVH* or *El* or *Elohim*—grammatically male names of God. But God also *goes out* into exile with Adam and Eve, in empathy with the difficulties that stretch out before them, and it is as the *Shekhinah* that God does that, is *present* with them, just as the *Shekhinah* of God wanders through the wilderness for forty years with the Israelites, travels with Abraham on his journey—and remains with any traveling male who treats his wife properly.[18]

In any case, though, while perhaps we may infer inspiration from Christianity, Islam, or both, this is a very different genre of applying the category "female" to the mystical quest from what we have observed and shall observe of Christianity, through Hildegard of Bingen, St. Catherine of Siena, and St. Teresa of Avila (among others) and less emphatically, Islam, through Rabi'a, where the mystical aspirant or the successful mystic may be a woman. The *Zohar*'s approach is, in an obvious sense, diametrically opposed to that of Christian and Muslim mysticism: In the Jewish case, the male mystic's intimate relationship with God and the *mysterion* may be couched in terms of God's "femaleness," which is understood to be a paradoxical aspect of God's essential genderlessness; in these particular Christian and Muslim cases, the mystic's relationship to God is couched in terms of God's maleness (and in the Muslim case, also understood to be a paradoxical aspect of God's essential genderlessness).

More importantly—to repeat, lest we forget—the whole idea of "maleness" and "femaleness" where God is concerned is problematic for Judaism and therefore for Jewish mysticism. In the end, both males and females must be encompassed by the *Shekhinah* and the spiritual rewards to the community that accrue from its presence, since God is neither male nor female. The ability to grasp the truth of this ultimate contradiction (of God's genderless maleness/femaleness) is both the goal of the *aspiring* kabbalistic mystic and a characteristic of the *successful* kabbalistic mystic.

∽◌∾

Moreover, we have arrived at a second figure, besides Moses de Leon, who is of particular significance to the kabbalistic phase of Jewish mysticism as the latter evolves in Spain. Abraham Abulafia (1240–1291) was an older contemporary of the author/editor of the *Zohar*. Abulafia asserted that at age thirty-one he received the prophetic call, hearing a voice calling "Abraham! Abraham!" to which he responded, "Here am I!" (recalling that brief dialogue that sets Genesis 22 in motion). Shortly thereafter, he began to gather a circle of pupils around him in his home town of Saragossa. His sense of the sort of thinking that fills out the *Bahir*, the *Zohar*, and similar texts is that they are merely preparatory for the fuller experience of "prophetic Kabbalah" (*Kabbalah n'vooeet*). He claimed to be able to train his pupils through an intimate investigation of the names of God to purify their souls and ultimately to achieve the capacity to exercise magical powers. The disciple's access to God's names is through the letters comprising the names into which he or she absorbs him- or herself, feeling inspiration (*in-spirit-ation*): He or she becomes possessed by God's name. (I have deliberately emphasized ambiguous gender in my use of the personal pronoun, since, in a stance that makes him unique in the Jewish mystical tradition, Abulafia claimed to be able to train both men and women, as well as both Jews and non-Jews.)

Abulafian Kabbalah's underlying principle is that meditation on any letter within a word that addresses an aspect of the creation transmutes into a meditation on the whole of that word and, by further analogy, on the whole of creation and ultimately on the Creator. Since such a deconstructive method of meditation—emphasizing most particularly the word of God, Torah, and, more broadly, biblical words and phrases—necessarily yields irrational meanings, words and phrases are deprived of their *profanus* sensibility and thus function as a mechanism of guidance out of the *profanus* into the *sacer* in its deepest recesses: The more irrational, one might suppose, the deeper.

The process is at once physical and mental. One begins with *mivta*: the articulation of the sounds of the letters. But not in a simple manner. Take, for example, the first letter of the Hebrew alphabet, *aleph*, which is part of the hidden divine name,[19] and repeat it in combination (1) with each of the four letters of the Tetragrammaton (YHVH), and (2) with every possible permutation of the five Hebrew vowels. The result is two hundred nonsense sound combinations.

As in other systems that emphasize dwelling on or repeating sound combinations—not only in Sufism or the hesychastic Christian mystics but also in Hinduism and Buddhism—breathing is an essential element, and Abulafia offers instructions regarding how properly to breathe in the course of this process, in his *Mafteah haShemot* (*Key to the Names*): "take each one of the letters [*YHVH*] and wave it with the movements of a long breath so that you do not breathe between two letters, but rather with one long breath, for as long as you can possibly endure it, and afterwards rest for the length of one breath. Do this with each and every letter." Moreover, one is to shake one's head in a manner that corresponds with each of the vowel sounds that one is pronouncing. Thus, in his *Hayyei ha'Olam haBa'* (*Life in the World to Come*), he instructs the practitioner, "after you begin to pronounce the letter, begin to move your heart and head . . . and move your head in the form of the vowel-[-point] of the letter which you are pronouncing. . . . When you extend the vowel of the letter in its pronunciation, move your head up toward the heavens, and close your eyes and open your mouth and let your words shine, and clear your throat of all spittle so that it will not interfere with the pronunciation of the letter in your mouth." Similarly, specific hand movements are to be performed during this process.

One continues with *mikhtav*, the writing of the letters. The implication of this pair of meditation-focused actions is clear. The first part reflects an ever-present paradox for Jewish mysticism: The letters of the Hebrew alphabet are significant because they are assumed to be God's own chosen alphabet. But as such, they are a writing system, not, per se, a phonemic system (the phonemes of Hebrew may be found in scores of other languages and can be represented in any number of other writing systems); Abulafia (and others) treats the *sounds*, not the visual forms, as if they are unique, in obsessive *mivta*, but then concentrates on the visual forms—a first within the tradition—with *mikhtav*. Moreover, both foci are physical *actions* (as opposed to mental exercises): The practitioner repeatedly vocalizes the sound of the letter of focus and repeatedly marks the form of the letter as he or she writes it again and again. Finally, with *mahshav*, the practitioner contemplates the letter. As much as this last is the third of three stages of focus on a given letter within a given word or phrase, it is also the overarching action taking place through both the other actions, which are actually undertaken simultaneously: Three phases or stages are indistinguishable aspects of one process.[20] It/they (the process and its "phases") yield(s) a state of *ek-stasis* in which the spirit hidden "behind" each letter becomes manifest.

The overall process is intended to serve as a means of moving from gross visualization to ever-finer spiritual focus. Abulafia asserts that his disciples will begin to experience fiery sensations (reminiscent on the microcosmic body scale of the macrocosmic full-body experience of Enoch) as they engage with intensity in this process.

> After much movement and concentration on the letters the hair on your head will stand on end . . . your blood will begin to vibrate . . . and all your body will begin to tremble, and a shuddering will fall on all your limbs . . . you will feel an additional spirit within yourself . . . strengthening you, passing through your entire body . . . [as if] fragrant oil [is] anointing you from head to foot.

Each letter corresponds to a different body part, and so each act of focus also yields a fiery sensation for a given limb. Particular body positions and modes of breathing correspond to particular vocalic and consonantal sounds. The danger is that, if a practitioner inadvertently, though loss of complete focus, moves a body part from its proper position while focused on a letter sound or shape, he or she may cripple that body part, Abulafia warns.

On the other hand, key letters emerge through the process as personifications of the beings whose names begin with those letters. Thus, as the letter *mem* ("m") stands at the beginning of the name Metatron, proper focus on it can yield to the practitioner the envisioned appearance of Metatron personified as the letter. So, too, focus on the letter *shin* ("sh") can lead to the appearance of the personification of that letter as *Shaddai*, God's power-protective name. Again, paradox: God by definition cannot appear, since God is invisible; it is God's *name—one* of God's *many* names—that appears, which is and is not the same as *God*. The masters of the name (*Ba'alei Shem*), as the Abulafian terminology calls successful practitioners, ultimately seem to unite with God, moving beyond vision. Having become one with God, the practitioner becomes (and yet does not, cannot, could never imagine that he or she is) God. The dangers are obvious: The ego intrudes to let the practitioner imagine that he or she truly is God, and he or she loses his or her mind; the practitioner cannot separate from this awesomely desirable union and loses his or her mind or dies. The higher one goes, the greater the dangers and the greater the barriers (*masteeneem*, or "withholders") to success.[21]

The pathway to success is divided between two gates—the Gate of Heaven and the Gate of Saints or Inner Gate—each of which comprises diverse paths that are divided into parts. Each of these "gates"—there are at least "fifty gates of understanding" within each of us, awaiting actualization, as a preliminary—refers to, or is the result of, a meditative state in which one visualizes one's self as angels: Raphael, Uriel, Michael, Gabriel, and others. Within the successful process, they cease to be independent entities and become, rather, the personifications of our own human tendencies, which, as we conquer them, separate us from our human-physical selves and push us toward our spiritual-divine selves. Their names are projections of the innate prophetic power in each of us. They also correspond to the letters, and since we are all imprinted with the divine letters that articulate the words that articulate the process of creation, then in focusing on the letters (in deconstructing the words that they comprise and reassembling them), we are focusing on these angelic beings and on our own tendencies and on ourselves (whom we are deconstructing and reassembling), as we are generating the latent divine energy within ourselves, activating the prophetic power within ourselves, and thus stepping outside ourselves toward becoming one with God's name and thus with God.

From the focus on words to the focus on letters, the disciple focuses on the numerology of the letters and words, first in a straightforward and later in increasingly complicated ways, in leaping[22] from one thought to the next, but by means of a carefully disciplined pattern of association (see below). Through this process, the entire Torah will ultimately merge into a combination of divine names. Thus, the mystic's goal, which is to be a perfect human being, perfectly generating divine energy and prophetic power from within and without him- or herself, is to *be* the Torah. God's most fundamental words are expressed in that ultimate text—which is, as an entity within the *profanus*, as close to God as the Jewish tradition possesses, articulated through the ultimate conduit, Moses. He is the ultimate prophet, the perfect human being, who perfectly generated divine energy; it cannot be coincidence that the phrase *Moshe Rabeinu* ("Moses Our Teacher") adds up to the number 613 in Hebrew numerology, for this is the number of commandments that Jewish tradition finds within the Torah. Thus, Moses and the Torah are one, and the successful Abulafian practitioner becomes one with Moses and one with the Torah; the devotee's 248 limbs and functions (by Abulafia's count), when added to the cycle of a year (365 days), add up to 613, thus connecting him or her to time and space both within and beyond the *profanus*, both microcosmically and macrocosmically.

Abulafia's focus on letters furthers that starting point found in the *Sepher Yetzirah*—just as other aspects of his system relate to principles operative in the Enoch literature and *merkavah* mysticism—and adds to the *Sepher* new notions, or at least a new intensity of interest in the notions, of *tzeruf*, or permutations of letters.[23] Thus, as one ascends through the "Fifty Gates of Understanding," one's method of deconstructing words and names includes the manipulation of those words and names by means not only of their numerological values, with their possibilities for linking concepts (such as *Moshe Rabeinu* and Torah), but also of concept-linking shifts made possible by shifting the order of letters in a given word or name in different ways. Thus, the most common form of *tzeruf*, as seen with *Moshe Rabeinu*, is called *gematria*, which simply works with numerical values. *Gematria*, for example, yields the following: When in Exodus 23:21 the text offers "the angel in whom resides the Name of God," the mystic understands that the reference must be to Enoch become Metatron. Why? Because the name Metatron equals 314 in *gematria* (M = 40; T = 9 [twice]; R = 200; O = 6; and N = 50),[24] and the name *Shaddai*, God's power-protective name, also equals 314 (SH = 300; D = 4; and I = 10).[25] Or, there is a midrashic tradition—and one must not forget that the mystical tradition is ultimately a subset of the midrashic tradition—that maintains that the rock on which Jacob slept, out in the *sacer* wilderness, in flight from Esau's anger, when he dreamed the extraordinary dream of the ladder connecting heaven and earth, ended up as the rock on Sinai upon which Moses inscribed the Ten Commandments. The mystic validates this by observing that the *gematria* for "ladder" (*soolam*; S = 60; L = 30; and M = 40) is the same as that for "Sinai" (*Seeynai*: S = 60; Y = 10; N = 50; and I [i.e., Y] = 10).

The second form of *tzeruf* practiced by Abulafians and others is called *notarikon*. This is essentially an acrostic form of *tzeruf*. One deduces new words from the first or last letters of other words. Thus, mystics are called "Knowers of Grace/Favor" (*Yod'ei Hayn*) because the two primary consonants—the first and last consonants of "grace/favor" (*hayn*; H and N)—are taken to be a coded reference to *hokhmah neestarah* ("hidden wisdom") by virtue of the fact that the first letters of these two words are "H" and "N." Perhaps the most famous example of *notarikon* is that self-reflective observation that places mystical speculation within the larger context of interpreting the Torah and other biblical texts. Thus, the word *pardes*—"garden" or "orchard"—which earlier served as a metaphor for mystical speculation and its dangers,[26] becomes a coded statement of the fourfold way of interpreting scripture. Thus, P = *pshat* = literal interpretation; R = *remez* = allusive interpretation; D = *drash* = allegorical interpretation[27]; and S = *sod* = secret interpretation. The last of these methods, then, is the mystical method, of seeking that which is hidden in secret from even astute mainstream midrashic exploration.

There is, finally, *temurah*, the mode of *tzeruf* that affords the alteration of meanings—even to their opposites—through transposing letters. Thus, for example, *'oneg* means "delight," but if one changes its letter order, one can arrive at the word *n'ga*, meaning "pain." Thus, these two concepts, which oppose each other in the everyday *profanus* context, merge into identity within the hiddenmost recesses of the paradoxical *sacer* (as we have observed of ascending/descending, male/female, left/right, inner/outer, active/passive, and so forth). One of the issues that one notes by way of this particular example of *temurah* is how close it is as a conceptual observation (the pain/pleasure paradox) to that offered by Socrates at the outset of the Platonic dialogue *Phaedo*. By itself, this would merely be an interesting coincidence. But when one recognizes how both the terms *gematria* and *notarikon* are derived from Greek terms, one arrives at the question regarding the degree to which Abulafian and other Jewish mystics of the thirteenth century, living cheek by jowl with Christians and Muslims in Spain in particular, were open to non-Jewish sources of potential wisdom where esoteric affairs were concerned. This presents two further notes: One, such openness is continuous with what we have observed since antiquity and the beginnings of Jewish mysticism; and two, such openness would have been perceived by the mainstream Jewish leadership as dangerous in its potential to draw everyday Jews who became involved in mysticism into apostasy.

Abulafia himself was certainly perceived as dangerous. Both the culmination of his role as a threat and the opportunity for the mainstream leadership to rid itself of his troubling way of teaching arrived in 1280, when he was inspired to journey to Rome with the intention at least of condemning the behavior of the intensely anti-Semitic Pope Nicholas III and at most of converting him to Judaism. The Roman rabbinical authorities, no doubt both to avoid having to deal with the various problematic issues brought about by his presence and out of fear of how his presence might stir up the Christian authorities against the Jewish community, reported him to those authorities, who promptly arrested him, even before he arrived into the city. His fate was placed in the hands of the pope, who ordered him burned at the stake. It was the eve of the Jewish New Year (*Rosh HaShanah*); Abulafia spent the night meditating in his prison cell outside the city. When he was brought into Rome the next morning, he found out that the pope had unexpectedly and suddenly—he had not been ill theretofore—died during the night. This certainly confirmed for him his own miracle-working powers, and it must have shaken his Franciscan jailors as well, who released him a mere four weeks later.

The leaders of the community were certainly equally unhappy to have him still around and seem to have persecuted him sufficiently so that he and his most loyal followers moved on to Sicily, where he spent the last decade of his life. Among the works that he wrote there were *Or HaSeykhel* (*Light of the Intellect*) and *Sepher HaTzeruf* (*Book of Permutations*). He also predicted the arrival of the Messiah in 1290, inspiring many Jews to pack up their homes and immigrate to *Eretz Yisrael*. Attacked as a dangerous charlatan by Rabbi

Solomon ben Adret of Barcelona, he defended himself by writing an account of his life and his philosophy, asserting that he was one of the few daring men who had found "the steps of the ladder" toward God and who, as a prophet, had "entered the Palace of the Temple," which remained inaccessible, he further wrote, to all those rabbis who buried their heads in the sand of Torah interpretation and Talmudic legalities. But Abulafia died the following year—shortly after the Messiah did not appear. Did he die from natural or untoward causes—or from heartbroken disappointment?

His legacy would extend into the next phases of Jewish mysticism: His delineation of the three ways through which the Jewish mystic may gain enlightenment yields terminology central to Jewish mysticism in the next six centuries. Thus, enlightenment through renunciation as a *tzadik*, through intense piety as a *hassid*, or through prophecy (achieved through his methods) yields, in the first two cases, terms and concepts that will continue to develop as the centuries push forward, while the last concept will also push forward, but without using the term "prophet"—as we shall see. Moreover, through his universalistic thinking, Abulafia's influence would receive from and extend into Muslim mysticism (Sufism) and the push toward the work of Renaissance-era Christian mystics such as Pico della Mirandola.

NOTES

1. I am referring here to the term *symbol* in its Greek derivation. *Symbolon* derives from the verb *symballein*, meaning "to throw together," but referring to an object that is exchanged by two peacemakers to "stand for" the abstract peace agreement at which they have arrived. Thus, just as the color red, as a *symbolon*, stands for blood and thus sacrifice in Christian art, and the circle, without beginning or end, stands for perfection and completion, the Jewish tradition in all of its aspects is understood by the kabbalists to be a compendium of *symbola* for God and the universe created by God.

2. This, at any rate, is what I assume; his biological father *could*, by coincidence, also have been named "Judah."

3. The term *yihud* is both linguistically cognate with the Arabic word *tawhid* and cognate as an idea with the idea of *tawhid*, as we encountered both in the previous chapter.

4. And we understand that the focus on the significance of the grammatical gender of a word is part of the sensibility that sees in the Hebrew language itself, as "God's language," a series of keys to the *mysterion*: Nothing can be accidental about it since it is God's, including the gender of its key terms.

5. Nonetheless, when they are discussed in some detail in sections 149 to 169, only the first two are referred to by the names that will adhere to them in subsequent kabbalistic texts, as *keter* and *hokhmah*; one other is obliquely referred to as *yesod*, but

as the eighth of these, whereas subsequent Kabbalah will represent *yesod* as the ninth *sephirah*. See the discussion of the *Zohar* below.

6. This is analogous to the notion that *merkavah* mysticism is primarily focused on descriptions of God's name, glory, throne, and so forth, rather than on the question of creation. Yet the *Sepher Yetzirah*—which some would say is part of, as opposed to being a prelude to, the *merkavah* literature—is explicitly about creation, as we have seen.

7. Let's not forget the fact that Ibn 'Arabi lived the first thirty-five years of his life in Spain, between the time periods of Yehudah HaLevy and Moses de Leon (about whom, see the following paragraphs).

8. In particular, see Gershom Scholem, *Major Trends in Jewish Mysticism* (New York: Shocken Press, 1969), particularly 164–65 and the observation there that "in general, the language of the *Zohar* may be described as a mixture of the Aramaic dialects found in the two books with which the author was above all familiar: the Babylonian Talmud and the *Targum Onkelos*, the old Aramaic translation of the Torah."

9. The variant vocalizations reflect variant possibilities in Aramaic, depending upon exactly what dialect is assumed. Absoluteness regarding the vocalization is not possible, since the text sources are usually unvocalized themselves.

10. Given this genealogy—the ultimate Israelite king descended from a daughter of one of the key traditional enemy peoples (the Moabites) of the Israelites—the Book of Ruth is also one of the two most universalistic, nonethnocentric books in the Hebrew Bible (Jonah is the other). But, given the time, place, and historical context, I doubt that this is what makes it important for the *Zohar* and kabbalistic thinking.

11. Imagine the process of singing a musical scale from *do* to *do*: You end on the note where you began and yet not so, since you end an octave away from where you began. Imagine creating a painting that begins with the creative principle and thus the capacity to create (*keter*), and, as you complete the first triad (moving from *keter* to *hokhmah* and *binah*), it evolves toward the idea as a vague conception and to the certainty that it will indeed be a painting (and not, say, a drawing or a sculpture). The idea of what the painting will be begins to assume specific shape in your mind, expands, and becomes still more specified as *hesed*. With *gevurah*, you are sketching the underdrawing on the canvas, and with *tipheret*, the distinctive attributes of that drawing are becoming manifest as you lay on the paint. The layers of colors and shapes and a wide range of details are becoming clearer and richer with *netzah* and *hod*; the elements of your distinctive style are emerging. With *yesod*, the work is moving towards completion, encompassing your review and reshaping of the little details that, when all of them have come to fruition, will yield, with *malkhut*, the completed painting. Note that every detail of this footnote works from analogy and acknowledges the impossibility of expressing a paradoxical and well-nigh ineffable idea except by analogy.

12. That the *Zohar* in general and the doctrine of the *sephirot* in particular might have a moral component should not be surprising. If the Hebrew Bible presents God creating the physical universe in six days, it pursues the shaping of a morally ordered universe to its last pages, in which shaping process humans, from Noah to the last Judaean prophet, are engaged in partnership with God. The Jewish mystic's goal, we

recall, is to emulate such individuals; his or her goal is not to achieve oneness with God but rather to achieve that oneness in order to return to the *profanus* and benefit it; if that is *not* his intention, his efforts at achieving oneness with the One will inevitably fail. The obligation to improve the world will be increasingly emphatically articulated as the kabbalistic tradition moves forward.

13. See the Latin term for "left," *sinistra*, which gives us "sinister" in English, and less emphatic words, such as "adroit" ("rightish") and "maladroit" ("badly rightish"), which arrive into English from Latin by way of French.

14. We recall that one of the prime candidates for the etymology of the name Metatron is the Greek phrase *meta ton thronon* ("beyond the Throne").

15. *Sanctus* and *sancta* are Latin variants of *sacer* (m.) and sacra (f.); thus *terra sacra*, as I have stated it to remain consistent with the Latin forms I have been using, is identical to the more familiar form of the phrase, *terra sancta*.

16. Thus, the *Shekhinah*, as "mirror of *YHVH*," as "Daughter of God" and "Sister to the World of Men," is the queen and the bride who is articulated in *time* as the Sabbath bride, the Sabbath queen. We shall see this developed further in later Kabbalah.

17. He is quoting from Job 5:24.

18. It is presumably a given in the world both of Rabbi Ishmael and of Moses de Leon that single travelers on long journeys will be male and not female—and the *Shekhinah* would be with a traveling female, due to her femaleness, in any case.

19. As he explains in his *Or haSeykhel* (*Light of the Intellect*) (MS Vatican 233, fol. 97a). For much of the discussion of the next two paragraphs, see in particular Moshe Idel, *The Mystical Experience in Abraham Abulafia* (Albany: State University of New York Press, 1988), for more detail.

20. One can once again understand why the mainstream rabbinic leadership would have been particularly uncomfortable with Abulafian mysticism: Not only does he assert that its practitioners can ultimately become as prophets but also the fundamental paradox of his triune methodology could easily be seen as a means of leading the Jewish mystic astray toward the apostasy of Christianity (even more so than the deca-une paradox of the *sephirot* might), especially given Abulafia's willingness to include Christians (and Muslims) among his pupils. I might note that a claim has also been put forth that Abulafia was himself importantly influenced by the Christian Cathars (a thirteenth-century heretical movement whose members were ultimately destroyed by the Dominicans). That claim, made differently by Yitzhak Baer and Shulamit Shahar, is discussed and eloquently refuted by Moshe Idel in his *Studies in Ecstatic Kabbalah* (Albany: State University of New York Press, 1988). Others have noticed the larger coincidence of the upheaval in the Christian world occasioned by the Cathars in Languedoc at around the time that the first centers of Kabbalah were taking shape in that same part of the world. Shahar, for one, has also suggested connections between the *Bahir* and Catharism.

21. Interestingly, from Abulafia's point of view, the third of the usual dangers, apostasy, is not a concern—see the previous footnote—especially since he claims to be able to train Christians and Muslims and not just Jews to succeed in accessing the *mysterion*.

22. He called this *dillug*, or "skipping."

23. One of Abulafia's early works (ca. 1270) was a commentary on the *Sepher Yetzirah*.

24. As always with Hebrew, it is only the consonants that count for such a purpose. The exception here is "O," but that is because the letter used to indicate that vocalic sound is the same as that used to indicate the consonant "V" (this is the same consonant that appears in the most basic name of God, *YHVH*).

25. In this case, the "I" is functioning as a diphthong/semivowel/virtual consonant; more precisely, what I am transliterating as an "I" would be more correctly rendered here as a "Y" (as in *YHVH*), but the conventional transliteration is *Shaddai*, not *Shadday*.

26. See chapter 3, p. 33.

27. Or, more literally, "digging beneath the surface" interpretation (i.e., midrash).

Chapter Seven

Medieval Christian Mysticism

From Assisi to Avila

In picking up the thread of Christian mysticism where we left it at the end of chapter 4, we enter into the heart of the Age of Faith. We move into the era of multilateral aspiration. Against the backdrop of unresolved conflicts with Islam (from Holy Land Crusades to Spanish *Reconquista*) and Judaism (from the efflorescence of the Blood Libel to the burgeoning of Disputations from Paris to Barcelona), the Gothic style offers increasingly literalized—soaring stone—expressions of reaching toward the heavens. In the same century, the struggle both to address the question of how to understand God and God's relationship to humanity and to ingather the varied compendia of human understandings of the world around us and the world beyond us carries from St. Thomas Aquinas to Vincent de Beauvais. Jacobo da Voragine ingathers all the stories of saints that have accumulated in the previous millennium, and the range and number of mystics flows in an expanding stream in the centuries that follow.

Within a few years of Hildegard of Bingen's death, and a few decades after the death of St. Bernard of Clairvaux, Francis Bernardone was born in Assisi in central Italy. The son of a prosperous cloth merchant, St. Francis (1181/82–1228) seems to have spent the early part of his life caught up in earthbound pleasures, in eating and dressing well and succeeding at games and feats of arms. At about the age of twenty, serving with his fellow towns-people in the incessant warfare between Assisi and other Umbrian and Tuscan polities, he was captured by the Perugians and spent a year in one of their prisons. Perhaps it was the fever that he contracted there that began to turn his thoughts toward the matter of eternity—or at least toward the matter of the emptiness of his lifestyle. Nonetheless, his initial inclination, after he gained his freedom and recovered his health, was to continue to pursue the glorious military career that he had envisioned before.

But the night before he set forth for Apulia in 1205 to participate in the armed struggle against the Holy Roman Emperor, he is said to have had a dream—reminiscent, in its way, of that ascribed by Eusebius to Constantine on the night before the Battle of Milvian Bridge,[1] but ultimately leading in the opposite direction, away from military engagement—in which he saw a large hall hung with armor all marked with the cross. He heard the words, "These are for you and your soldiers." He awoke convinced that he would achieve great military glory, but once again he was struck down by fever at Spoleto. There, forced to pause his march to the south, he dreamed again. This time, the voice instructed him to return to Assisi, away from the scene of battle, which he promptly did.

Francis's entire demeanor seems to have changed from that point on; his heart was less and less in the revels in which he continued to participate sporadically with his wealthy friends. Increasingly, he was drawn to an ascetic life, a life of poverty, rather than the mercantile and materially focused one his father would still have preferred for him. He spent increasing amounts of time in prayer and meditation. In the third transformational moment since Perugia—in which Augustinian *caritas* began its triumph within him—he was riding on horseback out in the countryside and encountered a poor leper. Initially overwhelmed with disgust and a desire to retreat, he controlled his aversion, dismounted, embraced the leper, and gave him all of the money he had with him. Shortly thereafter, he made a pilgrimage to Rome where, near the tomb of St. Peter, he exchanged garments with a beggar and spent the day as a mendicant by the doorway of the basilica.

Arguably, the culminating moment of transformation came after his return to Assisi. While praying before an old crucifix in an abandoned wayside chapel—named for the third-century Roman soldier-saint Damian—he heard a voice. As if coming from the crucifix, the voice instructed him, "Go, Francis, and repair my house, which as you see is falling into ruin." That command, which the saint took literally at first (so that he repaired the chapel), eventually led him to the turn from "my father on earth; [for] henceforth I desire to say only 'Our Father Who art in heaven.'" His nuptials with Lady Poverty, and the reduction of his worldly goods to a coarse woolen tunic of "the color of a beast" tied by a knotted rope,[2] ultimately led to the founding of the mendicant order named for him. Others were drawn to him and his extraordinary, charismatic[3] example. When their number had reached eleven, he found it useful to draw up a written rule—the First Rule of the Friars ("Brothers") Minor (to suggest humility)—inspired by the example of Jesus and the apostles captured in the Gospels.

By 1212, having received the verbal imprimatur of Pope Innocent III, the Franciscans established themselves outside Assisi—but this merely became a humble base from which the friars spread out to preach and teach and encourage the people of the country around, and, eventually, throughout the wide Christian and Muslim world. Out on a slope of Mount Alvernia, where he had gone in August 1224 to keep a forty-day fast in preparation for Michaelmas, the saint experienced the ultimate transformational moment of his life, the culminating seal of his ministry and the ultimate mark of mystical union with God. During his retreat, the suffering—the Passion—of Christ became increasingly the focus of his meditations. On September 14 (the Feast of the Exaltation of the Cross), in the midst of his prayers, he beheld the extraordinary vision of a seraph and, in returning to a *profanus* state of mind, found the five marks—stigmata—of Christ's wounds impressed onto his own body.

Brother Leo, who was with him at that time, describes how the saint's right side bore an open wound as if made by a lance, while through his hands and feet were black nails of flesh, the points of which bent backward.

> On that same morning he saw coming down from heaven a seraph with six resplendent and flaming wings . . . he had the likeness of a crucified man and his wings were so disposed that two wings extended above his head, two were spread out to fly, and the other two covered his entire body. . . . Christ . . . spoke to [Francis] certain secret and profound things which the saint was never willing to reveal to anyone while he was alive, but after his death, he revealed them, as is recorded. . . . 'I have given you the stigmata, which are the emblems of my passion, so that you may be my standard bearer' . . . this wonderful vision . . . left a most intense ardor and flame of divine love in the heart of St. Francis, and it left a marvelous image and imprint of the passion of Christ in his flesh.

Thus, we recognize echoes of the visions of Isaiah and Ezekiel, but carried to an extraordinary physical extreme that is commensurate with and extends the physicality that we have earlier observed as a consistent feature within Christian mysticism. We also note in the biography of St. Francis after this experience the first emphatic instance in the Christian mystical tradition of a connection between the satisfaction derived from ecstasy and the obligation to improve the condition of the community in the broad sense as a consequence of that experience. Francis's mystical encounter with the *mysterion par excellence* comes while he is the leader of a growing community of acolytes whom he serves as a guide to spiritual improvement and satisfaction—leading them, ultimately, to a more desirable eternity than that which they would have found without his guidance.

Moreover, he and they are conscious of their joint responsibility for extending that sort of guidance beyond their own small group, not only across the countryside of central Italy but also across the world—including the non-Christian world. In an era where the sword was the preferred instrument of Christian-Muslim contact for most men of the cloth and not only men of the world, he sought to bring his clear sense of the *sacer* to the *Dar al'Islam* by the word alone—he was even willing to risk losing his own life in order to speak with Muslim leaders and convince them of the spiritual truth as he understood it.

This extreme sense of responsibility for others is encapsulated in the tale told by his biographers of how, in 1216, while he was praying in his small hut chapel (the *Porziuncula*), Jesus appeared to him and offered whatever favor he might ask. Since the salvation of others' souls was most frequently what weighed on his own soul, he begged a plenary indulgence for those who, having confessed their sins, might visit that chapel. Christ agreed, provided that the pope were to ratify the indulgence. Francis set forth immediately for Perugia where Honorius III had just succeeded the recently deceased Innocent III. Honorius agreed that the indulgence would apply one day per year—on August 2. While the historical reality of this moment has been questioned (there is no papal or diocesan record of it), the point is that Francis always viewed his intimacy with the *sacer* as a privilege to be exercised in the service of others through complementary action in the *profanus*; he did not simply spend time in isolation from the *profanus* seeking communion with the *sacer*.

The fact that among the early followers of St. Francis was a woman, St. Clare, who ultimately under his guidance established her own order parallel to his, reminds us of the ongoing significance of women mystics within the Christian tradition. One of the more interesting of contemporaries of Francis and Claire was Hadewijch of Antwerp. Hadewijch was a mid-thirteenth-century Beguine. The Beguines were a group—perhaps "movement" would be an appropriate term of reference—that apparently arose spontaneously between around 1170 and 1175 in Lotharingia (in the area of what is now Belgium and the Rhineland). It offered a religious option for women outside the social mainstream of matrimony besides withdrawing to a convent or becoming an anchoress—both of which options, as abbesses and anchoresses had sometimes achieved considerable influence and, in effect, political power, were being suppressed in northern Europe at that time. The term seems to have originally been pejorative (thus we find the phrase *mulieres vulgariter dictae "beguinae"*) and is variously argued to derive from the grey color of their habits, or from the name of St. Begga, or that of Lambert de Begue (whose name meant either "stutterer" or "heretic"), or from the word "Albigensian." The last two derivative possibilities would associate the Beguines with heresy. Nonetheless, by the thirteenth century the Beguine movement had become quite popular. Its adherents dedicated themselves to lives of piety centered on prayers in honor of the Virgin, the rite of the Eucharist, and meditation on the life and Passion of Christ.

While in the early period, individual Beguines lived alone or with their parents, by the early thirteenth century, they had formed small communities within parish settings, and by the middle of the century, larger groups lived in enclosed settings attached to the service of hospitals. By the late thirteenth and early fourteenth centuries, independent Beguine parishes existed. Groups of Beguines living together in communities also provided havens for widows and other women who were disenfranchised by mainstream Christian society. They occupied themselves with the education of boys and girls—both the poor and the better off—with care for the sick and the elderly, with the training of housewives to run their estates, with providing help to any individuals who might be called societal outcasts, as well as with craft projects and with concentrated, contemplative prayers. One recognizes both a vibrant early feminist movement and a movement defined by the Augustinian concept of *caritas* and the kabbalistic concept of *tikkun olam*.

The same Pope Honorius III whom we associate with St. Francis of Assisi authorized the Beguines in 1216 to live in common and exhort one another to a life of goodness. A subsequent papal bull by Gregory IX, in 1233, *gloriam virginalem*, endorsed the movement, although it is symptomatic of the tenuousness of aspects of the Christian world of the thirteenth century[4] that three years later Aleydis, a Beguine, was executed as a heretic. There was a growing backlash against the movement as the thirteenth century wore on, but it was not until the council of Vienna of 1311, during the papacy of Clement V, that the movement itself was condemned as heretical. In 1421, Pope Martin V authorized the archbishop of Cologne "to search out and destroy" any remnants of the Beguine movement—which, however, began to experience a subsequent revival in the seventeenth century.

The Beguine life, lived outside the cloister, independent of the established religious rules ordained from Rome both within the mainstream and within the cloister, included a strong mystical element construed in terms of living a life truly consistent with what is prescribed in the Gospels. This is the world of which Hadewijch became part sometime during the thirteenth century. One may infer from her broad education and her familiarity with the language and customs of chivalry and courtly love that she came from an upper-class family. She, in any case, either founded or became the leader of a Beguine group; her surviving letters suggest that she was someone who served as a guide and adviser to younger Beguines. Besides these, she authored a range of kinds of poems and accounts of visions in which she consistently uses the allegory of a tree as a descriptive for the mystical path.[5]

BREVARD COMMUNITY COLLEGE
MELBOURNE CAMPUS LIBRARY
3865 N. WICKHAM ROAD
MELBOURNE, FL 32935

On the other hand, her courtly love allusions offer the prime imagery for the mystical relationship with God. Rather than beginning with a text such as the Song of Songs as an allegorical source for mystical love commentary, as we have observed with earlier Christian mystics, Hadewijch composed her own direct descriptions of explosive *ek-stasis* in which Christ is likened to the bridegroom: She speaks of melting in the arms of Christ as the beginning, not the goal and endpoint, of mystical life. Augustinian *caritas* and courtly love are synthesized in her descriptions of the nature and activity of *minne* ("love"). Love is a bond that enchains her; it is a great river that flows out of God; it is a source of terror—because it is too strong, too powerful for one who is ill equipped to bear it. Hence, the *danger* of mystical love: It can frighten us to death or madness or apostasy; ecstasy can bury us in the deepest recesses of the *sacer* from which, if we emerge, we are transformed but from which we may not be able to emerge without painful marks like those left by an inconstant lover.

> Love has seven names.
> Do you know what they are?
> Rope, Light, Fire, Coal
> make up its domain.
>
> The other, also good,
> more modest but alive:
> Dew, Hell, the Living Water.
> . . .
> Love is a Rope, for it ties
> and holds us in its yoke
> . . .
>
> Under the name of Fire, luck,
> bad luck, joy or no joy,
> consumes
> . . .
>
> Hell (I feel its torture)
> damns, covering the world.
> Nothing escapes. No one has grace
> to see a way out.
>
> Take care, you who wish
> to deal with names
> for love. Behind their sweetness
> and wrath, nothing endures.
> Nothing but wounds and kisses.

The experience of God's depths is a dizzying one, for God is an abyss and a spinning wheel, a whirlpool in which one can drown—but the mystic who is sucked into it is herself an abyss, bottomless as God is.

The thirteen century is marked in the Christian world by varied exempla of encyclopedic thinking and by a strong interest in grasping parallels between the universe at large (the macrocosm) and its smaller (microcosmic) elements, such as structures created by human beings and human beings themselves. Thus, Gothic architecture, for example, offers sweeping edifices that are both tiny within the universe but enormous within the context of the tiny human beings who enter within them. Such structures invariably offer organic, arithmetic exercises in the interrelatedness of all the parts that comprise the whole, as a parallel to the manner in which the universe is understood to be an order (the Greek word is *kosmos*) with myriad interrelated parts. Moreover, the vocabulary of the decorative schemata of Gothic churches and cathedrals is often divided among the human, natural, and supernatural realms.

Similar to the thought that underlies structures from Chartres, France, to Leon, Spain, is the kind of work represented by the Dominican Vincent de Beauvais (ca. 1190 to ca. 1264). Vincent's encyclopedic *Speculum maius* (*Great Mirror*, also known as the *Speculum mundi*, or *Mirror of the World*) divides the study of reality into four parts: nature (theology, psychology, physiology, cosmography, physics, botany, zoology, mineralogy, and agriculture); doctrine (logic, rhetoric, poetry, geometry, astronomy, instincts, passions, education, industrial and mechanical arts, anatomy, surgery, medicine, jurisprudence, and the administration of justice); history (the world up to ca. 1250 CE); and moral study. Contemporary with Vincent's work is the efflorescence of the sort of legalistic theological-philosophical thought that is encompassed by a second Dominican, St. Thomas Aquinas (1225–1274), who, in his *Summa Theologica*, sought to sum up the entirety of Christian thought in an encyclopedic manner.

One of St. Thomas's important, much younger contemporaries was Meister Eckardt (1260–1329), also a Dominican—he joined the order at age fifteen—whose intellectual life took him in at least two very different directions from that of Thomas's scholasticism. One is that in 1326 he was tried for heresy—at his death three years later, the case had still not been resolved, but Pope John XXII condemned his writings as heretical. The other way in which his thinking distinguishes him from Aquinas is precisely its standing outside the mainstream of accepted Christian thought. Included in his writings are comments that reflect his mystical yearnings: his desire to find union with God other than by way of the mainstream. In a manner that was perhaps too direct for contemporary scholastic thinking, Eckardt speculated about divine-human intercourse as a process that he labeled the "spark of the soul." That spark has always existed in the divine mind or soul, and is reflected in the human soul; if one negates one's own personality, one can experience the identity of one's soul with God. "My eye and God's eye are one eye and one seeing, one knowing, and one loving." We recognize in these words and ideas both the general medieval Christian and Jewish sense that perfect communion with God once existed (before Adam and Eve disobeyed God and were removed from Paradise) and a specific connection—but differently articulated—to the late kabbalistic notion that Adam and Eve's act smashed the primordial light into an infinite number of sparks (*n'tzotzot*) that, imprisoned within shells (*kleepot*), are nonetheless found in each of our souls. To locate the spark is to locate the God within us: *Ek-stasis* is *en-stasis*.[6]

Further, Meister Eckardt equates true seeing with true knowing and, in turn, with true spiritual loving. If the Greek verb "to know" inherently recognizes a relationship between the first two of these—"to know" (*oida*) means "to have seen"—then the mystic links these two capacities, in their fullest, purest, most self-negating form, with love. Not surprisingly, he uses the imagery of light in his *The Divine Desert*. And the sort of light he discusses is the light beyond even the primordial light of Genesis 1:2—like the endless light (*'eyn sof or*) beyond the *sephirot* in Zoharic Kabbalah—and yet not the same as the kabbalistic light, in the way in which he so emphatically finds it within the human soul, waiting to be discovered through self-negation and self-annihilation.

> Sometimes I have spoken of a light that is uncreated and not capable of creation and that is in the soul . . . [the soul's] light may have more unity with God than it has with any power of the soul . . . if a man will turn away from himself and from all created things, by so much you will be made one and blessed in the spark in the soul, which has never touched either time or place . . . this same light is not content with the simple divine essence in its repose . . . but simply wants to know the source of this essence, it wants to go into the simple ground, into the quiet desert. . . . In that innermost part, where no one dwells, there is contentment for that light, and there it is more inward than it can be to itself, for the ground is simple silence.

The problem for his assertions as the church understood them was that they may be seen to engender the threefold problem that is generally associated with mysticism: The individual may be torn apart by the experience; the mystic's influence on other individuals within the community, each inspired to develop along his or her own spiritual path, threatens the unity and order of the community, which may be damaged by the spiritual chaos that undercuts its proper relationship with God; the sacerdotal leadership of the community does not wish to have its own authority undercut.

Eckardt carries us into the fourteenth century, particularly rich with regard to the mystical quest—perhaps in part because it is a century so fraught with political and military conflicts, as well as with the most profound of attacks on Europe by nature, in the form of the Black Plague. The widespread interest in mystical thought in the fourteenth century—from St. Birgitta of Sweden to St. Joan of Arc in France—is further signified by the fact that our access to Hadewijch of Antwerp's work in part comes through those familiar with and influenced by her work in the fourteenth century, such as the Carthusians of Diest and the Canons Regular of Windesheim. But on the other hand, the uncontrollably spreading interest in mysticism, combined with the range of natural calamities, helped assure that individuals such as Meister Eckardt would be more likely to confront the accusation of heresy than they might have been in a different era under different conditions. In what has been called the calamitous century, the search for passage out and elsewhere into the deepest Other is not surprising; nor is the concern on the part of the mainstream leadership that the paths being taken were nefarious.[7]

The calamitous nature of the era was also clear from the church's perspective when one recalls that the papacy fled its traditional seat of political and spiritual power, Rome, and took up residence for three-quarters of a century in southern France, in Avignon—which period (1309–1377) is generally referred to as "the Babylonian captivity of the papacy." One of the more significant figures of the era, who bridged mystical aspiration with a strong sense of community obligation articulated in political terms (and therefore differently from how, for example, St. Francis had articulated that obligation 150 years earlier), was St. Catherine of Siena (1347–1380). At an early age, she began to have visions and practice austerities, and by the age of seven, she already asserted her sense of calling, vowing that Christ would be her only bridegroom when she came of age. (She has inspired many paintings of the moment of her mystical marriage to Christ.) Her father, a fairly well-off wool dyer, initially unhappy about the direction she was prescribing for herself, relented when, late one afternoon, he sought and found her seated by one of Siena's more out of the way public fountains. As he approached her, he saw a pure, white dove sitting on her head while she was lost in meditation. As he drew closer, rather than flying off, it simply disappeared, and he understood that it was the dove of the Holy Spirit that had been resting on her—that the favor (*charis*) of God rested upon her.

At sixteen, she took the habit of the Dominican tertiaries[8] and in effect became an anchorite, taking up residence in a little room in her father's house. It is asserted of her that, after three years of visitations and intimate conversations with Jesus, she was formally—perhaps during the carnival (that marks the beginning of Lent) of 1366—espoused to Christ. Rejoining her family, she began to engage in good works, tending the sick, in particular those, such as lepers, with the most repulsive maladies, and to work for the conversion of sinners. At age twenty-one, she left home to continue her work while residing with the Dominicans. Her dedication to an ascetic life and her convictions regarding contact with Christ were so extreme that even some of those within her order subjected her to scorn. But her unfailing charm and charisma gradually yielded a strong group of disciples around her, both female and male, bound by spiritual fellowship and a powerful sense of mystical love. It was perhaps among those disciples that, in 1370, at the age of twenty-three, Catherine experienced the mystical death in which, entranced for four hours, she had visions of hell, purgatory, and heaven and heard a voice commanding her to leave her cloistered life and go out into the world. In that four-hour experience of *ek-stasis*, she received the stigmata. A second biographical account suggests that this occurred was while she was in Pisa on the fourth Sunday of Lent five years later and that the marks did not appear outwardly on her body while she was alive.

More to the point for our purposes is that, in the collection of her letters entrusted to and published by the Dominican reformer, Raymond of Capu, who served as her confessor and spiritual guide, she directed four petitions to God—for herself, for the reform of the church, for the world, and for divine providence—to which petitions she asserted that she received a response from God while in a state of *ek-stasis*. In these letters, organized as a compendium and entitled *Dialogue*, she represents Christ as a bridge to the divine and describes the stages leading to complete mystical union as five kinds of tears. There are those of the wicked, who are damned, first of all. Next are those of the fearful, who have risen out of sin due to the threat of punishment. Tender tears, the third sort, are associated with those who, rising out of sin through having gotten a taste of God, are still imperfect in their love of and service to God. Souls that have achieved perfection in loving both their fellows and God without self-interest yield perfect tears, the fourth kind, which in the fifth and final stage of communion with God become sweet, tender, perfect tears.

The number of such "tears" corresponds to the number of wounds in Christ's body, further suggesting that, in the stages leading to mystical union, the devotee is coassociated in a symbolic manner with Christ's suffering on behalf of the world. Indeed, the desire to move through these stages cannot, in Catherine's understanding, be separated from the desire to be washed in Christ's blood—which baptism we may understand as intended to wash away self-interest and to submerge oneself in *caritas* toward others. She expressed her own longing for martyrdom in a letter comforting Niccolo di Toldo prior to his beheading for pro-papal agitation. She writes subsequently that when Niccolo's head fell into her hands, she had a vision of Christ receiving the blood into his side. She describes how the fragrance of Niccolo's blood mingled with her own and that of Christ, further impelling her desire for martyrdom.

> I received his head into my hands saying 'I will!' with my eyes fixed on Divine goodness. Then was seen the God-Man as one sees the brilliance of the sun. His side was open and received blood into his own blood. . . . After he had received his blood and desire, [Jesus] received his soul as well.

Ironically enough, this period of her short life was marked neither by martyrdom nor even by a cloistered existence; she was vigorously engaged in the sort of worldly activity that was intended to reform the church and save others' souls. She expended great energy in convincing Pope Gregory XI to leave Avignon and return to Rome (in which she was finally successful in 1377) and also in pushing for a crusade that would unify Christian Europe. Engaged on the pope's behalf in Florentine politics in 1378, she nearly lost her life in the popular tumult—and was bitterly disappointed to have escaped; she was convinced that her sins had deprived her of the red rose of martyrdom. In the last few years of her life, she was in Rome, working on behalf of and with Pope Urban VI, serving the poor and the ill—and beseeching the divine bridegroom to share with her the burden of the punishment for the sins of the world and to bear her away. This he did: After a prolonged and medically inexplicable agony of three months from Sexagesima Sunday until the Sunday before Ascension, 1380—endured by her with ecstatic delight and exultation— she died at age thirty-three (Jesus's age at the time of his crucifixion).

Quite different from St. Catherine of Siena both in remaining cut off from the world but organized as a community onto themselves and in their emphasis on *words*—in a manner that parallels Jewish mysticism's obsession with the Torah's words and then names of God and their deconstruction—is the hesychast group of Eastern Orthodox monastic mystics established on Mount Athos in northern Greece, one of whose key theorists was Gregory Palamas (1296 to ca. 1360). The term *hesychast* derives from the Greek word *hesychos*, meaning "quiet," and the group that may be said to have been founded in the eleventh century by Simeon "the new theologian" had, by the time of Gregory, a three-part ideology. Simeon had evolved an elaborate quietist theory—that through silent contemplation, developed by a complex system of asceticism, detachment from earthbound cares, submission to a bona fide master, and extensive prayer—all leading to perfect repose—the practitioner can see the hidden, uncreated light of God. By holding the body absolutely immobile for a lengthy period of time, with the chin pressed down against the chest, the breath held, the eyes turned inward, in due time the practitioner will see the incomparable light: To contemplate that light is the highest goal for humans in the *profanus*.

The hesychast theory argues, moreover, that this light, while it is the eternal light of God, is yet not God's essence, which is beyond reach by any human. We recognize this paradox as parallel to that in *merkavah* and Kabbalah: The mystic seeks the innermost recess of that which is unachievable and yet which he or she continues to pursue as if it were achievable. We can also recognize a parallel to the kabbalistic discussion of the *'eyn sof or*. As such, the hesychasts distinguish God's essence from God's actions. The Western Scholastics saw this viewpoint as heretical for the dualism that they perceived in it, and it is against the Scholastics that Gregory wrote works such as *The Hesychast Method of Prayer and the Transformation of the Body*. He had entered the monastery of Mount Athos after his university education, leaving in 1325 to establish a semimonastic community in Thessaloniki. The community practiced a hesychast way of life—this is the third element of hesychastic thought, associated specifically with Gregory and his followers—centered on a constant repetition of the Jesus prayer: "Lord Jesus, Son of God, have mercy on me."

Thus, repeating the prayer endlessly and ultimately mindlessly—another practice we recognize as parallel to those in some branches of Jewish mysticism, particularly Abulafian mysticism—while in the prescribed body position with chin pressed against the chest, would facilitate the descent of the mind into the heart. Therefore—if God graces the mystic with a response—the mystic will be treated to a vision of the Holy Spirit transformed into pure light. That light is furthermore associated by Gregory with the light that transformed Christ on Mount Tabor in the narrative of the transfiguration (in Luke 9:34ff). This means that the mystic has become one with the disciples (Peter, James, and John) who were present at that moment. Gregory carried this teaching back to Mount Athos in 1331 and back again to Thessaloniki, where he became bishop in 1347.

⁘

This is also the era in which the English anchorite mystic Richard Rolle of Hampole (ca. 1300–1349) wrote of divine love as yielding a state of ecstasy in which he was "intoxicated, ravished and annihilated." In his *Incendium amoris* (*The Fire of Love*), he describes passing through successive states of *calor* ("heat"), *canor* ("melodiousness"), and *dulcor* ("sweetness") over a three- or four-year period of purgation and increasing illumination toward pure contemplation of God, each of which states merged into the next, all of them, once achieved, remaining with him so "that I did not think anything like it or anything so holy could be received in this life."

Thus, the terms used to express the ineffable mergence with the inexpressible multiply. The era of Richard Rolle overlaps that of Julian of Norwich (1342 to ca. 1416; she carries our discussion further forward, into the fifteenth century), an anchorite who drew her name from the location of her anchorage, beside St. Julian's Church in Norwich, England. During a serious illness, she received a vision of the crucified Christ from which hidden understandings were revealed to her. These she wrote down in her *Sixteen Revelations of Divine Love* (which she expanded as a text, over the following twenty years of contemplation). While at the outset she refers to herself as a "simple creature unlettered," it seems that she read and did not merely contemplate the vision she had received, for her later, fuller work evidences influence from as far afield as the anonymous text *The Cloud of Unknowing* (and its Neoplatonism) and the letters of St. Catherine of Siena (in Julian's use of the specific image of the place in Christ's wounded side for all mankind that will be saved).

On the one hand, Julian, like Catherine and other medieval Christian women mystics, steers away from the idea of a dualism, a separation between body and soul. God is in our "sensuality," as well as our "substance," so that the soul and body render mutual spiritual assistance to each other: "Either of them take help of the other until we are brought up into stature." Thus, the physicality so prevalent in Christian mysticism and particularly logical for Christian women mystics, as I have earlier discussed, is evident in her thinking. On the other hand, some of her imagery recalls the thought of St. Francis and the panhenotheistic mood of his Muslim contemporary, Ibn 'Arabi, and also anticipates the panhenotheism of several later Christian mystics and members of the later Hassidic movement in Jewish mysticism who perceived that the One (*heno-*) God (*theos*) is found in everything (*pan*), since everything was created by the One God. Thus,

> He . . . surrounds us with his love. . . . And in this he showed me something small, no bigger than a hazelnut, lying in the palm of my hand. . . . I thought that because of its littleness it would suddenly have fallen into nothing. And I was answered in my understanding; it lasts and always will, because God loves it; and thus everything has being through the love of God.

The anonymous fourteenth-century text, *The Cloud of Unknowing*, which may have influenced Julian, also emphasizes love (rather than study and the sort of knowledge that study yields) as the means to grasping God. It articulates the *contemplatio* aspect of prayer that had been first formally referred to by Guigo II (see the very end of chapter 4) as an act shapable only by the heart, not the head. But it turns in a different direction from what we have encountered before—at least we have not encountered it as directly and emphatically—the direction of *negation*, which is also precisely the opposite direction from that suggested in Julian's image of the hazelnut. Thus, if one separates one's self from the created world (the *profanus*), "keeping your thoughts and desires free from involvement in any of God's creatures . . . and so diligently persevere in [this separation] that you feel joy in it," the created world will be left behind in a cloud of forgetting. This can be accomplished by concentrating on one's sins and on the image of the suffering Christ—and one can arrive beyond the cloud of forgetting to the cloud of unknowing, beyond which is the hidden recess of God.

> You will seem to know nothing and to feel nothing except a naked intent toward God in the depths of your being . . . your mind will be unable to grasp Him, and your heart will not relish the delight of His love. . . . But learn to be at home in this darkness. . . . For if, in this life, you hope to feel and see God as He is in Himself it must be within this darkness and this cloud. But if you strive to fix your love on him, forgetting all else . . . I am confident that God in His goodness will bring you to a deep experience of Himself.

Thus, on the one hand, the negation process is an affirmation process, but on the other hand, it does negate the ultimate validity of the created world, in an almost Gnostic sense, since one's goal becomes not merely to transcend it but to transcend it in its forgetability in order to get closer to the realer reality of the *sacer*. Moreover, the methodology of beginning the journey is a negative one—focus on suffering and on one's own sins, including by definition the original sin for which the only hope of remission is the act of suffering upon which the mystic is enjoined to concentrate. This particular form of presenting the paradox of negative-positive is unimaginable, by comparison, in Jewish mysticism, since Judaism lacks not only the Christ imagery but also, more fundamentally, the concept of original sin and, with it, the strong emphasis on sin found even within the mainstream of medieval Christian mysticism—which sensibility would have reached a high watermark in the fourteenth century with its crises and disasters. On the other hand, we recognize in the last assertion that all-important, faith-bound notion shared by both traditions in their varied manifestations: that the final step of the journey is facilitated by God drawing the mystic into itself, once the mystic has traveled the lion's share of the distance by properly prescribed means.

The doctrine of self-negation that was first overtly articulated in Christian mystical thought by Meister Eckardt and takes such a distinct and emphatic turn in the *Cloud of Unknowing* reaches a place of particularly strong synthesis with the positivity of concentrating on and seeking to emulate Jesus in the work of Thomas à Kempis (1379/80–1471). His most famous work, *The Imitation of Christ*, is arguably the most important Christian mystical text of the fifteenth century.[9] This four-part work seems to have grown out of the new devotional movement established under the roof of the Augustinians by Thomas's older brother, John. It emphasizes in a radical manner the notion that weaves its way through the history of Christian mysticism, of emulating Christ in order to merge with the hidden recesses of God. In prescribing the means to achieving that goal, one must begin by renouncing all vain and transitory things (as Thomas prescribes in the first treatise) and seeking with complete and absolute humility only that which is eternal (which is to say, God).

> This I pray for, this I desire, that I may be wholly united with thee and may withdraw my heart from created things, and by Holy Communion . . . may more and more learn to relish heavenly and eternal things. . . . Then all that is within me shall rejoice exceedingly when my soul shall be perfectly united with my God.

His second treatise counsels the reader to recognize that the kingdom of God is to be found within each person but cannot be located with the senses or the intellect; it can be found only by emulating and seeking union with the crucified Christ. Thus, negating the world of the *profanus* leads to negating the sense-and-knowledge self in favor of the eternal that is signified by Christ in his final self-sacrificing (and in the *profanus* as opposed to *sacer* sense, self-negating) act. Yet, self-negation has as its purpose to discover the *true* self—the divine self—that is already and was always present within everyone.

The third treatise, in building on the assertions and prescriptions of the first two, emphasizes the importance of grace (*gratia*) and love (*caritas*). Thus, by way of distinctly Augustinian terminology, this third work associates the notion that God can be found within any and all of us—and articulates the goal of finding that God in ourselves and in each other—with both the notion that success in finding God means accomplishing the universal love achieved by Christ and also the notion that such success is in part possible through God's grace. For that grace *enables* the successful mystic to achieve union with Christ by achieving love of the God that resides in himself and others. Thomas's fourth treatise offers a kind of culmination of the physicality of this process by its discussion of the sacraments and its assertion that union with Christ can be achieved, in part, through the Eucharist. Thus, the spiritual union derived from disconnection from earthly matters and concerns is met by the physical union of taking the miraculous bread and wine into one's body.[10]

By the fifteenth century, yet other mystics and their movements were spreading particularly to and through Christian Spain. Monastic reform continued in further response to the upheavals occasioned by the Black Death and its extended repercussions. Upheaval certainly pushed onward into the sixteenth century, with the Protestant Reformation that tore Western Christendom apart and, for Spain in particular, with a succession of crises that extended from the hideous development of the Dominican-led Inquisition there in the late fifteenth century, to its expulsion of non-Christian populations in the late fifteenth century and following, to its struggles for power with Catholic France in the early sixteenth century and subsequently with Protestant England in the late sixteenth—to say naught of those with the Muslim Turkish Ottoman Empire.

Francisco de Osuna (1492–1540?) was born in the very year in which the Catholic king Ferdinand conquered Granada, eliminating the last vestige of independent Muslim political power in the Iberian Peninsula and unifying Spain as a Christian entity by also expelling the remaining Jewish population (many Jews had either left Spain or converted to Christianity during the previous century) a few months later and suppressing Islam.[11] Francisco grew up in a Spain dominated by strong spiritual—emphatically Catholic—currents. His shaping as a Franciscan mystic presents a rich vocabulary that—astonishingly broad-based, given the time and location in which he lived—synthesizes focus on the Bible and the writings of the Church Fathers together with the work of Pseudo-Dionysius and readings in Greek philosophy and Islamic mysticism. In his *Third Spiritual Alphabet*, he begins by focusing on the matter of cleansing the conscience as the starting point toward the mystical spiritual life.

Francisco's primer for attaining that goal articulates a practice that had emerged in the generation before him, called "recollection" (their followers in the Spanish-speaking world were called *recogidos*, or "rememberers"). He applied to Christian thought the Platonic concept of recollection—*anamnesis*—which asserts that learning is actually a process of recalling what we already know from previous lives and have forgotten in the course of the journey through the realm of death and the process of rebirth.[12] The practitioner is enjoined to practice recollection with regard to imitating Jesus—that is, to *recall* the moments of his Passion as if one had been present to *witness* them. By means of this process of recollection (which he also calls "mental prayer"), one withdraws from people and the outside world to enter one's *sacer* self—recalling how Christ withdrew in the wilderness (the *sacer*) to pray alone.

But the process of prayer that he prescribes is also physical to the extent that it involves vocal expression together with contemplation. His *Alphabet* offers a furthering of the notion that we have observed previously of seeking union with God through a process of unknowing: that one must empty the mind and heart in order to be filled with God's love. Yet the vocal expression of prayer, filled with holy thoughts, rather than with no thought at all, pushes lesser issues and ideas out of the soul, preparing it so that divinity may enter.

> The first form or manner of prayer is vocal. . . . The second kind of prayer is that within our hearts, wherein we do not pronounce the words vocally with the mouth. This prayer consists of holy thoughts. The third kind of prayer is called mental or spiritual prayer, in which the highest part of the soul is lifted more purely and affectionately to God on the wings of desire and pious affection strengthened by love.

The special recollection that follows this hierarchy of preparation emerges as one prays silently to God with complete devotion and with all concern for other issues left behind. The ecstatic giving of one's self to God becomes the receiving of God. The soul "falls asleep in its very self, forgetful of its human weakness, for it sees itself made like God, united in His Image and garbed with His Clarity as Moses was after entering the cloud encircling the mountain." The image of Moses on Sinai is synthesized to the image of Christ on Mount Tabor, and that synthesis articulates the condition of the soul that has succeeded in achieving transformation, transfiguration, and union with God's hiddenness.

Francisco de Osuna's *Third Alphabet of Prayer* was the key transformative text in the life of St. Teresa of Avila (1515–1582). If, in one sense, St. Francis of Assisi presents the culmination of the process of imitating Christ as the first and most famous Christian mystic to experience the receiving of the stigmata, St. Teresa presents the culmination of the process of a mystical marriage mode of union with Christ of which St. Catherine of Siena marks the emphatic beginning point. St. Teresa, interestingly, was the grandchild of one of the fifteenth-century Jews who felt compelled to embrace Christianity but who apparently continued to practice Judaism in secret—or at least was accused by the Inquisitional authorities of so doing. One of the interesting and unanswerable questions about Teresa is the degree to which she identified with the Jewish side of her heritage; more to the point of this discussion, she might be seen as a symbol of the fusion of parallel traditions.

As Teresa was the third of nine children, her life by the time of her mother's death (Teresa was fourteen years old at the time) would have led her either toward matrimony or the convent. The first option was undercut both by her *converso* background and by the fact that she had had a love affair. She was thus sent to a convent, as a boarder, at age eighteen, where she was quite unhappy and from which she left a year and a half later due to ill health. Back at home and again faced with the same life choice, this time she *chose* the convent, running off to join the Carmelite Convent of the Incarnation. The Carmelites, a mendicant order founded, like the Franciscans and Dominicans, in the thirteenth century,[13] claimed spiritual descent from the schools of prophets established on Mount Carmel during the era of the prophets Elijah and Elisha.[14] They sought to wed spiritual focus to worldly focus by living together in groups for mutual support but often being involved in the world beyond the convent. By the middle of the fifteenth century, a number of communities of Beguines in different places asked for and received affiliation with the order. The prestige of the Carmelite sisters grew rapidly in the later part of the century, and convents were established in France, Italy, and Spain. In the last of these countries, the order was particularly admired and thus in 1535 attracted Teresa, who made her profession the following year.

She fell ill again about a year later—she suffered fevers and fainting spells—and thought to have tuberculosis and thus obviously to be unable to fulfill the usual obligations of a member of the order, she was sent back to her family. Briefly under the care of an uncle, she received from him a copy of Francisco de Osuna's *Third Spiritual Alphabet*, which introduced her to the pattern of mental prayer leading through recollection ("It is called 'recollection' because the soul collects together all the faculties and enters within itself to be with God," she would later write in *The Way of Perfection*) to *contemplatio* that she began to practice for an hour twice daily. Her beginning point would be variously a short reading from an inspiring text or a scene of natural beauty or a sacred image to help her focus and lead her mind to a state of effortless stillness. Nonetheless, her physical ailments continued with sufficient seriousness that a gravesite was prepared for her at the convent when she went into a coma lasting several days—a coma that everyone but her father was convinced was a death throe.[15]

In the aftermath of her recovery—she remained in the convent infirmary for several years—she practiced *contemplatio* with increasing intensity over the years that followed, and at age forty, she began to have visions, seen "not with the eyes of the body but the eyes of the soul." She felt increasingly drawn to a life of poverty and self-denial and, in August 1562, began a reform of the Carmelite order (later known as the "discalced"—"barefoot"—Carmelites), with the establishment of a small convent (for thirteen nuns), dedicated to St. Joseph, in her native town of Avila. It subsisted on alms. Teresa dwelled there for four years. But in her search for poverty and silence, she spent most of the last years of her life traveling throughout Spain. With the support of the general of the order, Rubeo—but often against strong opposition from the authorities of the church and their allies (the Inquisition authorities were examining her autobiography during this period for signs of heresy, of which, as a descendant of Jews, she was more easily suspect)—she established sixteen more convents guided by her strict Carmelite reformation over the remainder of her life. She also established a Discalced Carmelite order for men, which at the outset included her most famous disciple, the mystical poet St. John of the Cross.

If, for Teresa, the quiet sense of union with God that she was able to arrive at later in her life was the most satisfying of her accomplishments, posterity has been most moved by the writings that record the process of arriving at that union and the imagery describing it. In her *Life*, she writes of moments of *ekstasis* in which she would see "the Lord . . . nothing but His hands, the beauty of which was so great as to be indescribable. . . . I also saw that Divine face, which seemed to leave me completely absorbed . . . [and] His resurrected body . . . [bathed in] a light so different from what we know here below that the sun's brightness seems dim by comparison." Most famously, she wrote of how

> beside me, on my left hand, [stood] an angel in bodily form. . . . In his hands I saw a great golden spear, and at the iron tip there appeared to be a point of fire. This he plunged into my heart several times so that it penetrated my entrails. . . .
>
> The pain was so great that I moaned aloud; but at the same time I felt such infinite sweetness that I wished the pain to last forever. . . . It was the sweetest caressing of the soul by God.

This is the description that Gian Lorenzo Bernini captured in his famous sculpture of 1645 to 1652, which in its brilliance of rendering the moment in earthy orgasmic naturalism may well startle a modern, post-Freudian audience.[16] But the image is perfectly appropriate on two grounds. First, St. Teresa had been so attractive to and attracted to men in her earlier life and had thus, in a very literal sense, transformed that physical passion to a spiritual passion for God. Second, as such, she represents the culmination of that process of physical-become-spiritual union as it is explored and expressed by the women mystics of the Christian tradition.

In what is arguably her most important work, *The Interior Castle*, the *enstatic* reality of *ek-stasis* is underscored. St. Teresa describes the soul as a castle of clear crystal or diamond that contains chambers that parallel the heavenly chambers—in which imagery we recognize a parallel to *merkavah* mysticism, with its *heikhalot*. Within the heart of the castle sits God, in the center of spaceless reality, constantly beckoning to the individual to remain within his love and his truth. The mystical journey is equated with entering the castle and traveling through its seven mansions (chambers), each with its own myriad rooms. Those who enter the first are still largely too enticed and distracted by worldly concerns to focus on the search for the true light. But the first step is to persevere in prayer and meditation. Those who begin will gain access to the second mansion, where, engaged in such focused prayer, although still reluctant to part with wealth and honor and still too preoccupied with and too easily shocked by others' faults, they are nonetheless received.

Those whose longing not to offend God increases as they meditate gain access to the third mansion, within which they become increasingly fond of ascetic practices and periods of recollection, as well as a desire to extend their *caritas* to their neighbors.

These three mansions are centered on the active human effort that pushes toward ordinary grace—and the danger, still, of being led astray, back toward worldly concerns. The last four mansions are defined increasingly by human passivity, in which the act of divine reaching toward the mystic signals increased spiritual delight. The mystic's praying becomes increasingly infused with God's grace; thus, his or her state is not merely filled with the *contentos* ("consolations") that spring from human experience but with *gustos* ("delights") that flow from God into those who have arrived at this point of spiritual preparation and desire.[17] She warns, as one enters the fourth mansion, that one must let the intellect go and surrender to God: "the important thing is not to think too much but to love much" and to draw the faculties inward. In the fifth mansion, a condition of union with God begins to manifest itself: "silkworms come from seeds about the size of a peppercorn. . . . When the warm weather comes . . . the worms nourish themselves on mulberry leaves until they grow and settle on twigs. There they enclose themselves in cocoons, and the silkworm, fat and ugly, dies and a little white butterfly, very pretty, comes forth from the cocoon." The cocoon is Christ, within which the soul is transformed from silk worm to butterfly.

But this fifth mansion is still part of the process that precedes complete fulfillment—complete *gusto*. For in the sixth mansion occurs the spiritual betrothal that furthers the union of the soul to God and enables the soul to enter divine mysteries through visions. There, the mystic experiences wounds that offer simultaneous pain and delight.[18] There, the mystic feels both self-knowledge and complete humility, enormous joy and a desire to share it, to serve others. Thus, the individualized, personal journey moves toward an endpoint of communal improvement; the mystic who achieves the state of *ek-stasis/en-stasis* that St. Teresa is describing does so ultimately to benefit others—or finds him- or herself wishing ultimately to do so. (This is why she *writes*: to benefit others.)

The denouement of the journey into the seventh chamber is the arrival to the highest level of union with God. Here, beams of light pour into the room from different windows. Here, the butterfly (arrived out of the vision of the fifth chamber) dies with joy as its death is an arrival at the strength to serve others with *agape/caritas*. Here,

> in this seventh dwelling place the union comes about in a different way: Our
> good God now desires to remove the scales from the soul's eyes and let it see

and understand, although in a strange way, something of the Favor He grants it. When the soul is brought into that dwelling place, the Most Blessed Trinity, all three Persons, through an intellectual vision, is revealed to it through a certain representation of the truth.

The soul experiences what Paul did on the road to Damascus: a blindness and deafness that, by paradox, are the removal of the scales from the eyes to "let it see and understand." This is the moment of perfect union, like rain falling into a river and streaming into the sea. The soul is the rain, and God is the sea; God is the rain, and the soul is the sea.

St. Teresa's arrival into the seventh dwelling place of her soul's journey, marked by the spiritual marriage that she experienced on November 18, 1572, occurred six months after Juan (John) de Yepes y Alvarez, also known as John of St. Matthias (1542–1591)—who had entered the order four years earlier, renaming himself St. John of the Cross—had arrived at Avila to become St. Teresa's disciple. Although a generation younger than she, he also became her most trusted adviser and her spiritual director, having arrived at the Convent of the Incarnation at her behest as director and confessor to the nuns residing there. He witnessed her culminating moment of spiritual ecstasy. Among his most famous mystical writings are *The Dark Night of the Soul*, in which he explains how God pulls the devout mystic into the deep darkness (which is the beginning of true light) that first purges the senses and on "the other [such] night . . . the spirit is purged and denuded, as well as prepared for union with God through love," and the poem "The Living Flame of Love," in which the consequence of the dark night—mystical ecstasy—is described. Thus,

> Oh living flame of love
> that tenderly wounds my soul
> in its deepest center . . .
> Oh sweet cautery,
> oh delightful wound! . . .
> In killing, You changed death to life.
>
> . . .
>
> How gently and lovingly
> You awake in my heart.
> where in secret You dwell alone;
> and in You sweet breathing,
> filled with good and glory,
> how tenderly You swell my heart with love.

The heart, which is the soul that is swollen with divine love, must first empty itself in order to be filled; it must be purified of any trace of *profanus* dross before it can be united with the deepest purest *sacer*. That dross in its most nonmaterial aspect is comprised of sins of which we may not even be aware—like a body with sores that it does not feel. The soul must submit to the painful divine surgery that heals the sores, removes the sins, and purifies the soul so that it may return to the world filled with *caritas*. Ultimately, if the mystic is to achieve the mystical goal, he or she must return to the world not only enriched by the experience of *ek-stasis* and the *mysterion* but also capable of sharing the consequences of that experience; if there is to be value, there will be success, and if there is success, it is because there will be value: extending a sense of God's love to the world around the mystic.

NOTES

1. In which, according to Eusebius, the Roman emperor saw a cross in the heavens and near it the words *in hoc signo vinces*: "by this sign you will conquer." In the year following his victory, we recall, Constantine granted *religio* status to Christianity.

2. We recognize the obvious formal similarity between this sartorial choice and that which defines Sufism.

3. I mean this as a deliberate pun between the common-parlance sense of the term as it applies to Francis as a charismatic personality and the etymological sense: derived from the Greek word *charis*, meaning "favor" or "grace," and referring to the notion that the favor or grace of God rested on the saint and enabled him to love all of creation, which he was beginning to do.

4. This was the era not only of the Franciscans but also of the Dominicans and their shaping of the authority of inquiring into proper Christian faith better known as the Inquisition—to say nothing of being the era of the Albigensian heresy.

5. She was clearly familiar with Latin but wrote in the middle Dutch vernacular of her time and place.

6. See chapter 9, regarding Lurianic and post-Lurianic Kabbalah.

7. I am borrowing the phrase "calamitous century" from the title of Barbara Tuchman's masterful historical narrative focused primarily on France, *A Distant Mirror: The Calamitous 14th Century* (New York: Random House, 1978). Hers is a superb book for an overview of the various issues that define that period and shape much of the background context for our own discussion.

8. That is, Third Order Dominicans.

9. There have been any number of scholars who have asserted that various individuals other than Thomas actually authored the work, but that is a separate matter.

10. One might view this emphasis on such a mainstream aspect of pre-Reformation Christianity both as a statement of how inherently mystical mainstream, everyday Christianity *is* and as a rebuke to the Albigensian view of the previous century that argued that sacraments such as baptism and the Eucharist were misguided, since

they used *profanus* (and therefore inherently corrupt) materials to afford connection with the *sacer* and its purity.

11. The *Moriscos* (Crypto-Muslims, outwardly Christian but inwardly Muslim) were finally fully expelled from the Iberian Peninsula in 1614.

12. The primary source for the discussion of this idea in Plato is the *Meno*.

13. More precisely, St. Berthold founded the order—the group of crusaders or pilgrims who gathered around him originally lodged, as hermits, on Mount Carmel (chosen for its association with the biblical prophet Elijah) in what is today Israel—in the late twelfth century. But, positioned to host and help pilgrims on their way down to Jerusalem, the Carmelites soon gained sufficient attention that the patriarch and papal legate, Albert of Jerusalem, defined a formal order for them between 1206 and 1214, and they received papal approval from Honorius III in 1226. By 1238, the order had relocated to Cyprus and Italy and eventually to other parts of Europe and begat an order of nuns.

14. That would have been in the late ninth century to early eighth century BCE.

15. They had apparently already sealed her eyes with wax so that when she awoke from her coma, she could not open them. "My tongue was bitten to pieces; nothing had passed my lips, and because of this and of my great weakness my throat was choking me so that I could not even take water. . . . As a result of all of my torments I was all doubled up, like a ball, and no more able to move arm, foot, hand or head than if I had been dead."

16. It is found in the Cornaro Chapel in the Church of Santa Maria della Vittoria in Rome in a most dramatic setting. The artist has managed to transform stone and metal into flesh and swirling drapery and soaring clouds.

17. Note, incidentally, that she is writing in Spanish, not Latin, hence terms like *contentos* and *gustos*.

18. One might again recognize a parallel, this time to the kabbalist Abraham Abulafia's emphasis on the *temurah* style of *tzeruf* that offers focus on the paradoxical relationship between *'oneg* (delight) and *n'ga* (pain). See chapter 6, p. 128.

Chapter Eight

The Spread of and Variety
within Sufism

THE DISSEMINATION OF THE *TARIQA*: THE WAY

In the generation of Ibn 'Arabi and those generations following, three particular developments within Sufism might be noted. One is the growth of Sufi
education centers toward providing systematic mystical instruction; these
were modeled on the mainstream madrasas but with a focus less on standard
matters of Qur'anic jurisprudence than on the teachings of the Sufi masters.
In an obvious retrospective sense, one recognizes this dissemination of teaching through the proliferation of such centers (beginning in Persia and spreading mainly west toward Egypt and eventually across North Africa) as a fulfillment of the late twelfth- and early thirteenth-century dictum of al-Ghazali
that "the disciple (*murid/shagird*) must of necessity have recourse to a director to guide him."[1] Loose fraternities of mendicants—*fuqara* (in Arabic; singular, *faqir*) or *daravish* (in Persian; singular, *darvish*)—began to emerge
around a *shaikh* or *pir*. The residences of such masters thus began to function
as entities akin to Christian monasteries (in Arabic, *ribat*; in Persian, *khan-
qah*) growing through endowments from followers drawn to such centers for
ascetic focus on prayer and concentration on the teachings of the master as
the means of access to God's inner recesses.[2]

These centers continued to spread in the course of the twelfth and thirteenth
centuries, providing guidance for initiates along the mystical path of *tariqa* (the
"way"). Initiates into Sufi mysteries came to be marked by being invested with
a special cloak—a *khirqa*—associated by tradition with a line of divine service
extending back to the Prophet himself.[3] Naturally, with such a widespread
range of *ribat/khanqah* structures, the variation of particulars with respect to
dhikr, litany, and doctrine also spread. Thus, the second aspect of Sufi evolution during and beyond the time of Ibn 'Arabi is the proliferation of the Sufi

orders—the word *order* used here being the common-parlance, common-usage meaning of *tariqa*. The eleventh-century Persian scholar Hujwiri already mentions several schools of Muslim mysticism associated with particular teachers, each with his own sense of the way to access God's hiddenmost innermost recesses. Each *ribat* within each *tariqa* tended to include a double population within its ambience: the initiates and disciples, who directed most of their time and energy to religious devotions and the practical matters of the *ribat* functions, and the lay members connected to the *ribat*, who participated in the *dhikr* but lived outside lives with outside occupations and families. One recognizes in this a similarity to Christian monastic orders such as the Franciscan or Carmelite with their own hierarchies of participation in the life of the order.

The Qadiri Order (*Qadiriya Tariqa*)—generally regarded as the first to be established in a formal manner—is so named for its founder, Muhyi ad-Din 'Abd al-Qadir ibn 'Abd Allah al'Jili al-Jilani (1077/78–1166) and is the most urban of the primary Sufi *tariqas*. Al-Qadir was born in Persia and moved to Baghdad while still in his teens to study Hanbali jurisprudence, but eventually he experienced conversion to the mystical way of life. Adherents to the *Qadiriya Tariqa* assert that al-Qadir's connection to God enabled him to perform miracles. His followers in turn became known for their tolerance and progressive thinking, for their philanthropy, piety, and humility, and for their strong opposition to fanaticism of any sort. It seems that al-Qadir himself chose not to establish a strict mode of devotional exercises (a strict pattern of *dhikr*), and his writings—his most famous extant manual of devotional instruction is his *al-Ghunya li-talibi tariq al-haqq*—are firmly based in the Qur'an and the sunna, with little that would offend most Orthodox Muslims. For example, the *Ghunya* recommends that after the morning prayer, one recite each of the following phrases one hundred times as a *dhikr*:

> I ask forgiveness of the mighty God; May God bless our Master Muhammad and his household and Companions; there is no God but God.

Thus, the practitioner engages the *sacer* through insistent repetitions that both force one to focus and concentrate—if the *dhikr* is to have any effect—and, at the same time, through rapid repetition, create a transrational mental state in which the words cease to be words but revert to being clusters of sounds (culminating with the mellifluous phrase *la 'Allah illa 'Allah*: "there is no God but God"). More than that, one recognizes that the invocation of blessings on the Prophet, his family, and his companions as if they are part of the here and now underscores that the line between the *profanus*, with its past-present-future sensibility, and the *sacer*, with its atemporal condition, is being eradicated.

Al-Qadir had forty-nine children, and among these, eleven sons who carried out his work; the order spread, with variations, through many parts of the Muslim world, particularly India (where it is still very present among the Muslim population). The variations, a function of the nonrigidity of al-Qadir's devotional system, include, for example, that founded by his nephew Ahmad al Rifa'i (d. 1182). The *Rifa'ya Tariqa* eventually developed as an order independent of its parent order. Based largely in Iraq, it tends toward greater rigidity and includes stronger practices of physical self-mortification, leading ultimately to extreme thaumaturgical exercises, such as eating glass, walking through fire, handling dangerous serpents, and the like. Some historians assert that these practices came into the order in the thirteenth century as a consequence of the Mongol invasions and the importation of customs associated with their shamans.

It was, in any case, during that century, looking west rather than east, during the time of the Seventh Crusade,[4] that one of the leaders of the *Rifa'ya Tariqa* in Egypt, Ahmad al-Badawi (d. 1276), was also extremely active as a leader of local opposition to the European invaders. Eventually, he founded his own order—an offshoot of the *Rifa'ya* offshoot of the *Qadiriya Tariqa*—which is variously called the *Ahmadiya* or the *Badawiya Tariqa*. Where the grandparent order was and remains largely urbanized, the *Badawiya Tariqa* is more rural and rustic—the most popular in Egypt. The *Badawiya Tariqa* became known particularly for its wild dancing, which to the outsider may seem orgiastic, and its customs are derivable from earlier, pre-Islamic Egyptian customs. Later on, the *Badawiya Tariqa* spawned two popular offshoots in northern (Lower, coastal) Egypt: the *Bayyumi* and *Dasuqi Tariqas*, the existence of which underscores both the flexible possibilities of the original *Tariqa* and the principle of a disseminational range of Sufi orders over the centuries.

In purely chronological terms, the second order to be founded after the Qadiri is the *Suhrawardiya*, named for Shihab ad-Din 'Umar ibn 'Abd Allah al-Suhrawardi (1144–1234). Al-Suhrawardi was the nephew of the principal of a well-known madrasa (the *Nizamiya* madrasa), who was himself not only an authority on hadith but also the author of a Sufi primer and the contemporary of Abu 'l-Futuh al-Suhrawardi, whose panhenotheistic writings led to his execution as a heretic. So Shihab ad-Din al-Suhrawardi grew up in an atmosphere of intense spiritual exploration. He grew to prominence, and his sermons and lectures came to earn him the patronage of the powerful, as did his writings, most prominently his *'Awarif al ma'arif* (*Knowledge for Encountering God*), which became the basic instructional text for the order named for him. Al-Suhrawardi's range of contacts and disciples included Sufi poets and politicians. As such, in the generations since his disciple,

Baha' ad-Din Zakariya', carried the Suhrawardi Order into India, not only did the order flourished there but also the name of the order in time grew to prominence in Bengali politics.

More substantial, perhaps, as a mystical order, and the third major order in time of founding—at the opposite end of the Muslim world—is the *Shadhiliya Tariqa*, named for the Maghribi scholar Nur ad'Din Ahmad ibn 'Abd Allah al-Shadhili (1196–1258). He founded the order in Tunisia but became so popular that the authorities of that time and place were concerned, and it became necessary for him to flee to Alexandria, Egypt, where he experienced immediate success at attracting adherents, eventually spreading not only back to the west across North Africa but also northeast up into Syria and southeast into the Arabian Peninsula. The *Shadhiliya* are known on the one hand for the aphoristic instructions that supplement their prayers (*ahzab*; singular, *hizb*) composed by al-Shadhili himself—particularly those aphorisms collected by one of the third generation among al-Shadhili's followers, Ibn 'Ata' Allah al-Iskandari (*al-Iskandari* means "the Alexandrian"; d. 1309); on the other hand, they are known for a more extravagant ritual than that of the Qadiris, with more apparently physical expressions of *ek-stasis*.

The aphorisms were organized into a work, *al-Hikam al-'Ata'iya* (*The Wisdom of 'Ata'*) that, in the following centuries, was subject to a growing body of commentary by subsequent Shadhili scholars. These aphorisms focus on the distinction between everyday Islam and its prayers—wherein those prayers are presumed to have become perfunctory, therefore coming *between* the devotee and God, rather than functioning as a means of *access* to God— and the mystical search for direct access to God, as well as on the distinction and relationship between free, human will and divine will, as between destiny and divine will. Thus, for example, "a sign of relying upon [the efficacy of religious] performance [such as prayer and related actions, instead of relying on God] is the diminution of hope [for God's forgiveness] when slips occur [such as, for instance, disobedience to the Divine Will]."[5] This distinguishes between prayer that is offered in a conventional and therefore nonfocused manner and attachment to God without prayers that are viewed as mere circumlocutions. Or, "the [operations of the human] will controlling [the course of phenomena] do not pierce the walls of the [appointed] destinies [but are themselves merely the result of the Divine Will]."

Thus, destiny and the notion that outcomes are predetermined are opposed not to free human will but to divine will, of which apparent human will is merely a consequence: What we succeed in doing on our own, we succeed in doing because we are *not* on our own but are favored to accomplish what we accomplish by God. The *Hikam al-'Ata'iya* thus enjoins us to "give rest from [attempting] the control [of human affairs] and what Another[6] than you has undertaken [to perform], do not undertake for yourself." The implications for this extend from the personal to the political, since controlling human affairs is, by definition, the enterprise of politics. Thus, both the ruler and the ruled are enjoined to recognize that their shared situation is ultimately shaped by God.

The book concludes with a turn from aphorisms to suggested prayers (*ahzab*) to God, such as, "Oh God, seek me out of Your Mercy that I may come to You; and draw me on with Your Grace that I may turn to You"—in which formulation we recognize the familiar mystical notion that, as the mystic seeks intimacy with God, ultimately that intimacy is made possible when God—and only when God—turns toward the mystic (but that turning will only occur when the mystic is turning entirely to God), and that it is an act of God's grace that, by paradox, makes it possible for the would-be mystic to succeed in *being* a mystic. The *ahzab* include as a concluding recitation,

> Oh You Who are veiled in the shrouds of Your Glory, so that no eye can perceive You! Oh You Who shine forth in the perfection of Your Splendor, so that the hearts [of the mystics] have recognized Your Majesty! How shall You be hidden, seeing that You are ever Manifest; and how shall You be absent, seeing that You are ever Present, and watch over us?

Thus, the paradox of God's transcendent inaccessibility and yet immanent availability—and the imagery of veils—as well as of God's presence-absence, are articulated both as description and as prescription. One recognizes affinities both with earlier Muslim mystical thinking and with the mystical thinking within the Jewish and Christian traditions.

On the other hand, among the subsequent offshoots that sprang from the *Shadhiliya Tariqa* is the *Isawiya*, known for a sword-slashing ritual that underscores the emphatic nature of the *Shadhiliya* physical expression of *ek-stasis*. The ritual also underscores the nature of such *ek-stasis*: that one transcends one's physicality to the extent of obliviousness to physical pain and the spilling of one's own blood. Opposite in its nonphysicality and differently extreme in its austerity is the *Derqawa Tariqa* that developed in western Algeria and Morocco, thus reinforcing the notion of how far-flung the Sufi *tariqas* and their *ribat*s became over the course of the fourteenth and following centuries.

Arguably the best-known—certainly in the Western, non-Muslim world—of the Sufi orders, and the fourth of the great *tariqas* in order of chronological organization, is the *Maulawiya*. It is named for Maulana, the Sufi name for the great Persian poet Jalal ad-Din Balkhi, better known as Jalal ad-Din Rumi (1207–1273). Rumi was actually born in the city of Balkh in northern (what is now called) Afghanistan, where his father, Bahauddin Walad, was apparently headmaster of one the city's well-known madrasas, but after Balkh was sacked by Genghis Khan, his father and he—his mother was murdered by the Mongols—moved on to Nishapur in northeastern Persia (i.e., Iran), where they met the famous Sufi poet, 'Attar; thence, they went briefly to Baghdad (it is said that, shocked by the city's extravagant wealth, they remained for only three days), then to Makka on pilgrimage, to Armenia and Syria for several years, and ultimately to central Anatolia, finally settling in the city of Rum (Konya)—as a consequence of which the poet is known as Rumi.[7]

For it was there that, by 1240, he had become recognized as a master of orthodox scholarship and, four years later, stricken by a spiritual and emotional crisis—occasioned by the arrival of a Sufi, named Shams of Tabriz, whose eccentricities and seemingly wild behavior attracted great attention, and whom the young scholar embraced instead of shunning as others did—left orthodoxy behind in favor of mystical thought. He came by that path honestly, since his father had a strong mystical side to go with his skill as a jurist; Rumi's father's extant writings, among other things, exhibit what for orthodox scholars was a shocking sensuality in his description of his union with God.

Rumi studied his father's esoteric teachings, as well as the writings of the Sufi poets Sana'i and 'Attar, through a former student of Bahauddin Walad, Burhanaddin Mahaqqiq. Thus, one might suppose that he was predisposed to respond strongly when the wandering *darvish*, Shams, appeared in Konya/Rum and posed a question to the young scholar. Tradition has it that the question was, who is greater, the Prophet Muhammad or the Turkish mystic Beyazit-I Bestami, since Bestami asserted "How great is my glory!" whereas Muhammad acknowledged, in a prayer to God, that "we do not know You as we should." Rumi is said to have fainted. Recovering, he asserted that Muhammad was the greater, for while Bestami had swallowed one enormous gulp of God and stopped there, for Muhammad the *tariqa* was always and continuously unfolding with new nuances and aspects. But the dialogue that ensued between Rumi and Shams made of the two inseparable companions in the search for greater intimacy with God. Even with Shams's abrupt disappearance—he recognized after several months how his presence was making Rumi's position as an attentive teacher difficult—there was no turning back to his old style for Rumi. Indeed, it may well have been Shams's disappearance that forced Rumi around the final turn toward his transformation as a mystic. In his distress and in his new emotional excitement, he often underscored his teaching with whirling and skipping dancelike movements—appalling the many students he now lost, while attracting others. Soon he became a *shaikh* or *pir* in his own right, attracting his own followers into what emerged as his own *ribat* and his own *tariqa*. Due to the Turkish version of his Sufi name, that *tariqa* is perhaps best-known as *Mevleviya Tariqa*: the Mevlevis.

The *Mevleviya Tariqa* became marked by a unique *dhikr* in which devotees not only whirl with increasing speed in concentric circles but also learn to whirl around individually for extended periods of time, with absolute, perfect equilibrium, so that they are able both to start and to stop abruptly and without a scintilla of balance unease. With one hand pointing down and one up, each whirling *darvish* is a microcosm of perfect, centered reality, of close-eyed inner sight, a perfect connector between earth and heaven, a simultaneously still and silent, yet ever-moving, rustling access-seeker and -achiever to the hidden God. The nineteenth-century English writer E. W. Lane described a "performance" of the *Mevleviya Tariqa* in Egypt[8] (which included Turks and Persians as well as Egyptians)[9]:

> The durweeshes who formed the large ring. . . now commenced their *zikr*; exclaiming over and over again, "Allah!" and, at each exclamation, bowing the head and body, and taking a step to the right; so that the whole ring moved rapidly around. As soon as they commenced this exercise, another durweesh, a Turk, of the Order of Mowlawees, in the middle of the circle, began to whirl; using both his feet to effect this motion, and extending his arms: the motion increased in velocity until his dress spread out like an umbrella. He continued whirling thus for about ten minutes; after which he bowed to his superior, who stood within the great ring; and then, without showing any signs of fatigue or giddiness, joined the durweeshes in the great ring; who had now begun to ejaculate the name of God with greater vehemence, and to jump to the right, instead of stepping. After whirling, six other durweeshes, within the ring, formed another ring; but a very small one; each placing his arms upon the shoulders of those next to him; and thus disposed, they performed a revolution similar to that of the larger ring, except in being more rapid; repeating, also, the same exclamation of "Allah!" but with a rapidity proportionately greater. This motion they maintained for about the same length of time that the whirling of the single durweesh before had occupied; after which, the whole party sat down to rest.

The order flourished and spread in the course of the Ottoman period from the fifteenth through the early twentieth centuries when the empire encompassed Turkey and other lands. As such it often exerted strong political power by means of the influence of its *shaikhs* on sultans and the wide circle of their governing infrastructure. Meanwhile, many other Sufi orders—scores of them—developed across the Muslim world in the course of the thirteenth through early twentieth centuries. Some of these are of particular interest for the manner in which they came to incorporate elements into their *dhikr* that reflect either tribal and ethnic customs unusual in conjunction with Islam or customs that clearly owe their origin to contact with the Christian (or Jewish) world. Thus, one might note the *Yeseviya Tariqa*, also in Turkey, in which women participated—*unveiled*—in the *dhikr*, a reflection of rural Turkish customs. More astonishing, perhaps, is the *dhikr* of the *Bektashiya Tariqa*, a likely late-fifteenth-century offshoot of the Yesevis, surviving today only in Albania, in which the central element, rather than devotional liturgy, is the sharing of wine, bread, and cheese together. This sort of communion suggests a distinct non-Muslim influence, particularly when one considers the orthodox Muslim taboo regarding the consumption of alcohol; that this influence is Christian is affirmed by the fact that the Bektashi devotees also practice confession to their *shaikhs* or *pirs* (termed *babas*, or "uncles"), a custom central to Christianity (and particularly to those branches of Christianity that have yielded the greatest volume of mystical figures) but virtually unheard of in Islam.

To the east, as Islam established itself in India, with it a series of Sufi *tariqas* also established themselves—arguably it is there that the largest range and variety of *tariqas* have existed since the post–World War I era—some of which succumbed to influences from Hinduism. There are orders such as the *Qadiriya* and the *Naqshbandiyya*, with international connections, and those such as the *Chishtiya* (founded in the early thirteenth century by Mu'in al-Din Chishti, from Sistan), the membership of whose subdivisions is confined to India. There is also a large number of *tariqas* that are called *be-shar* ("irregular") orders, so peculiar are they with respect to a "normative" Muslim basis. Some of them, for example, present a good deal of focus on the sacred fire, *Agni* (itself a God in Hindu thought), or on images and the Hindu concept of *darshan*, or "visualizing" God through various concrete manifestations.[10] Others retain a distinct link to the Hindu caste system, describing a hierarchy of human roles and positions in reality, which concept is anathema to orthodox Islam.

THE GOLDEN ERA OF SUFI POETRY

Intimately interwoven with the spread of Sufism and its *tariqas* from the late eleventh through the end of the nineteenth century is the shaping of an array of stunning works of poetry and prose across the Muslim mystical world that articulate mystical ideas by staring through various allegorical lenses. This constitutes the third development within Sufism toward, during, and beyond the era of Ibn 'Arabi. Perhaps not surprisingly, given both the time period of Sufism's efflorescence and of the poetry that grew with the mystical movement at large, Persia seems to have been the first extensive center of variously

didactic, romantic, and lyrical expression. Among the more prominent figures, Abu al'Majd Majdud ibn Adam, better known by his pen name, Sana'i
(fl. ca. 1110–1150)[11]—or more fully, Hakim ("the Wise") Sana'i of Ghazni (a
city in that part of the Persian realm now called southern Afghanistan)—was
the first to write an extensive poem elaborating Sufi doctrines. He had been
court poet to Bahram Shah for many years until experiencing a conversion to
intense spirituality, after which he abruptly left the court, retired from the
public eye, and completely redirected his poetic efforts.

He composed in the two classical forms of Arabic, Persian, Urdu, and
Turkish poetry, the ode (*qasida*) and the lyrical poem (*ghazal*) but also turned
to quatrains (*ruba'iya*; plural, *ruba'iyat*) and rhyming couplets (*mathnawi*) in
the course of his career. Thus, his allegory of the mystic's pilgrimlike search
for God, in his *Sair al-'ibad* (*Pilgrim's Progress*) was written as a *mathnawi*.
The passage through the ugliness within our reality and beyond our reality—
a Muslim articulation of hell—is rich in its imagery. The pilgrim's descriptions anticipate those in Dante's journey through the inferno, as he (the pilgrim) passes through territory inhabited by all the (personified) vices that he
must leave behind in order to ascend toward union with God:

> [A] devils' paradise my gaze befell,
> a people smothered by the smoke of hell.
> Savage were they, and black as a thundercloud
> shrouding a mountaintop, that steely crowd
> all hushed and silent, as if unaware,
> bewildered at each other they would stare,
> all full of wind and air, as bagpipes be,
> decked with two necks and orifices three
> monkeys they were, all running at a bound,
> head chasing tail, as will a fox a hound,
> wind-full and crooked, like a lute or reed,
> yellow, and cold, and ponderous as lead.
> . . . eyes that were founts of modest plenitude,
> faces that ravenously searched for food.[12]

This we recognize as part of a colorful delineation of the third of the deadly
sins—gluttony and sensuality—as al-Ghazali had discussed them in the third
section of his *Ihya'*.[13]

So, too, Sana'i's epic *Hadiqat al-Haqiqa* (*The Garden of True Reality*),
which puts into poetic form a survey of the main mystical concepts elaborated
in prose by the mystical leaders, such as al-Sarraj and al-Qushairi, who preceded or were contemporary with Sana'i, was written in rhyming couplets.
The *Hadiqa* was the main work of Sana'i's that Rumi studied with his father's

student, Burhanaddin Mahaqqiq, early in his own burgeoning career as a Sufi master. He would later quote from it in his own *Mathnawi*, and in one of his *ruba'iyat* quatrains, he would refer to Sana'i's importance within the flow of mystical poetry:

> 'Attar was the spirit,
> Sana'i his two eyes
> And in time thereafter
> Following them came I.

Farid ad-Din 'Attar was the other Sufi poet whose work Rumi studied—and whom Rumi met when, as a child, he and his father passed through Nishapur. And he is the second major Sufi poet in order of chronology. Active between about 1160 and 1200,[14] 'Attar apparently made his living as a perfume seller and pharmacist (this is what his name, 'Attar, would suggest) in Nishapur. He traveled and studied for a long time, to Rey (near Teheran), parts of Egypt, Syria, Turkestan, and India, and, of course, he also made a pilgrimage to Makka before returning to Nishapur, where, it is said, he saw five hundred patients daily in his *dharu-khane* (perfume and pharmacy shop). Between dispensing herbal prescriptions, he wrote prose and poetry. There is some evidence that at some time he was tried and found guilty of heresy.

Some thirty works by 'Attar have survived; four of these are essential classics within the canon of Sufi literature. He wrote a treatise on the lives of the Sufi saints (the *Tadhkirat al-auliya'*). He wrote an extensive *mathnawi* poem articulating the general principles of Sufism, exploring and expounding the mystical life, called the *Book of Secrets* (*Asrar-nama*)—a copy of which he personally inscribed to the young Rumi before the latter left Nishapur. He wrote a long *mathnawi* poem on mystical love, called *The Book of God* (*Ilahi-nama*). The underlying ideas of this work are recast in the more famous and much longer allegory, the *Mantiq at-tair* (*Conference of the Birds*),[15] in which the culmination of a successful pilgrimage, a quest for loving mergence with God—toward *fana'* and *baqa*, toward a passing away of the ego-bound self within the self of God and toward consciousness of one's survival within God—is personified by the hoopoe and his fellow birds, who undertake a long journey to find their king. Thus, thousands of

> Birds of all natures, known or not to Man,
> flocked from all quarters into full Divan,
> on no less solemn business than to find,
> or choose, a Sultan Khalif of their kind,
> for whom, if never theirs, or lost, they pined.[16]

The hoopoe, who asserts that she is a messenger from the Other, leads them—she as the *shaikh pir* and the birds as seeking souls and disciples (*murids*)—scores of them—to undertake what proves to be an extremely arduous journey, through seven valleys, to seek the legendary simurgh bird whom the hoopoe has indicated as their true king.[17]

> [I]f you wish to travel on the Way,
> set out on it now to find the Simurgh, don't prattle and sit
> on your haunches till into stiffening death you stray.
> All the birds who were by this agitation shook,
> aspired to a meeting place to prepare for the Shah,
> to release in themselves the revelations of the Book;
> they yearned so deeply for Him who is both near and far,
> as they were drawn to this sun and burned to an ember;
> but the road was long and perilous that was open to offer.
> Hooked by terror, though each was asked to remember
> the truth, each an excuse to stay behind was keen to proffer.

The hoopoe warns them that it is not sufficient to memorize or recite passages from scripture (the book); theological discussion is just the beginning point of the journey. As each bird must confront his or her own limitations, misguided attachments, and fears along the way, one by one they reveal the degree to which they are held back by earthly interests. Twenty-two of them speak, ask questions regarding the journey, or are described. Thus, for example,

> [t]he nightingale raises his head, drugged with passion,
> pouring oil of earthly love in such a fashion
> that the other birds shaded with his song, grow mute.
> The leaping mysteries of his melodies are acute.
> I know the secrets of Love, I am their piper,
> he sings, I seek a David with broken heart to decipher
> their plaintive barbs, I inspire the yearning flute,
> the daemon of the plucked conversation of the lute.
> The roses are dissolved into fragrance by my song . . .
> . . . I cannot go further, I am lame, and expose
> my anchored soul to the Divine Way.
> My love for the rose is sufficient, I shall stay
> in the vicinity of its petalled image, I need
> no more, it blooms for me the rose, my seed.

The nightingale, symbol here of desire and yearning, is limited by its inability to look beyond the transience of everyday, *profanus*, physical beauty toward the eternal, unchanging, ultimate spiritual beauty buried deep within the *sacer* toward which the hoopoe, in its response to the nightingale, would, as the poet-*shaikh*, lead him and us:

> Escape winter's frost. To seek the Way
> release yourself from this love that lasts a day.
> The bud that nurtures its own demise as day nurtures night.
> Groom yourself, pluck the deadly rose from your sight.

The parrot speaks of his longing for immortality; the duck is content with the shimmering surface of the water through which he habitually paddles. The partridge is focused on gemstones—which, the hoopoe reminds him, are no more than stones that harden the heart, not the real jewel toward which their journey carries them. The sparrow takes too much pride in her humility. (Along the way to the *fana'* of one's ego-bound self into God lies the pitfall of an overly ego-bound humility, which takes such pride in its self-effacement that it becomes obsessed with pride and with the pride of being humble, rather than being focused on God and the goal of oneness with God.) One after the other, the birds describe or exhibit *profanus*-based weaknesses, which the hoopoe addresses, encouraging them to begin what will be a difficult journey.

> So long as we do not die to ourselves,
> and so long as we identify with someone or something,
> we shall never be free.

But, she asserts, they will enjoy happiness if they succeed in withdrawing from attachment to the world, and she encourages them to

> Strive to discover the mystery before life is taken from you.
> If while living you fail to find yourself, to know yourself,
> how will you be able to understand
> the secret of your existence when you die?[18]

The birds finally undertake the journey through the valleys of quest, love, understanding, independence/detachment, unity, astonishment, and poverty/no-thingness. Each has its own trials and complications; each offers up new understanding and clarity to those who survive its transit (the valley of understanding, for example, yields the awareness that *knowledge* is temporary, while true *understanding* endures). The majority of the birds fall away, weaken in their will to reach the goal, give up, turn back. Those who arrive through the valley of unity recognize that the appearance of many beings around us is no more than appearance: Reality is one and complete. We recognize the familiar panhenotheistic mode of thinking expressed in particular by 'Attar's much younger contemporary, Ibn 'Arabi.

Lost in the divine essence, the thirty birds who arrive into pure poverty and no-thing-ness recognize that they are immersed in love and goodness. They have arrived at the beginning of the fulfillment of the early dictum of the hoopoe to the birds that, if they succeed in their journey, they will not have found God but be immersed in God; they will *be* (and yet *not* be, in any ego-bound sense) God, who suffuses them with itself. Within each of their hearts, they recognize the divine image, the shadow of the simurgh who is them-selves—or put otherwise, only God truly exists; all else are shadows emanat-ing from him. Thus, to find God is to find ourselves, for to truly find ourselves *is* to find God. Arrived at their head at the goal of their journey, the hoopoe ejaculates,

> Be it even so:
> let us but see the Fount from which we flow,
> and seeing, lose ourselves therein' and lo!
> before the word was uttered, or the tongue
> of fire replied, or portal open flung,
> they were *within*—they were before the *Throne*,
> before the Majesty that sat thereon,
> but wrapt in so insufferable a Blaze
> of Glory as beat down their baffled Gaze,
> which, downward dropping, fell upon a scroll
> that, Lightning-like, flashed back on each the whole
> past, half forgotten Story of his Soul. . . .
> . . . Once more they ventured from the Dust to raise
> their eyes—up to the Throne—into the Blaze,
> and in the Centre of the Glory there
> beheld the Figure of—*Themselves*—as 'twere
> transfigured—looking to Themselves, beheld
> the Figure on the Throne en-miracled,
> until their Eyes themselves and *That* between
> did hesitate, which *Seer* was, which *Seen*;
> they that, that they: Another, yet the Same;
> dividable, yet One: from whom there came
> a Voice of awesome Answer, scarce discern'd
> from which to Aspiration whose return'd
> they scarcely knew; as when some Man apart
> answers aloud the Question in his heart—
> The Sun of my Perfection is a Glass
> wherein from Seeing into Being pass
> all who, reflecting as reflected see

Themselves in Me, and Me in Them; not *Me*,
but all of Me that a contracted Eye
is comprehensive of Infinity:
nor yet *Themselves*; no Selves, but of The All,
fractions, from which they split and whither fall. . . .
. . . All you have been, and seen, and done, and thought,
not *You* but *I* have seen and been and wrought:
I was the Sin that from Myself rebell'd
I the remorse that tow'rd myself compelled:
I was the Tajidar who led the Track:
I was the little Briar that pull'd you back:
Sin and Contrition—Retribution owed,
and cancell'd—Pilgrim, Pilgrimage, and Road,
was but Myself toward Myself: and Your
arrival but *Myself* at my own Door:
Who in your Fraction of Myself behold
Myself within the Mirror Myself hold
to see Myself in, and each part of Me
that sees himself, though drown'd, shall ever see.[19]

Thus, after their exhausting passage through the seven valleys—and we cannot help but recall the importance of the number seven, not only within the Muslim tradition or within the Abrahamic traditions but also going back deeply into pagan Middle Eastern antiquity, as a symbol of perfection and completion—the birds who have completed their journey finally stand before the glorious throne. (We recognize the imagery of "glory" not merely as an abstract figure of speech but as a fiery concretion found within the verbiage and the imagery of all three Abrahamic traditions.) Expecting that, when their eyes have adjusted to the furious light before them, they will finally see the simurgh, they are shocked, instead, to see the image, unified, of their multiple, composite selves!

Not only is the multiplicity of themselves indistinguishable from the One in the perfect state that they have achieved (and there is an essential pun in the Persian: *si-murgh* means "thirty birds"), but also in journeying such a distance, they have not moved a millimeter; they have become, in becoming one with—in recognizing perfectly their oneness with—the simurgh (God), like the perfectly spinning top that, in its perfect equilibrium, appears not to move at all, like the perfectly tuned string that maintains its pitch by constant tension while apparently at rest.

Thus, as in the earlier theorists in the Muslim mystical tradition, *fana'* means that the seeker and the sought have become one, that lover, beloved, and the love that binds them are one (the God who punishes the sinner feels

empathy—is one with—the sinner and rejoices in forgiveness), that the outward journey turns out to have been an inward journey—which, in any case,
must be so, if one has entered into the depths of the spaceless space of the
sacer. To seek God through *ek-stasis* is—if we are to *find* God—to seek God
through *en-stasis*. The glory and the beauty, as well as the danger, are all
there: Each of us, each of our souls, it turns out, *is* God. The glory, the beauty,
is that God is *there* and so accessible; the danger is that one mistakes the nature of the path, confuses the understanding and the fact of God's being
within ourselves as a cause for pride in *self*. And to the narrow-minded adherent to orthodoxy, the end of the journey as expressed in the poem would
be misunderstood as just that: a heretical assertion of splintering the One into
multiple parts and of confusing God with one's self. It should be no surprise
that 'Attar was—or is said to have been—tried and condemned as a heretic.

Perhaps the most significant Sufi poet after 'Attar in this golden era of Persian poetry was his younger contemporary, Abu Muhammad Ilyas ibn Yusuf
ibn Zaki Mu'ayyad, known by his pen name, Nizami—or sometimes Nizami
Ganjavi, since he was born, lived, and died in the northern Persian (now Azerbaijani) town of Ganja. Nizami (1141–1209) lost both his parents at an early
age and was raised by an uncle; in turn, he was married three times, losing
each of his wives to death. Very little is known beyond these data about the
course of his life—even the extant manuscripts of his poems date from well
beyond his own lifetime—but, at a time when the western Persian-language
poetic style—the "Azerbaijani" style, marked among other things by an in-
novative use of metaphor and technical terminology, as well as Christian imagery—was emerging into prominence, he towered above his contemporaries. Nizami became known both for a small corpus of lyric poetry (many
poems shaped as laments for the death of each of his wives)—he was arguably the supreme exponent of lyrical laments in the Persian language—and
for five long, narrative poems (the totality called *Khamsa*, the Arabic word
for "five"). As a scholar (he is often referred to as *al-Hakim*, "the Wise"), he
was particularly known, in fact, for the highly intellectual treatise entitled
Makhzan al-asrar (*Treasury of Secrets*), written in poetic form, that comprises the first section of his *Khamsa*.[20]

Nizami's poetic interests were, as it were, broader than those of Sana'i and
'Attar, who were both so entirely focused on mystical themes. Yet, his psalm-
like poems dedicated to God, generally written in *mathnawi* form, are particularly effective. Thus, for instance,

> "*In God's Name, the Kind, the Pitying*":
> This key unlocks the Treasury of the King.
> With God all Thoughts arise, all Words descend;

Then let His Name thy Recitation end. . . .
. . . He brings to naught what heedless Men design,
But spares their Sins who unto him repine:
He stills the Clamor of the fearful Heart
And, to the knowing, Counsel doth impart.
First He and Last, in All that is and lives,
Naught His Being, and to Nothing Being gives:
Before His Might the two Worlds sink to death,
The sum of all our days is but a breath. . . .
Nizami's Clay, that by His feet is trod,
A furrow is, where grows the Seed of God.[21]

The poet begins with an acknowledgment of the all-encompassing importance of that renowned beginning line—the *bismillah*—that requisite declaration for believers that initiates every prayer, every statement, every enterprise.
From this, he elaborates the myriad aspects of the aspectless God—by way of
God's name, extracted as a phrase from the *bismillah* declaration, but in the
Sufi context a reminder that through God's name one may access God because God and God's name are one and the same (and yet not) and because,
as in Ibn 'Arabi's exposition, that name, offered to us by way of many and diverse *names*, is not offered in hierarchy (thus there is no lower starting point
from which one reaches upward). "His Fingers," "His Hand," how "He
clothes" the world, how "He threads," "He lights," and "He marks"—all are
delineated before the poet turns, by comparison, to how limited humans are
without God's limitless assistance and how God can easily bring to naught
what humans do, particularly if and when they imagine themselves to be more
than severely limited in their abilities.

Only God can create out of nothing and reduce anything to nothing in an
eyeblink. Before God's might, both the outer world of appearances and the
inner world of contemplation sink to death: but the first is an uncomfortable death; the second can become the death of sinking into God and thus
into the eternal *sacer* life. The last two lines reflect Nizami's connection to
the history of lyric poetry, as far back at least as the Roman lyric poets,
who, as he does here, often embed themselves in the words of their poems
as a means both of signature and of subsuming the subjective into the objective. The poet's poetry is the clay that only yields the plants that are his
poems if and when God inspires him sufficiently. God is the seed without
which clay remains clay and no amount of anything will produce anything
but mud.

About two years before the death of Nizami, Jalal ad-Din Rumi was born.
Destined to be the eponymous founder of the Sufi *Mevleviya Tariqa*, as we
have seen, Rumi would also, by means of his extensive *Mathnawi* (often

presenting the rhyming couplet form of *mathnawi* within the quatrain form of the *ruba'iya*) offer in Persian verse form the equivalent of what Ibn 'Arabi articulates in Arabic prose form: a complete summary of Sufi doctrines as they have been shaped by the mid-thirteenth century.[22] In the couplet quoted above (p. 168) he sees himself as the third great Sufi poet after Sana'i and 'Attar. Rumi enjoins the reader, at the outset of the *Mathnawi*, to

> Hearken to this Reed forlorn,
> Breathing, ever since it was torn
> From its bed of rushes, a strain
> Of impassioned love and pain.
>
> The secret of my poem, though near,
> None can see and none can hear.
> Oh, for a friend to know the sign
> And mingle all his soul with mine!
>
> It is the flame of Love that has fired me,
> It is the wine of Love that has inspired me!
> Would you learn how lovers bleed,
> Hearken, hearken to my Reed!

One recognizes the image of the reed pipe, frequently used by Rumi both as a symbol of his poetry and as a symbol of the purpose of his poetry: to cry out to God—and indeed the reed is typically, in his work, a "reed forlorn" both as statement of humility (that his poetry is but a trifle) and as a statement of desperate sadness unless and until he succeeds in accessing God by means of the reed. The reed as his poetry therefore has a double audience: God itself, whose "attention" he hopes to attract with his poetry, however meager, modest, and forlorn, and those who would follow his lead in seeking to access the hiddenmost depths of God.

Thus, one also recognizes that the references to love in the third stanza are references to love of God; the poet is thus the bleeding lover who seeks to staunch the flow of his blood by achieving union with God the beloved, and the pouring out of his words is the pouring out of his blood—which is the pouring out of his soul and thus of his life, which flow will stop only when he has achieved the union that makes words both useless and impossible (because words are a *profanus* instrument by definition impossible within the *sacer*, and the more so within the *mysterion* within the *sacer*). The blood/words will flow both to attract God and to exemplify for the poet's audience how one must bleed in order to attract God. So, too, the poem is *itself* God in being entirely inspired by God, created through the poet's enflamed love for God and, as in the opening of the second stanza, its secret hidden although near. For God is hidden, His secrets inaccessible, yet they are, as God is, nearer than our own breathing. Uncovering them, however, is a task that sight and sound cannot ultimately facilitate, since such secrets—*mysteria*—are beyond the realm of sight and sound.

The allusion to a friend whose soul would be mingled with that of the poet suggests Rumi's awareness of imagery that goes back, in Arabic-language poetry, to its pre-Islamic and prewritten forms: The beloved, who is a woman, is spoken of as if she were a boy, following a pattern of circumlocution that carries still further back, to the Greeks and their concept of the *erastes* ("lover") and *eromenos* ("beloved"), both conceived of, on an intellectual and spiritual plain, as male.[23] In the spiritual poetic tradition that moves lyrical love poetry toward a psalmist's focus on God, the *eromenos* is God Itself (*Him*self), who, in the poet's wish, will mingle His soul with that of the poet. It is this tradition of layered allegory as well, then, that Rumi carries into Persian poetry. At the same time, the conviction and passion with which he writes can also be tied to his personal life: When Shams disappeared, and rumor had it that he had gone to Damascus, Rumi sent his older son there to find him. Tradition asserts that, united again, the two friends fell at each others' feet, and "nobody knew who was the lover and who the beloved." Shams stayed in Rumi's home and married a young girl who had been raised within Rumi's family.

As the intense discussions (*sohbet*) between the two began again, one can easily enough imagine the jealousies of others also reemerging. On the evening of December 5, 1248, as Rumi and Shams were in conversation, Shams was called to the back door. He went out of the house and was never seen again. Consensus is that he was murdered—in part (presumably out of jealousy) through the efforts of Rumi's younger son, Aladdin. Rumi himself went searching for his friend as far as Damascus. It was on that road—how marvelously coincidental with the experience of Saul (Paul) of Tarsus more than a millennium earlier on a different road from a different direction to the same place—that he was struck by the realization that

> I am the same as He.
> His essence speaks through me.
> I have been looking for myself!

In this statement we recognize a version of the conclusion arrived at by the thirty birds in 'Attar's poem, who arrived at the palace of the simurgh whom they recognized to be themselves.

So the allegorical and the actual merge. The love driven in the *profanus* and the love driven in the *sacer* are intertwined aspects of each other: *Fana'* in one realm can lead to an ability to achieve *fana'* in the other. The poet dedicated the first body of his odes and quatrains to Shams, calling them, in fact, *The Works of Shams of Tabriz*. He addressed the next body of work to the gold-smith, Salah ad-din Zarkub, who functioned as his second amanuensis. With Salah ad-din's death, Rumi's favorite student, Husam Chelebi, assumed that role and, as Rumi's secretary, wrote down the last six volumes of the great *Mathnawi*. Lover and beloved are one in the words that repeatedly seek to ar-ticulate that oneness, achieved ultimately in the God who is the ultimate lover and beloved. The sense of turning to an allegorical means of describing the indescribable (that is, however, *real*) and achieving unity with the One, in Rumi's life, carries back and forth between his poetry and the *dhikr* that is unique to his *tariqa*, the whirling *darvishes* are also allegories: physical alle-gories of the lover swirling around the beloved and microcosms (as we have earlier discussed) of the whirling planets and spheres. We might also see them in this way as an activated three-dimensionalization of the whirling of the *sephirot* within Zoharic Kabbalah.[24]

Indeed, Rumi's poetry also finds a frequent usefulness for the idea of spin-ning, of rotation, not only of planets and spheres but also of objects that may be seen as the smaller and more everyday counterparts of these celestial ele-ments, such as the millstone and the mill wheel. Thus, the poet asserts to his *eromenos*,

> Your mountain of the sun
> I'll fashion to a mill,
> And as my waters run,
> I'll turn you at my will.

And again, paradox: The true *eromenos* is God, whom one can never expect to turn at one's will—except and until God responds to one's pattern of seek-ing union with God. Then God becomes the *erastes* (who always *was* the *erastes*, for God has always wished us to turn to God!); then lover, beloved, and love—*mahabba* (to return to Arabic-language terminology)—can no longer be distinguished from each other, and therefore the will of the one is the same as the will of the other. Therefore, God will be turned at the poet's will, who is turned at God's will—because the two won't be separate wills or turns but one and the same. This union *can* happen; God *can* and *will* be our beloved when we truly pursue God as a lover pursues the prefect, ideal beloved, for

> [w]hen you are a lover, you want your beloved also a lover to be.
> God is humanity's greatest lover, and His beloved,
> who must become his lovers, are we.

In the vast sea of Rumi's *Mathnawi*, diverse aphoristic comments and varied allegorical images repeat and reappear, interweave, and move along their own paths. His images are exquisite:

> I sought a soul in the sea,
> and found a coral there;
> beneath the foam for me
> an ocean was all laid bare.

The vastness of God is incomparable and, yet, ever-expanding before him; the infinitesimal coral of himself, of his own soul, is locatable (because the infinitesimally small coral and the infinitesimally large sea are one and the same). As charming as his allegories are, he references the *limitations* of allegory, particularly when they are intended to capture what humans are, or even more, what God is. All allegories will serve, and none can ultimately serve well enough; a sea of words will serve, but no number of seas will ultimately be enough to express what is ineffable. So silence is the better course, which he recognizes even as he continues to pour out seas of words.

> Men have argued (but they lied)
> that this image does not bide;
> one declared we are a tree,
> said another, grass are we.
>
> Yet the rustling of this bough
> proves the breeze is stirring now;
> silent then, O silent be:
> that we are, and this are we.

The beginning of the process of finding God is silence vis-à-vis everyday reality. The beginning of the process is to recognize that focus on our own reality is foolhardy; it prevents us from making that pursuit, for which a prerequisite is to recognize that the pursuable God is *there*, is *real*, but will not be found in our false reality: "There are two worlds. There is the outer world which appears to exist, and seems solid and permanent, but in truth is an illusion. And there is the inner world which many people deny, and is invisible to the senses, and yet is real and eternal." And that second world is the *sacer* realm in which God awaits us.

It is a realm accessible to *all* humans—and not only to Muslims. It is this last aspect of Rumi's thought and his poetry that is perhaps most extraordinary: He shares with Abulafia in the Jewish mystical tradition the distinction of suggesting that—in spite of the orthodox notions that insist that there is only one *tariqa*, one *shari'a*, one *halakhah*, one correct path to connection with God, and in the Jewish and Muslim traditions, with varying intensity, the conviction that that path may be taken with only one language as one's guide—God is available and accessible to *all* who seek God. In the most full-fledged of panhenotheistic senses, the poet identifies with all of humanity as the beloved of God, with all of time and space as the source from which God emanates and to which God extends:

> Not Christian or Jew or Muslim, not Hindu,
> Buddhist, Sufi, or Zen. Not any religion
>
> or cultural system. I am not from the East
> or the West, not out of the ocean or up
>
> from the ground, not natural or ethereal, not
> composed of elements at all. I do not exist,
>
> am not an entity in this world or the next,
> did not descend from Adam and Eve or any
>
> origin story. My place is placeless, a trace
> of the traceless. Neither body nor soul.
>
> I belong to the Beloved, have seen the two
> worlds as one and that one call to and know,
>
> first, last, outer, inner, only that
> breath-breathing human being.

This is the poet speaking as it if were God, who transcends all worlds, speaking within the poet. Lover and beloved (to repeat) are one in the words that repeatedly seek to articulate that oneness, achieved ultimately in the God who is both the ultimate lover and the ultimate beloved—and the ultimate source of love.

⁘⊗⁙

Love and its concomitants as a motif within Sufi poetry carry forward into the following centuries and beyond the borders of the Arabo-Persian world, with the spread of Islam and the Sufi *tariqas* to the east. One of the most important of the Persian mystical poets whose writing had a profound influence on religious thought in India in the fourteenth and fifteenth centuries was Khwaja Shams-ud-Din Muhammad Hafiz-e Shirazi, known better simply by his pen name, Hafiz (1310/25–1388/89). *Hafiz* is actually an honorific title gained by the poet in his youth that refers to his having memorized the entirety of the Qur'an. Hafiz was thus recognized early on as a scholar. He memorized the Qur'an by listening to recitations by his father, a coal merchant; he also memorized large portions of poetry by Nizami and Rumi, among others. Beyond these few details, little is actually known about the poet's life. He was born in Isfahan in central Persia, but his father moved the family to Shiraz when Hafiz was still a young child; he lost his father soon thereafter and was raised by an uncle. While becoming learned, he worked as a copyist, in a drapery shop, and then as a baker's assistant, before acquiring the sort of patronage—he became a poet in the court of Abu Ishak—that enabled him to study and write full-time; later, he became a professor of religious studies. He himself never took the time to edit or organize his work for publication; that was left to a friend, Muhammad Gulandam, to accomplish after the poet's death (the organization was completed around 1410). In his one-volume compendium of Hafiz's work, Gulandam speaks of the poet's genius, compassion, and diligence as a student of Islamic thought.

Among the intriguing aspects of Hafiz's unknown life, as it filters into his poetry, is the question of his having been married and produced children— one of his poems seems to refer to the death of his wife and another to the death of a son. If he did, we do not know whether the woman to whom he refers as *Shak-i-Nabat* ("Branch of Sugar Cane") is the woman he married or the never-attained object of his love, whom he apparently never ceased to love even after he married. *Shak-i-Nabat* is, in any case, in his work a symbol of perfect spiritual love. Hafiz preferred the *ghazal* as a poetic form, unlike his heroes who, as we have seen, tended toward *ruba'iyat* and *mathnawi*. The *ghazal* is typically eight to fourteen lines long, and by the time of Hafiz, it had also become usual for the poet's name to appear in the last line.[25] Each "line" may be seen as complete by itself (and may be long enough to be rendered as a couplet or even a four-line stanza), even as each partakes of a coherent, larger whole. The rhythmic patterns are prescribed and are determined based on the meaning of the words: Form and content meet. The subject of a *ghazal* is usually love, be it romantic or mystical.

One of Hafiz's favorite image mixtures is love and wine; to be intoxicated with one is a trope for being intoxicated with the other—which in any case is a trope for being intoxicated with love for God, or being intoxicated with God, or both. One thinks of the "intoxicated Sufis" of an earlier generation, so "drunk" with the achievement of love union with God that they lose themselves entirely and speak as one with God. Wine may be a stand-in for love, or wine and love may be discussed "side by side." Thus, in *Ghazal* 34,[26] we read,

> Come, let us pass this pathway o'er
> That which to the tavern leads;
> There waits the wine, and there the door
> That every traveler needs.
>
> On that first day, when we did sweat
> To tipple and to kiss,
> It was our oath that we would fare
> No other way but this.

To tipple and to kiss are, as it were, one and the same. The tavern to which the poet would draw his auditor—the object of his desire—is love itself. There awaits the wine of love to which (by oath) the lover and beloved have sworn themselves. And a few lines later, the *ghazal* continues,

> Preacher, our frenzy is complete:
> Waste not thy sage advice;
> We stand in the Beloved's street,
> And seek not Paradise.

> Let Sufis wheel in mystic dance
> And shout for ecstasy;
> We, too, have dour exuberance.
> We, too, ecstatics be.

> The earth with pearls and rubies gleams
> Where thou hast poured thy wine;
> Less than the dust are we, it seems,
> Beneath thy foot divine.

> Hafiz, since we may never soar,
> To ramparts of the sky,
> Here at the threshold of this door
> Forever let us lie.

The frenzy of intoxication with wine and love is the frenzy of intoxication with God: Having achieved oneness with the One, there is no need to seek paradise, since paradise is both the goal and the achievement of that ecstatic union. The achievers of that state are at one and the same time—like whirling Mevlevi *darvishes*—within the above and within the below, connected to heaven and to earth. They are both beyond the need for conventional paradise and less then dust beneath the divine foot. The divine foot is the foot of the beloved. The poet addresses himself, ground beneath that foot, as content; he sits at the door "that every traveler needs"—in humility, he never soars, content to lie at the threshold, because the threshold and the door are one with the tavern that is beloved and love itself, that are the ramparts of the sky of union with God. He is not *there* because *there*—beyond *here*—is merely a full recognition of how *there* is *within* himself; how *here* and *there*, like lover and beloved and love, are one.

Again the poet writes about satisfying his love thirst in *Ghazal* 38, which begins,

> I cease not from desire till my desire
> Is satisfied; or let my mouth attain
> My love's red mouth, or let my soul expire,

Sighed from those lips that sought her lips in vain.
Others may find another love as fair;
Upon her threshold I have laid my head
The dust shall cover me, still lying there,
When from my body life and love have fled.[27]

Here the satisfaction of love is the expiring of the soul and the dissipation of the body: To love is to die—and be reborn as someone other than who and what the lover was before love transformed him. Love is subjective; others may find another whom they think is as fair or is even fairer than the poet's beloved, but he is content to lie in the dust at her feet until his body is covered in dust and reduced to dust. All of this is a metaphor for seeking not only his earthbound beloved but also that for which she, in her perfection, is a symbol: God itself. *Fana'* within God and the complete dissolution of the physical self and its *profanus* concerns is the soul expiration for which the mystical lover hopes.

Moreover, Hafiz interweaves various aspects of his outer life with his inner spiritual aspirations. Thus, in the aftermath of the overrunning of his beloved city of Shiraz by the Turco-Mongol conqueror Tamerlane (a.k.a. Timur), the poet writes, in part,

Sweet maid, if thou wouldst charm my sight,
And bid those arms my neck enfold,
That rosy cheek, that lily hand,
Would give thy poet more delight
Than all Bokhara's vaunted gold,
Than all the gems of Samarkand.

Boy, let yon liquid ruby flow,
And bid the pensive heart be glad,
Whate'er the frowning zealots say;
Tell them their Eden cannot show
A stream so clear as Rukhabad,
A bower so sweet as Moscalla.

Oh! When these fair, perfidious maids,
Whose eyes our secret haunts infest,
Their dear destructive charms display,
Each glance my tender breast invades,
And robs my wounded soul of rest,
As Tartars seize their destined prey.

In vain with love our bosoms glow;
Can all our tears, can all our sighs
New luster to those charms impart?—

> Can cheeks where living roses blow,
> Where nature spreads her richest dyes,
> Require the borrowed gloss of art?
>
> Speak not of fate—ah! Change the theme,
> And talk of odors, talk of wine;
> Talk of the flowers that around us bloom;
> 'Tis a cloud, 'tis all a dream;
> To love and joy thy thoughts confine,
> Nor hope to pierce the sacred gloom.[28]

The entire poem may be taken as a metaphor, with the lover to whom the poet addresses it representing wisdom, as is the case in the *Diwan* on the *Fideli d'amore* of Ibn 'Arabi, wherein the allusion to the young Nizami is an allusion to "a sublime and divine, essential and sacrosanct Wisdom, which manifested itself visibly to the author of these poems with such sweetness as to provoke in him joy and happiness, emotion and delight."[29] It is this religion of *sophia* ("wisdom") that yields "more delight than all Bokhara's vaunted gold, than all the gems of Samarkand," which bids the pensive heart be glad, "whate'er the frowning zealots say." Those members of coldly rational, supercilious orthodoxy are pursuing wisdom by means of a false path—and ultimately pursuing wisdom that is itself false or at least severely limited.

The deeper wisdom sought by the mystic will not be gained through uninspired, everyday ritual and a Qur'anic focus that is too mind-bound but too heartless. Wine (again), which is synonymous with love—love is the wine of life, a draught that never fails and yet never satisfies, but still leads to the highest bliss if it is properly consumed—together with beauty of the purest metaphysical, spiritual sort, leads to the experience of God and union with the One. For the "sweet maid" to whom the words are directed at the outset is God itself, as the swooning bard courts God with praise and flattery in order to be within him. In this particular *ghazal*, the "sweet maid" may also be understood as a metaphor for the poet's beloved city of Shiraz, to which he speaks as to a coquettish woman; this is the city wherein he was born and wherein he found the mystical inspiration for his poetry. This layer of allusion is first clearly suggested in the end of the third strophe, where he refers to the Tatars "seiz[ing] their destined prey"—a rare reference to the most significant of the bloody dramas enacted through the course of his lifetime in Shiraz—the time in 1388 when Tamerlane conquered the city and an orgy of slaughter followed.

Such an ugly historical moment would serve only to further underscore the necessity of looking beyond the *profanus* for genuine happiness and satisfaction (*rida*), as well as to further validate a mystical methodology for finding satisfaction. The two strophes that follow continue the imagery of the third strophe, as the poet mourns the crushed petals of Shiraz but again takes refuge in the power of God to bring his fervent lovers to a paradise that is realer than the horrid illusion of the earthly situation. He dares to question momentarily the fate of the city and of himself but, in the end, resigns himself—to the God who determines the fate of the city and who is the beloved who determines the fate of the lover—and concludes,

> What cruel answer have I heard!
> And yet, by heaven, I love thee still:
> Can aught be cruel from thy lip?
> From lips which streams of sweetness fill,
> Which naught but drops of honey sip?
>
> Go boldly forth, my simple lay,
> Whose accents flow with artless ease,
> Like Oriental pearls at random strung;
> Thy notes are sweet, the damsels say,
> And oh! Far sweeter, if they please
> The nymph for whom these notes are sung.

The poet speaks to that God who is the nymph. That nymph is the beloved whom the poet hopes to please, who inspires the words and thus makes them sweet. Should those words be pleasing to God, they will thereby be rendered sweeter still.

Thus, we recognize in the love poetry of Hafiz an obvious parallel to the poetry of Christian mystics such as St. Catherine of Siena and St. Teresa of Avila. One also recognizes a parallel to the poetry of the Hebrew Bible's Song of Songs, which is typically interpreted as an allegory of the love relationship between God and Israel. The two most obvious differences are, first, that in the case of Christian mystics—who in my two examples here are women—the imagery of the beloved is straightforwardly masculine, reflecting both the maleness of God as Jesus and the femaleness of the mystic; and, second, that in the Christian context the imagery is more intensely sexual/physical, as compared with the more romantic imagery of Hafiz and his fellow Sufi poets, who in any case direct themselves as males toward feminine imagery.[30] Conversely, the worldly context and reference point for Hafiz is the immediate outer world around him, since, as a noncelibate Sufi, he *dwells* fully within the world around him, whereas the reference point for his Christian counterparts is necessarily a different, hermetic one. Dwelling within the confines of the monastery, wars and their destruction are less likely to provide a layer to the layered allegories leading them toward God.

Love, in both the earthbound and heavenward senses, defined the teachings of Nur ud-Din Abd ur-Rahman (1414–1492), better known as Jami. So-called because he was born in a village near Jam—some twenty-five years after the death of Hafiz—Jami was one of the last of the great Persian mystical poets. His family moved to Herat when he was still a child, and there he would study a range of subjects at the university, eventually moving to Samarqand to complete his scientific studies in what was then the center of the Islamic world for such matters. Eventually, Jami became a Sufi, part of the *Naqshbandiyya Tariqa*, and asserted that love is the fundamental stepping stone for starting on a spiritual journey. To a student claiming never to have been in love, he proclaimed, "Go and love first, then come to me and I will show you the way (*tariqa*)."[31] Like Hafiz, he frequently interweaves love imagery with that of wine, and his themes tend both toward women and young boys. We recognize in this the intention to think in a manner that contradicts the overly narrowly conceived orthodox "norm." The invocation of wine not only suggests a link back to the "intoxicated" Sufis but also, more fundamentally, flies in the face of orthodox gastronomic prohibitions.[32] Thus, treating the consumption of wine as a positive act would appear, to a noninitiate, as objectionable as declaring "I am God" appears heretical. But one who understands his language would recognize that the point of such an image is to force the reader/devotee out of the box of ordinary thinking, to "let go," and thus to transcend *profanus* thinking and *profanus* reality. It is both that the imagery of intoxication, which is the imagery of letting go, and intoxicated dissipation is dissipation into God, that using such an image forces the reader/devotee out of thinking according to convention.

In the same way, the love of boys is a "forbidden" theme. But, "one of the central and fundamental conceptions in his mystical doctrine is that of the Absolute as the Eternal Beauty."[33] The purpose of creation, in Jami's expositions, is to manifest the beauty of God, and the passion for beauty is therefore a means to link the soul to God. In this, we recognize a frame of mind that can be traced back to the Greeks and specifically to Socrates, whose interest in beautiful young boys (of whom Alcibiades was the most notorious) was predicated on his assumption that their beauty ultimately reflected the internal, intellectual, and spiritual beauty that was the true object of his passionate interest.[34] Thus, Jami's focus on the love for and beauty of boys is not to be seen in surface terms. His impassioned description of visual, physical beauty exists both because that visual, physical beauty is a manifestation of the invisible, nonphysical God and because it is (nonetheless, merely) a doorway to the invisible, spiritual beauty that more obviously and directly connects us to God.

Jami wrote nearly ninety books and letters, ranging from prose to poetry and from the everyday to the spiritual, in the latter of which he asserted inspiration from Nizami as well as Hafiz. Among Jami's works, the most famous is a long epic poem, *Yusuf and Zulaika*, considered by many to be "the finest poem in the Persian language."[35] The poem, based on the biblical tale of Joseph and the wife of his Egyptian master, Potiphar, presents the former as a symbol of divine perfection and the latter as a demonstration of how the soul attains the love for the highest beauty and goodness only when it has suffered and been purified and regenerated. In his poem, Jami incorporates the allegorical elements he writes about elsewhere, both in passages that tell the story and in those that are non-narrative. He writes,

> No heart is that which love never wounded: they
> Who know not lovers' pangs are soulless clay.
> Turn from the world, O turn thy wandering feet;
> Come to the world of love and find it sweet.
> Heaven's giddy round from craze of love was caught;
> From love's disputes the world with strife is fraught.
> Love's slave be thou if thou would fain be free:
> Welcome love's pangs, and happy thou shallt be.
> From wine of love came joy and generous heat:
> From meaner cups flow sorrow and deceit.
> Love's sweet, soft memories youth itself restore:
> The tale of love gives fame forevermore. . . .
> The groves are gay with many a lovely bird:
> Our lips unsilent and their praise unheard;
> But when the theme is love's delicious take,
> The moth is lauded, and the nightingale.
> What though a hundred arts to thee be known:
> Freedom from self is gained through love alone.
> To worldly love thy youthful thoughts incline,
> For earthly love will lead to love divine.
> First with the alphabet thy task begin,
> Then take the Word of God and read therein.
> Once to his master a disciple cried:
> "To wisdom's pleasant path be thou my guide."
> "Hast thou ne'er loved?" the master answered; "learn
> The ways of love and then to me return."
> Drink deep of earthly love, that so thy lip
> may learn the wine of holier love to sip.
> But let not *form* too long thy soul entrance;
> Pass o'er the bridge: with rapid feet advance.[36]

Love and wine are analogues; earthly love—not scholarship or ascetic meditation—is a prerequisite to the ultimate wisdom that is the analogue of divine love. "The Gnostic is not the one who commits to memory from the

Qur'an and if he forgets what he has learned, relapses into ignorance. He only is the Gnostic who takes his knowledge from the Lord at any time, without committing it to memory or studying, and this knowledge lasts for a lifetime . . . he is the true spiritual Gnostic."[37] Jami's opening lines make it clear that only through love can we understand life and begin the search for oneness with the One.

More than that, only love's chains bring true freedom; only the occasional pain of passion can bring true pleasure and happiness. Enslavement to love is, in leading to freedom from one's self, freedom from all the issues and concerns of the temporal world; the realm of freedom is the realm of divine love. Only through love can that aspect of "self" conveyed by renown and the immortality of renown as it is inscribed in the pages of time be achieved. Love is the alphabet of divine (and thus everlasting) life, with which alphabet the word of God may be perceived.

These are the words of *wordlessness*, expressing the realm beyond words to which the bridge is temporal love. Without the bridge, one cannot cross, but equally to be avoided is the mistake of forgetting that the bridge is no more than a bridge: One is enjoined not to confuse it with the other realm itself. For ultimately, pure love is love for God, albeit expressed through love for earthly beings. Jami seems to place a heavier weight, a more solid significance, on earthly love than does Hafiz. Also, whereas Hafiz directs his words to the double—earthly and divine—beloved (who is also the lover), Jami writes as an editorial narrator even when he is not, per se, narrating. He also wrote a masterful theosophical treatise on Sufism called *Lawa'ih*.[38] This means *Flashes of Light*, and essentially, it is an attempt to explain and systematize the Sufi concept of the inner light, the intuitive experiences considered to be the basis for true *gnosis*—that is, not orthodoxy's understanding of religious wisdom as coming from without, after a strict course of prescribed study, but something that emerges through *en-stasis* from within one's own God-connected self.

⸙

Ultimately, all of these concepts expressed and motifs used by the Sufi poets are discussed in a small treatise, the *Risala-i Mishwaq*, written by Muhsin Faid Kashani in the seventeenth century with the intention of defending the Sufi poets from criticisms and attacks by the mainstream, orthodox leadership. Kashani offers a systematic and very specific discussion of poetic Sufi—primarily Persian-language—vocabulary, particularly as it is used in the imagery of the beloved's physiognomy. Thus, for example, he explains that *rukh* ("face" or "cheek") symbolizes the revelation of divine beauty expressed in particular graceful attributes, such as gracious, merciful, life-giving, guiding, bountiful, and light-filled, as well as absolutely real. *Zulf* ("flowing hair") symbolizes the revelation of divine majesty as expressed in powerful attributes, such as omnipotent, withholding, death-dealing, and dark—as well as refering to the veils that conceal absolute reality. *Khal* (the "mole" on the cheek) symbolizes the hidden (therefore black) point of absolute unity. *Khatt* (the "down" on the cheek) symbolizes the manifestation of reality in spiritual forms. *Chashm* ("eye") symbolizes God's constant action of watching his servants. The beloved's glance (*ghamza*) symbolizes God's granting spiritual repose after the anguished struggle of the mystic to gain God's attention—or the anguish that returns after the moment of peaceful repose. When the eye is *mast* ("intoxicated") or *bimar* ("languishing"), God is being spoken of as having no need of humankind and ignoring us. So, *abru* ("eyebrow") is a broad symbolic reference to the totality of God's attributes, veiling his essence. *Lab* ("lip") refers to God's life-giving and -maintaining capacity. The beloved's mouth (*dahan*) is described as narrow (*tang*) in order to suggest that the source of our being—the God who is Being itself—is invisible.

So, too, other key motifs are described by Kashani. *Sharab* ("wine") symbolizes the ecstatic experience occasioned by experiencing the revelation of the true beloved (God), which experience smashes the foundations of reason. The wine bearer (*saqi*) is absolute reality (God) manifesting itself in all the forms of nature. So the cup (*jam*) is the revelation of divine acts; the pitcher (*sabu*) and the jar (*khum*) symbolize the revelations of the divine unnamable names and inestimable qualities. The tavern (*kharabat*) symbolizes pure, undifferentiated unity, and the one who goes from tavern to tavern (the "tavern haunter," or *kharabati*) is the true lover, the one who recognizes how all that we see and do and know within our temporal reality is ultimately obliterated by the reality of God (the true beloved). Beyond these images are yet others. Among these, the sea (*bahr*) and the ocean (*qulzum*) symbolize the revelation of divine essence. Most interestingly, given the far narrower viewpoint of orthodoxy—on all sides of the Abrahamic fence—is the term *tarsa'i*, translatable as both "God-fearing" and also as "Christianity." The underlying meaning of the term is "deliverance from the customs and habits derived from the bondage associated with *taqlid*—traditional belief," which Kashani viewed as hypocritical. And the perfect guide is denoted by the phrase *tarsa-bachcha*, which may be translated as "Christian child or son."[39]

So one hears the echoes of Rumi's universalistic sentiments in the last pair of verbal images expounded by Kashani. By his time, the golden age of Sufi philosophy and poetry had passed, although important voices have continued to be heard here and there in the centuries since. The eighteenth-century Sufi al-Badr al-Hijazi would lament the degeneration of Sufi poetry and the excessive proliferation of *marabouts*—saints and their tombs, venerated, it seemed to al-Badr, everywhere, without distinction between the real *auliya* and those falsely imagined to be *auliya* by limited and foolish acolytes:

For they have forgotten God, saying,
"So-and-so provides deliverance from suffering for all mankind."
When he dies, they make him the object of pilgrimage, and hasten to his shrine,
Arabs and foreigners alike:
Some kiss his grave, and some the threshold of his door, and the dust—
Just so do infidels behave toward their idols, seeking thus to win their favor.
And that is due to blindness of vision: woe to the
man whose heart God has blinded![40]

The problematic of saints, particularly for Islam and Judaism,[41] will occupy increasing space in the mystical legacy of the last several centuries. But by then, the changes in the world from West to East will have affected patterns of development in various positive and negative ways—from greater hostility toward mystical thought on the one hand to increased interest in, and influence and counterinfluence from, such thought on the other—in and among all three Abrahamic traditions, as we shall see in the chapters that follow.

NOTES

1. See above, p. 90. *Murid* is Arabic, and *shagird* is Persian; the word that I am rendering as "director" is *shaikh* in Arabic and *pir* in Persian; it is more or less the equivalent of the well-known Sanskrit term *guru*.

2. The *ribat/khanqah* harbored ascetics, not celibates. Most Sufi masters were/are married—asserting that Muhammad himself (who was married, of course) proscribed celibacy (*rhabaniya*)—and in this feature they stand on common ground with Jewish mystics and on very different ground from Christian saints and mystics (for nearly all of whom celibacy is a given), although their organization as orders invites obvious comparison with Christian monastic orders.

3. We are reminded that the cloak is made of wool and that the term *Sufi* is arguably derived from the Arabic word for *wool—suf*—that marked the early mystical ascetics of whom these communities are the spiritual descendants.

4. This is the Crusade associated with St. Louis (Louis IX).

5. The phrases in brackets are those of subsequent commentators.

6. That is, God.

7. The Hittites (ca. 1500 BCE) called the city Kuwanna, the Phrygians (ca. 800 BCE) called it Kowania, the Greeks (ca. 600 BCE) called it Ikonion, which the Romans Latinized as Iconium, and eventually the Turks called it Karamanli and then Konya. As the capital of the Seljuks of Rum (Roman Anatolia) from 1071 through 1243, it was also called Rum.

8. He recorded this in his *Manners and Customs of the Modern Egyptians* (London: John Murray, 1836), 172–74.

9. I am not changing any of Lane's transliterated spellings to conform to those that I have been using.

10. "When Hindus go to a temple, they do not commonly say, 'I am going to worship,' but rather, 'I am going for *darshan*.' They go to 'see' the image of the deity. . . . The central act of Hindu worship, from the point of view of the lay person, is to stand in the presence of the deity and to behold the image with one's own eyes, to see and be seen by the deity. . . . In the Hindu tradition, however, there had never been the confusion of 'image' with 'idol.'" The images are parallel to icons in the Orthodox Christian tradition: revered windows through which we connect to the *sacer*, not manifestations of the *sacer* to be worshipped by us. See the superb discussion of this in Diana L. Eck, *Darshan: Seeing the Divine Image in India* (Chambersburg, PA: Anima Books, 1981); these quotes come from Eck, *Darshan*, 3–4.

11. We have no birth date for him, but he is believed to have died in extreme old age shortly after completing his *Hadiqat al-Haqiqa* in 1131.

12. I am quoting from A. J. Arberry's translation in his *Sufism: An Account of the Mystics of Islam*, (New York: Harper Torch books, 1970), 112.

13. See above, pp. 90ff.

14. His birth date is typically given as 1119 (some sources date his birth as late as 1157, but they seem, for various reasons beyond this discussion, less valid) and his death either as 1193 or as 1219/1220. Several sources indicate that he lived for about one hundred years. Tradition has it that he was killed by Mongol invaders, but that would have been in 1229, which either means that he was spectacularly old, born later than 1119 or 1120, or that certain historiographers were taken in by the romantic image of a saintly old man cut down by ruthless barbarians.

15. The title has been and can also be rendered as *Speech of the Birds* or *Parliament of the Birds*: the point is that they are all gathered together to discuss an issue and as they journey, they continue to discuss that issue.

16. I am quoting here from the classic Fitzgerald translation. Since his initial version, there have been a number of others (those that follow in my text will mostly be from the Raficq Abdulla translation), including at least one in prose.

17. The simurgh is to Persian and Turkish literature what the phoenix is to Greek literature: a singular bird that lives for a thousand years, builds its own pyre, and is reborn out of its own ashes, over and over again, forever.

18. These last two passages are from the non-rhymed translation of Garcin de Tassy and C. S. Nott.

19. I have reverted to the Fitzgerald translation in this last passage (and not changed its archaic spellings where they appear).

20. As such, it follows the pattern of mystical poetic treatises such as the *Hadiqat al-Haqiqa* of Sana'i and the *Asrar-nama* of 'Attar.

21. This is A. J. Arberry's translation (see his *Sufism*, 110); he has rendered the first line, presumably, to accord with the rhyme scheme he has in mind. The standard rendering of that all-important phrase is "in the name of God the Beneficent and Merciful" (*bismillah ar-Rahman waRaheem*).

22. I am distinguishing between *mathnawi* as a mode of poetry and Rumi's work in that mode, which is referred to as the *Mathnawi*.

23. In turn based, in prejudicial male-dominated thinking, on the assumption that women are incapable of real in-depth thought or an in-depth spiritual relationship—and in Arabic-language mystical poetry (which would, in Spain, also exert influence on Hebrew-language poetry, where the same reasoning applies), also based on the fact that the word "God" is grammatically masculine.

24. See chapter 6, pp. 115–16.

25. In this we see (perhaps merely by coincidence) both a tie all the way back to Roman lyric poetry wherein (as observed in a previous note) the poet either overtly refers to himself by name or at least clearly exposes his subjective presence to the reader—and also perhaps a connection to the emerging tendency in Italian Renaissance painting of the same era and increasingly in the following generations for the artist to depict himself within the scene that he paints, looking out toward the viewer.

26. This is an eight-line *ghazal*, each "line" rendered as a quatrain by A. J. Arberry in his translation of *Hafiz's Fifty Poems* (Cambridge: Cambridge University Press, 1947).

27. This *ghazal* is organized into five groups of eight lines (of which I am only quoting the first). The translation is by Gertrude Bell in her *The Teachings of Hafiz* (London: Octagon Press, 1985).

28. I am using Arberry's translation and spellings again.

29. Henry Corbin, *Creative Imagination in the Sufism of Ibn 'Arabi* (Princeton, NJ: Princeton University Press, 1969), 139.

30. The Song of Songs goes back and forth between genders (these are poems exchanged by the bride and groom at their wedding) and are not outdone by the most overtly sensuous of mystical poetry. There are times when both Arabic- and Persian-language love poetry is apparently homosexual in its imagery (the male poet/*erastes* writing to a younger male *eromenos*), but just as that imagery often focuses in further circumlocution on a fawn being pursued in order to symbolize the beloved being pursued, so the young boy *eromenos* has been effectively argued in many places to be a conventional means of symbolizing a female object of love in a cultural context where such straightforward heterosexual romanticism is considered inappropriate. See below, on Jami, regarding the love of boys as a "forbidden" theme.

31. Quoted in William Chittick, "Jami on Divine Love and the Image of Wine," *Studies in Mystical Literature* 1, no. 3 (1981): 193–209.

32. That is, as we recall, the consumption of alcoholic beverages is prohibited in normative Islam.

33. Bishop John A. Subhan, *Sufism: Its Saints and Shrines* (Lucknow, India: Lucknow Publishing House, 1960), 47.

34. See Socrates and Alcibiades most intensely on the same stage in Plato's *Symposium*.

35. N. H. Dole and Belle M. Walker, eds., *The Persian Poets* (New York: Thomas Y. Crowell and Co., 1901), 390. Strictly speaking, the poem is the fifth of seven poems/stories that make up the work called *Haft Awrang* (*Seven Thrones*).

36. From the Pendlebury translation.

37. So writes the Sufi commentator, Bayazid, quoted here in Margaret Smith, *Early Mysticism in the Near and Middle East* (London: Sheldon Press, 1931), 240.

38. This work is said to have been written in emulation of the work *Lama'at* by an earlier Persian poet (whom, due to space considerations, I have not discussed), 'Iraqi (d. 1289), who was inspired to write his *Lama'at* by Ibn 'Arabi's *Fusus al-Hikam*.

39. *Tarsa* really has a range of meanings, from "fearful; timid" to "Christian" to "fire-worshipper (i.e., Zoroastrian)," to "sun's rays-colored," so that, depending upon the context, the nuance can be interpreted as more negative or more positive.

40. Taufiq al-Tawil, *al-Tasawuf fi Misr*, 47, quoted in and translated by Arberry, *Sufism*, 121–22. I have made a few minor changes in the translation for greater clarity.

41. That is, the problematic of how to distinguish true from false figures who assert themselves to be a sacerdotal bridge between God and ourselves; the problematic for mainstream Judaism and, less emphatically, mainstream Islam and some but not all branches of Christianity—not Roman Catholicism, for example, for which the pope is a sacerdotal bridge by definition—of whether there can be such bridge figures at all before the messianic era (in Judaism) or before the advent or return (depending on which branch of Islam) of the *mahdi* (in Islam). And if a saint is a sacerdotal figure, can there *be* saints before these eras?

Chapter Nine

Variations within Jewish and Christian Mysticism

From the Renaissance through Emancipation

FROM ABRAHAM ABULAFIA TO ISAAC LURIA

Over the course of the centuries in which Sufism spread across the Muslim world, in part articulated by diverse poetic voices, Kabbalah continued to evolve, and Christian mysticism continued to spread in new ways—even to the point of embracing Kabbalah along its (Christianity's) own path. In comparative terms, it seems that, as Sufism spread "horizontally" (by way of its increasingly diverse *tariqas*), Jewish mysticism evolved in a more concentrated, "vertical" development, with the number of its "schools" and their geographic and conceptual centering points more circumscribed—until the late eighteenth century and the second generation of *Hassidut*. During the same era, the diversity within Christian mysticism continued to revolve around particular individuals and their writings.

One might say that two main streams of Jewish mysticism flowed out of the thirteenth and fourteenth centuries, both in Spain: that of Moses de Leon and Zoharic Kabbalah and that of Abulafia and "prophetic" Kabbalah. In one sense, Abulafian Kabbalah receded from prominence, although the master had his successors, such as Joseph Ben Abraham Ibn Gikatilla of Castilla (1248–1305); and the Abulafian penchant for understanding *sacer/profanus* reality through the medium of *gematria* and its cognate letter-number formulae continued to expand over the centuries that followed. "Mainstream" Kabbalah—if it can ever be deemed appropriate to label any mystical tradition "mainstream"—evolved further, in new locations. And it evolved in two directions, recalling the dichotomy of thought and action in proto- and early Jewish mysticism. Thus, on the one hand, Kabbalah *'Eeyuneet*—"contemplative/ theoretical Kabbalah," rife with speculative issues—continued to expand, while alongside it, Kabbalah *Ma'aseet*—"practical Kabbalah"—with its attention to the sense of the relationship between the inner religious activity of the soul and its ability, under the correct circumstances, to affect outer, magical activity—began to offer itself with increasing prominence.

The geographic shift in the central location of post-Zoharic Kabbalah reflects outer historical realities. Spain, so long largely hospitable to its deeply historical Jewish communities, began to change emphatically. By the end of the fourteenth century—on Ash Wednesday in 1391, beginning with a riot in Sevilla—Christian-held Spain began a downward turn of persecution of its Jewish population that would culminate, in the immediate aftermath of the completion of the *Reconquista* and the virtually complete Christianization of the Iberian Peninsula, with the expulsion of the Jews in 1492. The world through which figures such as Abulafia and Moses de Leon had moved with relative comfort was in the process of eradication in the century leading up to that year. The Western Christian world of the next century was torn by the Reformation and Counter-Reformation. It was also engaged in the throes of its last series of "officially declared" Crusades against the Muslims, whose key political leaders in the late fifteenth through early twentieth centuries were the Ottoman Turkish sultans. One of these, Beyazid II, invited Jews from Spain and Portugal to settle freely and peacefully in his realms after their expulsion from those two countries; he is said to have provided ships to bring refugees to his shores and to have said, "Ferdinand's act of self-impoverishment [through expelling the Jews and with it, among other things, virtually his entire mid-level managerial infrastructure] is my enrichment."

Ottoman domains extended, in the century that followed 1492, up into eastern and toward central Europe, across most of North Africa, and through the Middle East as far as the Persian Gulf. Among the key figures in the court of Beyazid's successor, Suleiman the Magnificent, was the Jew Joseph Nasi, whom Suleiman eventually designated the Duke of Naxos and to whom the sultan extended semiautonomous political control of a small but substantial stretch of largely uninhabited territory in Palestine, in northern Galilee, around Safed (Tzfat) and Tiberias. Not surprisingly, then, hordes of Sephardic refugees migrated to northern Palestine. There, among them, Joseph Caro (1488–1575), arguably the last great codifier of rabbinic Judaism, emerged as a significant figure who, coming to dwell in Safed, drew up the famous compendium *Shulhan Arukh*, which summarized all of the most significant rabbinic discussions and legislations of the previous fifteen centuries into a one-volume encyclopedia that functioned as a guide to how to live an everyday Jewish life in a complex, non-Jewish world.[1]

Within Caro's circle, perhaps his most notable disciple was Moses de Cordovero (1522–1570), who was a significant encyclopedist of older kabbalistic literature and its ideas. Cordovero authored some thirty works of his own, many of them not published until after his death. Among these, two works in particular stand out. The first, entitled *Pardes Rimmonim* (*The Garden/ Orchard of Pomegranates*), written in 1548 and first published in Cracow, Poland, in 1591, is a systematic exposition of the *Zohar* in thirteen parts—thirteen "gates."[2] Thus, since the *Zohar* is itself, in effect, a midrash, the *Pardes* is a midrash on that midrash, a commentary on a commentary. In short, while residing outside the spiritual and intellectual mainstream in being focused on a mystical text, it is part of the Jewish mainstream in both its typically Jewish mode of construction (as a midrash) and its ultimate focus: the problem of creation. The discussion within the *Pardes* of the *sephirot* reconceives them as *kayleem*, or "vessels," through which the Godhead flows into the *profanus* of creation. This notion, of the Creator flowing into and found in all the elements of the created world would, in the expanding triadic split and interweaving within late medieval and early modern Jewish thought among rabbinical, kabbalistic, and philosophical thinking, ultimately influence Baruch Spinoza's (1632–1677) doctrine of *natura naturans* and *natura naturata*.[3] It would also, as we shall shortly see, feed into the panhenotheistic notions found in *Hassidut*.

Cordovero's other particularly important work is an ethical treatise called the *Palm Tree of Deborah*. This is a small book, also published posthumously (the first time in 1588 in Venice). It draws its title from that moment in chapters 4 and 5 of the biblical book of Judges when the prophetess and judge, Deborah, in the context of seeking relief for her people from the oppression "of Jabin, king of Canaan, that reigned in Hatzor," "sat under the palm-tree of Deborah between Ramah and Beth-El in the hill-country of Ephraim." The narrative that follows leads to the destruction of the powerful army of Sisera, Jabin's general, at the hands of Barak, Deborah's general, through her guidance and the divine assistance that she foresaw.[4] Thus, Cordovero's book has as an underlying theme to suggest that the mystic's goal of union with the One is achieved through a combination of his own effort to reach God and God's reaching toward the mystic—a theme that we have seen as characteristic of Jewish mysticism from the outset (as well as endemic to Christian and Muslim mysticism). Its overt purpose is to apply a kabbalistic perspective to the doctrine of imitating God: how to walk in God's ways, to be merciful, just, and compassionate, as God is.

In offering such a purpose, the *Palm Tree* raises the problem of defining what God *is*, as far as the human ability to understand and describe it is concerned. One must recall the notion of the imitation of Christ as articulated by Thomas à Kempis and others: there the model possesses a flesh-and-blood form, lives a human life, and dies a human death.[5] Thus, having embraced the paradox that the model is God Itself in spite of its human aspects and experiences, the Christian mystic can focus on and easily enough articulate what it is that he or she wishes to imitate. Both the nature of divine compassion, justice, and mercy as exemplified by Christ and the martyrdom to which Christ subjects himself offer contextual parameters that connect directly to our *profanus* reality. The Jewish (and Muslim) insistence on God's absolute nonphysicality eliminates such a straightforward and direct connection, and it is that "connectionless" connection that Cordovero is attempting to clarify.

This attempt does not, of course, begin with Cordovero. Both the rabbinical and the prior philosophical Jewish traditions ask what it means to read both of God's mercy and of God's anger in the Hebrew Bible. The philosophical tradition observes how ascribing qualities of any sort to the perfect Godhead—which ascription derives from human experience and human descriptive features—is to limit God, in terms of both the quality of the qualities and the fact that, if one lists, say, ten qualities, one is by definition excluding others that one does not list, thereby undercutting God's limitlessness; so, too, in listing whatever number of them, we may be led to think less clearly about God's absolute oneness and God's absolute uniqueness. God's nature as eternal, unchanging, and all-encompassing is contradicted. The philosophers' solution is to understand these terms as symbolic, mere attempts to place thing in terms that we can understand.[6] They argue, moreover, that the attributive descriptives don't actually apply to God but to God's activities: We recognize an action as merciful or angry and understand the actor to be God, but we should not presume thereby to associate our limited concepts of mercy and anger with God Itself.[7]

To this discussion Moses de Cordovero adds a kabbalistic twist: He distinguishes God Itself from the God that we see revealed to its creatures. As Itself, God is unknown and unknowable, limitless: without end, as in the Zoharic phrase '*eyn sof.* The biblical God is the biblical "God": self-revealing up to the point of our capacity to understand but ultimately (hence the quotation marks) an approximation and stand-in for—a bridge between us and— the *real, inaccessible* God. How does the true God emerge into revelation then? For without the conviction that we can somehow access God, we would be left well short of where we want and need to be in order to be engaged in a complete and fulfilling relationship with God. God emerges through the *sephirot*; these emanations are the mechanism through which the '*eyn sof* is revealed. Thus, the paradox twists a further turn around itself: The *sephirot* are part of a unity, yet tenfold, and are part of a unity that encompasses both them and the '*eyn sof or*, the '*eyn sof*, and the '*eyn*, yet we articulate them all through separate terms referring to separate attributes. It is as if water were poured through conduits of different colored glass: The water remains unchanged, although to the eye it appears to assume different colors: God is the water, and the *sephirot* and allied terms are the glass vessels (the *kaylim*). The ten chapters of the *Palm Tree* correspond to the ten emanations/*sephirot*/*kaylim*; each offers the discussion of a different divine attribute that the devotee should seek to emulate. Thus, the first two chapters focus on the supernal crown—*keter*—which is treated as the incipient will to will creation into existence (not the beginning of creation but the beginning of the process that will ultimately yield that beginning). Within *keter* are the thirteen attributes of higher mercy. Cordovero's description of these offers a guide to human behavior, above all, humility and kindness to all creatures. From *keter* emanates *hokhmah* ("wisdom"), the wisdom that is the will to create and within which all of creation exists potentially. Thus, the focus of chapter 3 of the *Palm Tree* furthers the emphasis on the human obligation to love all of God's creation and to translate the notion of human dominion over it to caretaking of it. *Binah*, or "understanding," is discussed in chapter 4 in terms of the actualization of created beings within divine thought and, on the part of the human devotee, true turning and returning to God. The Hebrew term for this, *teshuvah*, implies for the mystical discussant both a turning of the soul in full sincerity toward God and "returning," as a created being, to the source of all creation: a remerging of the *profanus* self with the innermost recesses of the *sacer*.

The uppermost triad of the *sephirot*, as we have seen (see chapter 6), reflects divine *thought*. In continuing the emanation from *keter*, *hokhmah*, and *binah* to the lower seven *sephirot*, one moves through divine *emotions* and *actions*. *Hesed*, or "mercy," the fourth *sephirah*, may be construed as that divine grace through which creation is accomplished. But its abundant light is so great that few if any creatures could survive in its glare without the screenlike boundary to it provided by the fifth *sephirah*, *gevurah*, or "power." Thus, quite counterintuitively, the grace of God by itself is *dangerous* to the one unprepared for it or unbalanced—as with one who emulates Enoch, he or she would be burnt to a crisp—and the power that by itself yields law without justice and other unhappy results becomes the necessary and desired counterweight to help the mystic maintain a dynamic spiritual balance. The discussion of how these two *sephirot* complement each other is found in chapters five and six of the *Palm Tree*, as is discussion of how the righteous man—the mystic who succeeds as a *tzadik*—might emulate the dynamic and harmonious balance between these two by performing acts of kindness on the one hand and, interestingly, using the evil inclination to serve God and thus further the divine plan on the other. Power is associated by the text with evil, and the bringing of evil into the world is associated by the text with "the female side" of the *sephirot* "tree"[8] (referring to the tradition held in common among

the Abrahamic faiths that Eve, as opposed to Adam, was the first to respond
to the serpent's seduction through which humankind disobeyed God's commandment regarding the fruit of the Tree of Knowledge). Thus, when Cordovero writes that "for his wife's sake he should gently bestir his evil inclinations in the direction of the sweet Powers, to provide her with clothes and
with a house, for example" (chapter 6, paragraph 2), his presentation of how
this yet serves God follows:

> [A]nd he should say: "By providing her with clothes I adorn the *Shekhinah*," for
> the *Shekhinah* is adorned with Understanding which is Power (for it includes all
> Powers and these are sweetened in her abundant mercies). Therefore, all the
> needs of the household are the *tikkunim* of the *Shekhinah*, which is sweetened
> by means of the evil inclination, which was created to do the will of his Creator
> and for no other purpose. Therefore, a man should not intend to derive any kind
> of pleasure from the evil inclination but when his wife appears before him in her
> beauty in a fine house he should have the intention of adorning the *Shekhinah*,
> for she is adorned by the good Powers of the Left [side of the tree of the *sephi-
> rot*] from whence come wealth and honor.

We recognize in this short passage from the shortest chapter in the *Palm
Tree* several familiar and yet newly turned issues. There is a distinctly ambiguous sensibility with respect to women: They are connected to—the ultimate source of—evil, yet connected directly to the *Shekhinah* and thus to
God's presence among us. The negative side of this sensibility is less extreme,
as we have discussed earlier, than the Christian and even the Muslim viewpoint, generally speaking, and the positive side is more exalted than for Judaism's Abrahamic siblings. Yet, on the other hand, it is a sensibility in which
we can hardly imagine a place for a mystic such as Rabi'a or St. Catherine of
Siena. So, too, we may recognize a distinctly Jewish mystical emphasis—
shared with Sufism but less prominent in Christian mysticism—to turn aspects of seeking oneness with God toward practical, everyday living. The
"needs of the household" are obviously defined as the mystic's wife's needs,
but they are also *tikkunim* of the *Shekhinah*. *Tikkunim* here—literally, "re-
pairs" or "reparations" or "fixings"—means the setting of his house in order,
which action "gives adornment to the *Shekhinah*." To adorn the *Shekhinah* is
to glorify God.

If acceding gently to the evil inclination yields this process through a
happy partnership with "the wife whom God has chosen to be a help mate for
him" (chapter 6, paragraph 4) and leads to this result—of glorifying God—
then we are faced both with the paradox of evil being turned into good as a
mode of imitating God and with layers of partnership in completing the perfection of our reality. Male and female on the human level, together with God

on the divine level, can achieve what, for reasons we cannot understand, God decided should be achieved not by divine, all-powerful *fiat*. Rather, in gifting us with free will, God obligated us to help achieve perfection through the human-divine partnership. We seek (or should seek) the moral perfection that will mirror the physical perfection accomplished by God in the six days of creation. The mystic who truly accomplishes this is a righteous one, a *tzadik*, a centerpiece of the process of *tikkun*.

In turn, Cordovero's seventh chapter focuses on *tiferet*, or "beauty," conceived as devoting one's self to the ultimate expression of beauty in the world, the Torah, to studying its words and behaving in accordance with its precepts. The eighth chapter focuses on the imitation of *hod*, *netzah*, and *yesod*—"majesty," "endurance," and "foundation." This lower triad is the foundation supporting the middle and upper reaches of the *sephirot*; it offers divine involvement and action within the world. The coming together of a series of apparently opposed forces within *yesod* offers a final conduit to the tenth *sephirah*, *malkhut* ("kingdom; sovereignty") that is the focus of Cordovero's ninth chapter. It is this last *sephirah*, as the ultimate manifestation of the principle of divine creativity within the created world, that is most directly associated with the *Shekhinah*, God's indwelling presence within the entirety of creation.

In the last chapter of his *Palm Tree of Deborah*, Cordovero summarizes how human behavior can maintain an unbroken tie to the *sephirot*. "He begins with the night, the time when man sleeps on his bed. . . . He should rise at midnight, wash his hands from the shell (*kleepah*) which has dominion over them, remove the evil from his flesh and recite the benediction [over the washing of hands]. He should then make a *tikkun* for the *Shekhinah* by studying the Torah" (chapter 10, paragraph 2). Thus, Cordovero introduces the concept of shells of evil encapsulating us, which need to be removed if we are to exercise purer good and thereby repair the world: to exercise *tikkun* upon it. The text follows the mystic or *tzadik* through the course of the day, until he arrives at the following evening, "attached, ever, to the dominating light" (chapter 10, paragraph 5). At each step of the discussion, both in this last chapter and throughout his short book, Cordovero refers to passages both from the Torah and from elsewhere in the Hebrew Bible and also the rabbinic tradition, in midrashic style, as if his words are glosses on those passages. He outlines the first detailed prescription not only of how God may be imitated but also of how, through such a divine-human partnership, the *sephirot* themselves (as the created world itself) may achieve perfect repair (*tikkun*).

Cordovero did not work in isolation. He was part of a group of friends/members, or *haverim*, governed by its own strict rules of conduct within the hill town of Safed. This was a self-defined mystical community that, within its rules, prescribed acting without anger and embracing free association with fellow men of any and all sorts. Its members were expected to engage insistently in some discussion of spiritual matters with a *haver* everyday, to confess sins to themselves or to each other before meals and before sleep, and to review their actions of the previous week through a one-to-one, *haver*-to-*haver* dialogue every Friday before the advent of the Sabbath. As a group, they received the Sabbath as a queen (as a manifestation or aspect of the *Shekhinah*). The eventual, if brief-lived, center of the mystical subcircle of the circle of which both Caro and Cordovero were part was Isaac Luria, born in Jerusalem in 1534, who traveled as far afield as Cairo within the Turkish domains and eventually settled in Safed, around 1570 (the very year of Cordovero's death). There he would gather his own disciples through his charisma, but his flame burnt briefly: He died there in 1572 of plague.

Luria's activity as a mystic was largely oral; the doctrines that he developed and espoused were recorded by his disciples, in particular Hayim Vitale Calabrese. In Luria's thought, we begin to see an intense merging of kabbalistic thought with Jewish messianic thinking. Luria approaches the question of how the creation was affected from what, in a sense, is a viewpoint opposite to that of classical Kabbalah. He asks the question, how can there have been (and continue to be) room for the created world when God is all-encompassing? His answer is *tzimtzum*, a term meaning "concentration" or "contraction," but which in his vocabulary comes to mean "withdrawal" or "retreat." In midrashic sources, there are references to God as concentrated within the *Shekhinah*—God's presence in the *profanus*—specifically within the Holy of Holies in the Temple, the center of the center of the umbilicus of divine-human, heavenly-earthbound, *sacer-profanus* contact, where God's power is concentrated and contracted into a single infinitesimal point.[9] The concept seems also to have appeared in an obscure thirteenth-century essay that Luria apparently read.[10] But the point is that Luria goes further—as we might expect of a mystical thinker—in suggesting that even from such a point of concentration, God withdraws: In order to make room for the universe, God shrinks into no-thing-ness. At the same time, that shrinkage is a shrinkage from within God's all-encompassing self, so that it is a withdrawal from a spaceless space within the spaceless space that is God and an abandoning of that spaceless space in order to make "room" for the space of the universe.

Thus, instead of emanation outward, Luria posits contraction inward into a corner of God's all-encompassing spaceless self, a concentration of itself deep into the recess of its own infinite, spaceless, no-thing-ness being—and it is to those recesses that the mystic seeks access. Gaining access will yield *tikkun*—repairing the mystic's soul, bringing it toward perfection. The question, as always, then becomes, how can the mystic gain access that will complete the soul's ascent toward perfection, its act of *tikkun*? The Lurianic system suggests a fourfold path: *sigguf* ("chastisement") is the first aspect—the recognition of all of the soul's errors, which recognition comes about through rigorous self-examination, in which one is assisted by cross-examinational discussions with a *haver*. *Ta'anit* ("fasting") is the second, and frequent *tevillah* ("ablution") is the third. The fourth is *kavanah* ("intention"), which refers both to special prayers and devotions beyond what is in the normative liturgy, including the sort of combinations of sound-letters that recall Abulafia's system, and to the recitation of those prayers and devotions with particular, special, intense, complete care and focus.

Luria carries forward an increasingly complex theory of the human soul. It is divine in origin—as is understood to be stated in Genesis—and that divine origin is also its ultimate goal; the goal of the mystical soul is to return whence it came (*teshuvah*, or "return.") To the articulation of the process of seeking to return, Luria adds a number of significant terms and concepts. Thus, he speaks of the *partzufim*,[11] the divine countenance, found in all of God's besouled beings, which become fully *partzufim* when their divine source is realized by their being turned toward each other. When that happens, the presence of the Godhead in those spiritually turned toward each other becomes manifest, and the divine "qualities" expressed in the *sephirot* (in the manner in which Cordovero had explored and explained them) become activated in the human sphere.

We may not succeed in achieving the goal of *teshuvah* in the course of our lives, but Lurianic thinking introduced, with an assertiveness unprecedented in the Jewish tradition, the notion of transmigration of souls: *gilgul haNefesh* (literally, "rolling of the soul"; *galgal* is the common-parlance Hebrew word for "wheel"). Thus, every besouled being possesses a soul that has been incarnate and gone through life one or more times before, and everyone who dies can expect his or her soul to return from the *sacer* to the *profanus* again. The process of *gilgul*, it would appear, will continue until the messianic era, when all souls will be remerged in a definitive and final way with God. There is more. The master—the word that the *haverim* use to refer to him is *tzadik*, or "just one"—possesses the capacity to recognize the prior incarnations of the souls of all those he meets and can trace those souls' wanderings back to their beginning. As such, he is in a position to elicit spiritual qualities from each of those he encounters by drawing from the previous times, places, and experiences that an individual might not be aware his or her soul has been and had. Every soul is pregnant with possibilities—the word used for soul "pregnancy" is *ibbur*—derived from the attachment to it of its higher-placed aspect, which aspect derives, if not from a prior existence within the *profanus*, then from the time it spent when deceased, within the *sacer*.

On the other hand, sometimes a soul that has left its incarnation cannot complete its journey to the other side (into the *sacer*) and still maintains an attachment to the *profanus* or to a particular individual within the *profanus*. Such a soul, called *dybbuk* (meaning something "glued" or "stuck"), usually has spiritual business that was somehow left unfinished when the individual died. Sometimes the form the attachment to the *profanus* takes is that of "possessing" an individual with whom such spiritual business was interrupted.[12]

There is still more. The soul has within it sparks—*n'tzotzot*—that are the endless fragments of the primordial light of divine goodness that was shattered when Adam and Eve disobeyed God's command and were exiled from the Garden of Eden. Those sparks are found in all of nature, since all of creation contains elements of the Creator—or, rather, of the light that marked the beginning of God's creative act vis-à-vis the *profanus* world—inherently within it. The sparks housed within human souls shoot out from one to the other when the *partzufim* are engaged, the pregnancy of each soul gives birth to goodness, and both souls (if it is a matter of two, but it could be, and ultimately must be, more than two) are successfully engaged in the act of *tikkun*.

Indeed, the concept of *tikkun* so essential to Lurianic Kabbalah is never limited to the perfection of an individual soul—certainly not to the mystic's own soul. The practice of the fourfold path of bringing the soul toward perfection is intended not simply to aid the individual in gaining access to God's hiddenmost recess but to bring the Messiah. When all souls are ready, perfect, and suffused with *kavanah*—when the entire world is ready and in alignment with perfect goodness—the Messiah will arrive. Thus, Lurianic *tikkun* is ultimately not *tikkun haNefesh* ("perfection of the soul") but *tikkun olam* ("perfection of the world"). The *tzadik* is able to help facilitate all of these processes, but it is the intense *kavanah* with which the practice of *sigguf*, *ta'anit*, and *tevillah* is undertaken by each and every member of the community—us everyday people—that will hasten the coming of the messianic age.

KABBALAH AND THE SPREAD OF JEWISH MESSIANISM

Indeed, as we follow the history of Jewish mysticism forward from the sixteenth into the seventeenth century, we observe an increasingly frequent intersection between the spread of Lurianic and late Kabbalah and the messianic idea. Messianism in the Jewish tradition offers an important distinction from its counterpart in Christianity. Where, for the latter, Jesus is the Messiah, thus Christians are awaiting the return of a particular and specific individual, one whom they already know; for Jews, Jesus does not play that role. So, at the very least, Judaism does not know exactly for whom it is waiting. Moreover, the growing ambiguity as to what the nature of the Messiah is, as the term and concept had evolved in the Israelite-Judaean periods toward Judaism and Christianity—a descendant from the house of David: at least a warrior to protect the people from its foreign foes and at most a great and glorious king sanctioned by God and recognized by other peoples as such, ruling in righteousness in Zion—comes to full efflorescence as an aspect of Judaism when the two sibling traditions emerge as distinct from each other.

Thus, over time, the Jewish question of whether the Messiah will indeed be a descendant of David's house, whether he will be a mere man or something more (since if he will be the harbinger of a renewed prophetic reality, then that would suggest that he is not merely an everyday being, even an everyday royal being), whether, indeed, the term *Messiah* should refer to a particular individual at all, rather than to an era and the idealized conditions that it will offer—these kinds of questions grow and percolate beneath the surface of Judaism as it moves through the centuries of dispersion and the condition of being an often oppressed and at best tolerated minority.

Apocalyptic books both within and outside the Hebrew Bible (i.e., in the Apocrypha), such as Daniel, Tobit, and Ben Sirah, emphasize the condition of the people. They speak of the eternity of the nation of Israel and the connections between its idealized, glorious Davidic past and its glorious future, of the spread of the Judaean-Jewish concept of God among the nations as the pagans become converted to that concept and honor its progenitors accordingly. Within the rabbinic sources, there begins to appear a good deal of discussion of the messianic era as an end of days—the end of history as we know it, marked by supernatural events including the resurrection of the righteous dead—and the beginning of a new, final era. Philo writes of a man of war who will bring peace, a personal Messiah to which everyone can relate on an individual basis.[13] Simeon Ben Kotziba, leader of the revolt against the Romans in 132 to 135, was perceived by no less an intellectual and spiritual leader than Rabbi Akiva (to whom Jewish mysticism looks as the preeminent early mystic, as we have seen) as a messianic figure. Unusually tall and strong and a brilliant guerilla war strategist, Simeon held off the Romans for three years and received from Akiva the epithet by which history has come to know him: Bar Kokhba, an Aramaic phrase meaning "Son of the Star."

Over the next fifteen centuries, any number of individuals declared themselves to be the Messiah and gained constituencies. Thus, Serene of Syria (ca. 720), for example, asserted to his growing flock that he would drive the Muslims from the Holy Land and restore the Jews to their ancient inheritance. In opposition to rabbinic leaders, he abrogated the Jewish dietary laws, used nonkosher wine for the Sabbath and festivals, neglected various ritual and liturgical details that the rabbis considered essential, and was eventually captured by Caliph Yazid's men and destroyed. By contrast with him, Obadiah Abu-Isa Ben Ishak of Isfahan claimed to be the last of five precursors of the Messiah (as opposed to the Messiah himself). He perished in battle in 755, and for three centuries there persisted a sect of his followers. Hidden literature—mystical texts—also associated Rabbi Shimeon bar Yochai with messianism in ascribing to him a vision in which an angel sent by God informed him of God's intention to act soon to lift "the yoke of Edom from Israel."[14]

Philosophers such as Maimonides in the twelfth century and Nachmanides in the thirteenth century speculated on the time of the Messiah's arrival. Thus, the latter argued that the description of creation offered a symbolic statement not merely of the beginning of reality but of its entire history. The six days described in Genesis stand for the six millennia of the world's existence. Man, created on the sixth day, symbolizes the Jews (and thus the various species of animals represent the other nations of the world!). The Messiah will appear at the end of the sixth day, toward the evening that begins the seventh day—the Sabbath, which day represents the beginning of a new reality, the life of the future. That messianic future will be immediately preceded by the hardest time (the darkest hour is before the dawn)—and when, indeed the Tatars ravaged the Holy Land in 1260, there were those who took this as a confirmation that the messianic era was soon to follow.

Within this complex of messianic speculation, the *Zohar* also preoccupied itself with the question. In fact, the text self-reflexively views itself in some places as a revelation for the last, premessianic days only.[15] It offers a numerological formula for predicting the arrival of the Messiah based on the ineffable name of God, the Tetragrammaton (*YHVH: yud hey vav hey*). Thus, the double *hey* (the numerical value of which letter is five) represents five thousand: the five thousand years of suffering endured by "Israel" in its subjugation to foreign powers. Multiplying the *yud* (which equals ten) by the *vav* (which equals six) yields sixty. After that period of time—5,060 years—of oppression, Israel (the Jews) will arise from the ground, and the kindness of God toward them will continue in sixty-year increments until six hundred years into the sixth millennium will have passed. At that time, the gates of heavenly wisdom (*hokhmah* or *sophia*) will open, and the fountains of wisdom will gush out from below, inundating the world from above and below with the wisdom necessary to prepare it—just as one prepares for the Sabbath, the seventh day of the week—for the future, messianic world. In Gregorian calendrical terms, the calculation seems to suggest the year 1300[16]; later interpolators suggested, rather, 1328 or even 1648 (see below).

One passage states that a pillar of fire will appear prior to the arrival of the Messiah, visible for forty days to all the nations of the world. One recognizes in this a synthesis of ideas drawn from the description in the Torah of the passage of the Israelites through the wilderness for forty years—led by Moses and the Tabernacle, over which there hovered a pillar of fire by night and of smoke by day—and the prophetic passages in the Hebrew Bible which speak of a future era in which all the nations of the world shall go up to the mountain of the Lord and recognize that God is God. The *Zohar* continues: After that forty-day period, the Messiah will arise from a place beyond place, referred to as "the bird's nest," appearing first in the Galilee (where the Romans first suppressed the Judaean revolt in 66 CE). A brilliant star will appear in the heavens, surrounded by seven other bright stars, and a battle will be fought three times daily between the one and the seven, for seventy days, during which the one will swallow and vomit forth the seven again and again. After the seventy days, the stars will disappear, and the Messiah, concealed in the pillar of fire, will be taken up into heaven, where he will be crowned; he will descend to earth, and the pillar of fire will reappear and be recognized by the nations of the world. The world will grow dark for two weeks, and those who do not recognize the Messiah will gather in Rome to wage war against him, only to be destroyed by fire and brimstone (such as consumed biblical Sodom and Gomorrah), until finally those who are prepared for the messianic era shall enter the seventh millennium, purified with new souls: a new reality and, within it, new human beings.

These last paragraphs are a small sample of the often phantasmagorical passages within the *Zohar* that consider the advent of the Messiah, all of which make considerable use of numerology wedded to biblical imagery—and also imagery clearly drawn from Christian thought (we are reminded that the Spanish world in which the *Zohar* was written down was one characterized by intense interface among Jews, Christians, and Muslims). In sum, messianic speculation grows as a theme within the Jewish mystical tradition over the centuries, particularly following the shaping and repetition of the Crusades in the Holy Land to the east and the *Reconquista* of Spain to the west. The obvious primary source for such a theme even in general Jewish thought is the *Zohar*. As the Jewish mystical tradition moves chronologically forward beyond the *Zohar* (bringing this discussion back to the era of Isaac Luria), messianic speculation moves and grows yet further.

Consistent with the ambiguity of the concept in Judaism and thus with the range and variety of manifestations that might be called "messianic," we encounter the rabbi of Prague, Judah Loew (1512/25–1609), as one of the key figures in the later part of the late kabbalistic period centered in the circle of Isaac Luria. Rabbi Loew was revered as a Talmudist and mathematician, as the author of an important commentary on Rashi,[17] and, in kabbalistic circles, for his complex mystical writings. He became more widely known for the story of his alleged application of his esoteric knowledge—his access to secrets associated with creation—that enabled him to devise a creature that protected the Jewish community of Prague from its enemies in an era when potential accusations of blood libel and threats of expulsion were rampant. The creature has been re-ferred to through history simply as the Golem—from a word that appears once in the book of Psalms (139:16) and means "unformed/shapeless (mass)." On the one hand, the Golem may be seen as a localized messianic figure: It served the Jewish community and protected it from hostile Christians. On the other, its manner of creation reflects a turn to—or back to—that side of the Jewish mys-tical tradition that is occupied with effecting concrete results in the *profanus*, as magic does.

There are thus three aspects of the "life" of the Golem that are of particular interest for this discussion. First, Rabbi Loew shaped his creature out of earth, on the banks of the Vltava River, and having shaped it as an anthropomorph, recited prescribed, esoteric formulae as he walked around it seven times in the appropriate direction.[18] Second, the creative process culminated with the place-ment of the ineffable name of God, either (depending upon the version of the story) written on a piece of parchment and placed within the creature's mouth or inscribed directly on its forehead.[19] Thus, we recognize that Rabbi Loew was recapitulating the original culminating creative act of God, taking earth (*adamah*) as God did in creating the first human being (*adam*) and, as God breathed life into the being that was thus besouled with God's own breath, so Judah Loew breathed life into the Golem by using the name of which he (Rabbi Loew) was a master (and thus he knew the true, hidden, secret, ineffable name and could use it as such). The third aspect of this story of consequence for us is that, when inevitably the Golem got out of hand—only Rabbi Loew truly un-derstood how to control it; others could command it, and it would respond, but they neither appreciated the manner in which it would respond literally to every command nor understood how to make it desist from whatever action had been demanded of it—its creator had to deactivate it. Rabbi Loew did so by remov-ing the name of God (or the word, *truth*)[20] from its mouth (or its forehead), whereby it returned to a condition of being a lump of earth. This culmination of the Golem's career thereby offers a concrete reminder of the dangers attached to using mystical formulae.[21]

The key, then, to this local "messianic" figure is the use of the ineffable name of God, known to only the most successful kabbalists, mastered by only the most qualified of what would be termed *tzadikim*[22] in Lurianic terms. Later on in the seventeenth century, perhaps the most notorious of messianic pretenders in Jewish history—whose renown would extend from one end of Europe to the other—would assert of himself that he possessed that knowl-edge and that mastery. The pretender was Shabbetai Tzvi (1626–1676). He was born into a century in which the Christian world was as expansive in its expectation that the Messiah would be *returning* to transform the world as Jews were that he would *arriving* to accomplish that task.

Thus, for instance, European explorers' tales of encounters with descendants of the Lost Ten Tribes as far east as Kai Fung Fu along the Yellow River in China, where a small Jewish community had resided for centuries and had been newly discovered, and as far west as the Yanoama Indians in the Brazilian jungle, who were (mis)perceived to be speaking Hebrew, suggested that such groups represented the exiles or Lost Ten Tribes soon to be ingathered as a prelude to the *parousia*. And in England, the era leading to and encompassing the rise of Oliver Cromwell (ca. 1649–1658) was ushered in, in part, through the support that Cromwell received from a group calling itself Fifth Monarchy Men. The adherents of this group were certain that there had been a progression of major empires that had defined history up to their time: Assyria, Persia, Greece, and Rome were the first four. The kingdom of Jesus was to be ushered in (in accordance with a passage in Daniel 2:36–45) by the prelude kingdom—the first stage of the fifth monarchy—established by Cromwell. With that in mind, Cromwell was easily convinced by the chief rabbi of Amsterdam, Manasseh ben Israel (1604–1657), both that Cromwell should officially rescind the decree of expulsion that had been meted out to the Jews of England three hundred years earlier and that Manasseh was the obvious leader of the soon-to-be-redeemed Jews—the soon-to-be-ingathered exiles—who would all flock to the new Israel (England) and its capital, a new Jerusalem (London), where the new reality and the redemption of all of humankind would begin to take shape.

Moreover, 1648—the year preceding the execution of the English king Charles I and the beginning of Cromwell's rise—was marked by the end of the Europe-wide conflagration known as the Thirty Years' War. If that war could be easily enough seen as that darkest of premessianic hours, then the end of the 1640s would have been particularly rife with messianic excitement and hope. The atmosphere in which Shabbetai came of age was propitious. Born and raised in Smyrna, on the coast of Anatolia (Ottoman-governed Turkey), he had, as a youth, studied the *Zohar*, together with Luria-Vitale interpretations, and taught it to a circle of friends who gathered in his father's house. Extremely handsome and charismatic, he began to acquire followers, who emulated his conduct—he led an ascetic life and frequently bathed at night in the sea—and in 1648 (which, as we have noted above, is one of the years in which, apparently, the *Zohar* predicts the arrival of the Messiah), at age twenty-two, he declared himself to be the Messiah by pronouncing the ineffable name of God.[23] Deemed false and heretical by the rabbinical leadership of Smyrna, he was excommunicated by them three years later—as a result he acquired a halo of martyrdom and increased influence.[24]

Shabbetai traveled from Smyrna to Salonica (modern Thessaloniki in northeastern Greece), which was a hotbed of kabbalistic inquiry where, sometime in the late 1650s, he and his followers celebrated a feast in which he, as the "son of God" was wedded to the Torah as the "daughter of God."[25] The Jewish mainstream authorities were neither impressed nor pleased, as the stir that he was creating threatened to rock that ever-delicate boat of the Jewish community both within itself and afloat within unpredictable Christian and Muslim seas. In the early 1660s, he was exiled from Salonica and made his way to Jerusalem, where he would await the miracle of his confirmation, as he understood that confirmation to be forthcoming according to the *Zohar*. He moved on briefly to Egypt—where he met and wedded the beautiful Sarah, who had been asserting for some time that she was destined to be "the future wife of the Messiah"—and returned to Jerusalem. Along the way, he met Nathan of Gaza, who joined his retinue as both a publicist and an idea man, and Samuel Primo, who apparently began to write the words that Shabbetai continued to speak even as he began to have long moments of doubt regarding whether he was in fact the Messiah.[26] Nonetheless, he repeated his declaration on New Year's Day (*Rosh HaShanah*) in the fall of 1665, creating a sensation that reverberated from Jerusalem to London and back. (He is discussed in the famous diary of Samuel Pepys, in 1666, as putatively "the King of the World and . . . the true Messiah.")

The next two years must have been hectic indeed. Shabbetai returned to Smyrna and Salonica, his excommunication largely forgotten. He preached that the *n'tzotzot*—the fragments of the equiprimoridal light, of the aboriginal world soul—cannot be reunited because they are imprisoned within us by *kleepot* ("shells") that encompass them in each of us. These can only be destroyed by a true *tzadik*, who knows and understands the relationship "between the upper and lower worlds"—the upper and lower triads of *sephirot*; the world of *'asiyah* and those of *yetzirah, bri'ah,* and *atzilut*; the *sacer* and *profanus* realms. Only the true *tzadik* is capable of effecting a reunification of the *n'tzotzot* so that, under influence of the *sephirot, tikkun olam* may prevail. That true *tzadik* is the anticipator or forerunner of the Messiah, who is referred to by him as the *adam kadmon* ("primordial man," that is, the equivalent of the Adam with whom God had such an intimate relationship at the outset of creation) and as the *malkha kedeesha* ("holy king" in Aramaic); he assumes control of the upper world that has heretofore been governed by the all-seeing Metatron in order to perfect the lower world: the "true God incarnate."

This astonishing spiral upwards of phraseology and its accompanying concepts yields two obvious connected consequences and a profound danger from the perspective of traditional Judaism. The first consequence is that the

Torah loses its significance as the ultimate umbilicus between God and ourselves; cognate with that consequence, the rabbinical literary tradition of Talmud and Midrash becomes even less significant and, with it, the rabbinic leaders themselves. The profound danger is that the notion of the *tzadik*/Messiah/ *adam kadmon*/*malkha kedeesha*/incarnate God is obviously strongly Christological in style and inspiration. Of course, sabbateans would argue that this is precisely the point: The true Messiah—Shabbetai—is the meeting point of the false path previously followed by Christians who mistook Jesus of Nazareth for the Messiah and the true path followed by Jews who embrace the mystical tradition and who recognize in Shabbetai the true Messiah.

As a practical matter, it would appear that Shabbetai Tzvi, in this late, intensely manic period, considered himself to be merely the true *tzadik*, although for the majority of his followers, the distinction between that concept and that of the Messiah seems to have been blurred to invisibility. In any case, based on the tradition that the Messiah will not appear—or that the messianic era will not arrive—until the supply of unborn souls is exhausted (this, then, is a variant of the Lurianic concept of *gilgul*: Souls continue to be reborn in new bodies, but at some point the original, finite number of souls is depleted; all of them have been put into play within the reality of birth-death-rebirth). The Jews of Smyrna and Salonica began to marry off their children by the bucketload, at extremely young ages, in order to multiply the number of simultaneous births and therefore remove the obstacle of having too slow a birth rate to complete the soul-exhaustion process. On the other hand, his followers labeled his detractors *kofrim*, a term which ranges in nuance from "unbeliever" or "infidel" to "godless" or "impious."

Within a year of the Jerusalem declaration of his messiahship, Shabbetai was on his way to Istanbul with the intention of converting the sultan himself: to "take the crown from the Sultan" and hand it over to God. The sultan's response was to place him in the Gallipoli prison and offer him the option of execution or conversion. Shortly thereafter, Shabbetai converted to Islam and either, as some assert, married a Turkish woman or, as others claim, was joined in his conversion by Sarah. Most of his followers, disillusioned, faded back into the woodwork of Jewish life. A core of them, however, followed him into Islam and settled in Salonica. Some asserted that the conversion was feigned, that he pretended to become a Muslim in order to smash the *kleepot* from within (i.e., to smash the *kleepah* of Islam's spiritual misdirection from within it; it is said that even as a Muslim he continued to teach the *Zohar*), or that it had been merely a phantom Shabbetai who converted: The real Shabbetai ascended to heaven or went east in search of the Lost Ten Tribes (the location and ingathering of which would usher in the messianic era). At its most extreme, the Sabbetain movement boasted followers who, by the beginning of the eighteenth century, located in northern Palestine, fasted, mortified their flesh, and worshipped images of Shabbetai Tzvi. Nonsabbatean historiography understands that he eventually made his way west from Istanbul, dying in obscurity in Dulcigno, Albania, in 1676.[27]

FROM MESSIANIC PRETENDERS TO *HASSIDUT*

At least three subsequent developments following the rise and demise of Shabbetai Tzvi are relevant to this discussion. The first is the fact of other, subsequent false mysticism-connected messiahs and, with them, repeated disappointments for a Jewish community that, particularly in eastern Europe, found its condition of oppression and depression relentless. More specifically, the period of Shabbetai's rise and fall coincided almost precisely with the beginning of the long swoon of the far-flung Polish kingdom. The struggle for Ukrainian independence, led by Bogdan Chmielnitski, began in 1648—the year of Shabbetai's first proclamation and the year in which the Thirty Years' War ended—and continued until around 1660, and the Jewish community was caught in a constant, murderous crossfire between Polish Catholics and Ukrainian Orthodox and between Cossacks and peasants. In the following century, perhaps the most famous of post-Shabbetai false messiahs, Jacob Frank, emerged in Poland.

Frank emerged in the middle of the eighteenth century, and his life as a messianic pretender seems to have followed a threefold progression. Soon after declaring himself the Messiah, he began to lead an increasingly debauched lifestyle, asserting that his wallowing in alcohol-accompanied (or -induced) orgies was a necessary part of his program: that he would enter the *kleepot* and smash them from within. He next embraced Christianity—but reminiscent of Shabbetai Tzvi's apparent embrace of Islam, he is said by some to have asserted that his purpose was merely to enter *that* ultimate mode of *kleepah* and smash it from within. Lastly, he is said to have ended up engaging rabbinic figures in disputations, where his knowledge of Judaism's ins and outs might be put to use against its defenders.[28] He subsequently fades from the historical picture into obscurity with even greater alacrity than had Shabbetai.

The second postsabbatean development, also in the eighteenth century, was that associated with the last major figure in late kabbalistic thought, Chaim Luzzato, born in 1707 in Padua, Italy. At the age of twenty, he began to assert that he was experiencing the vision of a heavenly, partially messianic *maggid* (a teacher; literally, "one who tells or instructs"). Attacked as a heretic by mainstream rabbinic leadership, he left northern Italy for Amsterdam (which had become a haven for the religiously persecuted in the previous century)[29] and thence, eventually, to Palestine, where he took up residence within the post-Lurianic community of Tzfat. Luzzato died in Acre, on the northern coast of Palestine, in 1747. His legacy included the furthering of the assertion that the kabbalist has extraordinary sources of knowledge that make it feasible for him to effect direct results within the *profanus*.

That is, Luzzato extended the concept of a distinction between theoretical and practical Kabbalah, whereby the first, with its elements of elaborate discussion, offers the roots of which the second, with its concrete consequences, offers the branches—of the same sacred tree. This notion completes a circle that began with the question raised in this discussion with regard to the early phases of Jewish mysticism in antiquity and the distinction between mysticism and magic. While throughout the history of *merkavah* and Kabbalah, the question was implied as to precisely how contact with the *mysterion* might yield positive results within the *profanus*, with increasing frequency since the time of Judah Loew, an expectation evolved that the effective mystic could perform miracles of various sorts. And the kinds of objects that had served for millennia to protect individuals from the negative potential of the *sacer—kemiot* ("amulets")—were joined by a growing array of "cures" (*refuot*) and "rituals" (*segulot*) provided by those who asserted that the source of their cures and the goal of their rituals was the *mysterion*. Luzzato was a key figure in expanding and validating such a perspective.

Luzzato's post-Lurianic thinking also further suggests the manner in which Kabbalah solves the two fundamental problems of Jewish (and Christian and Muslim) religious thought, to wit, the question of how the finite creation derives from an infinite source and how evil apparently derives from absolute good. Thus, the notion of the *sephirot* as aspects of the *adam kadmon* (an extension of that aspect of Zoharic Kabbalah that superimposes the image and concept of the tree of the *sephirot* over that of a man and a variant of the concept of the Messiah as an eternal being whose existence predates creation but is not to be revealed until the end of days) and the idea that the divine will is expressed by the figure of the *adam kadmon* and achieves its ultimate manifestation in *malkhut*'s connectedness to the *profanus*—this nexus of notions returns to and further refines the idea of an emanational relationship between Creator and creation.

And the notion that evil has no existence in itself but assumes shape only to the extent that good withdraws, leaving it space in which to come into existence—thus good effects a form of *tzimtzum* in order for evil to exist—is expanded to encompass the notion that the goal of the kabbalist as a *tzadik* is to destroy evil by stepping out of the shrinking realm of good and directly into evil, thus conquering it from within. This last notion is a further expansion of the idea of the *kleepot* as *the* manifestation or articulation of evil. For the *kleepot* are thus seen as shells that imprisoned the sparks of perfect goodness scattered at the moment when the first humans disobeyed God (the *kleepot* were rendered into reality by that act of disobedience) and therefore enabled evil (defined as disobedience to God) to come into existence.

Thus, key aspects of late Kabbalah intersect the revitalized messianic idea in the seventeenth and eighteenth centuries for better and for worse. False messianic figures assert that they are ultimate *tzadikim*. What prevents both the collapse of Jewish mystical thought and, perhaps, the destruction from within of European Judaism at large in this volatile combination is the third development that comes in the aftermath of the sabbatean era, into which aspects of the first two developments that I have summarized in these last four paragraphs extend. That third development is Hassidism (*Hassidut*).

The term *Hassidut* means "pietism"—thus the hassidim are "pious ones"—and has a long history. The adherents of a number of prior groups called themselves by that term, from contemporaries of the Maccabees in the second pre-Christian century to medieval groups of German Jewish mystics. The group that emerged in the eighteenth century in eastern Europe may be seen in one sense as the antithesis of the direction of Jewish mysticism through most of its history, since, rather than offering an ascetic and esoteric ideology directed to a small and select group, it developed as a populist movement, sweeping across half of Jewish Europe. In another sense, Hassidism may be seen as a logical culmination of the history of Jewish mysticism. It is focused on and within entire communities, rather than encompassing self-isolating individuals; thus, it emphatically embraces the ultimate Jewish mystical imperative of benefiting the community at large and not merely the individual mystic. The *hassid* abandons himself within the greater perfection of God, but a primary means of so doing is to recognize God within all aspects of God's creation. That creation includes not only the human community around us but also all of the elements of nature that surround and interpenetrate the human community.

One of the syntheses effected by late, post-Lurianic Kabbalah, as we have seen, is that between the *tzadik*, who is understood to have achieved a liaison with the deepest, most hidden recesses of God and, as such, is capable of perceiving the prior phases of an individual soul's past lives, and the miracle worker, who can accomplish more everyday effects to help his community out of individual and group difficulties. The power to accomplish both practical and esoteric feats, as suggested in late Kabbalah and its messianic offspring, is derived from the power of God's ineffable *name*: that is, through intimate knowledge of the name expressed by a unique ability to manipulate the Tetragrammaton. The name of the all-good God is the Good

Name; thus, such a *tzadik* would be called a "master of the good name," a *ba'al* ("master") *shem* ("name") *tov* ("good").[30] While that phrase could be used to refer to any number of individuals possessing such a capability, it came eventually to refer, almost as a personal name, to the individual viewed as the founder of Hassidism, Israel ben Eliezer, known to history simply as the Ba'al Shem Tov.

The Ba'al Shem Tov may be seen as a solution to a complex problem of void and despair that may be seen to have swept European Judaism, particularly within its eastern and central regions, in the seventeenth and eighteenth centuries. In the West, the seventeenth century had yielded two antithetical directions for thinking about the *sacer*. On the one hand, as we have seen, there was an intensified spirituality with a specifically messianic focus affecting even the most overtly political of places and situations. On the other, in the sweep of philosophical thought that carries from Descartes (the French Catholic) to Spinoza (the Dutch Jew) to Leibnitz and Bacon (both Protestants, one German and the other English), we recognize a gradual but emphatic shift in a secular direction, one that would move from the God-related questions that had previously torn Western Christendom apart in Reformation and Counter-Reformation bloodbaths toward questioning the very existence of an all-powerful, all-knowing, all-good God.

That sweep would have multiple consequences into the eighteenth century and beyond. In conjunction with industrial, technological, scientific, and political revolutions, Western European intellectuals like Voltaire would understand themselves to be in the midst of an age of enlightenment, emerging from what they considered to be the darkness of religious thinking. Since that thinking was also *sectarian* religious thinking, enlightenment—at least in *theory*—meant liberation from the animosity between Protestant and Catholic and from the Christian majority toward the Jewish minority. Thus, the era of the Enlightenment is also the era of the emancipation of the Jewish communities of much of western Europe. From the fringes of the Christian world, Jews could now begin to move to the center of social, economic, cultural, and even political involvement in a *secular* Christian world.

In the East, such changes in thinking on the part of the Christian majority and in the condition of the Jewish minority were far rarer. Thus, the Eastern European Jewish communities of the seventeenth and eighteenth centuries were downtrodden and despairing, oppressed on the one hand by the policies of church and state, bitterly disappointed and disillusioned in the aftermath of the failures of first one then another messianic pretender, and pushed down by increasingly complex rabbinic legislation. These communities were thus caught between a hostile outside world and a rigid Jewish leadership that had largely come to pride itself on making minute legalistic points for the sake of making those points.[31] They were further caught in the cross fire between that disputational Jewish leadership and a new wave of "Enlightenment" (the Hebrew word is *Haskalah*) thinkers influenced by the secularized tendencies coming from the West.

The Ba'al Shem Tov, with his notions of religious joy, communicable not only by Torah study and formalized prayer but also by singing and dancing one's fervency and recognizing God's glory in the beauty of the world around us, uplifted those who followed his lead. Symptomatic of his importance to his ever-expanding community of followers is the tradition that later emerged that he had participated triumphantly in a disputation that involved a key rabbinic figure and the treacherous and traitorous Jacob Frank. He blew off the dust-laden responses of the one and sliced through the deceptions of the other.

The Ba'al Shem Tov created a movement that was both a logical culmination and a contradiction of the prior Jewish mystical tradition. For, in some respects, Israel ben Eliezer and his alleged abilities represent an intensified expansion of the precepts and assertions of Lurianic Kabbalah in its most esoteric aspects, as well as of late Kabbalah in its practical, wonder-working aspects. In its turn further outward to the world and its emphasis on improving it—*tikkun olam*—Hassidism continued both the general direction of Jewish mysticism and the specific directives associated with Lurianic Kabbalah. On the other hand, in being such a far-flung community, the *hassidim* who followed the Ba'al Shem Tov by definition constituted a contradiction of the quietistic, inner-circle esoteric emphases of the Jewish mystical tradition.

The Ba'al Shem Tov was born in Ukup, in Podolia, Poland, in or around 1700. His father Eliezer had a strong reputation as a man of kindness, particularly kindness to strangers. He is said to have unknowingly entertained none other than the prophet Elijah, disguised as a beggar, one Sabbath day. Hassidic tradition asserts that he was a vizier to princes, and he was also said to have enjoyed, at the age of one hundred, the birth of a son, whom he named Israel.[32] The story is told that as a young adult, Israel ben Eliezer was a failure as a teacher of children in a *heder* (Jewish elementary school) and that he served as the village synagogue *shamash* ("sexton"), which instilled a strong sense of humility within him. The son of the synagogue's rabbi—Rabbi Adam is the name that has been passed down—was adept in the Lurianic and Sabbataean mysteries and taught such things to young Israel. This would suggest in a very direct way that the Ba'al Shem Tov represents a continuation of the first (Lurianic) part of that tradition and an answer to the second (Sabbataean) part. He is said to have left his community and withdrawn from the world at large into the Carpathian Mountains to commune with nature, before returning and revealing himself as one in contact with God's *mysterion*, at the age of forty. We immediately recognize that number as consistent with key biblical and postbiblical personality patterns, from Moses's going out into the *sacer* from Egypt at age forty to Rabbi Akiva's assumption of command within the *Sanhedrin* at age forty.

Returned to the community and to the wife whom he had temporarily (?) left behind, the Ba'al Shem Tov is said to have become a tavern keeper in the town of Brody. Actually, his wife ran the tavern, while he traveled about performing miracles—cures, exorcisms, telling about the future—all of which acts were occasioned by his connection to the ineffable divine Name. Put another way, everything about the Ba'al Shem Tov seems to pertain to actions rather than words—to say it as the Greeks would have, it is the *ergon* ("action") of the Ba'al Shem Tov, rather than the *logos*, for which he was known. Not just miraculous acts, but more importantly, every everyday banal act in which he engaged became imbued with a *sacer*-connected quality. When words emerged, either for him or for his successors, they took the form of *mythos*, not of *logos*: of tales and parables—including tales *about* him—not of theory or esoteric formulae.

This matrix of issues may be perceived in a story told regarding his immediate successor, Dov Baer. Dov Baer began as a strong opponent of the Ba'al Shem Tov and his style of engaging God and the world, but his mind and soul were seduced by the master, and he eventually became both his son-in-law and his most important successor. There was a time when Dov Baer heard that the Ba'al Shem Tov was passing through a village near enough that he might visit him. As Dov Baer prepared for his journey to that village, one of his own disciples asked why he was bothering—why not wait until the two were in the same town for a visit, instead of putting himself out? What exactly was he going for? Dov Baer's response was, "To see how he ties his shoelaces." His point was that the most apparently insignificant of actions became imbued with a *sacer* quality, that observing the Ba'al Shem in such an action could spiritually enrich the viewer more than a wagonload of prayers and Torah readings. Moreover, other stories suggest that when the BeSh'T (as his name came to be abbreviated as an acronym) spoke to a group of his followers, no matter how large, each individual felt as if he were being personally addressed by the teacher.

The most esoteric of ideas may evolve through the teachings of the BeSh'T and his followers, but always extends out to a broad community of followers. Thus, the Hassidic movement might be called one of social esotericism. The *tzadik*—the BeSh'T and then those who follow him as masters around whom circles of followers grow—is understood by his constituents to have achieved a unique condition of enlightenment regarding how to achieve *d'vekut*, or clinging (literally "gluedness"),[33] to God's hiddenmost, innermost recess. He expresses it in his actions, in the way he lives his life (which is why the most banal of actions will be observed by his followers, who hope thereby to glean a spark of enlightenment). Previous generations—and the generations who follow mainstream Jewish tradition who are contemporaries of the BeSh'T and the *tzadikim* who follow through the eighteenth and nineteenth and twentieth centuries—look to the Torah, seeking in its depths answers to the question of how to find the inner depths of God. But the BeSh'T and the *tzadikim* who follow him are understood to have "become the Torah." He (they) contain(s) all the answers within him (them) and, so, must not only be hearkened to as he (they) teach(es) and chant(s) and dance(s) on the Sabbath but also studied with respect to every gesture.[34]

It is this emphasis on personality rather than on doctrine that helped produce such violent opposition to *Hassidut* from much of the mainstream eastern European rabbinic leadership. From the outsider's perspective, the blind adoration and veneration of the *tzadik* was tantamount to the worship of Jesus on the part of Christians; thus, it offered not merely a threat to the political leadership of the rabbis but a threat to the community by leading it down a slippery slope toward apostasy. Of course, the outsider failed to recognize that, from the inside, as venerated as the *tzadik* might be, he was understood to contain within himself only half of the process necessary for fulfilling the ultimate goal of the Jewish mystic: *tikkun olam*, or repairing the world. For only with a complete and seamless partnership between *tzadik* and *hassidim*—down to the most socioeconomically, culturally, intellectually, and spiritually impoverished of them—might such *tikkun* ("repair") be hoped for.

This symbiotic relationship between the *tzadik* and his *hassidim* is one of the obvious differences between what the *tzadik* is in *Hassidut* and how he was often misperceived by outsiders: He cannot accomplish *tikkun olam* alone; he is not—contrary to the sense of him expressed by those who feared apostasy—a Christ figure, either in the sense of being worshipped (he is merely venerated) or in the sense of self-sacrifice on behalf of the community. This is in spite of the accumulation of stories about him: that, for example, on the Sabbath he steps onto his handkerchief and disappears on that humble vehicle to the innermost recesses of heaven to converse with God, to report to God the needs of the community and return with a statement to the community of the needs of God! It's as if he *could* shoulder all of the responsibility of *tikkun* but he doesn't—because he *can't* as that's not how it is *supposed to be*, any more than the all-powerful and all-good God always intervenes to prevent an evil act: God could but God doesn't because God cannot, because then we would be deprived of free will, and that's not the way it's supposed to be.

The partnership between the *tzadik* and his *hassidim* that can ultimately yield perfection in the world is ultimately rooted in a series of underlying concepts that, over time, came to be associated with the Ba'al Shem Tov. His teachings emphasize the importance of religious fervor, of pure and powerful intention—*kavanah* is the Hebrew word he used, meaning to direct one's self fully toward God. This is a fervor that is expressed not only with the traditional Jewish instrumentation of the word—prayers, chanted with enthusiasm, and stories, shared with passion—but also with melody, often wordless melody (*n'ginah*), and also with the entire body: dancing that explodes with passion and enthusiasm. That all-encompassing fervor extends from the master—the *tzadik*—to his disciples, followers, companions—his *hassidim*—and rushes through their bodies as through their souls. This is the analog of the enthusiastic embrace of God (the soul of the universe), who is found rushing throughout the universe (the physical "body" of the macrocosm). Hassidic thought with regard to God and the universe is panhenotheistic. Not *pantheism* (all things as gods) but the one (*heno*) God (*theos*) in everything (*pan*), a concept we have earlier encountered in the thought of Ibn 'Arabi and Julian of Norwich.

Thus, the starting point of the BeSh'T's teaching is love (*ahavah*): the love of God expressed in love for the created world in all of its aspects, since God is found embedded in everything around us. Prayer (*t'filah*) itself is understood as a merging between addressing God with praise and addressing God with supplication—not in the sense of asking for fulfillment in the here and now as much as yearning for *oneness* with God—which, in order to be real must be conducted with fervency, with *kavanah*. Beyond prayer, there is *avodah*—service to God expressed not only in terms of scrupulous observance of God's commandments but also in terms of one's everyday thoughts, words, and actions within the *profanus*. Good deeds should not be additives to one's life but its essence, based on a love of those around one that is rooted in the love of God and the recognition of God's presence in everyone and everything.[35]

If, then, one might extract doctrines out of the *Hassidut* that began with the BeSh'T and continued to evolve over the next 150 years, one would start with creation, referred to as *y'tzirah* (rather than *bri'ah*). We may recognize in that choice of term both a direct sense of continuity back to the first Jewish mystical texts[36] and an allusion to the same sort of humility we encountered in them: that even in discussing God's creation of the universe, we recognize the impossibility of really explaining or exploring it at its divine heart. Thus, rather than using the biblical term *bri'ah*, which refers to divine *creatio ex nihilo*, we discuss it using a term that means "shaping, forming"—as a potter shapes clay into a bowl or a carpenter shapes wood into a table. Even so, the doctrine taught by the BeSh'T is one of *creatio* ex nihilo, of course, but in offering a statement of the relationship between God and ourselves that begins with creation, his doctrine emphasizes God's filling every crevice of creation

with Its love and mercy: This is emanation in extremis rather than the contraction that we have seen to have emerged as a creation theory in Lurianic
Kabbalah.[37]

God's primary instrument in accomplishing creation was wisdom—
hokhmah—which is also the sacerdotal intermediary between the innermost
recesses of the *sacer* and the sacerdotes, like Abraham and Moses, through
whom wisdom is disseminated throughout the moral and intellectual universe
(as God itself is disseminated through the physical universe through *y'tzirah*.)
In each of us, an element of both Godness and wisdom is contained within
our souls. The soul (*n'shamah*) is inherently pure but became corrupted
though its union with the body. In order to regain its purity, the soul must
strive to be minimally dependent on the body and its needs—so there is an ascetic aspect to *Hassidut* that finds roots in the Lurianic tradition—and strive
to accomplish good acts that elevate and purify the doer.

This last concept leads directly to two principles. The first is *musar*
("morality"): The highest form of morality is defined as *awe* of God, which
is intimately interwoven with and a precondition for *love* of God—and, given
that God is found in everyone and everything, it translates practically into
love of, and proper actions toward, all one's fellow beings. More specifically,
if reverence for, and awe and love of, God comprise the primary and ultimate
moral mode, the second (which leads to the first) is love of and study of Torah
(which is God's word and the umbilicus between God and ourselves). Thus,
as much as love and reverence for the *tzadik* are essential, and as much as the
tzadik is himself a kind of embodiment of the Torah, the Torah continues to
be a centerpiece of the *hassid*'s life. Prayer and song follow in the hierarchy
of shaping a moral being, since, interwoven, these lead to yearning for God
and thence to devotion to God. And finally, benevolence is, after God, Torah,
and prayer and song, the fourth pillar of Hassidic *musar*. But all of these elements are as intertwined as the threads in the tightest of tapestries.

And so, the second principle to which the concepts of creation, wisdom,
and soul directly lead is that of *mitzvah*. This word, in common use in the
Jewish tradition, means "commandment," but it is in particular through *Hassidut* that it has arrived at the common-parlance meaning of "good deed." For
in *Hassidut*, every act of kindness is understood to be a response to a divine
imperative to improve the world: The act of doing good deeds is not a function of a desire to go beyond what is expected of us but of a desire to fulfill
the most limited and basic of divine precepts, the fulfillment of which brings
us closer to God.

Moreover, these precepts apply in two directions, that of human-human
interaction and that of human-divine interaction. In the first case, we recognize the commandment to treat each other with a sense of awareness of

the God that resides in us all. In the second case, the *hassid* (by definition, pious) prays, first of all, with fervency, with a burning, an "enflamement," as one might literally render the word *heetlahavut*—translated in ordinary parlance as "enthusiasm" but built on the Hebrew root *lahav*, meaning "flame." Second of all, one's sense of clinging to God—*d'vekut*, literally (as we recall from Judah the Hassid's work, in chapter 6 "being glued," from the root *d-v-k*, meaning "to stick, glue"—carries out of prayers and out of the synagogue into one's everyday life and everyday thoughts, words, and actions, in all of which one remains conscious of God's abiding presence and of God's abiding love for all of creation. Thus, even if and when apparently unhappy events occur in one's life, one does not despair but rather maintains one's fervent faith in God's overarching kindness and expresses gratitude for that.[38]

Cognate with the understanding of mitzvah is the Hassidic articulation of the concept of *ahavah*: love, to come full circle. It is not only that one's love of God is sincere, whole-hearted, engineered with *heetlahavut*, and driven by a yearning for *d'vekut*, but that it exists as an end unto itself. The *hassid* loves God in order to love God, because both he and the world are ultimately enriched by that relationship, rather than because of hope for some personal reward or compensation: The small part he plays in *tikkun olam* by virtue of his effort toward *d'vekut* is reward enough. Moreover, his intention is to carry to an extreme the principle of *imitatio dei* that is endemic to all religious traditions. As God is holy and pure, the *hassid* seeks to become holy and pure, and the most obvious means of achieving that state of being is by clinging to God through one's prayers, by the *hassid*'s merciful and benevolent thoughts, words, and actions vis-à-vis all those around him, and by his or her genuine appreciation of nature and the world around him—the creation in its totality—that is imbued with godliness.

There is, finally, a threefold articulation of the relationship between God and the world that the BeSh'T offered to his followers. The principle of *m'tziut adonai*—the "substantial existence" (literally "foundness") of God—is the first. By this phrase, the Ba'al Shem Tov means that God not only exists (a given for any believer) but also that God's existence is manifest in the world because God *is found* throughout the realm of creation—and not only in the physical creation but also in the deeds and words and even the thoughts of humankind. Thus, even as God is more distant than the most distant star, unencompassed by the most distant realm of the heavens, God is as near as one's own breathing—nothing is nearer to us than God—who is thus, by pure paradox, both *infinitely transcendent and infinitesimally immanent*. At every moment of our conscious awareness of God's presence (*shekhinah*), God *is* present, whether in the synagogue, the bedroom, the fields and forests, or the bathroom: The most banal of places and actions have *sacer* potential not only for the *tzadik* but also for each and every *hassid*, thereby reinforcing the essential interwovenness of the *tzadik-hasid* relationship and the importance of that interwovenness for fulfilling the goal of *tikkun olam*.

God's relationship to us as an all-abiding presence is expressed, secondly, in the notion of Providence—*hashgahah*—the fact of God's awareness of everything, everywhere, always. God's absolute foreknowledge of every word and action is not to be confused with the notion that our words and actions are predetermined. Since humans have free will, we do what we do without divine intervention to push us or pull us this way or that—but God knows before we do what choices we will make. God's interest and interventionist activity is expressed, rather, in offering a model of absolute virtue that we ought to emulate. To the extent that we do emulate that model, our actions are virtuous; we are part of the process of improving the world (*tikkun olam*) and are accomplishing the mergence (*d'vekut*) with God that we seek and that will ultimately make us most happy.[39]

The third aspect of rearticulating the divine-human relationship is by way of the term *hashpa'ah* ("effluence"), which seems to bring *Hassidut* back to classical Kabbalah and its sense of God's creative process as one of emanation out of itself into what becomes creation (albeit, in Kabbalah, this is articulated as the flow through the specific "channels" of the *sephirot*) rather than furthering the late kabbalistic, Lurianic notion of the creative process as one of *tzimtzum*. So, to repeat, whereas *Hassidut* is in so many other ways an outgrowth, continuation, and even furthering of Lurianic ideas, in this one important aspect of its thought it runs in a contrary direction to that of the Lurianic "school."

But the notion of *hashpa'ah* is not quite the same as that of emanation (*'atzilut*). It refers less to God's extending itself into the world as a statement of the process of divine creation than to the manner in which God provides for all of creation according to the particularized needs of its myriad constituents—from humans to elephants to cockroaches, from trees to blades of grass to pebbles. There is a hierarchy of needs that yields a hierarchy of emanational response from God—as well as of divine expectations. Humans have been endowed with an intellectual soul that makes it possible for us to achieve some grasp of God, and we are therefore expected to seek God in a manner not possible for other species. It is that ability and the responsibility that comes with it that transforms a human from *adam*—a clod of earth (*adamah*)—to *ish* ("man").[40]

In striving for *d'vekut* with God, a human achieves an *ish* state of being. In emulating God's goodness by thinking, saying, and doing good thoughts, words, and acts with a constant consciousness of and enthusiasm (*heetla-*

havut) for God and a desire to emulate God, one is striving for and coming closer to *d'vekut*—and the world comes closer to perfection. To cease that striving through ceasing to think, speak, and act with divinely graced, pure *kavanah* is to lose the thread of connectedness to God's purity. Although God by definition remains connected to every human, as God does to all of creation, the human who falls short through evil thoughts, words, and actions loses the *ish* status of closer, deeper, richer connection. The human becomes less human, more spiritually impoverished, and the world suffers as a consequence.

CHRISTIAN MYSTICISM, KABBALAH, AND POST-RENAISSANCE DEVELOPMENTS

In the period that carries from classical Kabbalah through its Lurianic and post-Lurianic phases and on into *Hassidut*, there is a series of interesting turns taken by Christian mysticism to which we must turn before following into the era that leads to our own time. Specifically, in addition to the developments within Christian mysticism that we have discussed previously (in chapter 7), there is the interesting phenomenon of Christian mystics delving deeply into Kabbalah and, in some cases, into Sufism in their broad-based desire to find the ultimate path to God's hiddenmost recesses.

As far back as the thirteen and fourteenth centuries, there is evidence of this. Thus, the Catalonian Raimundo Lulio (1234–1316), whose *Ars inveniendi veritatis* (*The Art of Discovering the Truth*) derived from no less than five visions that he had experienced of Christ on the cross, was perhaps the first great Christian mystic from the Iberian Peninsula. He was in any case the first great writer in the Catalan language and an innovator in a number of theological and scientific directions.[41] More to the point, he grew up in Majorca, where there were large non-Christian minorities, and was thus both aware of and quite clearly sympathetic to forms of spirituality other than his own. He arrived at spirituality through a religious epiphany in 1265 that caused him to become a lay brother of the Franciscan order. Raimundo's *Ars magna* of around 1275 (the final version was not published until 1305)—initially composed after one of his visions, in which he saw and understood how everything in the universe could be related to the Godhead through divine attributes, such as goodness and greatness—was written to argue against the "errors of the infidel."

He refers to those attributes as "dignities," and his discussion of them sounds remarkably like the discussion of the *sephirot* in Kabbalah. On the other hand, it has been said by some that the inspiration for the system laid out in the *Ars magna*, where different divine attributes are engaged in different combinations, was inspired by his observation of Muslim astrologers employing a *zairja*. That device uses the twenty-eight letters of the Arabic alphabet, assigning to them numerical values and organizing them into categories, then manipulating them to offer new paths of thought and insight. Raimundo's diagrams and symbolic notation of what he refers to as a "ladder of being" that connects all forms of knowledge to manifestations of God's "dignities," as well as his manipulation of the letters of the alphabet, also suggest either influence from or a fortuitous parallel with the pre-Zoharic and Zoharic discussion of the *sephirot*. Elsewhere he makes use of numerology in his discussions, and in other works he seems influenced by Sufi mystics. That Raimundo was acquainted with Jewish mystical thought is demonstrated by the fact that one of his works was entitled *De audito cabbalistice*.

In general, the use of Kabbalah and Sufi thought by Christians between the thirteenth and sixteenth centuries was for the purposes of attempting to convert Jews and Muslims by demonstrating the correspondences between their respective faiths and Christianity (but the subtle superiority of Christianity) and, with regard to the Jews, to convince them of the practical advisability of joining a larger, more "successful" faith without having to give up the key tenets of their own smaller, less "successful" faith. On the other hand, the long-held Christian belief in the association between the Jews and the Satan and the Antichrist, which also translated into associating Jews with magic (as a *suspect* mode of engaging the *sacer*, analogous, as such, to association with the Satan as a *negative* aspect of the *sacer*), also led to an interest in practical (as opposed to esoteric) Kabbalah, with its more "magical" (i.e., "lower" *sacer*) aspects.

Perhaps the most significant variation on this was in the work of Giovanni Pico della Mirandola (1463–1494), whose interest in Kabbalah derived both from his desire to understand—or reshape—Kabbalah as a Christian mystical discipline, out of a belief that it (Kabbalah) confirms Christianity, and from his generally far-reaching interests and open-minded sensibilities. For Pico was one of the important philosophers associated with the *accademia* circle of Lorenzo de Medici—particularly Marsilio Ficino, who translated Plato's works from Greek to Latin under Lorenzo's patronage and who became one of Pico's teachers—in late fifteenth-century Florence. He was best known for his nine hundred theses on religion, philosophy, natural science, and magic, published in 1486 when he was only twenty-three years old and to which he appended a preface, "Oration on the Dignity of Man," which vaulted him to prominence. The "Orations" and their preface came to be known as the pre-eminent statement of humanist thinking—as the "Manifesto of the Renaissance."[42]

Trained in Greek as well as Latin, Pico also studied Hebrew and Arabic and probably Aramaic and counted among his friends and associates not only Christian humanists like Lorenzo, Ficino, and their associates but also the rabid antihumanist preacher Savanarola, who would briefly control Florence in the mid-1490s before being overthrown and burned at the stake. He was also very friendly with the Jewish scholar Elia del Medigo, with whom he studied Near Eastern languages. Pico's broad-based thinking encompassed Greco-Roman mystery religions, the Hermetic writings associated with Hermes Trismegistos, Zoroastrianism, the so-called Chaldaean Oracles, and Greek Orphic hymns[43]—in all of which he saw correspondences with Kabbalah as he also studied it and in all of which he in turn perceived anticipatory references to Christianity. He was a champion of the idea of syncretistic thinking, perceiving different schools of thought to be directed toward the same issues and capable of reconciliation, be it Platonic with Aristotelian thought or Greek philosophy and Jewish and Muslim thought with Christian thought.

In addition to the nine hundred theses and their appended "Oration," which brought Pico into the way of papal opposition and the authority of the Inquisition, who saw much to be considered heretical in them, Pico subsequently wrote works focused on the problem of divine creation, as well as one tearing apart the underlying theories of astrology. He saw in this discipline an address of "lower magic" rather than the "higher magic" that has as a goal to benefit humankind by its penetration of the *sacer*. For Pico was not only convinced of the unique position of humankind within the hierarchy of God's creatures but also saw the human position as standing outside the standard animal chain of being, yet sliding within it in accordance with how we behave.

Thus, when we operate at a more profound and philosophical level we ascend within the chain toward the angels and toward communion with God; when we don't use our intellect, we descend toward the worms. Moreover we are unique as a species in having the capacity to change how we are through the exercise of free will. If, on the one hand, his writing feeds into the Renaissance idea of the solitary, divinely inspired genius (who resides at the peak of the hierarchy), on the other hand, one can readily see how an interest in esoteric mystical systems would have been consistent with this viewpoint.[44] He apparently studied a number of kabbalistic texts, such as the commentary on the *Sepher Yetzirah* of Moses ben Nahman of Gerona.[45]

One of the most interesting ways in which his kabbalistically attuned thinking expresses itself is in his observation that there are eighty-six Orphic hymns and that eighty-six equals *Elohim* (biblical Hebrew for "Lord") by way of numerology, thus suggesting an equivalence between the two systems—one pagan Greek, the other Judaeo-Christian (not *Jewish*, but *Judaeo-Christian*)—of addressing the *sacer*.[46] Syntheses of different kinds of doctrines and thought from different traditions, including but not limited to Kabbalah, offers the solution to the ultimate problem for the world: not creation—the answer to which question is a means to an end—but the end itself, the solution to the problem of good and evil. If we are to understand how evil exists in a world created by a God that is both all-good and all-powerful—and this is ultimately the purpose for which we should seek to understand creation—then we must seek in and through every tradition and all traditions and find their common threads. As such, we can weave a new tapestry of explanation that will be the tapestry of solution to the problem.

While Pico connects Christian and Jewish mysticism by his deliberate and specific use of kabbalistic thought in general, the overall breadth of his theological and philosophical studies connects him as a thinker to Abraham Abulafia, the first Jewish mystic to believe that he could provide equal access to the *mysterion* to Christians and Muslims as well as to Jews of both genders and a range of backgrounds. Pico also connects to the Muslim mystical poet Rumi, who, as we have seen, also taught that the path to the *mysterion* was multi-branched (although Rumi went even farther in suggesting that the path is not paved by God to favor any group over any other).

⌒⊗⌒

This occasional emergence of an emphatic universality among mystics within the Abrahamic traditions, carrying them outside the more usual tendency to think in more discreet terms, will also, on occasion, extend beyond those traditions to interface non-Abrahamic faiths (the more so, interestingly enough, in the nineteenth and twentieth centuries, as we shall see in the last two chapters of this discussion). Perhaps the most interesting of figures who follows such a course, a contemporary of Pico and of Jami (see chapter 8, pp. 185ff) and, like the latter, a poet, is Kabir (ca. 1440–1518).[47]

One of the more compelling figures in the entire history of Indian mysticism, Kabir was born in or near Benares, and little is known about his childhood: The weaver family in which he grew up was apparently Muslim, but some assert that he was born of a Brahman widow and adopted by a childless Muslim couple. Otherwise, the only information regarding his early life is that he became a disciple of the renowned Hindu ascetic Ramananda and a devotee of that form of Hinduism known as *Bhakti* (Sanskrit for "devotion"), which emphasizes the divine-human love relationship, particularly (but not only) as expressed in the literature that presents Krishna (an avatar of the god Vishnu) as engaged in a love-relationship with Radha, a *gopi* ("goatherd girl").[48]

Kabir came to be revered as a teacher (in Sanskrit, *guru*) who emphasized inward, loving devotion to a divine principle. As much as his poetry has a rapturous, passionate, and prophetic feel to it, it is directed to the common man.

He eschewed the sort of social distinction enshrined in the Hindu caste system and despised the religious exclusivism that went with it, as well as the sort of religious perspective that emphasized differences between Hindu and Muslim thought. He would eventually disavow an affiliation with either tradition—or better put, he asserted his membership in both as "at once a child of 'Allah and of Ram"; he "dreamed of reconciling the intense personal Mohammedan [*sic*] mysticism [expressed in the poetry of Hafiz, who was then exercising a strong influence on Indian thought] with the traditional theology of Brahmanism."[49]

Kabir understood life to be an interplay between the individual, personal soul (*Jivatma*) and God, the universal soul (*Paramatma*). Salvation (in the dual sense of the survival of the individual and the perfection of the *profanus* world) derives from the synthesis of the two. That synthesis involves a merging of Hindu (especially Bhakti) and Muslim (especially Sufi) ideas; thus, the Hindu notion of an ongoing cycle of reincarnation governed by the law of karma[50] is joined to the Muslim assertion of a single God and its rejection both of the worship of images and of a social or religious caste system.

Kabir's poems are spontaneous expressions of his vision and the divine love that enveloped him; they are reflections of the passion for the infinite expressed through the vocabulary of a mystically intimate and personal realization of God. Kabir constantly extols the life of the home, family, and love and criticizes those who assert that the road to connection with the divine is a road of flight away from the world of love, joy, and beauty:

> Lamps burn in every house, O blind one,
> and you cannot see them!
> One day your eyes shall suddenly be opened
> and you shall see: and the fetters
> of death will fall from you.
> There is nothing to say or hear.
> there is nothing to do:
> It is he who is living, yet dead,
> who shall never die again. (XXI)[51]

For "he who is living, yet dead" is the one who revels in and experiences the joys of nature, the love of life on earth that is found through the things that God has created, immersed within which one dies to the wrong-directed austerities of an ascetic life and is reborn in a full savoring of the *profanus*—and "dead" in the sense of being merged with the *sacer*, which is yet the source of eternal life. The true guru guides his devotees on such a path, not the path of mindless chanting, endless rituals, or self-flagellations, which are substitutes for reality and, in fact, impediments to intimacy with the *mysterion*. For these actions are walls separating the human soul from the divine soul within the God of love and beauty.

Love between man and woman is both a symbol and a preparation for divine love and, like the first link in a chain, connects to love of nature and one's fellowhuman (as a second link) and thus to devotion (*bhakti*) to the deity through an appreciation of his universe (the third link). Kabir's metaphoric expression ties *sacer* and *profanus* love together:

> Dear friend, I am eager to meet my Beloved!
> My youth has flowered, and the pain of separation from Him
> troubles my breast.
> I am wandering yet in the alleys of knowledge
> without purpose, but I have received
> His news in these alleys of knowledge.
> I have received a letter from my Beloved;
> in this letter is an unutterable message, and now
> my fear of death is done away.
> Kabir says: 'O my loving friend!
> I have got for my gift
> the deathless One.' (LI)

The separation from the beloved is the separation from God; the knowledge is esoteric spiritual knowledge that, like human-human love, is a prelude to union with the divine; the message is unutterable because the language of the *sacer* (the more so the *mysterion* deep within it) is ineffable. Through union with the divine, death is done away with, for the devotee, in becoming one with the *sacer*. One, is both "dead" already to the meaningless *profanus* and deathless in being one with the eternal and unchanging God.[52]

Kabir spoke always of the "simple union" with divine reality—"O Sadhu! The simple union is the best" (XLI)—as the joy and *duty* of the soul. God is wherever God is sought, in the heart of the common man and in the beauty of nature, without specificity as to the institutional religious affiliation of the devotee:

> Oh servant, where dost thou seek Me?
> Lo! I am beside thee.
> I am neither in temple nor in mosque: I am neither in Ka'aba nor in Kailash,
> neither am I in rituals and ceremonies, nor in Yoga and renunciation.
> If thou art a true seeker, thou shallt
> at once see Me: thou shallt meet Me in a
> moment of time.
> Kabir says: 'O Sadhu! God is the breath of all breath!'

. . . Are you looking for me? I am in the next seat,
My shoulder is against yours.
You will not find me in the stupas, not in Indian shrine rooms,
not in synagogues nor in cathedrals:
Not in your masses, nor kirtans, not in legs winding
around your own neck, nor in eating nothing but vegetables.
When you really look for me you will see me instantly—
You will find me in the tiniest house of time.
Kabir says: Student, tell me, what is God?
He is the breath within the breath. (I)

Not in the edifices or actions associated with any in the range of institutional forms of faith—be it Hinduism or Islam, Judaism, Christianity, or Yoga[53]— will God be found, who is rather in the innermost recesses of the everyday person's love of, and preparation to serve, God. Neither ascetic practices nor specialized gastronomy, which separate one from ordinary *profanus* life, will get one there; rather, the full-hearted recognition that God is all around and within everything will lead to God.

~∞~

Between the time of Pico and Kabir and our own era, diverse Christian mystics articulated their own variations on the traditional theme of seeking oneness with God as the Christ by means of reference not only to earlier Christian mysticism but also to other sources of esoteric knowledge, such as alchemy and astronomy.[54] Thus, more than a century after Pico, the German mystic Jakob Boehme (1575–1624)—the shepherd of his father's flocks as a boy, who went off to make his fortune and became a master shoemaker— experiencing an epiphany, began to compose a series of mystical works in the decade or so after 1612. Boehme is the first Protestant mystic we have encountered; that is, until the sixteenth century, by definition, every Western Christian mystic might be termed "Roman Catholic" since Rome was the center and only center of Western Christendom.[55]

Boehme's first work, *Aurora,* merely passed around at first among a small circle of friends in manuscript form, hand to hand, generated a following— and also provoked a charge of heresy from the locally powerful Lutheran pastor, Gregorius Richter. Boehme was forced to desist from writing but, after a few years, could not avoid returning to his inspired task, writing a continuous series of works that flowed through him like water through a sieve. Among others, he wrote *On the Threefold Life of Man, Six Mystical Points, Concerning the Birth and Designation of All Being, The Mysterium Magnum* ("*Great Mystery*"), and *The Way to Christ.*

If Pico sought to understand the workings of good and evil by plumbing whatever intellectual and mystical sources he could find, ancient or contemporary, Christian or Jewish, Muslim or pagan, Boehme contended that the endlessness of God—the unfathomable and unplumbable depth and height that is God—means not only that we cannot understand God but also that we cannot grasp the logical illogic of the coexistence of what *we call* good and evil both within the universe and *within God itself*. It is, as it were, less a moral question than one of the limited mathematics of volume that we possess and of our imposing labels on aspects of reality that fail to fit into the sort of mental boxes that labeling is supposed to reflect.

God is the ultimate source of all that is and thus contains within it both good and evil, as God is both the nothing and the all: Everything that *is* derives from God and thus contains God within it, but God ultimately precedes all of material reality and is therefore utter no-thing-ness. One might say that for Boehme the dual human inclinations for enacting good or evil are mirrors of the dual aspects located within God that are embodied in Christ and Lucifer, which two aspects are both accessible to us through intense focus and concentration. For

> all things have their beginning from the outflow of the divine will, be it evil or good, love or sorrow. Since the Will of God is not a *thing*, neither *nature* nor *creature*, but in that Will there is neither pain, suffering, nor contrary will, from the outflow of the Word, as through the outgoing of the ungrounded mind (which is the wisdom of God, the great *Mysterium* in which the eternal understanding lay within the *temperamentum* [i.e., eternal, timeless time]) understanding and knowledge flowed forth. This same outflow is a beginning of the willing by which the Understanding divided Itself into forms [i.e., the forms of the created world].[56]

We may recognize in Boehme's panhenotheistic view—which many of his contemporaries misunderstood to be *pantheistic* and overly broad in what it embraced as God-connected—an affinity for the thought of Ibn 'Arabi and Julian of Norwich before him and the Ba'al Shem Tov after him. But Boehme naturally understands God to be accessibly manifest to us in Christ and, of course, wrote a substantial handful of works, whereas for Ibn 'Arabi or the BeSh'T, a human shape to God would be unthinkable, and we have access to the latter's thoughts only through the sayings and stories ascribed to him by others.

God is the primordial depth out of which the creation—particularly humans, who are the apex of creation—struggles forth to become manifest and self-aware. The human soul has achieved a certain level of self-awareness and thus of awareness of God, who resides within our soul, as It does in everything around us. But, in order to achieve perfection, the soul must be reborn into a deeper awareness of God. The process of achieving that awareness will culminate in grace residing upon and within the human soul, which is to say that the soul will be fully suffused with and embedded within Godness. If God is already by definition within us and embedded within our souls—a manifestation of the outflowing will of God through God's creative word—it is only a matter of cleansing our souls of the polluting corruption with which they have been infested by the Satan.

As God created the world and us with the *word* (in Genesis: "and God *said*, 'Let there be light,' . . . 'let there be a firmament,'" and so forth), and as God self-manifested as the Christ by means of the word (in John: "and the Word became flesh"), then we were all created by a process analogous to that through which Christ came into our world, which means that Christ offers an inherent route through which we can access the *mysterion*. And so, Boehme asserts, "The beginning of all being was the Word, as God's breathing forth . . . [which] Word is also the flowing out of the Divine Will or the Divine Knowledge. . . . It says: In the beginning was the Word, for the Word as the outflowing from the Will of God was the eternal beginning, and remains so eternally. . . . By Word [we understand] the *revelation* of the Will of God and by God we understand the *hidden* God."[57] Minus the Christ imagery, we can recognize a parallel to the discussion in the *Sepher Bahir* of the *sephirot* as *ma'amarot* ("sayings").[58]

So, ultimately, humans may avoid evil and its extreme expression, hell, by uniting themselves with God in the form of Christ, thereby attaining the place in heaven from which the Satan was displaced at the beginning of time. The means of access, described in Boehme's *The Way to Christ*, is by means of a process elaborated in nine parts framed in four books. Perhaps not surprisingly, given the importance of the issue of free will as a means of attaining grace—as opposed to viewing grace Calvinistically as located in the predetermined configuration of reality shaped by an all-powerful and all-knowing God—the first is the call to repent of one's sins. Boehme formulates a series of prayer sequences that will assist the devotee in assuming the proper attitude before God and thus to awaken his soul.

This shifting in attitude intersects the discussion within his second treatise: of how one might grasp the divine *mysterion* through intense concentration and contemplation. Prayer sequences follow this part, as well, as they also follow part three. The third treatise emphasizes constant self-examination on the part of the devotee: He or she must ask how, in his or her way of life, he or she can commit all of his or her activities—even the most banal and everyday of them—to God. Conversely—for the third treatise by definition prescribes a particular form of self-focus—the fourth (which constitutes the second book) calls for a particular turning *away* from the self. Boehme argues that the soul seeking oneness with the One must die within his or her own will every day (that is, give up the will through an act of will) and allow the desire for God to be subsumed into God, acted upon by God. This allows for what he discusses in his fifth treatise and third book: being reborn in God's spirit (understood as the Christ) to dwell alone within him. Thus, the self is both absorbed into God's Self and yet, by paradox, retains its individualized contours.

Boehme's fourth book with its diverse parts prescribes a series of paths by which the soul can arrive at full contemplation of the divine, and also offers a description of the great mystery in which resides the paradox of coexistent good and evil and everything and no-thing and to which, having emerged from it to self-awareness, the individual soul seeks a return. What is emphatically parallel to Jewish mysticism (minus the specific Christological elements) in this series of treatises and dialogues is the eighth treatise, in which Boehme discusses how the enlightened soul can and must return, its condition perfected from its participation in the realm of the perfected, to seek out and assist other souls yearning for perfection, helping them toward the pilgrim's route to God. In his allegorical discourse, Boehme discusses the origin and configuration of melancholy in both the general Christological terms that reference the Fall in the Garden and the mystical terms that refer to the pain of separation from God that the mystic feels and the yearning to be reunited with God—and, like an Israelite prophet who concludes his words of warning with words of comfort, he ends this discussion with hope and the comforting words that suggest the genuine possibility for accessing the *mysterion* by following the path he has laid out.

Boehme died suddenly of fever shortly after the appearance of *The Way to Christ* excited hostility once again from the Lutheran Church, but his thought yielded an ever-widening circle of followers that continued to expand beyond his death—not only in Germany but also in Holland and England. Among those inspired by him was Johannes Scheffler, born in the year of Boehme's death (1624) and, it seems to me, a symptom of how interestingly crisscrossed this story of mystical searching can be, even as—perhaps particularly as—we follow that story forward through the last four centuries. Scheffler was a Polish Lutheran by birth who studied philosophy and medicine in France, Italy, and Holland; in Holland, he encountered and was very taken with the writings of Boehme. Several years later (in 1653) Scheffler converted to Catholicism, taking the name by which he is better known: Angelus Silesius. The first part of that name refers to his sense of being a sacerdotal intermediary through which God speaks forth, the second part to the area, Silesia, from which he came. He entered the Franciscan order, ultimately became a priest (in 1661), and died at St. Matthias monastery in Breslau in 1677.

If Angelus's more political religious writings are an emphatic part of the Counter-Reformation battle to bring Protestants back into the Catholic fold, his poetry transcends sectarian boundaries—poems from the 205 that comprise his 1657 *The Soul's Spiritual Delight* have found their way into both Catholic and Protestant hymnals.[59] In the hymn "The Hidden Deer and Its Source," we recognize the imagery of Song of Songs understood as allegorical and transformed into love poetry—in which deer = human lover = human soul—that attracted Christian mystics from the beginning:

> The deer runs off to seek a cooling hidden spring
> So that it then may be refreshed and calmed therein.
> The soul, in love with God, is rushing toward the source
> From which the purest stream of life comes flowing forth.
> The source is Jesus Christ, who with his bracing draught
> Imbues us with true faith, restoring us from sin's dark wrath.
> When you drink freely from this Fount and are revived,
> Then, holy soul, you have at blessedness arrived.

This collection of hymns, together with the more than sixteen hundred rhymed couplets that make up his *The Cherubic Pilgrim* published in its first version in the same year, are Angelus's most renowned works. *The Cherubic Pilgrim* combines the stylistic elements of French Alexandrine verse with content drawn from familiar liturgical phrases, together with paradoxical scriptural verses favored by the Silesian Pietists. Thus, for example,

> *God as all names and none*
> Indeed one can name God by all His highest names
> And then again one can withdraw each one again.
>
> *Who goes past God, sees God*
> Oh Bride, if you should seek the bridegroom's face to see,
> Go past God and all things, he'll be revealed to you. . . .
>
> *The Godhead is unfathomable*
> How deep the Godhead is, no one may ever fathom;
> Even the soul of the Christ in its abyss must vanish. . . .
>
> *God is within me and around me*
> I am the vase of God, He fills me to the brim,
> He is the ocean deep, I am contained in Him. . . .
>
> *God becomes me, because I was He before*
> What I am, God becomes, takes my humanity;
> Why has he acted thusly? Because I once was He. . . .
>
> *I am like God; God is like me*
> God is that which He is; I am that which I am;
> And if you know one well, you know both me and Him.

We recognize the influence of Boehme's thought here in the panhenotheistic underpinnings of these verses and in the emphasis they offer on God as love, angled somewhat more subtly than in a hymn like "The Hidden Deer and Its Source."

In finding myself in Him and asserting that I was once He, that in my depths I am as He is in His depths (it is merely a matter of locating the most *essential* Him/me within myself), we may recognize not only a Boehmean sensibility but also one that echoes the Intoxicated Sufis. Just as they were persecuted—for they were believed heretical in asserting that "I am God"—Angelus Silesius was attacked as a heretic who, in his "I am like God and God is like me," continues in another diptych, "I am large as God. He is as small as I. He cannot be above me nor I beneath Him." There is a double explanation for the nonheretical nature of these words that echoes the explanation for Intoxicated Sufism: First, the "I am God" dictum refers to the entire abandonment of the mystical self into God, a total absorption that makes of the soul of the mystic and God a single being—even as, by paradox, if the mystic is not simply to die or go mad, he or she must be able to retain a sense of self as he or she emerges from the condition of *ek-/en-stasis*.

Second—which is more unique to Angelus's thinking as it transforms Boehmean thought—God who is love cannot by definition love anything inferior to Itself (for that, he argues, would not be true love). Thus, God can only love Itself, but God cannot be an object of Its own love without going out of Itself, without becoming a paradoxically separate being from Itself—without manifesting Its infinite being in a finite form—that is, without becoming something such as man is. Thus, man is an effluence not only *from* but also *of* God's unique Godness; God and man are in their *being*, one. To say that God and I are one is merely to have recognized the paradox of our commonality, as opposed to offering a statement of outsized ego.

By the time Angelus Silesius has come and gone on the stage of history—for our discussion, he serves as another symbol of interweaving and parallelism within the Abrahamic mystical traditions—the world of which he is otherwise part is deeply in the throes of an intense argument regarding who has the franchise on the proper path to contact with the *sacer*. I refer to the wide range of aspects of the Reformation/Counter-Reformation era that include ongoing Protestant-Catholic/Catholic-Protestant bloodshed between the mid-sixteenth and early eighteenth centuries. Moreover, by that time there is a range of thinkers—Descartes, the French Catholic; Spinoza, the Dutch Jew; Leibnitz, the German Protestant (to once again name three of the most prominent)—who raise questions that lead to doubts and further questions regarding not only the nature but also ultimately the very existence of a God defined as all-powerful, all-knowing, and all-good. We speak, then, of the seventeenth century in the West as, in part, a century in which a secularizing process has set in.

We may understand two aspects of this development. One is that it was provoked in part by the long reality of the Reformation/Counter-Reformation: that reality might provoke the question not only of whether there can be a single path to God when there are so many different groups, each of which is convinced that it is in singular possession of that path, but also whether there can be "a path" at all. Or, otherwise put, how can a God described as both all-powerful and all-good allow such an inordinate volume of carnage *in the name of God*? The second aspect is that the intellectual-theological consequence of such a layered question is that, instead of viewing all of human experience as ultimately mandated from God, the notion that it needs to be mandated from ourselves spreads. That is, rather than viewing reality in *teleological* terms—the Greek term for "goal" or "purpose" is *telos*; thus *teleological* refers to the notion that God created us for a purpose (which we must figure out, and that's what religion seeks to accomplish)—a growing group of cultural and intellectual leaders argue for a *mechanistic* view: that the universe got going, whether through the efforts of a conscious being or through an accident, and just keeps going on like a well-wound-up machine.

The second of these viewpoints—the "mechanistic" view—further asserts that we must locate meaning and purpose for our reality from within *our profanus human selves* and not from some metaphysical superstructure (call it "God"), which is either too otherwise preoccupied or simply too disinterested to focus on the needs of humanity and our world. Or God does not even exist. From this issue, in turn, a question arises: How will mysticism as a discipline fare in a world that seems by the seventeenth and eighteenth centuries to be turning gradually away from religion altogether? But the need addressed by religion, which need is yet more profoundly expressed and addressed by mysticism than by normative religion, does not necessarily disappear because religion in its institutionality seems to many to have become so dysfunctional. Mysticism flourishes and begets new forms of itself in the modern era, right up to our own time, as we shall see in the last chapters of this discussion.

NOTES

1. The title *Shulhan Arukh* means "set table." The phrase plays on the manner in which rabbinic guidance renders the most banal of everyday elements in our existence, the table at which we eat, into a virtual altar of connection to God by way of the prayers and rituals associated with eating.

2. Two important matters should be recalled here. First, the word *pardes* has an important history within the Jewish mystical tradition of representing the fourfold approach to accessing God through God's word in the Torah—which approach includes the mystical approach—while also representing mystical speculation itself (and that sort of speculation as dangerous). Second, the pomegranate also has a long history in the conceptual and visual symbology of Jewish thought: Pre-Jewish tradition associates it with fertility and thus with life; Jewish tradition adds to this the notion that the pomegranate possesses 613 seeds, thus making it a symbol of the Torah, the ultimate Tree of Life. See Ori Z. Soltes, *Our Sacred Signs: How Jewish, Christian and Muslim Art Draw from the Same Source* (New York: Westview Press, 2005), 227–28.

3. "Nature naturing" and "Nature natured" are Spinoza's articulation for the idea of God/substance becoming nature (the world)/modes, in a manner that both distinguishes the one from the other and ties them inextricably together. Both this choice of a more "secular" terminology ("nature" rather than "God") and his manner of understanding God in us and us in God were perceived by his community, the Sephardic Jewish community in Amsterdam, as heretical.

4. Judges 4:14–15: "And Deborah said unto Barak: 'Up; for this is the day in which the Lord hath delivered Sisera into thy hand; is not the Lord gone out before thee?'... And the Lord discomfited Sisera, and all his chariots, and all his host, with the edge of the sword before Barak." The destruction of Sisera's army is further glossed in the poem chanted by Deborah that comprises chapter 5, most specifically in lines 20–21: "They fought from heaven, the stars in their courses fought against Sisera. The brook Kishon swept them away."

5. More broadly, we must recall that the idea of *imitatio dei* is endemic to the history of religion: Every people seeks, at some level, to emulate and even imitate its gods to the best of its ability. What the gods are said to prescribe or proscribe is understood to be the kind of behavior exhibited by them, which we thereby emulate— or try to.

6. Thus, Maimonides (1135–1204), the most prominent of medieval Jewish philosophers, writes, "Whenever any one of His actions is perceived by us, we ascribe to God that emotion which is the source of the act when performed by ourselves, and call Him by an epithet which is formed from the verb expressing that emotion." (*The Guide for the Perplexed*, trans. Max Friedlaender [New York: Dover Publications, 1956], I. liv)

7. Thus, "all attributes ascribed to God are attributes of His acts, and do not imply that God has any qualities." (Maimonides, *The Guide for the Perplexed*, I. liv) Maimonides is parsing the passage in Genesis 1:27, which asserts that humans have been created "in the image of God."

8. Even as, strictly speaking, there are ultimately no "female" or "male" sides to the tree, as I have earlier explained, in chapter 6. That purist view apparently does not overcome Cordovero's gender prejudices: He is in this regard more a child of his time than of his text focus.

9. See Gershom Scholem, *Major Trends in Jewish Mysticism* (New York: Schocken Books, 1969), 260–61.

10. Scholem, *Trends*, 260 and his footnotes 41, 42.

11. The word *partzuf* means "face" or "countenance" in Hebrew; it is rendered in the plural in Lurianic Kabbalah to suggest that it is never present or activated in the singular but only when two or more *haverim* are engaged so that their spiritual countenances are turned toward each other. The pluralization also plays on the fact that the biblical name of God most readily identifiable as to gender and number, *Elohim*, is a grammatical plural, although it refers obviously to a God considered emphatically singular. The midrashic explanation for this is that the name suggests how everything (hence plurality) is encompassed within the One God.

12. Among the more famous explorations of this idea is the play *The Dybbuk* written in 1914 by S. Ansky. In the play, a poor student of mysticism, who is passed over as a groom for the woman he loves (and who loves him) by her father in favor of the son of a rich merchant, commits suicide (he virtually wills himself to death through manipulation of kabbalistic formulae). But his disembodied soul then inhabits his beloved and will not—perhaps, one might say, cannot—leave her and complete his journey to the other side until an exorcism is accomplished (to be overly brief in my summary) through the invocation of a heavenly tribunal by a renowned *tzadik*.

13. He discusses this in "On Curses," sec. XI and "On Rewards and Punishments," sec. XV–XX.

14. The work, "The Mysteries of Rabbi Shimeon bar Yochai," represents Metatron as the deliverer of the news that "[Islam,] the kingdom of Ishmael [has been] established for the sole purpose of redeeming you from this wicked kingdom [Edom]." Such a text demonstrates its apocryphal nature by referring to Edom, which term came to be used as a reference to Judaism's oppressor only when that oppressor became Christianity (i.e., Edom = Christianity; Edom does not mean the pagan Roman imperium); that development follows the time of Shimeon bar Yochai by at least two and a half centuries.

15. Harry Sperling and Maurice Simon, trans., *The Zohar*, 5 vols. (London and New York: Soncino Press, 1984), 1:25b.

16. Sperling and Simon, *Zohar*, 1:117b.

17. Rashi is the acronym of an eleventh-century (1040–1105) rabbi from northern France who authored the first comprehensive commentaries on the Talmud and the Hebrew Bible.

18. More precisely, he is said to have used two assistants, with whom he prepared all four elements. His son-in-law, a Kohayn, and a pupil who was a Levite, prepared fire and water; Rabbi Loew prepared air; the Golem itself was made of earth. After purifying themselves and studying the *Sepher Yetzirah*, at midnight of the prescribed day, they began the process. While reciting combinations of letters and words—*tzerufim*—the Kohayn walked around the creature seven times from right to left, after which the Levite walked around it seven times from left to right, after which Rabbi Loew walked around it once, then placed the name within its mouth (upon its brow), which caused it to open its eyes.

19. Yet another variant suggests that the word written down by Rabbi Loew was the Hebrew word for "truth," *emet*, contrived of the first (*aleph*) and last (*tav*) letters

of the Hebrew alphabet with a middle letter (*mem*) in the middle, thus signifying within the spelling of the word *truth* itself the notion that truth encompasses all.

20. A further variant: that by simply erasing the *aleph* from the beginning of the three-consonantal word, *emet*, one could instantly deactivate the Golem, since the remaining two consonants spell the word *met*, meaning "dead."

21. The narrative, well-known within both the Jewish and Christian communities of central Europe, may well have inspired cautionary tales such as *Frankenstein* and "The Sorcerer's Apprentice."

22. *Tzadikim* is the plural of *tzadik*.

23. I have always wondered what exactly this means: if nobody actually knows the proper pronunciation of the Tetragrammaton, because, since the destruction of the Temple and the dismantling of the high priesthood, nobody can unequivocally know it until the advent of the Messiah (who *will* know it, by definition), then how would anyone know that what Shabbetai articulated *was* the real ineffable name? And if he actually *did* exclaim it, then he *would* be the Messiah, because how else could he know the proper pronunciation? So perhaps the story of that moment should state that he *claimed* to be pronouncing the ineffable divine Name.

24. We must recall that "excommunication" does not mean for Judaism what it does for Christianity. There is no clear articulation of "hell" in the Jewish tradition, and nobody would in any case have the authority to consign anyone else to eternal torments if they were distinctly available. The term essentially means that the individual subject to such a writ is excluded from the community for a prescribed period of time. Depending upon the influence of the excommunicating body, "community" might be limited to the city in which the excommunication takes place or could encompass a large swathe of the dispersed Jewish world.

25. This moment, by extension, brings the Jewish mystical tradition as close as it gets to that aspect of the Christian mystical tradition that encompasses the "Wedding with God," as for example in the mystical marriage of St. Catherine of Siena. Whereas she is (and, fundamentally, all nuns are) wedded to Christ, who is God incarnate, Shabbetai declares his marriage to the Torah, which is not only, as God's word on parchment, the closest that Judaism comes to a physical embodiment of God but also, in the mystical tradition, is tantamount to (yet not cosubstantial with) God in being God's word—and in late Kabbalah, in being "feminine" (by way of the grammatical gender of the word "Torah"), the Torah is tantamount to God's "presence" (the *Shekhinah*, which is also grammatically female, as we recall from chapter 6) and thus tantamount to God. So Shabbetai's act offers an extraordinary twist to the issues of madness, apostasy, and communal chaos that cause the mainstream rabbinic leadership to push their followers away from mysticism over the centuries.

26. He seems to have been what today might be called bipolar or manic-depressive, shifting between moods of expansive self-assurance as to his unique role on the stage of history and deeply depressed moments of self-doubt.

27. The ultimate discussion of Shabbetai Tzvi is Gershom Scholem's *Sabbatai Sevi: The Mystical Messiah*, Bollingen Series XCII (Princeton, NJ: Princeton University Press, 1973). Briefer and broader discussions of Jewish messianism include Sc-

holem's *The Messianic Idea in Judaism and Other Essays on Jewish Spirituality* (New York: Schocken Books, 1971), and Julius H. Greenstone, *The Messiah Idea in Jewish History* (Philadelphia: Jewish Publication Society of America, 1906).

28. The word "disputation" has two meanings in two different contexts within the medieval and postmedieval worlds of Christendom. The first sense refers to a discussion between two Christians, both of whom agree upon some miraculous proposition—such as the transubstantiation of the Communion wafer and wine into Christ's flesh and blood—regarding how exactly the miracle takes place. The second sense refers to a theological debate between a Christian and a Jewish religious leader, in which the latter is required to defend Judaism from the attacks regarding its alleged falseness set forth by the former. Typically (but not always), one of two results are obtained: Either the Christian would win the debate, in which case the Jewish community involved would be expected to convert to Christianity, or the Jew would triumph, in which case the Jewish community involved would be exiled or subject to physical violence.

29. Holland in general and Amsterdam in particular had, since the success of the Dutch war for independence from Spanish control at the end of the sixteenth century, become a largely open religious community to which, among others, Jews flocked both from the increasing oppression of the Orthodox East and the Inquisitional complications of the Catholic West.

30. For reasons beyond this discussion, in Hebrew, adjectives always follow the nouns that they modify; in the case of this phrase, "of the" is understood.

31. This is called *pilpul*—literally, "peppering"—in Hebrew. It is similar to the kind of argumentation that those hostile to the Jesuits refer to as their preference for casuistry.

32. One recognizes in this story the echo of the biblical narrative of Abraham and Sarah producing Isaac in extreme old age.

33. See p. 219 for a somewhat fuller definition of *d'vekut*.

34. Put another way, every word and action of the *tzadik* is a text to be studied and dug into by his followers the way the midrash-creating rabbis study and dig into the text of the Torah.

35. We may recognize a parallel in this sensibility to that of Christian *caritas* as it is articulated by St. Augustine in his *Enchiridion*. See chapter 4, p. 64.

36. See chapter 3.

37. Thus, one might say that, whereas in most respects *Hassidut* may be seen to grow most directly out of Lurianic Kabbalah, with regard to the question of creation, it reverts to an earlier Jewish mystical understanding of that process.

38. One recognizes in this, as in a number of the elements articulated by the Ba'al Shem Tov for *Hassidut*, an intensified extension of normative Judaism: Thus, the "mourner's prayer"—the *kaddish*—in the Jewish tradition is not a prayer at all but rather an exaltation of God's greatness; the term *kaddish* means to "sanctify" and thereby to "aggrandize." For the time when one is most likely to be most angry with God, after the death of a loved one, is precisely the time when one is called upon to reassert one's faith in the greatness and essential goodness of God.

39. This notion of distinguishing between God's foreknowledge and predestination, which distinction is necessary in order to assure the reality of human free will, has been discussed elsewhere and earlier in all three Abrahamic traditions.

40. The question is whether by this distinction the Ba'al Shem Tov—he is a child of his era, however enlightened, one might suppose—intends to separate male from female as upper from lower states of being (for *ish* in common-parlance Hebrew means "man" in the genered sense of "a male human being"). But then, he could and should have said *ish* and *ishah*, not *ish* and *adam*. Both of the latter words are, grammatically speaking, masculine, and whereas *ish* has a feminine form (*ishah*), *adam* does not (although *adamah* is a grammatically feminine word, it is not the feminine rendering of *adam* the way *ishah* is the feminine rendering of *ish*). So, I prefer to believe that the distinction is between realizing one's full human potential by striving for *d'vekut* with God and failing to do so, without regard for whether the striver is male or female and without imposing a gender distinction on the two (human and less-than-human) conditions of being in the world.

41. His *Ars inveniendi veritatis* was in fact first written in Catalan (the title was *Art abreujada d'atrobar veritat*) and then translated into Latin. His *Blanquerna* was the first major work of literature written in Catalan and perhaps the first European novel written since antiquity.

42. The term *Renaissance* was first coined in the previous century by Petrarch with reference to his notion that writers and artists of his era should emulate the culture of the Greeks and Romans, which, he felt, offered a range of important ideas with respect to being in the world that were not to be found in the writings from his own Christian tradition. They should, moreover, not merely emulate but exceed Greco-Roman culture by adding new nuances and ideas to that which they were emulating. The *accademia* was founded by Lorenzo's grandfather, Cosimo de Medici, in 1462–1463. *Humanism* is a term referring to the growing conviction during the Renaissance period that humans can and should be at the center of the stage of history; God is relegated to the side or even back stage—not by any means removed from it, but perceived and presumed not to play the dominating and highly interventionist role in our world assumed during the previous millennium.

43. Hermes Trismegistos ("Hermes the Thrice-Great") refers by tradition to a conflation of the Greek god Hermes (messenger god in general and in particular between gods and humans) with the Egyptian god Thoth (inventor of writing); the actual so-named individual was on the other hand apparently a powerful ancient mage with access to profoundly hidden knowledge that yielded some seventeen volumes—this and more. But the entire "Hermetic" tradition was actually formulated by the Gnostic community in Alexandria around 200 CE. The so-called Chaldaean Oracles date from about the same time, survive only in fragments, and derive from a synthesis of Neoplatonic with ancient Babylonian or Achaemenid Persian material. The Orphic Hymns are a series of poems ascribed to the mythical poet Orpheus (who went down into Hades to rescue his bride, Eurydice, and charmed not only the three-headed dog, Cerberus, with his music but also even Persephone, queen of the dead, herself. He returned to the light but, lacking perfect faith, turned back at the last minute to be certain Eurydice was just behind him and lost her forever.

44. One might also be reminded of the previously discussed distinction between *ish* and *adam* status within early *Hassidut*—but that distinction and *Hassidut* itself will come much later than the time of Pico and in any case presents a much narrower band of hierarchical placement for humankind acting better or worse.

45. See Chaim Wirszubski, *Pico della Mirandola's Encounter with Jewish Mysticism* (Cambridge, MA: Harvard University Press, 1989), 57–58. Wirszubski's book, especially chapters 2 and 3, offers interesting details on the general topic of Pico and Kabbalah.

46. Remembering that only the consonants "count" in Hebrew (and that what is rendered here as an "E" is a glottal-stop consonant): E = 1, L = 30, H = 5, M = 40; Y (almost invisible in transliteration, as it is replaced by its vocalic equivalent, "I") = 10.

47. By some accounts he was born as early as 1398.

48. "Hinduism" is to a certain extant a misnomer: those we label "Hindu" (which is ultimately merely a Sanskrit word for "Indian" or "Indic") recognize a universal oneness that is variously manifest in three primary gods, each of whose devotees acknowledge all three and see all three as aspects of one being. But a Brahman perceives Brahma (the Creator) as the ultimate form of divine expression; a Vaishnite perceives Vishnu (the Maintainer) as the ultimate form; a Shaivite perceives Shiva (the Destroyer) as the ultimate form. Particularly among Vaishnites and Shaivites, there are also subset groups. The most popular one, coming to dominance from northern to southern India during the fourteenth through seventeenth centuries, focused on Krishna, Vishnu's most written-about avatar (and in one further subset Kraishnite tradition, the single source of all of Vishnu's avatars), whose persona is reminiscent in many ways of the persona of Christ as the Son/avatar of God the Father.

49. Rabindranath Tagore, trans., *Songs of Kabir* (New York: MacMillan Co., 1916), 7.

50. This law essentially states that what one does in a given lifetime will have consequences for the next life (and sometimes, lives) into which one will be subsequently born.

51. The Roman numerals refer to the numeration in Tagore's volume (see note 49).

52. The motif of the beloved as male is common to Islamic poetry, mystical or not, as noted in chapter 8. This is a paradox: Islam looks askance at homosexuality, but the most elevated love (which is spiritual, not physical) is directed toward a male due to a distinct misogynistic—or gynophobic—sensibility. Kabir follows that tradition, interestingly, thereby also imposing a more distinct maleness onto the Godhead that is, by Islamic definition, genderless. By Hindu definition, God is variously conceived as distinctly masculine (e.g., Brahma, Vishnu, Shiva; Vishnu's incarnation as Krishna) or feminine (e.g., Devi—to say nothing of the divine consorts of Vishnu and Shiva). Indeed, the *Tantra* in particular emphasizes gender-based sexuality in both its literature and its art. If all of this seems contradictory, it should: We are, after all, dealing not only with the *sacer* but also, in the case of Kabir's poetry, with the *mysterion* within the *sacer*.

53. Thus, the *ka'aba* is the center of Muslim faith. Mount Kailash, in western Tibet, is venerated by billions of people of four different faiths. *Kirtan* is one of the

pillars of the Sikh religion and refers to the singing of the sacred hymns of the guru Granth Sahib—its Hindu equivalent is more commonly called *bhajan*. The winding of legs around one's neck refers to the various *asanas* (body and spiritual positions) of the varied Yogic tradition.

54. We must keep in mind that the distinction between astronomy and astrology is a relatively recent one in Western thought. In Jakob Boehme's thought, how the stars and planets are configured at a given moment in time is assumed to have an effect on what happens here below.

55. Thus—forgive my stating the obvious, just in case it is not—even English mystics like Richard Rolle and Julian of Norwich are obviously Catholic, since they lived well before the time of the Reformation and the Protestantization of England. There are also Orthodox mystics, of course, such as Gregory Palamas.

56. From *The Way to Christ* (from the facsimile edition of the 1764 English edition by William Law (Liskeard, Cornwall, UK: Diggory Press, 2007), fourth book, second dialogue.

57. Quoting from Boehme, *The Way to Christ*. The italics are mine.

58. See chapter 6, pp. 109–10.

59. In the German Lutheran hymnal, one will find Angelus's hymns *Liebe, die du mich zum Bilde deiner Gottheit hast gemacht* ("Oh, Love, You Who Have Made Me in the Image of Your Godhead") and *Mir nach, spricht Christus, unser Held* ("After Me, Says Christ, Our Hero"), for instance.

Chapter Ten

Still Searching

The Persistence of Mysticism in the Modern Era

The Western world of the late eighteenth century was in the midst of a series of changes that would affect the mystical traditions of all three Abrahamic faiths in significant ways. In the first place, Christian Euro-America was still in the throes of a secularizing process that was shifting the position of God and humans on the stage of history and reality vis-à-vis each other—at least as far as human perspective is concerned. If the Renaissance era saw the beginnings of human assertion, so that God was ushered to the side and even the back of the stage, one might say that by the second half of the eighteenth century—an era marked by industrial and then political, intellectual, scientific, and technological revolutions, which referred to itself as the Enlightenment—God was being ushered off the stage in many places.

The sense of unending human potential interwove with a growing conviction that, rather than the universe's having been made by a single, all-powerful, all-knowing, and all-good God with a purpose in mind—a *telos*, in Greek terms—which purpose or *telos* we humans need to figure out (thus one speaks of a *teleological* sense of reality), perhaps the universe either simply began or was begun by some force that then turned away from it. So, like a well-wound-up watch, a flawless machine, it just keeps on going (thus one speaks of a *mechanistic* viewpoint): whatever purpose there is to reality must come from within and thus be sought within ourselves. With the gradual emergence of such a perspective, the age-old prejudices against Jews and Judaism found decreasing theological justification, and as a consequence, "modern, secular" European states began to grant fuller and fuller rights of participation within mainstream society to their Jewish communities—from socioeconomics to culture to politics. We speak, then, of the Emancipation.[1]

Most of these emancipatory developments with regard to Jews took place in western and central Europe. To the east, dominated by the Romanov tsars of an expansive Russian Empire, the mood, if anything, carried in the opposite direction. When Catherine the Great (1762–1796), to her chagrin, brought a million Jews into her empire through three successive partitions of Poland (Russia, Prussia, and Austro-Hungary having divided those political spoils each time), she sought to solve what for her was a new and large problem by a program that included exile, conversion, and extermination as key parts of its methodology. She defined a Pale of Settlement: an area within her domains to which Jews were confined. It was within those domains that—in part due to the increasingly onerous life lived by Jews under the tsars, wedded to increasingly oppressive legislation from a rabbinic leadership caught up in its own limited perspective on the *sacer-profanus* relationship and that emphasized restrictive legislative ideas increasingly for the sake of the ideas themselves, rather than for the sake of those governed by them—Hassidism was born and flourished, as we have observed in the previous chapter of this discussion.

THE SPREAD OF *HASSIDUT* AFTER THE DEATH OF THE BA'AL SHEM TOV

We must keep in mind that we come to most of the issues and ideas that we associate with *Hassidut* not by way of some treatise written by the Ba'al Shem Tov or necessarily even those written by his disciples, but by way of the tales and parables ascribed to him, told about him, and ascribed to his successors. The history of Hassidism is long and varied as, from the time of the BeSh'T's death around 1760, there had already arisen questions as to who should succeed him. So, as we follow the movement into the late eighteenth century and forward toward our own time, it becomes not only widespread but also varied in the specifics of its teachings. That the movement underwent fairly rapid splintering in the aftermath of the BeSh'T's death may in part be ascribed to his charismatic success: *Hassidut* became far-flung so rapidly that its constituent communities almost inevitably moved in divergent directions. Given the absence within Judaism of a tradition of looking to a papal sort of figure to carry forth divinely ordained ideas first set forth by the key figure in the foundation of the faith, it would have been a challenge indeed for one individual to assert and maintain command over the entirety of the burgeoning and dispersed Hassidic community. More practically, however, the divisions that begat splinters were a function of human, and therefore political (in the broad sense of that term), contentiousness regarding who was most qualified to succeed the BeSh'T, and in subsequent generations, of a typically geometric progression of contentiousness regarding the successors of his successors as leaders. Often the issue fell along genealogical versus spiritual or intellectual lines.

Thus, while many of the BeSh'Ts followers looked to Dov Baer as his heir—he was certainly the primary spiritual heir and the one mainly responsible for organizing the movement that the master had founded—others looked to Jacob Joseph of Polnoye, who created the movement's first substantial literature, as his successor. Both Dov Baer and Jacob Joseph were important disciples of the Ba'al Shem Tov. As a practical matter, Dov Baer established the center of his leadership in Mezeritz (well north of Medzibozh, which was the center of the BeSh'T's activities), creating a second center of Hassidic life there, and Jacob Joseph established a third center in Polnoye.

Dov Baer came from a line of traditional rabbinic Talmudists and was born around 1710 in Lukatsch. An impoverished student, he traveled to Lemberg (Lvov) to study, returning home to marry and begin a modest career as a teacher who included among his broad spiritual-intellectual interests the study of Kabbalah. That modest career required a good deal of travel—the town of his birth could not supply enough work for a teacher to feed his family, so he moved about as a *maggid*: an itinerant preacher/teacher. The term attached itself to him as an epithet: the Maggid. As he went from village to village, his reputation grew, and at a certain point, he encountered the Ba'al Shem Tov. That first meeting apparently underwhelmed him (a mystic would say that he was not yet *ready*), for the BeSh'T seemed too much the peasant, when Dov Baer (himself hardly more than that) was expecting someone of nobler mien. But the evening before he was due to depart the village where they were both staying, the Ba'al Shem Tov sent for him and opened up a copy of the *Eytz Hayim* (*Tree of Life*) of Hayim Vitale for exposition.[2] They ended up studying together all night long, and the Maggid would later report how the BeSh'T opened up the spirit of the text that was behind and beyond its words.

Dov Baer succeeded the Ba'al Shem Tov as leader and lived until 1772 or 1773. He is credited with furthering the panhenotheistic notion that finds God omnipresent, the source and origin of all things and the vital energy within them; that God is, as it were, diffused throughout creation in varying degrees from the lower to the higher sorts of beings. Moreover, since all things come from God, his essence must also be found in that which is and those who are apparently evil: the *n'tzotzot* of which Lurianic Kabbalah speaks—the sparks of Godness—are found in everything and everyone. If, on the one hand, the trouble is to dig them out at times, on the other hand, this means that even the most banal of everyday acts, such as eating and drinking, can constitute a holy act. Thus, the traditional Jewish notion that the dining table becomes a kind of altar as the meal is entered and exited with blessings and rituals is even more emphatic, and when, say, a group of *hassidim* engages in an extensive round of postprandial song-as-prayer, the most intense *ek-stasis* is possible.

In fact, *only* prayer expressed with enthusiasm, with an ecstatic physical and spiritual sensibility, can help the devotee break through the corrupt influences of material nature toward true meeting with the center of the *sacer*. Conversely, as both matter and spirit are present in all of creation, even in discussions of the Torah—for even in Torah there is nonspiritual matter—then even the study of Torah, if it is excessive, can lead to a loss of piety rather than a gain. Study must be balanced by other expressions of enthusiasm for God, such as song.

Dov Baer's teachings further underscore the importance of the *tzadik* as a kind of vicar of God on earth (thus, we may perhaps discern Catholic influence) to whom the divine sparks whisper from within the most drossy of matter and whose most trivial acts therefore may reveal something about the *sacer*. The story is told (and I have referred to it above, in chapter 9) that when the Maggid was planning a visit to the Ba'al Shem Tov, a disciple asked him why he was going to inconvenience himself by such a journey, to which Dov Baer responded, "I want to see how he ties his shoelaces!" But presumably the same sort of story could and would come to apply to the Maggid himself. More broadly, down through the generations, the *hassidim* would not only study every act and meditate on every word of their *tzadikim* but also provide for the *tzadik*'s every need, as well as for those of his family, in order to free him up to engage in undisturbed service of God (and therefore, conversely, of his community).

Dov Baer taught that the Lurianic *tzimtzum* of God may be reversed as humans strive to ascend to him, and he responds by extending out toward us. He asserted that it is actually easier to serve God in exile (and thus offered comfort in a distinct way to the oppressed eastern European Jewish communities who hearkened to his teachings) not only because the challenge of concentrating on divine service under difficult conditions is more elevating than when one is located in *Eretz Yisrael* but also because the people Israel can be more effective as an instrument in God's hand to bring grace to all of humankind in being dispersed among the peoples of the earth.

Tradition asserts that if Dov Baer was at least underwhelmed in his first encounter with the BeSh'T, Jacob Joseph, a second successor, was originally disturbed by the master. Like the Maggid, Jacob Joseph was deeply trained in Torah, Talmud, and also Kabbalah and became a rabbi in the little town of Sargorod. He awaited his congregation in vain one morning for prayers in the synagogue, for they had all hurried to the marketplace when the BeSh'T passed through and were mesmerized by him there. The rabbi sent the beadle to find out what had happened, and he, too, mesmerized, forgot his mission and remained in the marketplace. After praying alone and with difficulty of focus, Jacob Joseph summoned the BeSh'T to inquire as to whether he was the one responsible for disturbing the morning communal prayer. The BeSh'T replied that he was but asked the rabbi not to be upset with him and, instead, to listen to a story—the hearing of which clarified issues that had until then been unresolved for Jacob Joseph.[3] He quickly became a fervent follower of the BeSh'T.

We may recognize in this story several important components: There is perfunctory prayer, done by most of us most of the time, and then there is the kind of enthusiastic prayer that contact with the BeSh'T facilitates and that can lead to ecstasy. The site for communing most effectively with the *sacer* need not be the synagogue—there may be times when not only the woods and fields but also even the banal setting of the marketplace may serve as well or better. Understanding God by way of God's word and the interpretations of God's word may come through a story as well as or better than through the intellectualized engagement of traditional study and discussion.

Ironically—since we must assume from this story that Rabbi Jacob Joseph's congregation had all hastened to the marketplace to listen to the Ba'al Shem Tov—Jacob Joseph was soon forced out of Sargorod by the communal leaders, in 1748, for they found his transformation into a Hassidic leader heretical.[4] As such, he was the first Hassidic leader who may be considered to have been persecuted by the mainstream communal leadership out of their fear of *Hassidut* itself as being heretical. From Sargorod, he moved on to Rashkov (1748–1752), then to Nemirov (1752–1770), and finally to Polnoye, which became the third center of Hassidism and where he remained until his death in 1782. Early on, he embraced the extreme aspect of Lurianic teaching that enjoined devotees to fast extensively: For more than five years, he refused to take food before nightfall—until the BeSh'T himself commanded him to desist from "this way [that] is dark and bitter and leads to depression and melancholy. The Glory of God does not dwell where there is depression but where the joy in performing his mitzvah prevails."[5] We recognize in this how emphatically *Hassidut* rejects physical asceticism as a means of gaining spiritual oneness with the One, a perspective opposite to what we have observed of the Abulafian-Sabbatean style and even more so of the general Christian mystical tradition and that, conversely, recalls Kabir's poetic injunctions against asceticism.

Jacob Joseph was not the one designated by the Ba'al Shem Tov as his primary successor; Dov Baer was, perhaps because Jacob Joseph was deemed too impatient, too tempestuous, or, perhaps, simply too intense. In his disappointment, Jacob broke off relations with the Maggid, although it did not really take the two very long to resume their friendship. In any case, if the Maggid was viewed as the primary successor to the BeSh'T, Jacob Joseph is best known for converting Hassidic teachings into a formal written state. He authored four major works that have survived. *Toldot Ya'akov Yoseph* (1780) is a Hassidic commentary on the Torah and specifically on its 613 commandments. His *Ben Porath Yoseph* (1781) offers a commentary on Genesis and on key *Shabbatot* ("Sabbaths") during the Jewish year. His *Tzofnath Pa'aneah* (1782) offers a commentary on the book of Exodus, and his *Ketonot Passim*—which seems not to have been published until nearly a century after his death (1866)—is a compendium of diverse sayings and comments on various issues. The titles of these works often follow the Jewish custom, by then many centuries old, of directly or indirectly referencing the author's name: *Toldot Ya'akov Yoseph* is straightforwardly *The Annals of Jacob Joseph*; *Ben Porath Yoseph* translates to *Offerings of the Fruitful Vine of Joseph*; and *Ketonet Passim* translates to *Coat of Many Colors*,[6] a reference to the biblical Joseph. *Tzofnat Pa'aneah*, which translates to *Revealing the Hidden*, is the only work that makes no such allusion, although it is the work that most overtly presents itself as a text that digs beneath the surface of texts to guide the reader to greater closeness with God.

Jacob Joseph argues that God is the totality of everything, that there is nothing outside God, that nature is then the outer covering that conceals the inner essence of God. Thus, God does not withdraw, as the Lurianic kabbalists assert (*tzimtzum*), but rather transforms itself in creating the universe. He asserts that *soul* is found in *all* things and that therefore we humans must serve God by our focus on all things in the world around us and with all of our faculties, both material and spiritual—engaging in a style of prayer that is rapturous and very physical and lifts the veil to disclose God's living glory. He likens the *tzadik* to the *sephirot* in being a fountain through which the creative process continues to flow in an ongoing manner.

He was less of a philosopher, though, than he is our most direct source for the words of the BeSh'T (whom he quotes nearly six hundred times in these works) and of the Maggid (whom he quotes fifty-seven times)—and a polemicist. Often he includes in his discussions attacks on the rabbinic leaders whose hostility to the BeSh'T, he asserts, derives from their "sophistry" and their "hypocrisy." He assails such leaders as engaged in interpreting the traditional text not for the sake of heaven but to show off and accuses them of running schools for young students in which incompetent teachers expend all their energy flattering the parents rather than truly teaching their children. Such leadership, of course, found difficulties in the Hassidic interpretations for they misperceived Hassidic panhenotheism as pantheism or even polytheism and were fearful that the reverence accorded the *tzadik* could spill over into idolatrous worship. In that case, the *tzadik* would be divinized—and what would separate a *hassid* from a Christian who divinizes Jesus of Nazareth? Late in his life, Jacob Joseph's books were burned at rabbinic instigation in a number of cities.

While these two figures dominated the period following the death of the BeSh'T, each had his followers and successors. Among these, a few must be noted as particularly important. Levi Yitzhak of Berditchev (1740–1809) is often seen as the consummate *tzadik* in his humility and gentleness, in his readiness to see only the positive side of every individual's actions,[7] and in his role as defender of his flock, arguing with God on its behalf—even accusing God of injustice in defending his people to God. One of his prayers to God, which was subsequently set to music by his followers, reads in part,

> Good morning to you, Oh Lord of the Universe
> I, Levi Yitzhak, son of Sarah of Berditchev,
> Have come to You to plead on behalf of Your people Israel.
> What have You against Your people Israel?
> Why do You oppress Your people Israel?
> . . . I shall not move from my spot! I will not stir from here!
> There must be an end to the sufferings of Your people Israel.
> Hallowed and magnified be the Name of God!

As so often in the Jewish tradition, debate with, or even criticism of, God is acceptable in the personalized, immanent relationship that flourishes, but it always concludes with the Jobian acknowledgement of God's *sacer* greatness, couched in terms of praising the name of God. As a writer, Levi Yitzhak is also known for one work, *Kedushat Levi* (*Sanctification of Levi*, punning on his name and the name of the priestly tribe of Israel), with its discourses on holidays and on ecstatic prayer and its theme of demand from God itself that the messianic era arrive soon.

There seems to me to be a certain irony in the fact that, as we push from the eighteenth into the nineteenth century, when—in theory, at least—the condition of Jews is improving in western and central Europe (and that improvement is in part based on a growing secularistic mood), the preoccupation of Jewish mysticism in its Hassidic iteration (which is largely taking shape and being reshaped in eastern Europe) is increasingly marked by yearning for a messianic era that will transform the realm of the *profanus* into an idealized *sacer*. That is, the emphasis is less on the mystical goal for the individual *hassid* of oneness with the One than on bringing the grace of the One into a world that will then see itself at last *as one* in its connection to its *profanus* parts and its *sacer* source—which bringing of grace will be effected by those assumed already to be in intense interior contact with the One.

Levi Yitzhak's younger contemporary, Shneur Zalman of Lyadi (1747–1813)—said to be a direct descendant of Judah Loew, fashioner of the Golem—would certainly be called one of those in intense interior contact with the One by his followers. He was already a serious student of the entire range of traditional and nontraditional Jewish literature—he is said to have spent eighteen hours a day studying—well before the age of thirteen. He was already being addressed as *rav* ("teacher") by then, and by age fifteen, after many had vied to acquire him as a son-in-law, he was married off to the daughter of a merchant from Vitebsk. Over the next five years, as he continued to study by day and by night, he also found himself increasingly spiritually restless. He was torn between the urge to seek out the intellectual leader of eastern European Jewry in Vilnius, Lithuania,[8] which is where he began to direct his journey, and the yearning to learn how to pray with ardor and passion, which latter need turned his journey around, midway, in the direction of Mezeritz. He became the preeminent disciple of Dov Baer. The great Maggid seems to have recognized the young man's brilliance quickly, engaging him as tutor to his own son, Abraham.

By the age of twenty-five, Shneur Zalman had completed a new, five-volume distillation—both detailed and clear in its exposition—of the extensive Jewish legal codes with their commentaries on commentaries. In effect, this compilation by a leading light among the *hassidim* provided proof that the accusation by the *mitnagdeem*[9]—that *Hassidut* sidestepped Jewish law—was false. When the Maggid died in 1772 or 1773, his followers largely dispersed. Some, such as Shneur Zalman, remained in the company of Abraham, who died in 1777, however, at age thirty-six. Others considered the real intellectual and spiritual heir to be Rabbi Menachem Mendel, but he immigrated to *Eretz Yisrael* a few years later. Most of Dov Baer's circle of *hassidim* had, in any case, already begun to seek out Shneur Zalman as the most effective conduit through which the teachings of the Ba'al Shem Tov and the Maggid could be heard, before the death of the one and the emigration of the other would-be successors to the Maggid. Zalman had repaired to the small town of Lyadi. Shneur Zalman of Lyadi (as he has since been known) tried to heal the rift between the Hassidic and mitnagdic worlds, and often his erudition, wit, and charm succeeded, but he was not successful in even gaining an audience, much less a real discussion, with the Vilna Gaon himself.

This was a time not only of intense internal conflict within the eastern European Jewish world but also of external conflict: It was the era of the Napoleonic push eastward into the realms of Tsar Alexander I. In the context of the crisscrossing of internal and external conflicts, Zalman and his followers were often persecuted from different sides—he spent two terms in tsarist prisons—but his aura as a martyr gained him an ever-growing circle of followers. Meanwhile, he was fashioning a new form of *Hassidut* that had as its goal to synthesize the intellectual heritage of the rabbinic tradition—to turn back to Torah study as a desideratum—with the pure spirituality of BeSh'Tean teachings. His movement was called *HaBaD*, an acronym for the three *sephirot* that dwell just below *keter: hokhmah*, *binah*, and *da'at*.[10] These attributes—"wisdom," "understanding," and "knowledge"—are deemed to comprise the intellect.

The guidebook of *ChaBaD*, written by Shneur Zalman over the course of twenty years, is called the *Tanya* (an Aramaic word/phrase meaning "it has been taught"). The *Tanya* addresses the problem engendered by the Lurianic doctrine of *tzimtzum* that, it asserts, presents the problem of duality: God as separate from the world, as transcendent and having drawn away (perhaps still drawing away) from the world, as distinct from the God recognized as immanent and manifest within the creation, as part of the world. Zalman's solution is to turn back to the emanation doctrine of the *Zohar* and to reconsider the notion of the *'eyn sof* beyond the uppermost *sephirot*. The *'eyn sof* is the consequence of the infinite wealth of light with which (as per Genesis 1:2) God began to create the universe: light as a spiritual substance that radiates from within God itself, a force that partakes of divine perfection and infinity without, at the same time, *being* God and thus without making God directly responsible for the creation that ultimately emanates from that light.[11] In turn, creation—the created universe—is a secondary result of what amounts to a double process of emanation. The entire universe ultimately derives from (is contained within) the God who contains everything potentially within itself—as a flame is contained within the candle that feeds it. The universe emanates from the One, which is its inner cause, an eternal reality expressed in its first manifestation as the *'eyn sof* as light,[12] the sparks of that suffuse everything.

Those sparks, equally present in all of us but often held in a kind of suspended state, mean that each of us has the potential, if the sparks become liberated, to be a *tzadik*, and nobody may be deemed a *tzadik* who does not exhaust himself or herself in seeking to liberate the sparks in others. But, as such, the *ChaBaD* sees the *tzadik* as less of a miracle worker than a teacher of moral principles and a guide to moral action—to be respected for his ability to guide us, not venerated for his ability to commune with God. Torah is the ultimate guide, and proper, enthusiastic Torah study uplifts the mind and the soul, in part because it pushes the student to virtuous action: Proper Torah study is to live Torah and its commandments day and night, every day of one's life. These are the principles established by Shneur Zalman of Lyadi. As the movement, led by his sons, Dov Baer and Abraham, recentered itself in Lubavitch, not far from Ladi, soon after Shneur Zalman's death, the movement also came to be known as Lubavitch *Hassidut*.

Meanwhile, in the year before the first Dov Baer, the Maggid, died—in the year in which the Vilna Gaon first attempted to excommunicate the *hassidim*—another future luminary of a different sort was born in Medzibodz: Nahman, great-grandson on his mother's side of the BeSh'T. Poet, scholar, and mystic, Nahman of Bratslav would prove to be the greatest weaver of tales as access portals to deeper wisdom in the history of *Hassidut*. In his youth, he was drawn, like Dov Baer, Jacob Joseph, and Shneur Zalman were in their youths, to the varied range of Jewish literature and learning, both legalistic and legend bound—and although a descendent of the BeSh'T, he was drawn, as Jacob Joseph had been, to the austere side of Lurianic Kabbalah, with repeated fasts and immersions in ice-cold baths. Yet, he most emphatically articulated the principle of reveling in God's presence (*shekhinah*) by reveling in nature: "when a man becomes worthy of hearing the songs of the plants, how each plant chants the praises of God, how beautiful and sweet it is to hear their singing! And therefore it is good to serve God in their midst, roaming over the fields among the growing things, pouring out one's heart before God in truthfulness."[13]

On the other hand, he not only came to prefer tales to philosophy but also was hostile to rationalism: "He who wants to see the truth . . . must rely on faith alone." "It is better to be a believer, although unlettered, than a scholar and a skeptic."[14] So, he is in a sense the opposite of Shneur Zalman in his approach to spiritual intensity. He saw excessive reason as undermining faith, without which closeness with the One could never be achieved: "happy is he who knows nothing of [the rationalists'] books, but who walks uprightly and fears retribution." He furthermore injected a sense of awe and even fear of God's retributive behavior and an almost Christological sense of sin into his teachings. From Lurianic thinking, he resurrected—and further emphasized—the notion of confession; his followers were called *viduiniks* ("confessors"), who sought out their *tzadikim* to confess their sins to him. Whereas Luria's circle engaged in confessing each other, Nahman separates the *tzadikim* as auditor of confession from his *hassidim* as offerers of confession.

Perhaps this evolved out of Nahman's own nature, which—paradoxically, given the nature typically ascribed to a *tzadik*—seems to have been more self-preoccupied than was so for his predecessors. He felt called to journey to *Eretz Yisrael*, leaving his family, which included very young daughters, to fend for itself, as it were, and he returned from that journey not only with an amplified sense of mission and purpose but also with his own superior powers. Thereafter, as he preached and taught, he not only spoke negatively of rationalists, from Maimonides to the Vilna Gaon, and of the *maskeeleem* ("enlightened ones")—those influenced by the new modes of thinking and being that were seeping into the eastern European Jewish world from western and central Europe—but also belittled his contemporary *tzadikim*. He was adored by his followers but detested and vilified by others, many of whom he deliberately antagonized. Thus, the schismatic side of *Hassidut* flourished.

Nahman is best known for his aphorisms and even more so for his often complex tales. These began to be written down soon after he settled in Bratslav in 1802—hence his designation as Nahman of Bratslav—where he met Rabbi Nathan ben Naftali Sternhanz of Niemerov, who began to record his (Nahman's) every word. In the end, the printing press established by Nathan in Bratslav in 1821 (a decade after Nahman's death in 1811) produced half a dozen major collections of Nahman's tales that amount to an essential compendium of eastern European Jewish folklore, overrun with moral points and issues that have as their purpose to provoke the sort of meditative, interpretative thought that will open the door to intense contact with the *mysterion*. But Nahman had no successors—his sons predeceased their father. His followers were called *Toiteh Hassidim*—"Dead Hassidim"—because, by definition, they would die out as a distinct group, since they remained so faithful to his memory that they never sought a leader to supplant that memory.

More broadly speaking, as *Hassidut* moved more deeply into the nineteenth and twentieth centuries, the number of *tzadikim* with congregations and communities of *hassidim* around them proliferated. On the one hand, movements as vast as *ChaBaD*, with tens of thousands of adherents, spread over dozens of communities, centered around dynasties of single *tzadikim* from the time of Shneur Zalman to our own time; on the other, there developed Hassidic groups numbering no more than a few dozen, loyal to their *tzadik* and located in a single village.[15] The Hassidic world would be as devastated as were other parts of the European Jewish world by the wars of the twentieth century, in particular, of course, the Holocaust. The center of *Hassidut* shifted from East to West, to the United States, where any number of factions thrive—*ChaBaD* is perhaps the best known, but many other groups, such as the *Satmars*, also flourish. Some groups also reconfigured themselves in the new state of Israel. From a movement both mystically focused and offering a radical reform of traditional Judaism, *Hassidut* has evolved as a bastion of what is ultratraditional compared with the style of life lived by most non-Hassidic Jews.

Some might argue that the writing of Abraham Joshua Heschel (1907–1972) offers a kind of twentieth-century mystical approach that is not specifically Hassidic but carries the Hassidic sense of the individual *hassid*'s potential and responsibility toward *tikkun olam* through answering the question of how to evolve a relationship with God in a secular world where God is not a given. Heschel argues that the ineffable is part of us, not apart from us and, thus, that God, in its ineffableness, is as much a part of us as apart from us, that God's existence is God's Name (God's Name and existence are one and the same),[16] that God's existence is no more or less valid than phenomenal reality (*profanus* reality; in philosophical terms, the reality of appearances as opposed to the reality of actual unchanging being).[17]

By the ineffable we do not mean the unknown as such; things unknown today may be known a thousand years from now. By the ineffable we mean that aspect of reality which by its very nature lies beyond our comprehension, and is acknowledged by the mind to be beyond the scope of the mind. Nor does the ineffable refer to a realm detached from the perceptible and the known. It refers to the correlation of the known and the unknown, of the knowable and the unknowable, upon which the mind comes in all of its acts of thinking and feeling.[18]

Thus, the love of a parent for his or her child, the beauty of a sunset, the spectacular roar of a summer storm at the shore of the sea—are all examples of the ineffable that lies beyond our ability to parse yet that lies very much within our own realm. For the one receptive to the ineffable—by definition, the mystic (but anyone, we recall, has the potential to be a mystic)—"[i]t has entered our consciousness like a ray of light passing into a lake. . . . We are penetrated by His insight. We cannot think any more as if He were there and we here. He is both there and here. He is not *a being*, but *being in and beyond all beings*."[19]

Yet, "those who are open to the ineffable will beware of spiritual schizophrenia; namely, the loss of contact with the mystery of living that surrounds us everywhere and at all times."[20] This danger is, of course, endemic not only to those who are prophets, who by and large are represented in the sacred texts describing their words and actions as overcoming the danger—God only chooses those as prophets who have the necessary centering strength not to split apart—but is also even more endemic to those who would take the initiative and seek to enter the *mysterion* that resides within the ineffable *sacer*, as we discussed near the beginning of our narrative.

In his 1951 work, *Man Is Not Alone: A Philosophy of Religion*, Heschel begins by discussing "the problem of God" with a discourse on the sense of the ineffable and of the uniquely human ability

not only . . . to develop words and symbols, but his [the human's] being compelled to draw a distinction between the utterable and the unutterable, to be stunned by that which is but cannot be put into words. . . . The attempt to convey what we see and cannot say is the everlasting theme of mankind's unfinished symphony, a venture in which adequacy is never achieved. . . . The awareness of the ineffable is that with which our search must begin. . . . Citizens of two realms, we all must sustain a dual allegiance: we sense the ineffable in one realm, we name and exploit reality in another.[21]

Threads from the tapestry of the discussion that follows in this work are woven and rewoven into Heschel's lifelong exploration of the issue of God and ourselves. In his 1955 work, *God in Search of Man: A Philosophy of Judaism*, he elaborates on issues raised in the previous work and arrives (in chapter 19), for example, at "the mystery of revelation," for the beginning point of every religion (as we recall from the beginnings of our own discussion) revelation is its own *mysterion*. We can account neither for why God chooses to reveal itself to certain individuals nor for exactly how the process occurs: "And God spoke to Moses" (or to Isaiah, or to John the Evangelist, or to Muhammad) may not (or perhaps *cannot*) simply mean that God *spoke*, the way *we* speak. And we have also observed from the outset of our discussion of formalized mysticism that the mystic seeks (or, as the case may be, manages successfully) to experience what prophets experience: the revelation of the *sacer* and, more than that, the innermost depths of the *sacer*.

Heschel puts it this way: "just as a work of sculpture is more than the stone in which it is carved, so is revelation *more* than a human experience. True, a revelation that did not become known by experience would be like a figure carved in air . . . [but] we must not equate the event of revelation with man's experience of revelation."[22] There is that sense of necessary reciprocity that *every* mystical tradition emphasizes in Heschel's comment: the idea that the *mysterion* finds those who seek the *mysterion*. But this idea, for Heschel, reverts, by means of the notion that prophecy is accorded to those whom God seeks out, to the assertion that divine revelation and the revelation of the *mysterion* only become *relevant* when the *mysterion* has *been* perceived—and, Heschel would add, has been *acted* upon. But it is its ultimate ineffability that makes it mysterious: "In speaking about revelation, the more descriptive the terms, the less adequate the description. The words in which the prophets attempted to relate their experiences were not photographs but illustrations, not descriptions but songs . . . as a report about revelation the Bible itself is a *midrash*"[23]—which Heschelian description helps one to see his work, in part, as an extension of Hassidic thinking: not treatises but tales.

Further, "[r]evelation can only be described *via negationis*; we can only say what it is not . . . literally: *a voice of silence*. . . . Yet this is the axiom of Biblical thinking: God who created the world is unlike the world"[24]—which paradox (signifiable by a voice of silence) is at the heart of mystical thought, and which axiom (regarding the act of creation) is also the beginning point of the Jewish mystical inquiry (how did the singular, invisible, intangible God create the multifarious, visible, tangible world?), as we have seen. So, at the heart of Heschel's inquiries into spirituality is an exposition of the mystical heart of spirituality. I have been asked from time to time whether Heschel is a mystic (as opposed to a student and teacher of mystical thought). My answer is always the same: I can attest to the fact of his being a student and teacher through his writing, but I (who have had no personal conversations with him) cannot know whether he is a mystic in the sense of one who has sought intimate contact with the *mysterion* (and if so, by what method that one might label "mystical")—and only he can know whether he is a mystic in the sense of one who has succeeded in establishing that contact and returned from the experience to the *profanus* to share the *gnosis* gained through that experience.

THE CONTINUED SHAPING OF SUFISM IN THE NINETEENTH AND TWENTIETH CENTURIES

During the period in which Jewish mysticism was assuming and expanding its latest shape, as *Hassidut*, and passing through the doorway of modernist thought through individuals like Abraham Joshua Heschel, Muslim mysticism was also producing a continuous series of diverse Sufi orders and figures whose teachings carry beyond the golden age of Sufism into the modern era. The proliferation of relatively small groups adhering to doctrines promulgated by a particular teacher seems rather parallel, in fact, to the proliferation of Hassidic groups attached to a particular *tzadik*. Thus, for instance, the *Khalwatiya Tariqa* in Anatolia, which had its beginnings in Egypt and Syria, centered on the teachings of Shaikh Mustafa al-Bakri (d. 1749). Its meditation centers spread throughout Turkey in the late Ottoman period. A central element in its methodology is that its adherents rise an hour before the dawn prayer, wash themselves, and begin chanting a *dhikr* that includes 111 repetitions of *bismillairrahmaniraheem* ("in the name of God the merciful and beneficent") and 100 repetitions of *laillahillallah* ("there is no God but God")—among other, less familiar phrases. The devotee continues to chant until the total of repetitions of these and other important phrases numbers "at least 700," which process is part both of gaining access to God and of bringing God's blessing into the world.

The *Shaikhiya Tariqa* was associated with Shaikh Ahmad of al-Ahsa (d. 1826). It centered on the distinctive idea that the devotee focuses on images that appear identical to, but are insubstantial as substitutes for, the objects of this world (a kind of Platonic perspective but in reverse: Rather than forms as the reality of which the objects and concepts of our own reality are mere, inferior imitative *eidola*, the *Shaikhiya* devotee focuses on imitative images *of* our reality in order to disconnect from the physical, material objects of which those images are, in effect, mere *eidola*). Through focusing on the images, which, in his or her mind, become impossible to distinguish from the objects themselves, the devotee comes to think of and recognize the true objects themselves as if *they* were *eidola* and ultimately insubstantial. As a Shi'ite movement, the *Shaikhiya Tariqa* understood that the path to oneness with the One lies through an ongoing spiritual connection to the "hidden imam," so the focus of the devotee's concentration is penultimately the hidden imam, reached by disconnecting from this reality through focus on the images within the *'alam al'mithal* ("world of similitudes") and thus, through the imam, to the ultimate goal, God's innermost hiddenness.

By the early nineteenth century, the golden age of Sufi poets and theoreticians was long passed yet the number of *tariqas* each with its particular *shaikh* and its particular *dhikr* had exponentially increased—again somewhat parallel to the expansion of Hassidic communities and *tzadikim* in eastern Europe during this same period. E. W. Lane, whom I have quoted above in chapter 8, describes the Doseh ceremony in which the *shaikh* of the *Saadeeyeh* Sufis rides on horseback over his supine devotees, then seats himself on a prayer rug at the end wall of the courtyard of the Sufi meditation house. Some twenty of the *darvishes* enter, with three times that number of "audience" members beyond them, as they gather standing in a semicircle around him. Six of them begin chanting *Allahoo hai* ("God lives!"), maintaining a rhythmic chanting pattern and beating the left hand with a small leather strap with each beat. After a few moments of this they "performed a second zhikr; each alternative zhikeer exclaiming *'Allahoo hai!'* And the others, *'Ya hai'* ('Oh [thou who] lives!') and all of them bowing at each exclamation, alternately to the right and left. This they continued for about ten minutes. Then, for about the same space of time, in the same manner and with the same emotions, they exclaimed *'Daim!'* ('Everlasting!') and *'Ya Daim!'* ('Oh Everlasting!')."

So, too, new Sufi literature continues into the twentieth century. Among the authors in the classical tradition was Shaikh Muhammad Amin al-Kurdi al-Sahi'i al Naqshabandi, born in Irbil, Iraq (d. 1914), who authored the *Tanwir al-qulub*. In the final text, edited by his *khalifa* ("successor"), Shaikh Salama al'Azzami, we read in the biographical sketch of Muhammad Amin's life provided by al'Azzami about how when he sat down to eat and only a bit of bread was placed before him, somehow the amount expanded to become enough for the large group of people who inevitably sat down to join in his meal, or about how his disciples could see his *eidolon* ("image") when he was miles away—he in Cairo, they in Makka, for instance. We are reminded of the miracle-working propensities ascribed to *tzadikim* by their *hassidim* and recognize an ultimate parallel to the stories regarding Jesus found in the Gospels. But as for the *Tanwir* itself, it is, in a particular manner, reminiscent of earlier texts by masters such as al-Ghazali in that it focuses first of all on classical theology and jurisprudence and turns only secondarily to esoteric matters, with relatively little that is new to the "field"—except, of course, the particulars of the prescribed *dhikr*.

Muhammad Amin divides the *dhikr* into two parts, the first in God's Name in its essential aspect (*'Allah*) and the second in the statement that there is no

God but God (*la ilaha illa 'llah*)—which statement comprises, of course, the opening phrase of the *Shahada*.[25] The first consists of an eleven-part series of preparatory exercises, and the second, of a meditation on that *Shahada* phrase. Thus, one purifies one's self ritually (1) and prays two *rak'as* (2), turning to Makka in an empty and quiet, uninhabited space (3), kneeling on folded legs as when praying (4), and asking forgiveness for one's sins (5)—of which one generates images arrayed before God in one's mind. One recites the *fatiha* (first *sura*, or chapter, of the Qur'an) one time and then the *Ikhlas* (Sura 112; "Congregation") three times to the spirits of both the Prophet and all the Naqshabandi *shaikhs* (6).

With the eyes and mouth tightly closed to keep all distractions out, one presses the tongue against the roof of the mouth (7) and imagines oneself dead, washed, wrapped in a winding-sheet, laid in the tomb and alone—the mourners all gone—to face final judgment (8). One performs the "guide exercise," in which the heart of the neophyte faces the heart of his *shaikh* and experiences *fana'*, or passing away within him (9). One focuses all of the bodily senses, directing one's entire being toward God, repeating the words, "Oh God, you are my quest and your pleasure my desire," and being evermindful of God's all-abiding presence, watching and encompassing one's self, so that, in effect, one also experiences *fana'* within God (10). When *warid* occurs—a sense of God's presence, an epiphany of God within and around one's self, one remains still and silent, before slowly opening the eyes (11).

Having explained how each of the appropriate organs is engaged in this process, where precisely each is located within the body, how each connects to one of the prophets and is manifest by a particular colored light—the heart (*qalb*) is two fingers' breadth below the left nipple, is under the spiritual control of Adam, and is manifest as a yellow light; the spirit (*ruh*) is two fingers' breadth below the right nipple, is under the spiritual aegis of Noah and Abraham, and is manifest as a red light; the inmost conscience (*irr*) is two fingers' breadth above the left nipple, is under Moses's aegis, and is manifest by a white light; the hidden depth of one's being (*khafi*) is two fingers' breadth above the right nipple, is under Jesus's aegis, and is manifest by a black light; and the hiddenmost depth of one's being (*akhfa*) is in the middle of the chest, is under the spiritual aegis of Muhammad, and is manifest by a green light—the *Tanwir* then instructs the devotee as to how to meditate on the shahadic phrase.

One must keep the tongue cleaving to the roof of one's mouth—in other words, one willingly gives up the ability to verbally articulate anything (appropriate indeed, since both the process of encounter with God and God itself are ultimately ineffable)—take a deep breath, and, by paradox (for one cannot really speak), begin to produce the sounds that comprise *la*, visualizing them ascending from below the navel and gradually ascending to the front lobe of the brain, "the rational soul" (*al-nafs al-natiqa*). Then, one visualizes carrying the *hamza* (the light glottal stop preceding the first vowel) of *ilaha* from the brain through the right shoulder blade to the *ruh* and the *hamza* of the *illa 'illah* from the shoulder blade to the *qalb*, where it presses against the word of God's glory, forcing heat throughout the body, incinerating all of the corrupt physical elements, just as the light of God's glory envelops all of the spiritually perfect, noncorrupt elements. With full intensity of focus, this process is repeated twenty-one times, at the end of which the devotee will suddenly lose all sense of being human and a part of creation and will feel him- or herself completely dissipate within the divine essence.

We recognize that the *Tanwir* prescribes a process that is in large part a matter of visualization, in terms of both preparation and meditation; that the preparation involves associating one's self with key sacerdotal figures who have had an intimate relationship with God—five of them, like the number of pillars in Islam—and culminates with imagining one's self as having crossed over into the *sacer* realm as all of us eventually do—by dying; and that the culmination of meditation is to die by losing all sense of self as a separate entity within God's all-encompassingness (and thus that the challenge will be not only to arrive at this state but also to return from it emotionally, mentally, spiritually, and physically intact). There is thus a strong intertwining of spiritual and physical imagery and components.

We may follow Sufism further into the twentieth century by way of the *tariqa* surrounding Pir-o-Murshid Hazrat Inayat Khan (1882–1927), born in India, who is credited with first bringing Sufism to the West.[26] A master musician whose early efforts were directed at reviving a focus on the spiritual heritage of Indian music, he also eventually trained—a vision is said to have led him to seek out his *murshid*—in the four major Indian Sufi traditions: Chishti, Naqshabandi, Qadiri, and Suhrawardi. In 1910, his training complete, he began traveling and lecturing in Europe and America, bringing Muslim mysticism into contact with the West and its own expressions of spirituality. His interest in and capacity for accomplishing a synthesis of thought grows out of his universalistic sensibilities—which recall Rumi on the one hand and Kabir on the other—as suggested in a passage from his seminal work *The Inner Life*: "The man who makes God his Beloved, what more does he want? His heart becomes awakened to all the beauty that there is within and without. . . . To [such a man], God is all-in-all; to him, God is everywhere. If he goes to the Christian church or to the Jewish synagogue, to the Buddhist temple, to the Hindu shrine, or to the Muslim mosque, there is God. In the wilderness, in the forest, in the crowd, everywhere he sees God."[27]

The beginning point of arriving at this sensibility is to recognize that "the first and principal thing in the inner life is to establish a relationship with God, making God the Object to which we relate, such as the Creator, Sustainer, Forgiver, Judge, Friend, Father, Mother and Beloved . . . the work of the inner life is to make God a reality, so that He is no more an [aspect of the] imagination; that this relation that man has with God may seem to him more real than any other relation in the world. And when this happens, then all relationships, however near and dear, become less binding. But at the same time a person does not thus become cold, he becomes more loving."[28]

We recognize in Hazrat Inayat's thought at least two familiar mystical notions that are being articulated in an extreme (in the positive sense of that adjective) manner. First, we recognize the panhenotheistic perspective that we have encountered with other mystics within the Abrahamic traditions. But he focuses on God's presence not only within nature along its broadest contours but also within humanity—a concept often more difficult for humans to embrace than that of finding God in trees or the ocean. Inayat Khan recognized the myriad human spiritual paths to the One as paths into precisely the same unique *mysterion* within the same unique *sacer* reality. He articulated an absolute universality of viewpoint. Second, we recognize his assertion that through the love of God, one's love of others becomes enriched, not diminished—even if, through the limitations and paradoxes of language, it might be assumed to be diminished. The reason is obvious: The relationship with God's *mysterion*, if it is to succeed, will require a certain elimination of the devotee's ego, so that his or her *self* may be absorbed into the self of the *mysterion*. In "returning" from that journey, while a modicum of self must be restored in order for the devotee to function in the *profanus* world, enough of it, one might say, will necessarily remain "unreclaimed" due to the experience within the *mysterion*, so that everyone—and everything— with whom and with which he or she has a relationship will be approached from far less of an egocentric perspective. Love becomes freed of its bindings to flourish in a fuller, purer atmosphere.

Hazrat Khan never abandoned his love of music; he merely reangled his relationship to it, recognizing the universe as the ultimate music and the One as the composer. His sayings were typically organized into groups referred to by musical terminology. Thus, for instance, books of *gayan* ("psalmody") and *vadan* ("instrumental music") in turn offer chapters with titles such as *alapa* ("extemporization") or *raga* ("scale, mode"). In the book of his complete sayings, edited and introduced by his son, Pir Vilayat Khan, the first *alapa* reads, "When a glimpse of Our image is caught in man, when heaven and earth are sought in man, then what is there in the world that is not in man? If one only explores him, there is a lot in man."[29] Thus, as humans seek the One, the One seeks humans, and humans peering into the depths of humanity—*en-stasis*—will find the One there (finding a form of everything there), just as that search, undertaken by a human, will guide the One seeking to arrive there, in the hiddenmost depths of the human heart.

Hazrat Khan lived his universalism, finding his life mate in an American, Ora Ray Becker, from Albuquerque, New Mexico. His older son and successor, as well as his primary biographer, the just-mentioned Pir Vilayat Khan (1916–2004), practiced a spiritual life that emphatically expressed his parents' universalistic viewpoint. His perspective was simultaneously that of a Muslim *darvish*, a Christian monk, a Hindu *rishi*, and a Buddhist *bikku*—and he was also well versed in Kabbalah.[30] Pir Vilayat was also an author of significant books; perhaps the most relevant to this discussion of the transformation and continuation of Sufism into our own era is his 1978 *The Message in Our Time*. This work, in its very title, underscores two essential issues."The message" is not simply "the Sufi message," if the latter turn of phrase is intended to be limited to a Muslim viewpoint (or even a Shi'ite Muslim viewpoint) with respect to seeking oneness with the One. The message is of oneness with each other and not only with the One—which is logical since, after all, we are all understood to possess within ourselves the presence of the One (it is, as we have repeatedly seen, merely a matter of how to locate it). And the message is relevant—as relevant and necessary as ever—in our own time, as opposed to being some outdated form of spirituality that should be left behind in the interests of "modernity."

Interestingly, Pir Vilayat's son, Pir Zia Inayat Khan, is a much more overtly devout and practicing Muslim than his father, but as the current head of the Sufi Order International—the Sufi order founded in the West by his grandfather—he remains firmly embedded within the universalism of his father's and grandfather's universalistic ethos. In one of his 2005 lectures, Pir Zia discussed the way in which five aspects of prayer may be understood as intertwined with the concept of the five elements (earth, water, fire, air, and ether), so that the devotee and the world are overtly connected (the human microcosm is interwoven with the macrocosm). At first glance, one might suppose that the basis for his focus on "fiveness" is the tradition of the Five Pillars of Islam, or the five "grades" of Sufi seeking (physical, intellectual, mental, moral, and spiritual), or perhaps the establishment by his grandfather of the *Zira'at* as the fifth branch of the Sufi order (beyond the four in India into which he had been instructed as a student) in 1927.[31] But fiveness is essential to Christian mysticism: The number refers to Christ's wounds, and Christ is, particularly through his suffering, the portal through which the Christian mystic seeks oneness with the One, as we have seen in earlier chapters of this discussion. It is also a number essential to Jewish mysticism, since the Torah is comprised of five books, and the Torah is the ultimate doorway through which the Jewish mystic seeks oneness with the One. Thus, the emphasis on fiveness expresses connectedness both to a layered Muslim Sufi perspective and to a broader Abrahamic perspective.

Moreover, in Pir Zia's writing on *Zira'at*, he quotes from his father, Pir Vilayat, who observed that it (*Zira'at*) "is a continuation of the inheritance of Zoroastrianism." And in Pir Zia's essay, "The Paradox of 'Universal Sufism,'" the young Sufi master looks to a Zoroastrian master, Azar Kayvan (ca. 1529/33–1609/18), with his students of diverse faiths (seeking not conversion to his faith but inspiration from his charismatic spirituality), as the conceptual ancestor of Hazrat Inayat Khan's shaping of the Order International and its message.[32] As we follow deeper into the twenty-first century, that message continues to be revitalized by further essays and discourses with universal themes.

CHRISTIAN MYSTICISM IN A SECULAR AGE

As with Jewish and Muslim mysticism, so with Christian mysticism: The secularizing tendencies in the West during the past few hundred years have not prevented the emergence of a number of significant figures as intensely focused on merging with the *mysterion* as any mystic of prior centuries. In the midst of the great Enlightenment era of the late eighteenth century, Emanuel Swedenborg (1688–1772), himself expertly versed in a range of intellectual disciplines, emerged as what might be termed the first modern Spiritualist, cognate with, though perhaps not identical to, what one might call a mystic. For Swedenborg, the son of a Lutheran minister and drawn to a broad view of how one may make contact with the *sacer*, began at the age of fifty-six to experience visions and visitations from angels and demons. He asserted that through these contacts he—and he alone—was truly privy to the concerns and preferences of God for humankind.

Thus, Swedenborg's teachings and writings are sibling to mysticism in seeking as a goal to return from commerce with the *sacer* with a deepened and expanded knowledge of how the realm of the *profanus* may be brought closer to perfection and in admitting to an ongoing struggle between the love of one's self and an unadulterated love for God. But, in a sense, his *path* to that goal seems to be the opposite of that of a mystic: Rather than seeking the hiddenmost, most deeply implanted *mysterion* within the One, he derived his information from those beings that themselves are believed by believers to be intermediate between God and ourselves, thereby hovering round the periphery rather than the innermost recesses of the *mysterion*. The results of these celestial contacts were visions of things happening in the here and now, such as a fire in Gothenberg upon which he is said to have reported while 405 kilometers away in Stockholm, and his great, eight-volume work, *Arcana caelestia* (*Celestial Secrets*). In it he explores what he asserts to be "true" Christianity: A rejection of the notion of a triune God of paradoxically three *distinct*, if yet mutually indistinguishable, "persons," which notion, he argued, presents three separate "gods." Rather, he maintained, the Trinity should be understood as three *aspects* of the One God, just as soul, body, and spirit (the effect of being who we are and thus doing what we do) are aspects of every human being: The Father is the soul, the Son is the body, and the Holy Spirit is the spirit (the effect in action).

Swedenborg argued that what causes Jews, Muslims, and others to oppose Christian doctrine is what they recognize as polytheistic in the concept of the Trinity as first articulated by Athanasius at the Council of Nicaea in 325 and codified in the Athanasian Creed around 500 CE. This argument, not surprisingly, led many to accuse Swedenborg of heresy.[33] He also turned from the prevailing centerpiece of most post-Luther Protestantism in arguing against the doctrine that salvation may be achieved through faith alone (*sola fide* is the proper Latin phrase). He asserted not only that charity—good works—is of equal importance but also that the very purpose of faith is to lead one to charity in the Augustinian sense of *caritas*.[34] For

[i]t is very evident from their Epistles that it never entered the mind of any of the Apostles that the Church of this day would separate Faith from Charity by teaching that Faith alone justifies and saves apart from the works of the Law, and that Charity therefore cannot be conjoined with Faith, since Faith is from God, and Charity, so far as it is expressed in works, is from man. But this separation and division were introduced into the Christian Church when it divided God into three persons, and ascribed to each equal Divinity.[35]

Thus, the two cornerstones of Swedenborg's thinking—that of God's three aspects and that of the interweave of faith and charity—are connected as part of a discussion that presents these issues as developing from the same time, place, and circumstance.

The tie between his thinking and the history of Christian mysticism in its various aspects is this: He views Christ's actions as a model to emulate for the one who would be closer to God. But the actions upon which he focuses are those committed by Christ during his earthly life and not that of self-sacrificing crucifixion. The coming into the world of God as Christ had as its purpose to offer a more direct route of reconnection to the *sacer* God of goodness by offering an accessible, earth-bound, *profanus* model to emulate. Moreover, the ongoing transformation of Christ through the *profanus* experiences that culminate with his crucifixion is a transformation that ends with his becoming fully one with God itself—the God who became a human being remerges with God. He thus offers a model of transformation and becoming one with the One for his follow- ers to emulate as they meditate intensely on Christ's experiences and on his good works—and emulate those works.

Christ does not atone for us; he guides us to break through the evil that pre- vails the more distant we are from God and that is defeated the closer we come to God. As such, we achieve a partnership with God in which, having merged ourselves into God, our sense of self is enhanced as we become new, more angelic beings. And his vision of an angelic future encompasses all faiths, not merely Christianity; in his visits to (or visions of) the spiritual world, he saw followers of diverse spiritual traditions embedded within the pure innermost precincts of the *sacer*.

About a century after Swedenborg's death in Lutheran Sweden, Therese of Lisieux (1873–1897) was born in Catholic France; the family moved from Alenon to Lisieux when Therese was three years old. At age ten, she was very ill for three months, during which period she experienced convulsions and hallucinations. She recovered, she later asserted, when she was praying be- fore a statue of Our Lady of Victories, her first experience of intense spiritu- ality. Three years later—on Christmas Eve, 1886—she felt a full and power- ful sense of *caritas* entering her soul, and in the days that followed (specifically, while meditating on an image of the crucified Christ), she re- solved to devote her life to serving others with love. As she was only fourteen years old, she needed to petition Pope Leo XIII to permit her to enter the Carmelite convent in Lisieux, since ordinarily the order required that a pos- tulant be at least twenty-one years old.[36]

Entering the convent at age fourteen, she lived in accordance with what she called her "Little Way," the way of humility and service, based on "the way of confidence and abandonment to God [in which] we acknowledge our noth- ingness; that we expect everything from the good Lord," as she expressed it in her autobiography, published after her death from tuberculosis at not quite age twenty-four. It is as if by abandoning her will to God, she willed herself to a death that was a *profanusly* speaking premature (for from the perspective of the *sacer*, it could not be called premature) mergence with the *sacer*. As she further wrote, "martyrdom was the dream of my youth and this dream has grown with me within Carmel's cloisters. . . . Like you, my adorable spouse, I would be scourged and crucified . . . when thinking of the torments which will be the lot of Christians at the time of the Anti-Christ, I feel my heart leap with joy and I would these torments be reserved for me. . . . I am only a child powerless and weak, and yet it is my weakness that gives me the boldness of offering myself as victim of your love, Oh Jesus."[37]

Therese brings the story of Christian mysticism full circle with the desire to be martyred in emulation of the Christ—and she refers to various martyred saints as she continues her comments—in order to be more fully merged with him. The embedding of one's soul in God is achieved through denying the demands of the body as the Christ and early saints did. The tedium of the Carmelite daily timetable offers a reminder of the danger to the Desert Fathers of the demon of boredom, but that demon seems never to have tempted her. She is also another in a long line of female Christian mystics for whom the imagery of mergence with God as the male-conceived Christ contains a strongly sensual spirituality.

We recognize, too, the paradox of weakness/strength that she articulated and exemplified: This was a young woman who chose absolute humility as her profession but had a will of iron with respect to gaining her profession—and how does one draw the line between being chosen by God and being self-chosen for a particular life, between humility before God and the desire from an early age to achieve greatness, to gain *gloire* ("glory")? We recognize, at the same time, her sense of imperfection, that whereas, in the past "to satisfy divine justice perfect victims were necessary . . . the law of love has succeeded the law of fear, and love has chosen me as a burnt offering." She wants to be and has become that offering, yet feels herself unworthy to be offered.

As to her goal of serving others, it is subtle. Through her devotions and her self-abnegation, she may be accepted as a sacrifice on behalf of others, thus bringing them to salvation: "I long to enlighten men's minds as the prophets and doctors did; I feel the call of an Apostle. I'd like to travel the world, making your name known and planting your cross on heathen soil."[38] "Jesus, I would like to die a martyr for your sake, a martyr in soul or in body; better still, in both. . . . Jesus, may I be the means of saving many souls; today, in particular, may no soul be lost, may all those detained in Purgatory win release."[39] Her path is, at first glance, opposite to what Swedenborg had preached, in form at least, both in being so hermetic in its service activity and in conceiving of salvation as attainable only in traditionally understood Christological terms. Yet, its goal of atonement on behalf of others is at the same time parallel in substance to his emphasis on good works—not accidentally, the same Latin term, *caritas*, is used by both writers to refer to their respective goals.

There is a sense in which the mystical thought of Pierre Teilhard de Chardin (1881–1955) carries in a direction 180 degrees removed from that of Therese of Lisieux—as certainly his life did. Trained in geology, botany, zoology, and paleontology at the Sorbonne, as well as in Jesuit studies (at a time when the Jesuits were largely forced into exile from France and took refuge mostly in Great Britain), he taught physics and chemistry in Cairo, Egypt, for several years, at the Jesuit College of the Holy Family, and spent nearly twenty-five years in China, part of it as an advisor to the Chinese National Geological Service.[40] Thus, while Therese's life was emphatically hermetic, his was lived with both feet out in the world. And where her writing is strictly autobiographical—descriptive of her spiritual experience—his is more prescriptive of how to understand the spirit within the context of macrocosmic and microcosmic developments. Teilhard's continuous and intense focus on the spirit in fact intertwines with his paleontological work.

His first spiritual writing came during his service as a stretcher bearer during World War I—his experience of "the war [as] a meeting . . . with the Absolute" was captured in letters to his cousin Marguerite Teillard-Chambon, who later edited them together as a book. This was the period in which he wrote the essays "Cosmic Life" and "The Spiritual Power of Matter." Later (in 1920), he wrote "The Fall, Redemption and Geocentricity" and (in 1922) "A Few Possible Historical Representations of Original Sin." Still later (in 1937), he wrote "The Spiritual Phenomenon." The primacy that his writing offers to an evolutionary narrative that diverges from a more strict and literalist read of creation as presented in Genesis led to conflicts with the Roman Catholic Curia, which saw his words as undermining the Augustinian doctrine of original sin; he was forbidden from publishing his work during his lifetime.

His most famous work, *The Phenomenon of Man*, was published posthumously and summarizes his thinking on the matter of how the unfolding of the universe and the evolution of the human species reflect rather than contradict the notion of a divine artificer who shaped and continues to shape us with a purpose in mind. It associates human spiritual growth and development with evolution on the one hand and on the other with continuing the work that the advent of the Christ did not complete by his crucifixion, the entirety leading toward what he calls the Omega Point in the idealized future.[41] That Omega Point, the culmination of the "evolution . . . toward consciousness" that comes from the human striving that, in its totality, leads to ecstasy is, in so many words, God.

The process of striving and seeking, in its most intense inner-awareness mode, is articulated in Teilhard's 1926–1927 essay, "The Divine Milieu," as a series of five (like the wounds in Christ's body) interconnected circles into which we can ascend in order to achieve union with the One while not losing our individualized sense of self.[42] "Presence" is the panhenotheistic awareness that we have encountered in Ibn 'Arabi, the Ba'al Shem Tov, and others:

> The mystic only gradually becomes aware of the faculty he has been given of perceiving the indefinite fringe of reality surrounding the totality of all created

things, with more intensity than the precise, individual core of their being. . . . If, then, a man is to build up in himself the structure of a sublime love for God, he must first sharpen this sensibility . . . his perception of, his zest for, the Omnipresent which haloes everything in nature.

In the circle of "Consistence," the mystic searches within all that is in and around him or her for the stable, unchanging, unequivocal, and absolute element, the awareness of which gives the mystic intense pleasure, which can only be found by looking beneath the surface of appearances. This is not the seeking of the essence of each aspect of reality, as Plato would prescribe (seeking the "tableness" within every table, the "beautifulness" within everything we label beautiful, the "justice" within every act we call just), but the seeking of the One that underlies it all (the *heno* that underlies *pan*):

He knows the joy of feeling that Reality penetrates all things—wherever the mysterious light of the Omnipresent has shown—even into the very stuff of which his mental awareness, in the different forms it assumes, is made up.

The third circle is "Energy": the force and the desire to make contact with that unifying source underlying everything. One can exercise this energy through prayer—"I pray . . . that You do so make Yourself known to me in Your true essence"—or through a more energized, physical response that yields a feeling "within himself [of] a fever of active dependence and arduous purity seizing upon him and driving him on . . . that through his active obedience, he endlessly adheres more closely to the encompassing Godhead." Teilhard seems to be suggesting increasingly intense levels of what the Ba'al Shem Tov's followers refer to as *kavanah* and *heetlahavut* ("powerful intention" of praying that can encompass singing and even—especially—dancing, in order to yield a sense of "enflamement").[43]

The "mystical milieu" centers on the sense of the interpenetration of all the elements of reality with each other through their interpenetration with God and on the sense of the reciprocal process of seeking God and being sought by God, which is most emphatically expressed by Teilhard's fourth circle, "Spirit." For that circle reverses the processes of seeking the unifying One by pushing the mystic toward awareness of the infinite *multiplicity* of all the elements of reality. The "mystical milieu" is thus equally focused on seeking the center of reality and, through the realization of its presence, on feeling an intense connectedness to all of the inhabitants of reality. As such, the mystic's awareness of being part of a unified whole, but also a particularized, individuated entity, is enhanced.

Thus, the fifth circle, "Person," describes the attainment of full-fledged spiritual illumination. Teilhard in this part of his exposition turns briefly to the sort of ground upon which Therese of Lisieux stands throughout the story of her soul: "I understood . . . that without ever ceasing to be buried in you, the Ocean of Life, that life penetrates and quickens us. . . . Every presence makes me feel that you are near me; every touch is the touch of your hand; every necessity transmits to me a pulsation of your will. . . . It is impossible . . . for any man who has acquired even the smallest understanding of you to look upon your face without seeing in it the radiance of every reality and every goodness. In the mystery of your mystical body—your cosmic body— you sought to feel the echo of every joy and every fear that moves each single one of all the countless cells that make up mankind. And . . . we cannot contemplate you and adhere to you without your Being, for all its supreme multiplicity, transmuting itself as we grasp it into the restructured multitude of all that you love upon earth, oh Jesus!"

The term "person" articulates the mystical union in specifically Christian terms: Not only is the culminating aspect of Teilhard's essay *addressed* toward Jesus but also the reciprocity of interpenetrating feeling that he describes is facilitated by the fact of God's assuming a human "personhood"—with a physical body—as the Christ. God becomes one of us, and we can thus aspire to become one with God-as-Christ; our fully realized, spiritually illuminated "personhood," if it is fully realized and spiritually illuminated, *is* by definition Christ. Like the Intoxicated Sufis, "I am God" in the sense of having achieved complete and perfect union with the One from whom I cannot therefore be perceived as separate—even as I never lose my individualized self (thus, I am neither mad nor dead in my mergence with the *sacer mysterion*; nor am I making some egotistical statement).

One might say that Thomas Merton (1915–1968), who carries this part of our discussion still further into the twentieth century, falls directly into the line of Swedenborg's and Teilhard's actionist mystical viewpoint, as opposed to Therese's more passive and hermetic mode of being. And if Teilhard's emphasis is on what one might call a "vertical" reciprocity between God and the mystic, Merton might be said to extend the principle of reciprocity in a "horizontal" direction, toward an explicit awareness of non-Christian—indeed, non-Abrahamic—spirituality. Merton was born in France to a pair of artists, an American mother (who died of stomach cancer when he was six years old) and a father from New Zealand (who died of a brain tumor when Merton was sixteen years old).

Brought up as a nominal Protestant, he found himself in Rome some time after his father's death, visiting churches without really knowing why. One night, he sensed his father's presence for a few moments in his room, and with that presence, his own feeling of emptiness. He prayed seriously for the first time, asking God to deliver him from his darkness. But it was only after a long period of losing and refinding himself, which period carried him from Europe to America, eventually to Clare College in Cambridge, England, and thence to Columbia University in New York City, that he discovered Catholicism in a real way. It was during this period that he became a peace activist in the aftermath of Italy's 1935 invasion of Ethiopia.

In 1938, he met the Hindu monk Mahanambrata Brahmachari, who surprised him by suggesting that he look more deeply into his *own* faith, rather than attempting to convert him to Hinduism. Merton's spiritual quest in fact led him back to the Roman Catholicism with which he had been flirting on and off for several years; he was baptized as a Catholic on November 16, 1938. Still searching, one might say, in May 1941 he picked up the old copy of the Bible that he had acquired by chance (or not!) in Italy eight years earlier, and his eye fell arbitrarily (or not!) on the passage in Luke stating, "Behold, you shall be silent." He immediately thought of the Cistercian Order with its vows of silence. A few months later, he entered the Trappist monastery, Our Lady of Gethsemani, in Kentucky on December 10, 1941. After three days in the monastery guesthouse, he was accepted as a postulate into the order.[44] There, Merton found his vocation not only as a man of the spirit but also as a writer.

He wrote poetry, a number of works for the monastery (such as *Guide to Cistercian Life, Cistercian Contemplatives,* and *The Spirit of Simplicity*), works of hermetic focus (such as *Seeds of Contemplation*), and, in a turning point with regard to his vocation as a bridge between the inner life and outer action, a memoir, *The Seven Story Mountain,* which he authored in 1946 and which brought him unanticipated renown a few years later. The decision to write a memoir may have been inspired, in part, by the model of Therese of Lisieux; he admitted to having a "devotion" to her, and some of his phraseology recalls hers. But in clear respects, his writing is different. Most obviously, his work is deeply syncretistic, drawing not only from the Christian mystical tradition but also from Far Eastern religions, as well as from secular literature and art and also psychology.

The Trappist Cistercian Order emphasizes silence, but Merton spoke continually—and eloquently—through his writing. His abbot recognized the importance for the order—and for the spread of spirituality in broad directions—of Merton's talent and encouraged him to use it when Merton himself feared that his writing might make him too self-focused. His writings are shaped by silence and solitude; their purpose is to guide others as he seeks his own inner path back toward the union with God from which all humans, since Adam and Eve, have been in exile. True union requires true contemplation, which necessitates a true emptying of the self—a kind of spiritual death:

One has begun to know the meaning of contemplation when he intuitively and spontaneously seeks the dark and unknown path of aridity, in preference to every other known way. The contemplative is one who would rather not know than know, rather not enjoy than enjoy. He accepts the love of God on faith, in defiance of all apparent evidence. This is the necessary condition, and a very paradoxical condition, for the mystical experience of God's presence and of His love for us. Only when we are able to "let go" of everything within us, all desire to know, to taste and to experience the presence of God, do we truly become able to experience that presence.[45]

Paradoxes, again, then: One seeks not to know because what one seeks is beyond "knowledge." Only when we let go of the desire for God—which stems from our *self*, which self generates even that desire—can we find the unknowable God who can then find us. The image of an inner desert suggests a return to the beginnings of Christian monasticism, but without the necessity of physical isolation in the wilderness: One can find the desert of senseless, empty contemplation within one's self (which is where the One will find the contemplative one).

And it is only after one has achieved self-understanding through contemplation that one will be able to be useful as an instrument in helping to improve the condition of the world. Without self-understanding, the world gets nothing from the individual but obsessive, aggressive, ambitious, overweening *self*. And "there is nothing more tragic in the modern world than the misuse of power and action to which men are driven by their own Faustian misunderstandings and misapprehensions," and nothing more dangerous to the world than that self-obsessed condition, given the technological power we have attained as a species, with "more power at our disposal today than we ever had, and yet we are more alienated and estranged from the inner ground of meaning and of love than we have ever been."[46]

Moreover, the source of the inner ground of meaning and of love offers itself along diverse paths, not along any one exclusive path. As his years in the monastery moved forward, Merton became more and more focused on spiritual dialogue with other faiths, particularly the Far Eastern spiritual traditions. In this, he was also encouraged by his abbot. Having previously met the expatriate Vietnamese Zen Buddhist monk, author, and peace activist Thich Nhat Hanh,[47] as well as D. T. Suzuki, renowned author of books and essays on Zen Buddhism, Shin Buddhism, and Buddhism in general, he undertook a tour of Asia in 1968 during which he met with the Dalai Lama, supreme head of Tibetan Buddhism, among others. His syncretistic spiritual inclinations were on the verge of exponential further expansion. In what was then Ceylon, he visited Polonnaruwa, where he is said to have had a transformative religious experience while meditating before the enormous statues of the Buddha. But it was on this far-reaching journey that he died suddenly in Bangkok on December 10—the precise anniversary of his entering the Gethsemani monastery twenty-seven years earlier—when, stepping out of the bath, he touched a poorly grounded electric fan.

NEW SYNTHESES, REDIRECTED SEEKING, AND TRANSFORMED THINKING

Merton's influence has continued to grow in the decades since his death as more of his writing has become available in posthumous publications and as growing numbers of people in the West, particularly in the last decade of the millennium, began to look with increasing desperation at the condition of the world and to seek guidance in helping to improve it. Nor has Merton been alone, although he is arguably the best known of the twentieth-century Christian mystics to seek beyond the traditional bounds of Christian mystical thought for the means of merging with the *mysterion*. Perhaps this is to be expected: Within the colonialist atmosphere of the nineteenth century, a new level of awareness and even intimacy with non-Christian cultures could and did lead in two directions. One centered on newly articulated theories of race, in which non-Europeans were deemed inferior—not fully realized humans and therefore fit for exploitation at various levels—which "classification" came to include European non-Christians, particularly Jews, who were thus reassessed as non-European.[48] The other centered on an intense fascination with the Other—from North African and Near Eastern Muslims to Far Eastern Hindus and Buddhists—as endlessly exotic. This second sensibility expressed itself in the visual arts—for example, in the paintings of Delacroix—and in religious, and particularly mystical, thought in the reaching into other traditions for insights into divine-human connections.

Certainly, this last urge—to seek in all directions for workable paths to legitimate doorways and windows into the *sacer*'s hiddenmost spiritual storerooms—would and could have only increased in the twentieth century. If the enlightenment of technology was moving ever more quickly forward, so was the darkness of the abuse of technology, of harnessing technology to destroy on quantitative levels unheard of in prior history. From Verdun and La Somme to Auschwitz and Hiroshima, from the Killing Fields of Cambodia to the massacres in Rwanda, the twentieth century presented an ongoing proof of the human failure (and perhaps inability) to guide itself on a straightforward course toward perfecting the *profanus*. So, necessarily, the search for guidance from within the *sacer* not only continued but also intensified in certain ways, not least of these being a reaching out beyond traditional Abrahamic borders for that guidance.

We have already noted how Pir-o-Murshid Hazrat Inayat Khan and his son and grandson wove a thread of universalistic thought from Rumi and Kabir into a message broad enough that one may or may not refer to it as "Sufi" in the traditional use of that term; we have also discussed how from Emanuel Swedenborg to Thomas Merton the interest in considering the promise of non-Christian traditions not only expands a perspective first articulated by Pico della Mirandola but also, in Merton's case, pushes the spiritual boundary beyond the Abrahamic realms into a relationship with Buddhism in particular.

This last twist would find an even more intense turn in the work of Merton's contemporary, the French Benedictine priest and mystic, Henri Le Saux (1910–1973). Searching for a way in which to deepen his relationship with the *mysterion*, Le Saux was drawn to India. After a long period of hoping, he finally received permission from his abbot to go there, arriving in 1948 on the first anniversary of Indian independence. He ended up spending most of his adult life in India, where he developed a mode of Christian mysticism in which elements of Hindu thought are embedded. In India, Le Saux took the name Swami Abhishiktananda ("The Bliss of the Anointed One") and adopted the simple garb of a Hindu *sannyasi* (literally "throwing down" in Sanskrit, referring to the casting off of all material goods to live as a complete ascetic). He cofounded an ashram in Kulittalai, in Tamil Nadu, with Father Jules Monchanin: They named the ashram Saccidananda, after the Trinity—that is, the trinity of Being, Awareness, and Bliss, which are all coaspects of Brahma, just as Father, Son, and Holy Spirit are copersons of God in Christian thought.

Shortly before this, Le Saux had met the great Indian sage Sri Ramana Maharishi, who seemed to him the embodiment of self-denial and therefore self-actualization. Le Saux ended up spending the better part of three years (1952–1955) meditating in a cave on the sacred mountain of Arunchala where Sri Ramana lived. Later he met and placed himself under the guidance of Sri Gnanananda and in 1959 made a pilgrimage to the Ganges River. Eventually, he found himself drawn to the Himalayas in the North and, in 1968, left the Ashram Kulittalai in the care of one of his disciples, Father Bede Griffiths; he built a hermitage at Uttarkashi near the source of the Ganges in the Himalayas, where he spent the remaining years of his life in contemplation and writing his major works. These include *Hindu-Christian Meeting Point* and *Saccidananda: A Christian Approach to Advaitic Experience*, in both of which he seeks to provide a synthesis of Christian and Hindu advaitic ("nonduality") thought.

What he first experienced in the caves of Arunchala he wanted to share with others:

In my own innermost center, in the most secret
mirror of my heart, I tried to discover the image
of Him whose I am, of Him who dwells and reigns
in the infinite space of my heart.
But the reflected image gradually grew faint,
and soon it was swallowed up in the radiance
of the Original. Step by step, I descended
into what seemed to me to be successive depths
of my true self—my being, my awareness of being,
my joy of being.
Finally, nothing was left but He Himself,
the Only One, infinitely alone, Being, Awareness,
and Bliss, *Saccidananda*. In the heart of *Saccidananda*,
I had returned to myself.

The self of the individual is merged with and thus disappears into the triune
divine self, which may be referred to with Greek, Latin, or French Christian
terminology, or with the Sanskrit terminology of Hinduism—its threefold primary Godhead (Brahma, Vishnu, and Siva) understood as triune, as three elements that are ultimately One—or with the terms Being, Awareness, and
Bliss, to which trinity of conditions the successful mystic arrives, thus arriving at the deepest, innermost recesses of his or her egoless self.

Le Saux, or Abhishiktananda, strove to synthesize Christian and Hindu
thought in these works of his last years and to express the liberation of his inner *mysterion* to the world as a guide to others to accomplish the same. Thus,
advaita refers, in his usage, to the elimination of the line that separates the individual innermost self (*atman*, in Hinduism's Sanskrit terminology) from the
innermost *mysterion* of Brahman (which is the ultimate Hindu term for the
Absolute[49]); self and Absolute are one when the advaitic mystic succeeds in
his goal to elevate his consciousness beyond feelings and desires that are
profanus-bound. Le Saux further articulates this in more overt Christological
terms:

[E]ach of God's chosen ones [is] a personal center within the one center of *Saccidananda* and enables him to recognize himself within the boundless ocean of
Being, Awareness and Bliss. He knows himself as one who receives from the Father in the Son, and from the Son in the spirit, born in eternity and in each moment of time, he is the one who, in return, gives himself to all and thereby in the
Spirit returns to the Father. . . . The experience of *Saccidananda* carries the soul
beyond all merely intellectual knowledge to her [the soul's] very center, to the
Source of her being. Only there is she able to hear the Word which reveals
within the individual unity and *advaita* of *Saccidananda* the mystery of Three

divine persons: in *sat*, the Father, the absolute Beginning and source of being; in *cit*, the Son, the Divine Lord, the Father's self-knowledge; in *ananda*, the Spirit of love, Fullness and Bliss without end.

Thus, *advaita* also refers to the inseparable unity of the three parts that comprise *Saccidananda*, which term as a *term* Abhishiktananda parses into its constituent *concepts*[50]: *sat* is a Sanskrit root meaning "being, existing, happening, being present"; *cit* is a root meaning "to perceive, fix the mind upon, be attentive, observe"; together, they form a compound, *saccit* or *saccid*, meaning "(pure) existence and thought," which word/phrase is also used as an epithet or name for Brahma. In turn, this compound may be compounded with any number of additional terms, such as *ananda*, which means "joy, happiness, bliss" and is one of the three attributes of Atman or Brahma in Vedanta Hinduism. The full combination, literally meaning "existence and thought and joy," is translated into the Christian terms of Father, Son, and Holy Spirit.

Henri Le Saux was not the first Christian mystic, as it turns out, to take the path toward the East; nor was his the only path in that direction seeking a wider road along which to travel into the *mysterion*. One of the threads unraveled by Jakob Boehme in the early seventeenth century was extended into a full-fledged movement by Helena Petrovna Hahn (1831–1891) in the nineteenth century. Madame Blavatsky, as she came to be known, was born in the Ukrainian province of the tsarist empire of a German officer serving in the Russian army and a mother who came from an old, noble Russian family. Madame Blavatsky was one of the founders of the Theosophical Society and in travels from 1848 through 1858 that are said to have been far-flung, spent two years in Tibet, where she studied with men she referred to simply as the Brothers. The death of her son, Yuri, at age five is said to have caused her to cease to believe in the Russian Orthodox God, but as she claimed never to have consummated any of her several marriages, the truth of this assertion is uncertain, as is much of her biographical data. In any case, she was in Cairo in the early 1870s, where she founded the Spiritual Society (*Societe Spirite*) for Occult Phenomena with a colleague, Emma Cutting (later Emma Coulomb), which closed some time later, after complaints were lodged of fraudulent activities.

She immigrated to New York City in 1873, where she impressed many people with her apparent psychic abilities, including levitation, clairvoyance, out-of-body projection, telepathy, and an apparent ability to materialize objects out of thin air. Two years later, she cofounded the Theosophical Society, the underlying assertion of which was (and remains) that all religions are equally true in their inner teachings and imperfect in their external institutional manifestations. She claimed that deeper, hidden, esoteric spiritual knowledge is to be found in the possession of a handful of individuals, such as the Brothers with whom she studied in Tibet, who today preserve fragments of an ancient, once more-universal wisdom. "Theosophy," meaning "divine wisdom," is the term she coined to refer to that fragment of secret knowledge that she brought from the Tibetan masters to the world.

For Madame Blavatsky's claim was to be a messenger, one of those individuals periodically sent forth by the masters of esoteric knowledge into the world to spread their universalistic message. One may recognize in her claim somewhat of a successor to the sort of spiritualist role articulated in the previous century for himself by Emanuel Swedenborg. Compassion, within that message, is the law of laws. Universal brotherhood is a natural fact on the spiritual (in our terms, *sacer*) plane, which merely needs to be translated into the material (*profanus*) plane in which we live, which translation will offer moral guidance and inspiration in an age when traditional, institutional religion is losing its force in the world. She discussed these ideas in a number of works, perhaps the most important being *Isis Unveiled: A Master Key to the Mysteries of Ancient and Modern Science and Theology*, written in 1877, and *The Secret Doctrine: The Synthesis of Science, Religion and Philosophy*, written in 1888. In both of these, she argues for the legitimacy of understanding science and spirituality as siblings, not antagonists, and in both she speaks as one to whom hidden knowledge has been vouchsafed so that she may serve as an instrument for improving the world.

She had, meanwhile, moved from New York to India in 1879; a few years later, the Theosophical Society became international in scope and moved its headquarters to Adyar, near Madras. She would later return to the West, first to Germany and then to England, where she died of heart disease and a variety of other ailments. It is symptomatic of the range of possibilities for interpreting Madame Blavatsky's work that, on the one hand, one may recognize it not only as a successor to the teaching of Swedenborg but also as the forerunner of and inspiration for the New Age thought that began to emerge in the United States and then elsewhere in the West in the 1960s; on the other hand, she has been said to have influenced Nazi ideology with those aspects of her writings that offer racial themes. She contrasts "Aryan" with "Semitic" culture to the detriment of the latter and refers to Aborigines as "semianimal creatures"—and it should be noted that her late, brief residence in Germany coincides precisely with the time of William Marr's prominence.[51]

Both understandings of her thought appear true: She was both a universalistic and an ethnoracist. Otherwise put, she was caught up in that part of nineteenth-century Western European thought that felt the need to express its sense of superiority over other peoples in a colonialist-imperialist world by articulating a hierarchy in which only a portion of humanity was viewed as fully "human." At the same time, she was shaping an esoteric mode of thinking that argued for the universal brotherhood of all humans—but that thinking would by definition exclude those she defined as not fully human.

There is perhaps some irony in the thread that connects the Theosophical movement and Madame Blavatsky's thinking with that of Rudolf Steiner (1861–1925) and what he termed "anthroposophy" (from the Greek words for "human" and "wisdom," thus, literally, "human wisdom"). Steiner defined his movement as "a path of knowledge, to guide the spiritual in the human being to the spiritual in the universe."[52] He advocated a form of ethical individualism to which he brought a strong spiritual component, especially in the time after his turn toward and then away from Theosophy. An expert on the writings of Goethe and Nietzsche, Steiner had penned an article in 1899 on the esoteric elements in Goethe's fairy tale "The Green Snake and the Beautiful Lily," which resulted in an invitation to speak on Nietzsche to the Theosophists, and by 1902, he had become head of the newly formed German branch of the Theosophical Society. But over the following years, he developed his own approach to and terminology for matters of the spirit that distinguished his thinking from that of Madame Blavatsky and ultimately led him to part ways with the Theosophists by 1912.

In his autobiographical writings, Steiner speaks of an ongoing sense of connection to the spiritual world since his childhood. He argued that anyone could develop the ability to experience the spiritual realm, including the higher nature of one's self and of others that connects to the inner realm of the spirit (in our terms, the *mysterion* within the *sacer* realm), through freely embracing ethical modes of thought and behavior and through training in meditative techniques. Already in his 1904 *Theosophy: An Introduction*, he was exploring the idea of the human being as comprised of a body-soul-spirit triad, the notion of the unity of spiritual and sense-perceptional aspects of humans as "two sides of a single coin," and also the issue of reincarnation and karma as an effect from one lifetime to the next. In his Theosophical works of the next half-decade, he discussed the idea of higher (more hidden, esoteric) worlds and a spiritual hierarchy of connective ascent to them. In the period that followed his split with the Theosophists, he was engaged not only in writing but also in organizing institutions: schools that reflected his anthroposophical perspective.

One obvious goal of anthroposophy is to recognize the objective reality of the spiritual as much as the natural realm, to become aware of spiritual influences on human history and of the ongoing process within the physical universe of metaphysical beings, and to discipline one's self toward contact with those beings. But the second goal is to yield broad consequences of this contact: to evoke a sharper moral intuition and imagination and to effect positive results in fields from child education,[53] to the various plastic and performing arts, to eurhythmics,[54] to medicine, to organic and biodynamic farming.

One of the central ideas within Steiner's thought, which helped pull him away from the emphatic non-Christianity of Theosophy, focuses on the ultimate element of traditional Christian religious and mystical thought: Christ. But his articulation of that element diverges from tradition in at least three ways. First, he asserted that two different children named Jesus were involved in the incarnation of the Christ: One descended from David and Solomon (as set forth in Matthew) and the other from Nathan (court prophet and adviser to David, as suggested in Luke).[55] Second,

> the being of Christ is central to all religions, though called by different names by each. Each religion is valid and true for the time and cultural context in which it was born. The historical forms of Christianity need to be transformed considerably to meet the continuous evolution of humanity.

Thus, he is viewing both Christ and Christianity as a pair of universal concepts that happened at a certain time and place to be designated by a certain pair of names, which are, as such, neither definitive nor final. Third, he speaks of the Second Coming of Christ not as physical at all but as a *parousia* in the "etheric realm," where Christ's presence will be visible only to spiritual vision and through its effect on the human community. And he expressed concern that the essence of this "Christ"—love—might be ignored, even as the traditional name Christ might be used by those only partially recognizing the process that would be taking place. Steiner specifically anticipated that process as one slowly beginning to take place by about the year 1933.

There is a good deal of irony in the last few components of this discussion. There is irony in exploring what should appear as a perverse paradox in Madame Blavatsky's thought: synthesis of Western and Eastern esoteric thinking but a limited view of the human race to which such a synthesis applies. There is irony that Steiner was inspired toward spiritual and mystical thinking through her teaching but turned from it because he felt called to a simultaneously more Christian and yet more complete universalism in engaging the *mysterion*. There is irony in his belief that the perfecting of the world that he associated with a universalistic *parousia* would begin in the very year when, instead, Hitler came to power in Steiner's German world. It is still further ironic that, as early as 1919, the political theorist of the German National Socialist movement that Hitler would lead to such profound depths, Dietrich Eckart, had attacked Steiner for his broad, internationalist thinking—and suggested that Steiner was Jewish—and that Hitler himself would attack Steiner in a 1921 right-wing newspaper (*Der Voelkischer Beobachter*, or *The People's Observer*) article.

There is also some irony, perhaps, in the confluence represented by turning from Madame Blavatsky by way of New Age thinking and Rudolf Steiner by way of the proto-Nazi attacks on his thinking toward one of the more interesting late-twentieth-century forms of East-West synthesis: the phenomenon of the Jubus.[56] This term is one of a handful applied to a phenomenon that has expanded in the late twentieth century, mostly in America: the embrace by Jews of Buddhism. The coinage became popular with the publication of Rodger Kamenetz's 1994 book, *The Jew in the Lotus: A Poet's Discovery of Jewish Identity in Buddhist India*.[57] In some cases, the term refers to individuals who practice both traditions side by side. This is more than theoretically feasible in the sense that Judaism as a religion—which by definition exists in relation to the Jewish concept of God—can coexist with Buddhism, which is not a religion in the sense of not having as its central focus "God" but rather the achievement of a state of enlightenment (the term *buddha* means "enlightened" in Sanskrit).[58]

Some of these consider themselves primarily Jews but have a strong interest, both intellectual and spiritual, in Buddhism. In other cases, those calling themselves Jewish mean that term to be ethnic, or only cultural—even as limited as bagels and lox—not a spiritual reference point, and they look primarily, or even exclusively, to Buddhism for spiritual nourishment. The irony is that Jubus of this ilk, at the time of turning toward Buddhism, were or are often unaware of the intense spiritual possibilities that the mystical tradition offers from within Judaism, and in many cases, they remain unaware. Still others—perhaps the largest number—have synthesized Jewish religious belief and spiritual practices with Buddhist practices and beliefs. It should be noted that the form of Buddhism encompassed by this fusion is a Western form that emphasizes a communal aspect—meditation *retreats* rather than self-isolated, monastery-centered meditation—and promotes gender egalitarianism a great deal more than is found in its Eastern counterparts.[59]

The first American known to have embraced Buddhism, in 1893, was a Jew, and a wave of Jews interested and involved in Buddhism grew out of the 1950s (primarily on the East and West coasts, with the Beat Generation associated with the poet Allen Ginsberg and others), followed by the burgeoning of alternative spiritual directions that was part of the late 1960s—the same period during which Thomas Merton was expanding the Christian spiritual horizon in the same direction. But at the end of the millennium, within the explosion of renewed spiritual focus, particularly in the United States, the percentage of American Jews who might be labeled "Jubus" sufficiently exceeded the percentage of Christian Buddhists to justify the new coinage.[60]

In the thinking expressed by Madame Blavatsky's ladder of humanity, consistent with the thinking of Marr and other racial theorists of her time, the lower-than-Aryan Semites included the Jews. So the Jubu phenomenon encompasses a group that Blavatsky would have looked down upon. A century after her era of turning so emphatically to the East, a substantial number of Jews has looked in the direction to which she was the first Westerner to point in a major way. And that phenomenon has continued strongly into the new millennium.

⟨∞⟩

One might note yet another twist to this discussion that furthers my contention that the spiritual need addressed by diverse mystical traditions has an ongoing life even within the context of a self-proclaimed secular context. On two separate occasions in the 1980s, I was asked to address a conference of a group that calls itself the Secular Jewish Community, a branch of Judaism that has been in evolution at least since the aftermath of World War II. It defines itself as Jewish along cultural and historical, rather than religious, lines: God is not part of the matrix of secular Jewish beliefs, by definition. On both occasions, I was surprised by the request that mysticism be the subject that I was asked to address.

And on both occasions, during the discussion that followed my remarks, any number of individuals, in expressing what was clearly a desire to find and feel a connection between the mystical tradition and their self-defined secularity, suggested that perhaps one could substitute an idea such as "the realm of Being" for "God" and find an applicability for a secular individual of the mystical process. That is, secular Jews, such as comprised my audience, felt comfortable seeking *ek-stasis/en-stasis* with Being itself through whatever appropriate methodology, rather than *ek-stasis/en-stasis* with the God of pure Being that is presented by the Jewish tradition.

On the other hand, several psychoanalysts who were either members of both those two audiences, and/or present in courses I have taught on this subject over the years, have argued that the process of *ek-stasis* is inherently a process of *en-stasis*, a process that can and should be understood in purely psychological terms. It is a search for something that is entirely within ourselves. That is, what humans have referred to over the millennia as "God" is a function not of what is *out there* but of what is *within us*. But the remarkable thing is that even within these variously articulated secular viewpoints, the interest in the search, as well as the need to conduct it, are so strongly expressed.[61]

NOTES

1. England was first, granting rights to Jews by way of a bill in 1753. The Austro-Hungarian Empire came next, when under the Hapsburg ruler Joseph II it granted various rights in 1782 and in the following five years. The French followed with their statement of inclusion in 1791, and the Prussians final granted emancipation in 1812

(although in Prussia the rights of Jews continued to come and go over the following four decades).

2. Hayim Vitale's name, we recall, means "life"—both his "first" name, in Hebrew, and his "second" name, in Italian—so that this most essential work is entitled to pun on his name.

3. To my knowledge, this story doesn't tell the story that the BeSh'T told Jacob Joseph—or what exactly the story clarified!

4. The accusation of heresy would have been threefold: veneration of the BeSh'T, which they would have feared as effectively idolatrous; panhenotheistic teachings, which they would have mistaken as pantheistic and polytheistic; and too much encouragement of singing and dancing instead of studying the Torah.

5. From a relatively rare item: a letter from the BeSh'T. Quoted in Samuel Dresner's *The Zaddik: The Doctrine of the Zaddik According to the Writings of Rabbi Yaakov Yosef of Polnoye* (London, New York, and Toronto: Abelard-Schuman Press, 1960), 50. Dresner is in turn quoting from Samuel Horodetsky, *Shivhei HaBesht.* (Tel Aviv: Dvir Publishers, 1947), 64.

6. It might be noted that *passim* are literally "stripes"—so the idea is that the diverse sayings and comments are like stripes that make up the decor of the coat of commentary; Joseph's biblical coat is traditionally understood to have been striped.

7. Thus, in seeing a young man eating on a day designated for fasting, he inquired first, did you not know that it was this day? Then, did you perhaps not know that one is supposed to fast on this day? Then, are you perhaps in bad health (in which case fasting would be prohibited, lest one endanger one's life). To all of these inquiries, the response was no—and in the end Levi Yitzhak proclaimed with joy, "Your children are admirable, for even when they transgress Your Commandments, they do not stoop to lying!"

8. The key figure in Vilnius was Elijah the Gaon, the brilliant Talmudist, former student of and writer on Kabbalah, and yet profound enemy of Hassidism—the movement with which he is associated was called *hitnagdut* ("opposition"), and its constituents were *mitnagdeem* ("opposers")—who falls outside our discussion.

9. See note 8.

10. The standard transliteration is *ChaBaD*, so I will use it hereafter, although it contradicts my preference for transliterating the Hebrew "Het" as "h," rather than "ch." *Da'at* ("knowledge") began appearing in some kabbalistic thought from the end of the thirteenth century onward as a kind of hidden, complementary *sephirah* that harmonized *hokhmah* and *binah* and also presented an "external aspect" of *keter.*

11. As inevitably we continue to circle around and around the same issues, we may recall the Stoic discussion in pagan antiquity of *sophia* ("wisdom") as the agent of divine creation, which, moreover, because the word *sophia* is grammatically feminine in Greek, was spoken of by the Stoics in a manner analogous to the way in which early Jewish mystics come to speak of *hokhmah* as an emanational agent of the creation process, and later, Kabbalah comes to speak of the *Shekhinah* as a feminine aspect of the creation process.

12. Interestingly, this is not to be confused with the Zoharic *'eyn sof or* ("endless light"); it is, one might say, the *'eyn sof* that is the "source" of the light of the *'eyn sof or* in the *Tanya* discussion.

13. Quoted in Martin Buber's *Tales of Rabbi Nachman*, trans. Maurice Freedman (Bloomington: Indiana University Press, 1956), 24–25.

14. Asserted in Nathan of Niemerov's *Hayyei MoHarRayN* (*The Life of Rabbi Nahman of Bratslav*) (Jerusalem: Breslov Research Institute, 1965), 1:24. The larger quote from which I have extracted the first of these two fragments makes it clear that he is even hostile to Kabbalah to the extent that it has become corrupted by excessive intellectualizing. See Arthur Green, *Tormented Master: A Life of Rabbi Nahman of Bratslav* (New York: Shocken Books, 1981), especially 292–311.

15. *ChaBaD* has had a succession of seven generations of direct leadership descendants from Shneur Zalman. The last of these, Menachem Shneerson, died in 1994 at the age of ninety-two, and no clear successor has been designated as of this writing.

16. We recall that in the standard rendering of "God" in Hebrew, the four consonants *yud, hey, vav, hey*—YHVH, as one might more or less transliterate them—are those of the root for the verb "to be," so that God's "name" is "is-ness" or "be."

17. In symbolic mystical terms, the four-lettered name of God and the four-directioned *profanus* are joined by the abstract concept of *fourness* that resides in both, as we may recall from earlier discussions of letters and numbers.

18. Abraham Joshua Heschel, *God in Search of Man: A Philosophy of Judaism* (New York: Farrar, Strauss, and Giroux, 1955), 43–51.

19. Abraham Joshua Heschel, *Man Is Not Alone: A Philosophy of Religion* (New York: Farrar, Strauss, and Giroux, 1951), 78.

20. Heschel, *Man Is Not Alone*, 82.

21. Heschel, *Man Is Not Alone*, 4–8.

22. Heschel, *God in Search of Man*, 184.

23. Heschel, *God in Search of Man*, 185.

24. Heschel, *God in Search of Man*, 186–87.

25. This is the Muslim profession of faith. See above, chapter 1, note 4.

26. His given name is Inayat Khan. The terms *pir*, *murshid*, and *hazrat* are all honorifics. The first literally means "elder" and refers specifically to his role as head of the far-flung Sufi *tariqa* that he leads; the second, more generally, refers to his role as a spiritual teacher (it is similar, then, to the Arabic term *shaikh* in nuance); the third refers most broadly to his role as a leader.

27. Pir-o-Murshid Hazrat Inayat Khan, *The Inner Life* (Boston and London: Shambhala Publications, 1997), 10–11.

28. Khan, "The Object of the Journey," in *The Inner Life*, section 2, 8.

29. Hazrat Inayat Khan, *The Complete Sayings* (New Lebanon, NY: Sufi Order Publications, 1978), 6.

30. His discussion of the *sephirot* in a lecture heard by the author in Cleveland, Ohio, in the early 1980s was both profound and impressive for the detail that he presented, without notes, in response to a question from the audience.

31. The purpose of *Zira'at* is to promote not only spiritual realization in and for individuals but also a sense of attunement and harmony—a covenant—with the earth and all of its inhabitants.

32. Azar Kayvan was a native of Fars, Persia (i.e., Iran), who immigrated to Gujarat in the Mughul Indian empire of the highly cultured and spiritually involved Emperor

Akbar. He established the Sufi-influenced *ishraqiyyun* ("Illuminationists") school of Zoroastrianism there, subsequently known as the Sipassian school or sect.

33. The sort of splitting of a conceptual hair that separates Swedenborg's sense of "three aspects" of one God from "three cosubstantial persons" of one God would emphatically have led to his treatment as a heretic in the medieval period.

34. See chapter 3, p. 64.

35. Emanuel Swedenborg, *The True Christian Religion* (*Vera christiana religio, continens universam theologiam novae ecclesiae*), section 355 [2], 1771.

36. The Carmelite Order was originally established as a male order, founded in Palestine by St. Berthold around 1154, during the Crusades. By around 1250, an extremely ascetic rule had been set down, and two centuries later (in 1452) an Order of Carmelite Sisters was founded. Where the Benedictine Order and its offshoots emphasize a life of communal prayer, study, and manual labor, the Carmelites emphasize a kind of communal solitude. While the Carmelite friars maintained contact with the outside world through preaching and hearing confessions, the sisters originally never left their houses, even for family funerals, and spoke only briefly, through a grille, to their occasional visitors. But this had all relaxed considerably by the sixteenth century, when Therese of Lisieux's namesake, Teresa of Avila, set about introducing strict reforms. It is the Reformed Order that drew Therese of Lisieux.

37. Therese of Lisieux, *Autobiography of a Saint: The Story of a Soul*, trans. Ronald Knox (London: Fontana Press, 1960), 221.

38. Lisieux, *Autobiography of a Saint*, 220.

39. From her *Billet de profession* (a kind of statement of purpose, written out on the eve of being formally inducted into the convent), quoted in Lisieux, *Autobiography of a Saint*, 315.

40. The Jesuit exile was occasioned by the 1901 Waldeck-Rousseau laws, which placed congregational associations' properties under control of the state, in effect eliminating free associations of religious orders. Teilhard de Chardin, while in China, was a participant in the discovery of "Peking Man" in 1929.

41. Omega is both the last letter in the Greek alphabet and an early Christian symbol, together with alpha (the first letter of the Greek alphabet), for the infinity of Christ as the beginning of the beginning and the end of the end.

42. *Le milieu divin* was written in 1926–1927. It was published in 1957, then in English translation as "The Divine Milieu" in 1960 (more recently issued in a Harper Perennial edition in 2001). Some have preferred to translate the title as "The Mystical Milieu."

43. See chapter 9, pp. 217, 219.

44. The Trappist Order was established in 1644 in La Trappe, France, as a suborder of the Cistercians. Otherwise known as the Order of Cistercians of the Strict Observance, it was founded in response to the relaxation of practices in many Cistercian monasteries. The Trappists are a contemplative order that follows the Benedictine Rule; its members practice lives divided between manual work and prayer and with a sensibility focused on penance.

45. Thomas Merton, *The Climate of Monastic Prayer* (Kalamazoo, MI: Cistercian Publications, 1969).

46. Thomas Merton, *Contemplation in a World of Action* (New York: New Directions Publishing, 1971).

47. *Thich* is a title used by all Vietnamese monks and nuns to signify that they are part of the Shakyamuni Buddha clan. Nhat Hanh as a spiritual activist coined the phrase "engaged Buddhism" to refer to teaching outside the monastery in the world, in order to help improve it, in his key work *Vietnam: Lotus in a Sea of Fire* (New York: Hill & Wang, 1967), written during the Vietnam War era.

48. The German agitator and theorist Wilhelm Marr (1819–1904) may be credited with articulating that assessment in 1879 by appropriating the linguistic term "Semite" (used to categorize a family of languages that includes Hebrew, Arabic, Ethiopic, Babylonian, and so forth) to label the Jews as Semites, as opposed to Europeans. The intention was to underscore the notion that the Jews are different from "us Europeans" and included the nuance that they are inferior to "us Europeans." From that coinage, the terms "anti-Semite" and "philo-Semite" derive. For a broader discussion of nineteenth-century religioracial ideation, see Maurice Olender, *The Languages of Paradise: Race, Religion and Philology in the Nineteenth Century* (Cambridge, MA: Harvard University Press, 1992).

49. I am somewhat oversimplifying here, since the different branches of what we term "Hinduism" are more correctly labeled Brahmism, Vaishnism, and Saivism. Each emphasizes one of the three gods that are nonetheless all regarded as ultimately aspects of one absolute Godhead—and even this statement is an oversimplification. A further discussion would take us too far beyond the goals of this text.

50. The rules of Sanskrit phonology yield the elision of the parts into the whole: *sat + cit + ananda = Sac/cid/ananda*.

51. See above, note 48.

52. Rudolf Steiner, *Anthroposophical Leading Thoughts* (London: Rudolf Steiner Press, 1999) (originally published in 1924).

53. His education system asserts that children advance through three stages of spiritual development. Through age seven the spirit inhabiting the body is adjusting to its surroundings; imagination and fantasy dominate children between age seven and fourteen; in the third stage, an astral body is drawn into the physical body. The curriculum should reflect this threefold reality.

54. "The vowel is born out of man's inmost being; it is the channel through which this inner content of the soul streams outwards. . . . If we utter the sound 'A' and take this out-going stream of breath as the prototype for the Eurythmic movement, we find that this breath stream reveals itself to our imagination as flowing in two crossed currents. This is how the Eurythmic movement for 'A' is derived." Rudolf Steiner, *Eurythmy As Visible Speech* (London: Rudolf Steiner Press, 1984). This aspect of Steiner's Eurhythmy recalls Abulafia. See chapter 6.

55. See Robert McDermott, *The Essential Steiner* (San Francisco: Harper Books, 1984).

56. These people are also known as "Bujus" or "JewBus."

57. Kamenetz followed a group of eight rabbis on their journey to Dharamsala for a meeting with the Dalai Lama to which they had been invited by his desire to know "the Jewish secret of survival in exile" (with the thought of its potential applicability

to the exile of Tibetan Buddhists from their homeland due to the politics of China and Tibet). The book, *The Jew in the Lotus*, was published by HarperCollins; see the bibliography for full citation.

58. Strictly speaking, as Buddhism spread eastward from India and its practitioners moved along a spreading array of spiritual paths, there did emerge a number of Buddhist sects that have a "God-focus"—one might argue that Mahayana Buddhism's reverence for boddhisatvas turns them into demigods and that the line between reverence and worship is blurry, especially when prayers are offered to the golden statues that they are said to inhabit—but I am thinking of "classical" forms of Buddhism.

59. See James W. Coleman, *The New Buddhism* (Oxford: Oxford University Press, 2001), 14–15.

60. Some have asserted that between 16.5 and 30 percent of Western non-Asian Buddhists in the United States are Jewish—although Jews account for about 2 percent of the overall American population. See Coleman, *The New Buddhism*, 192–94, and Louis Sahagun, "At One with Dual Devotion," *Los Angeles Times*, May 6, 2006, and October 25, 2006.

61. The issue of the psychological or psychoanalytic dimensions of mysticism has been taken up by a number of writers. Two of particular note are Evelyn Underhill, in her classic of nearly a century ago, *The Mystic Way: A Psychological Study in Christian Origins* (London: Lighting Source, Inc., 1913), and Edward Hoffman in his more recent *The Way of Splendor: Jewish Mysticism and Modern Psychology* (Boston and London: Shambhala Publications, 1981).

Chapter Eleven

Unfinished Epilogues

There are four particular directions that one might briefly pursue as a kind of series of epilogues to this discussion—ideas, individuals, or movements that unravel threads from the diversely woven Abrahamic mystical tapestry into the present era.

MYSTICISM IN AND BEYOND THE ACADEMY

There is the academic thread, as it were. Most of what we understand regarding Hassidism, for instance, has come through the extensive study of Hassidism accomplished by the philosopher-theologian Martin Buber in the first half of the twentieth century. Interestingly, Buber's starting point as a very secularized Jew was the development of his interest in the spiritual traditions of the East. From his study of them, he gradually worked his way back to his own tradition, spending years as a student and expositor of *Hassidut* along two distinct lines. He wrote a series of books accounting for the birth and evolution of the movement and parsing its features in an analytical manner, and he wrote down an extensive series of parables associated with and ascribed to the various Hassidic masters—the *tzadikim*—that corroborate his assertion that the primary mode of teaching and transmitting within Hassidism has been through tales, not treatises.

On the other hand, Gershom Scholem may be called the father of the academic study of Jewish mysticism overall, but particularly of Kabbalah. And we note that Scholem, as a scholar, was also a critic of Buber's exposition of *Hassidut*, asserting in so many words that Buber idealized the movement and imposed upon it an overly existentialist nuance. By this Scholem means that the kind of role ascribed by Buber to every individual *hassid* with regard to helping to perfect the world—as opposed to relying too heavily on the *tzadik*—is outsized. Buber is in any case one of the preeminent existentialist theologians of the twentieth century, whose best-known work, *I and Thou*, offers the quintessence of the discussion of how to make God relevant in a world in which God is perceived to be nonexistent to many individuals.

Buber's instrument is the very human attribute that dominates secularist philosophy, from Kant and Hegel to Nietzsche and Sartre: the human will. In differing ways, the will is the attribute that defines the human capacity for complete independence from a metaphysical superstructure, according to such thinkers. The exercise of truly free will means that, functionally, God does not exist in the universe in which I make my moral and ethical and other decisions, which are governed ultimately by my own analyses and conclusions regarding how to think and act. Existentialism enshrines this philosophical stance in suggesting various scenarios in which human action is free and independent of divine interference—it denies either the very existence of God or at least the relevance of divinity to human reality. Buber adapts this line of thinking in order to suggest that one can, through an act of will, suspend—momentarily—one's disbelief in God or in God's relationship to us and in that moment find God present and engageable in what he terms an "I-Thou" relationship.[1]

While it is not conventional to consider such a work as mystical, it strikes me that its goal is parallel to that of the mystic. Nor do I think it accidental that Buber's thesis takes shape during the period of his study of Hassidism—and perhaps, while some, like Scholem, may argue that he imposed an existentialist viewpoint onto *Hassidut*, one might argue conversely that his study of *Hassidut* inspired him to shape his thought with regard to "I-Thou" human-divine relationships. Every *hassid*, as much as he or she accesses the *mysterion* through his or her *tzadik*, is yet confident of and *responsible for* a personalized sense of relationship with God; it is largely the host of those relationships that supports and makes possible the work of the *tzadik* in effecting *tikkun olam*. At issue is a double reciprocity—between the *tzadik* and his *hassidim* (as we have seen) and between God and humans—which Buber imposes on the secular existentialist will in positing God's relevance to an individual's life and being.

This, as with every aspect of the discussion within this volume—whether with regard to Jewish, Christian, or Muslim mysticism—is by definition part of the vast sea of interpretation and exegesis that defines the history of religion over all. I single out the Buber-Scholem debate regarding *Hassidut* for mention because we are much more fully at the mercy of an oral tradition where the Hassidic tales are concerned, few of them written down *until* Buber, than we are with either Christian and Muslim mysticism or other aspects of Jewish mysticism—or even the treatise aspects of second- and third-generation *Hassidut*—for all of which we are focused on texts ascribed to particular mystics whose thought we have discussed. So their "debate" is maximally dependant on unsubstantiatable interpretation.

Others have also provided interesting expositions of different aspects of or figures within the history of Jewish mysticism, as a perusal of the bibliography at the end of this volume will indicate. But for the purposes of this discussion, we note Arthur Edward Waite (1857–1942), a Christian occultist and cocreator of the Tider-Waite tarot card deck, who was also a student of Kabbalah. His extensive study and analysis of the discipline, *The Holy Kabbalah*, is one of the best, most detailed discussions of Kabbalah around in English. Waite's writing suggests a modernized Pico della Mirandola at work. With the growing interest in mysticism in general since the 1960s (the birth era of New Age thought), there has been an expanding academic library of discussions of mystical thought in general and of the Abrahamic mystical traditions in particular.

And there has been an expanding library of popular books particularly on Jewish mysticism, most of which typically *synthesize* kabbalistic with Hassidic thinking—I am thinking in particular of works by Lawrence Kushner and Aryeh Kaplan—although they rarely indicate where the line between those two aspects of Jewish mystical thinking might be drawn. In enjoying Aryeh Kaplan's book-length discussion of the *Sepher Yetzirah*, for example, one must be aware and wary of the fact that that discussion reflects the neo-Hassidic perspective that he brings to his analysis and which the unaware reader would be likely to mistake for the unadorned intention of the *Sepher* at the time of its writing. (Perhaps this comment is parallel to that of Scholem vis-à-vis Buber's discussion of *Hassidut*!)

OLD AND NEW CHARISMA

But with this last thought in mind—that academic and popular interest in mysticism has largely followed the lead of New Age interest in trying to climb into the interior of various esoteric traditions in response to the need for a deeper spirituality than traditional organized religion seems to offer (at least to the New Agers)—there have been not only other new movements that have offered new syntheses (such as Jubuism) or new directions, which have grown directly out of the New Age in directions asserting distinct differences from the Abrahamic or even the Eastern esoteric traditions (such as Erhard Seminars Training [EST]) and Scientology or, differently, those small groups led by "Bo and Beep" and Jim Jones),[2] but also groups that have claimed to offer up-to-date expressions of traditional mystical thought. Thus, a movement such as the Branch Davidians asserted of their leader, David Koresh, that he was the messianic heir to the Christian tradition that offers its beginning point with the figure of Jesus. This movement might not be considered strictly Christian "mystical" in nature in that the movement's claim might not be perceived to offer a means of accessing the *mysterion* from within the perspective of Christian faith—but to its adherents, this is precisely what the movement was offering: access to the *mysterion* (of which the rest of humanity, even Christians, is deprived) through its leader, who was understood to be the access panel in and of himself, by virtue of his being, as it were, the final avatar of the God-man, the final answer posed by biblical questions regarding the divine-human relationship as those questions and their answers were understood or interpreted by that leader.

In a somewhat analogous manner, the largest of the Hassidic groups in the last century, the *ChaBaD Lubavitch* group (see chapter 10) took a newly messianic turn in the 1980s. Late in his life, the fifth and latest (and to date, last) in the Schneerson family line to inherit the mantle of Lubavitch *tzadik* leadership, Mendel Menachem Schneerson (1902–1994), was periodically referred to in and by the circle of his leading followers and disciples as the long-awaited *Mashiah* ("Messiah")—the anointed one who would turn the world around and bring it back to proximity to God and thus bring God back to greater closeness to the world, and particularly to Jews, who would turn to a Hassidic way of life and its mode of embracing God.[3] The Rebbe, as he was popularly called,[4] never asserted this of himself—but neither did he deny it. When he sustained a stroke in 1992 that left him partially paralyzed and unable to speak, that circle of followers more emphatically began to circulate the notion that he was the *Mashiah*, in large part based on the idea that the darkest hour (the master's stroke and subsequent virtually complete incapacitation) precedes the dawn (of the messianic era).

As the Rebbe hovered for two years in the border territory of his stroke, the conviction grew, to the point that far-flung members of the Lubavitch movement were wearing "*mashiach* beepers" on their belts, anticipating the moment when he would rise up from his bed and declare the beginning of the new era. Even in the time since his eventual death, there has remained a cadre of followers who continue to sit praying by his grave, day and night, awaiting his resurrection, for which followers he remains the messianic key to the *mysterion* that contains the seeds of human redemption.

So, too, there have emerged, particularly as the millennium was pushing toward its conclusion—and with that push an intense upsurge in spiritual searching in many corners of the West became apparent—not only movements claiming to offer traditional mystical teachings in an accessible manner but also those that have attracted adherents across traditional religious lines. The most obvious of these is the Kabbalah Center. What is said to have begun in Jerusalem as the Research Center of Kabbalah in 1922, a place in which Rabbi Yehuda Ashlag and his successor, Rabbi Yehuda Brandwein, taught the *Zohar* and other Jewish mystical texts to Orthodox Jewish male students with strong backgrounds in the Torah, was transformed by Rabbi Brandwein's son-in-law. Having come from the United States as an insurance salesman, Rabbi Phillip Berg (as Feivel Gruberger subsequently called himself) married Rabbi Brandwein's daughter[5] and thus became involved in the center. When Rabbi Brandwein died in 1969, Rabbi Berg declared himself Rabbi Brandwein's successor. He subsequently divorced his wife, leaving her to raise their six children, married his secretary, Karen, and later left Israel, taking with him both a group of texts that had been authored by Rabbi Ashlag (at least some of which Rabbi Berg claimed as his own) and the name Kabbalah Center, ultimately reestablishing it in Los Angeles by 1984.

It presented (and presents) itself as a source of cutting-edge spiritual instruction drawn from a kabbalistic system which, Rabbi Berg has asserted, predates any religious tradition (including Judaism) and is therefore nondenominational (or omnidenominational, since Kabbalah is thus said to be the basis upon which *all* religious systems, from Judaism to Catholicism to Islam to Buddhism, have been constructed as parallel edifices). Instruction at elementary, intermediate, and advanced levels is obtainable at the center's dozens of outlets and online, and its better-known adherents, gained as the push toward deeper and wider spiritual focus burgeoned in the 1990s, include (or has included) Madonna, Demi Moore, Roseanne, and others of diverse religious backgrounds and traditions.

On the one hand, we recognize how far from traditional Jewish mystical thinking this system diverges, in spite of its assertion to offer true kabbalistic instruction: The need for Hebrew, much less for mastering the Torah and rabbinic thought, has been pushed away; even the need for being Jewish has been eliminated. Of course, we also recognize that there have been precedents for at least part of this, such as Abraham Abulafia's opening up of his ecstatic kabbalistic system to others than scholarly Jewish, over-forty-year-old males with families. On the other hand, there is a strong messianic strand in the reverence accorded to Rabbi Berg by his followers and in the conviction that seems to emanate from the Kabbalah Center that he alone holds the key to ultimate *tikkun* through his personal doctrines, his teachings, and his transformation of the teachings of Rabbis Ashlag and Brandwein and their embrace by a wide and varied audience. This, too, has precedents in the movements that grew around kabbalists, such as those associated with Shabbetai Tzvi and

Jacob Frank; perhaps it is even parallel to the veneration of the Rebbe by his *ChaBaD Lubavitch* constituents.

But the detractors of the Kabbalah Center as it has been remade by Rabbi Berg, his wife, and their two sons (Yehuda and Michael, who are currently its codirectors and "spiritual guides")[6] assert that the inevitably watered-down version of the Jewish mystical tradition being offered to its members is at least absurd and at most morally reprehensible, given its claims to lead to perfecting the world: "It's like brain surgery. Someone who tells you he wants to start cracking skulls to fix the brains inside but who hasn't yet cracked open a book of anatomy is, obviously, either a lunatic or a fool."[7] Berg admits that since "the Zohar is a very long book . . . [and] the Sepher Yetzirah . . . can be appreciated only by a highly trained eye," he has excised most of their material from the course of study that he sells to his followers.[8] At the very least, the rabbi's pupils, while they may agree that the *Zohar* offers light, will have no true understanding of what the light source is; they may follow his prescription for wearing a red ribbon on the left wrist to ward off evil, but without knowing why (to which comment his defenders might argue that they are exhibiting a purity of faith—doing out of believing without questioning or knowing—which is the key to accessing the *mysterion*).

Thus, the center's detractors assert that the parallel to Shabbetai and Frank, the most renowned among false messiahs within Jewish history, is profound—that, like these figures, who led so many along such a disastrous path, Rabbi Berg has not only corrupted the teachings of Kabbalah but also is duping his followers and leading them into chaos. It *is* extraordinary that the center website places Rabbi Berg and his wife, Karen, on the list of key Jewish historical figures, which includes Adam, Abraham, Moses, and Isaac Luria, and that its students are taught that their High Holy Day prayers will not be heard by God if they are not participating in retreats led by the rabbi, that any religion besides Kabbalah (that is, Rabbi Berg's version of Kabbalah) is flawed. What is most disturbing and sets Berg apart from prior messianic figures—or the venerated Rebbe, for that matter—is the materialism that anchors the Kabbalah Center: Every one of its services has a literal price tag, and millions of dollars have flowed into its coffers. For $2.65 per one-liter bottle and $60 per case, one may purchase "Kabbalah water"—water from a spring in Canada, the molecular structure of which Rabbi Berg claims to have transformed through his secret blessings and prayers so that it can cure cancer and other maladies. For $400 one can purchase a copy of the Berg edition of the *Zohar*, concerning which he asserts that simply running one's finger over the Aramaic and Hebrew text (without a scintilla of capacity to read, much less understand, it) can cure disease.

More disturbing still is the evidence that, should it become known to the center that someone objects to his or her spouse's giving gifts to the center, the gift-giving spouse is likely to receive a communication suggesting in no uncertain terms that he or she should divorce his or her spouse on grounds of "mystical incompatibility." The accounts of the diverse destructiveness of the Kabbalah Center's manner of being in the world are ironic, to say the least, in engaging in so much tearing apart of the world while building its own material empire and claiming to provide for the unsure and unhappy a path to oneness with the One and to *tikkun olam*. Given the prominence of interpretation in the vast history of religion, I would ordinarily hesitate to state as comfortably as I do here that the proffered path is a blatantly false one—who am I to judge?—but the varied aspects of the center's nefarious modes of conduct leave me no choice but to suggest that conclusion.

On the other hand—in a manner analogous to the manner in which the Kabbalah Center asserts that Kabbalah predates all three Abrahamic faiths—there is a small library of volumes emerging from the Tehuti Research Foundation, devoted to studies of ancient Egypt, that make an analogous claim for Sufism, as we noted earlier in this discussion.[9] The chair of the foundation and author of many of its books, Moustafa Gadalla, in his *Egyptian Mystics: Seekers of the Way*, offers a view of Sufism as a non-Muslim mystical discipline (in the normative use of the term *Muslim*), in which many of the elements of Sufi *dhikr* are traced back to ancient Egyptian practices.[10] One may recognize in this new thread of syncretistic thought an echo of Madame Blavatsky's Theosophical writings through the embrace of diverse ancient thought in the generation following the New Age.[11]

MYSTICISM IN TWENTIETH-CENTURY LITERATURE

A third epilogue to this discussion is the use of mystical motifs in the literature of the twentieth century.[12] Thus, for instance, Jorge Luis Borges, the renowned Argentinian writer, made use of kabbalistic motifs in any number of his "entertainments," as he calls his short stories. "The Aleph," to give one example, centers its concentric circles of narrative around that first letter of the Hebrew alphabet that, the protagonist informs the narrator, "is one of the points in space that contains all other points . . . the only place on earth where all places are—seen from every angle, each standing clear, without any confusion or bending . . . all places in the universe are in the Aleph . . . all lamps, all sources of light are in it, too."[13] That is, it is the center of spaceless space, "the pure and boundless godhead," the *mysterion—hidden* in the basement of

the protagonist who shares this secret with the narrator—the source of all
light (with which the universe was initiated according to Genesis 1:2), the
"not" beyond the "limitless" beyond the "limitless light" beyond the *highest*
of the *sephirot* (hidden *below* the lowest floor of the protagonist's house).

Its pursuit drives the narrator "to the ineffable core of my story"—ineffable, for how can he possibly "translate into words the limitless Aleph, which
my floundering mind can scarcely encompass?"[14] in which not only all of
space but also all of time ("I saw in a backyard of Soler Street the same tiles
that thirty years before I'd seen in the entrance of a house in Fray Bentos")
and his own innermost being ("I saw the circulation of my own dark blood. . . .
I saw my own face and my own bowels") seem to be contained.[15] Nor does
Borges forget that the struggle to articulate what the *aleph* is, in referring to
it as an "Aleph," is itself a circumlocutionary convenience used by Kabbalah,
which may be referred to in other mystical traditions by other terms: "one
Persian speaks of a bird that somehow is all birds [alluding to 'Attar's great
poem]); Alanus de Insulis, of a sphere whose center is everywhere and cir-
cumference is nowhere [alluding to a thirteenth-century French Christian poet
and mystical reactor against the Scholasticism of his era]; Ezekiel, of a four-
faced angel who at one and the same time moves east and west, north and
south" [referring to the description of the lower part of the *merkavah* in pre-
Jewish/Christian/Muslim sacred textuality].[16] Thus, Borges's *aleph* is also a
centerpiece of crisscrossing elements from diverse mystical traditions.

The French novelist Andre Schwarz-Bart builds his very moving Holo-
caust-centered work, *The Last of the Just*, around a different, later Jewish
mystical tradition, one that specifically emerges to clarity within the Lurianic
School and its successors. That tradition—a subset of the more mainstream
tradition regarding the *tzadik* who is recognized as the sacerdotal center of his
community—has it that there are, within every generation, thirty-six *tzadikim*
who are unrecognized not only by those around them but also often even by
themselves; yet, due to their righteousness, the world continues to survive its
own horrific behavior.

Recalling the fact that every Hebrew letter has a numerical value, and
that the two letters *lamed* (= 30) and *vav* (=6) combined offer 36, the
thirty-six righteous ones are called the *Lamed–Vav*. The number, of course,
is precisely double the numerology of eighteen, the ultimate numerical He-
brew/Jewish symbol of life. For the letter *het* (= 8) and the letter *yud* (=
10) together add up to 18—and in together spelling the Hebrew word *hai*
(which means "life"), that number is the ultimate Jewish "good-luck" number. "But if just one of them [the *Lamed-Vav*] were lacking, the suffering of
mankind would poison even the souls of the newborn, and humanity would

suffocate with a single cry. For the Lamed-Vav are the hearts of the world multiplied, and into them, as into one receptacle, pour all our griefs."[17] From this beginning, Schwarz-Bart traces a thousand years of the history of one *tzadik*'s line—which includes one member who, "after fifteen years of that mad solitude . . . became so popular that a number of stories identify him with the Ba'al Shem Tov himself, of whom he was said to have become the wandering incarnation"[18]—down to the protagonist's friend, Ernie (the *last* of the just ones).

For Ernie, in the end, suffocates with six million other Jews in a gas chamber. And

> in the flash that preceded his own annihilation he remembered, happily, the legend of Rabbi Chanina ben Teradion, as Mordecai [Ernie's grandfather] has recited it: "When the gentle rabbi, wrapped in the scrolls of the Torah, was flung upon the pyre by the Romans for having taught the Law, and when they lit the fagots, the branches still green to make his torture last, his pupils said: 'Master, what do you see?' And Rabbi Chanina answered, 'I see the parchment burning, but the letters are taking wing.'" . . . "*Ah, yes, surely, the letters are taking wing,*" Ernie repeated as the flame blazing in his chest suddenly rose to his head.[19]

Placed against the background not only of centuries of martyrdoms but also primarily the ultimate martyrdom, the Nazi horror, the novel is moving and majestic, an interweaving of despair and hope, for "at times one's heart could break in sorrow. But often, too, preferably in the evening, I can't help thinking that Ernie Levy, dead six million times, is still alive somewhere, I don't know where."[20]

Death, we recall, can come, according to an early rabbinic assertion, from the very study of mysticism, through the twists and turns it imposes on and inserts into the mind. The American writer Cynthia Ozick builds her short story "The Pagan Rabbi" around that fundamental notion: that to study Kabbalah or Jewish mysticism in general—to seek an entryway into the hiddenmost, innermost recesses of the *sacer*—can lead to death, or to madness or apostasy, which are variations of the same fate. And ultimately, the rabbi who is the subject of her tale does all three. Isaac Kornfeld, we learn from the first line, "a man of piety and brains . . . hanged himself in the public park,"[21] several weeks short of his thirty-sixth birthday. We recall thirty-six (the symbolic significance of which is noted a few paragraphs above) as the age when one ought only to *begin* studying Kabbalah, in part of the Jewish mystical tradition (the other part asserts that one ought not to do so until age forty), lest one's presumed mental fragility permit the imbalance that would lead inevitably to disaster.

The scholarly father of seven little girls had, it seems, not only been immersing himself ever more deeply into Kabbalah and *Hassidut* but also allowed that study, with its panhenotheistic possibilities, to lead him with increasing fervor out into nature and out into English and American Romantic poetry—in both cases, farther and farther from both the sacred books for which he had developed renown as a commentator and from his sane, stable center—and beyond panhenotheism to pantheism. His notebook and a letter, given to the narrator by the rabbi's young widow to read, express his growing struggle to relocate himself within the world—of both matter and spirit. That struggle leads him to apostasy, at least in his widow's eyes: "He was a pagan . . . [and she goes on to read from Rabbi Kornfeld's words in that letter:] . . . '[at] a watering place . . . some quick spry boy would happen to glimpse the soul of the spring (which the wild Greeks afterward called *naiad*), but not knowing of the existence of the free souls he would suppose only that the moon had cast a momentary beam across the water. Loveliness, with the same innocence of accident I discovered thee. Loveliness, Loveliness.'"[22]

In the increasing pace of the posthumous revelation, the rabbi writes of the need for "my soul [to be] released at once or be lost to sweet air forever."[23] In his growing madness—or visionary insightfulness—he recounts his embrace (literally) of a tree, seeking its inner spirit and seeking to merge with that spirit: "'Come, come,' I called aloud to Nature . . . so now let a daughter of Shekhina the Emanation reveal herself to me. Nymph, come now, come now."[24] His universalistic embrace conflates the pagan terminology and the pagan concepts that he has discovered with the terminology of Kabbalah in which, as we recall, God itself is manifest as a presence within the *profanus* and within all females and all balanced males as the *Shekhinah*, which may be understood as part of the process of emanation from the Absolute One into what becomes the multifarious universe.

Rabbi Kornfeld experiences a response to his call and access to another reality in the form of a creature that he can hardly describe whose own *sacer* language he can hardly express in ours: "Her sentences came to me not as a series of differentiated frequencies but (impossible to develop this idea in language) as a diffused cloud of field fragrances; yet to say that I assimilated her thought through the olfactory nerve would be a pedestrian distortion."[25] Through her he sees the world differently—including his own soul, outside his body, along the road (of life), "a dusty old man trudging up there," burdened with volumes of Talmud, who tells him that "the dryad, who does not exist, lies. It is not I who clung to her but you, my body," and accuses him of having "expelled me, your ribs exile me from their fate, and I will walk here alone always, in my garden."[26] That garden is the garden of the Torah and, perhaps, a pun on the garden of mystical speculation into which Rabbi Kornfeld had entered at too early an age to withstand its impact, however brilliant and pious he was, who now stands, light and empty and devoid of his soul. He unravels the prayer shawl from the old man and, in a burst of fury and fervor, calling out to the spirit—"Loveliness, come"—winds it around his neck and around the branch of the tree from which she had originally appeared (or so he had imagined, at least) at the end of this cautionary tale.

Among the more interesting, more recent literary works that both take up the theme of mysticism and also offer a cautionary tone is Myla Goldberg's 2000 novel, *Bee Season*. It is the story of a nine-year-old girl, Eliza, who, in contrast to her brilliant, self-obsessed lawyer mother, scholarly father, and smart, rabbinically inclined older brother, seems to have nothing but mediocrity to offer to the world—until she stumbles upon her genius for spelling, a genius that carries her from the classroom for "slower" students all the way to the national spelling bee finals. I am leaving the poignant larger storyline aside—of her relationship with her parents and brother and her struggle to put the world into focus and to hold her own world together—in the interests of space and our own focus. What eventually emerges as the centerpiece of her rise to prominence and self-decreed "fall" is the obsession with letters—Hebrew letters—and their relationship to matters physical, intellectual, psychological, and spiritual that is associated with Abraham Abulafia.[27] Abulafia, it turns out, has been Eliza's father's obsession pretty much ever since he moved beyond the hallucinogenic drugs of his college years. Alas, he has long since realized that he lacks whatever it takes to elevate to the heights that Abulafia offers. But Eliza's sudden exhibition of her singular aspect of genius—which he recognizes to be just *the* singular genius that accords with Abulafia's—offers him the apparent chance to shape his daughter to be and experience the prophetic ecstasy that he cannot.

It turns out that he is probably right, but the problem he has ignored is the classic one about which Jewish mysticism warns: that the practitioner must be of a certain minimum age, among other things, in order not to be torn apart by the experience. Eliza's father fails to see this in the larger classic manner in which obsessive parents, not able to separate their children's needs and ambitions from their own, too often fail to separate their desires from their children's welfare. The irony is that, although she is nearly blown apart by her Abulafian experience, Eliza survives—she returns from her mystical experience a person much wiser than her years or than those around her, with enough perspective to recognize that she is better off losing the next spelling bee at the local level than winning at the national level.

The story interweaves *various* mystical cautionary notions, the most famous perhaps, that of the four rabbis—Ben Azzai, Ben Zoma, Alisha ben Abuya, and Akiva—who enter the *pardes* from which only Akiva survives intact.[28] Of the other three, the first dies, the second goes mad, and the third apostatizes. Goldberg plays on this, as Eliza's mother eventually goes mad, her brother gradually apostatizes, and, although Eliza herself nearly dies, we realize that, in the end, when she does *not* perish, it is her father's *dream* that she has allowed to die. The ways in which the author pursues the intricate details of Abulafian and general Jewish mystical thought and carries them into the contemporary world, with its New Age, Jubu, and other, similar phenomena, are both manifold and clever.

MYSTICISM AND THE VISUAL IMAGINATION

One might add, as a fourth epilogue to this discussion, the interest in, focus on, and use of mysticism in the visual and related arts—keeping in mind the importance of art as an instrument for religion in general across history. Art is another means by which humans have long sought to communicate and by which we seek to understand—to fathom—the *sacer*. Music, dance, and visual art can transcend words, carrying both their maker and their audience toward that very superverbal, ineffable realm of the Other, which is addressed by religion generally and mysticism in particular.

Indeed, visual art has functioned as a visual concomitant of the primary verbal instruments of religion—myth and prayer—in addressing, describing, and seeking to apprehend divinity since the beginning of art history. Both kinds of instruments, verbal and nonverbal, seek to represent divinity, to explore its relationship with humanity, to point out what the forces that have created us wish from us to assure that we are furthered, rather than destroyed, by those same powerful forces.

The artist, in the course of religious history, is a figure whose position is analogous to that of the priest and the prophet. He or she functions as a *sacerdos* in intermediating between humanity and divinity, in representing and interpreting that other realm. From Neolithic fertility idols and Sumerian priest figures to medieval sculptures and baroque paintings, art has addressed the other realm.[29] This role has acquired a different nuance in the art of the West of the past three centuries or so. With increased secularization in Western society, increased secularization of their subject matter for artists has also become apparent. That change has accelerated during the past century, as Western art has moved from narrative to landscape to cubist breakdown to absolute abstraction.

Yet, the artist remains sacerdotal in the sense that he or she may be viewed as inspired—*in-spirited*—from that other realm (even as the Other is increasingly construed as internal rather than external, mind derived rather than God derived). He or she remains an intermediary, guiding the viewer to see with eyes not limited by ordinary reality, creating, as God creates, by transforming reality—enacting *yetzirah*—into a new microcosmic formation on the paper or on the canvas or in the sculpted form. On the other hand, in our own time—perhaps, in part, in response to the spiritual emptiness that secularization offers to many of us—there have evolved many artists who choose as their explicit subject matter the Other and its concomitants. Such artists have returned to that centuries-long tradition of art as a handmaiden of religion—albeit often by way of radically untraditional visual routes.

The role of the artist as *sacerdos* becomes yet more intense when his or her subject is that central aspect of the Other addressed by mysticism. For a Jewish or Muslim artist, the attempt to address that hiddenmost center of the invisible Other in visual terms is an absolute oxymoron. It challenges the capacity to visualize the by-definition invisible, as it focuses toward the center of a centerless Other, which cannot be *located* even as it may be *found*. Every artist—all of whom are themselves doorways for us into that paradox—enters through a different doorway.

The degree to which all of this is obvious in the arts varies. Thus, only recently have more than one or two art historians discussed the interest in Lurianic Kabbalah in the work of Jewish chromaticist abstract expressionist painters like Mark Rothko and Barnett Newman, whose inevitable interest in the question of the Holocaust—how, they asked, do we as Jewish artists respond (how can we *not* respond?) to that trauma, which destroyed six million of our coreligionists?—intersected with the engagement of the Lurianic concept of *tikkun olam*.[30] Barnett Newman's (1905–1970) "zip" paintings, large and frameless, their pigment extending to the canvas edge, with a central line to which the eye is inevitably drawn—particularly those with names like *Covenant* or *Onement*—overtly suggest an abstract aesthetic expression of reordering the universe: The central zip holds together the unity of the opposing sides of the composition. One can, moreover, recognize in that central zip an abstract reality simultaneously *withdrawing* from the universe of the color-field that it holds together (as in Lurianic *tzimtzum*)[31] and emerging, expanding, *emanating* (as in non-Lurianic kabbalistic *atzilut*) out into the color-field that it pushes to the edge of the unframed canvas.

In Newman's 1950 *The Name II*, the eye is drawn to the center of an image that is completely white, except for two thin golden lines that divide the visual plane into three equal components. Those familiar with the Jewish tradition would know that, since even the traditional circumlocution of God's ineffable name may be uttered by traditional Jews only in prayer,[32] verbal references to God outside prayer are made through what amounts to a double circumlocution which, in Hebrew, is *HaShem*, meaning "the name." So

Newman's painting is titled so that it informs the knowledgeable viewer of its subject: the God that cannot be depicted as its very name is ineffable. What in centuries of Christian art would be the figurative representation of God, as the Christ, in the center of a threefold canvas—a triptych, the very configuration of which is to symbolize the triune God—is here blank canvas, devoid even of color.

But white is that pigment closest to light, the totality of color. Thus, like color, the image of God is simultaneously present (in the totality of color that symbolizes the totality of the God-made, panhenotheistic universe) and absent (in the absence of color that symbolizes God's absence from, withdrawal from, the universe into absolute no-thing-ness, as expressed in the Lurianic concept of *tzimtzum*). This addresses the Holocaust question as well: Where was God when so many were being tortured and massacred? God was both absent (for those whose intense suffering became proof of God's absence) and present (for those who asserted that they were able to survive their intense suffering only through their certainty of God's presence). Newman has depicted—without depicting—the *mysterion* of endless light and the endlessness beyond light that cannot be depicted or even spoken.

Differently, the canvasses of Mark Rothko (1903–1970) scintillate with light. By soaking them in watered-down pigments, Rothko was able to inundate his images with broad bands of color that seem to approach and recede—typically three bands, like the number of the Trinity—toward and from a central, emanating, and withdrawing light source. The central element draws the eye, presenting itself as a symbol of oneness, wholeness, and transcendent unity. Unlike Newman, Rothko delivers no names for his paintings to hint at his spiritual intentions, but it may perhaps be no accident that his works hang not only in museums but also around the walls of meditative spaces, which they suffuse with an atmosphere of *sacer* mystery.[33]

The younger, Washington-based contemporary of the New York School chromaticists, Morris Louis (1913–1962), offered even less overt explanation for his work than Rothko: Only two of his canvasses were stretched during his lifetime, in fact, and he left no journals; nor, according to his widow, did he ever discuss his work, even with her. Yet, it is difficult to imagine, with the repercussions of the Holocaust rippling through so much of the Jewish side of the New York art world that he kept visiting, that he, as a Jew, would have been immune to thoughts like those of Rothko, Newman, Adolph Gottlieb, and others, in whose studios he spent time and whose conversations he heard. His first great, canonical series, created in the mid- and late 1950s, is referred to as the *Veils* series, in which lyrical curtains of color vie for a foreground presence on heroic-sized canvasses awash with pigment that soaks—melts, one might say—directly into the unprimed canvas.

His visual relationship to the work of Mark Rothko and Barnett Newman is clear: "Louis translates the chromatic calculations of Rothko into something that might be called chromatic mysticism," Stuart Preston wrote at that time, while Martica Sawin observed that the *Veils* belong "to a particular realm of experience to which the works of Rothko and Newman, in their different ways, also pertain."[34] The interesting thing is that, while such statements asserting a mystical quality to Louis's work were not and are not uncommon, nobody has seemed to wonder *what* mystical source (if any) might have inspired him and *what* (for all three, Newman, Rothko, and Louis) the "experience" mentioned by Sawin might be. Given the discussions of Jewishness, Jewish art, the Holocaust, and Lurianic Kabbalah that occupied these figures and those around them, *Jewish* experience and *Jewish* mysticism—with its specific references to veils (that, however minutely thin, separate even the most successful mystic from God's *mysterion*)—may be consciously (or unconsciously) Louis's reference points. But, as so often with both literary and visual commentaries, we can only theorize, not assert with absoluteness.[35]

On the other hand, Ad Reinhardt (1913–1967), a Christian painter and contemporary of Morris Louis, may be seen—in spite of himself—to pursue a path, as he arrives at his late works, that also merges painting with the question of the *mysterion*. His *Black Paintings* of the mid-1960s carry an aspect of Barnett Newman's *The Name II* another step further. Reinhardt deliberately sought to present a kind of "antipainting" by covering his canvasses with such a strong noncolor—or anticolor. But like white, black can be understood as both the totality (mix all the colors together and you come up with black) and complete absence of color—and in fact, a close look, for example, at *Black Painting No. 34* (1964) makes it clear that slightly different shades of black have been imposed on the canvas and that those slight differences of shade yield the subtle form of a cross across the image. Thus, they have a deliberately spiritual aspect to them; they offer an intense focal point defined by the ultimate symbol of the ultimate image that connects a Christian to the *mysterion*. It is easy to understand why Ellen Johnson could write that the *Black Paintings* "are as mystic, *malgre lui*, as anything of Rothko or Newman."[36]

As in other aspects of engaging the *sacer*, including an exponential increase in interest in mysticism and pop mysticism, the last decade of the twentieth century and its aftermath have offered a dramatic expansion of the directions in which visual artists have moved with respect to religion and spirituality in general and mysticism in particular. This has been particularly true where Jewish artists and Jewish mysticism is concerned. For example, the California artist Bruria Finkel's engagement of Abraham Abulafia's thought began thirty years ago when she slowly cotranslated a prophetic work of his called *Sepher Ha-Ot* (*Book of the [Alphabetic] Letter*). That work, offering both mental and physiological techniques—such as breathing, chanting, and visualization—for *seeking*, through the permutation of letters that emanate from the name, reverberates with tonalities that point in the music-and-dancing directions of Lurianic Kabbalah and *Hassidut*. From it emanates Bruria's (she typically uses her first name as her "artist" name) turn toward Abulafia and, in turn, toward the parts of his commentary on Maimonides that present concentric circles of text and isolated letters in mandala-like focus.

This encounter with Abulafian thought led directly to Bruria's bronze sculptures and paintings on paper collectively called *The Divine Chariot* (see figure 1.1). The text in Ezekiel speaks of wheels of eyes whirling in all directions simultaneously—they defy the norms of time, space and direction (see chapter 2, pp. 26, 28, and chapter 3, pp. 51, 52). Finkel's four bronze wheels reach across time into the Bronze Age Hittite innovation of a spoked wheel and, by way of the number ten—each of her wheels has ten spokes—into the kabbalistic emphasis on ten by way of the *sephirot*; in turn, the *merkavah* focus on ten by way of the *heikhalot*, and in turn the *Book of Formation* focuses on ten by way of the numbers that join with the Hebrew letters as conduits of creation.

Four wheels, of course, suggest both the four directions of the creation and the four-lettered name of the Creator—*YHVH*—and the four worlds (emanation, creation, formation, making) of pre-*Zohar* kabbalistic thinking that emanate toward our world from God (see chapter 6, 118ff). Each of the four wheels offers a different emphasis: one offers "The One"; one, "The Influx," which is the divine act of creation; one, the four-directioned "The Power of One" associated with the names of the four Archangels; one, the efflorescence that becomes "The Many." These are all emanations from the central idea, like the four rivers of paradise, referred to in Genesis, that emanate from the source and are the beginning of the fertilization of the created world.

Abulafia-like, the imaged wheels are nuanced with letters—ten each, organized according to their numerological values, the focused meditation on which yields mystical rapture—and across one wheel, the names of the four archangels are inscribed, hovering around the centerlessly centered One. Each wheel may be viewed from any of the four directions; the front of each presents the theme encompassed by its circle, and the back—through the motif of carefully modeled human hands—suggests the human role in the world, as creator and manipulator.

The triangular forms articulated by the spokes in concert with the outer rims are emphasized by subtleties of patina, and in "The Power of One," are subsumed into the form of a five-pointed star. The star, in its fiveness, further underscores the relationship between God and ourselves: it is like a hand with

Figure 11.1. Bruria Finkel, Placement of Power Detail, from the Divine Chariot Series Sculpture (1983–2004).

Source: Bruria Finkel, reprinted by permission.

five fingers. One, the thumb, is attached to, yet separate from, the other four. The one is the One; the four is our four-directioned reality: Both thumb and fingers are connected to the same hand, yet separate from each other.[37]

The spokes of the wheels are ten in number, yet one is different from the other nine. It is presented in the process of growth, as a part of nature, beginning to flower; the other nine are identical and unnaturally stagnant. The notion of transformation and growth, endemic to the universe, is reinforced by this imagery. Finkel's *merkavah* re-vision is superimposed onto the kabbalistic idea of representing the macrosomic universe and its processes as a *tree* of *sephirot*—the tree as a microcosm of nature, thus of the universe and also of the Torah as the ultimate Tree of Life—which, in turn, is also understood as a Vitruvian human figure (in other words, man, tree, *sephirot*, universe, and the Torah as analogues of each other), which Abulafia carried to an extreme.

Moreover, in the esoteric well associated with Abulafia from which the artist drinks, nine is a particularly propitious mystical number. It is the square of the number of "mother letters" referenced in the *Sepher Yetzirah* (*aleph, mem, shin*)—three (letters) times three. And if, using an Abulafian version of Hebrew-letter numerology, one eliminates zero (which then, of course, leaves nine basic numbers), then the Hebrew words for "truth" (*emet*, whose triconsonantal makeup is *aleph* = 1, *mem* = 4, and *taf* = 4) and for "light" (*'or*, whose triconsonantal makeup is *aleph* = 1, *vav* = 6, and *resh* = 2) add up to nine.[38] Light is that most essential instrument of visual imaging; it is the substance of the ladder of ascent to the celestial realm; it is the first material called into existence by God. And truth, which is the ultimate goal sought through that ascent, is the totality of existence from beginning to end—for its three letters are the first, the middle, and the last in the Hebrew alphabet.

⸎

Many artists have responded to the mystical imperative to be an instrument for improving the world by synthesizing mystical thought with overt political thought. Iranian Muslim artist Hossein Zenderoudi's 1960–1961 painting, *The Hand*, for example, functions like a political mandala, of which the political element is only apparent to those who know. The image is dominated by a *hamsa*—the upraised hand that, with its five fingers, represents the Five Pillars of Islam and, in the separation between the one thumb and four other fingers, symbolizes the relationship between God (the One) and ourselves (the four-directioned *profanus*)—attached to and rising from a six-pointed star element (another symbol of the meeting of realms: a triangle up, symbolizing earth and maleness, interweaving with a triangle down, symbolizing heaven and femaleness) that in turn is attached to and rises out of a bowl (suggesting water and thus purity, as well as life). This configuration, in a silvery white, stands out against a gold-colored background, the background overrun with Arabic writing and numbers ensconced within squared and circular forms. The painting includes its own triple-framed elements: two thin gold lines flanking a thick black one inscribed with gold writing.

The entire piece is a rich compendium of meditative elements; it encourages the viewer to stare and stare and focus and focus, the visual equivalent of the verbal repetitions that form the heart of a Sufi *dhikr*. But in the context of the vocabulary of intended Iranian political national sentiment, the hand represents the truncated hand of the Shi'ite Muslim martyr Hazrat Abbas, who died in the year 680 in the Battle of Karbala. Hazrat Abbas became a source of inspiration for the 1979 revolution that overthrew the shah and installed a theocratic government. Thus, the political intention of Zenderoudi's work is synthesized not only to elements that are traditional to Islamic art but also to a concentrated mystical sensibility that implies that the revolutionary movement (which would not achieve success until eighteen years after this work was created) is a divinely sanctioned part of the process of using the focus on the *mysterion* to effect a positive transformation within the *profanus*.

Differently, Jane Logemann, in a large body of her work, uses pale hues as washes over repeated words or letters. The repetitions—particularly in that if the writing reaches the edge of the canvas in the middle of a word, she simply breaks it and completes its broken form on the next line—recall the Jewish mystical technique of repeating sounds and words to the point where the words are reduced to mindless sounds and the sounds transcend any sense at all. But the often graduated, nuanced changes of pattern in color and form also recall purely formal exercises in conceptual art and music (figure 11.2).[39]

Part of the result of Logemann's work is to make the viewer aware of the *process* of *creating* it—one can't look at these works and not be conscious of the slow, painstaking concentration—*kavanah*—involved. In this sense, the works that identify her as what might be termed a meditative devotee of visual *Hassidut* also offer two particular directions of secularized visual thinking, one ancient, the other contemporary. The calligraphic component associates these multilingual expressions with cultures in which writing is an old, respected art form (not surprisingly, she has chosen languages whose writing systems relate to that sensibility). So, too, the subtle modulations of color ground connects them to Paul Klee, as well as to Ad Reinhardt, on the one hand, and the minimalist gestural quality of the marks that make up the letters and words, as well as the conceptual underpinnings, connect them to Sol Lewitt on the other. This latter aspect of her oeuvre is yet more obvious in those works that have no letters at all but are purely exercises in color and its modulations.

If, on the one hand, in its repetition and form the calligraphy itself—particularly given that the words and letters are never in English but rather are in Hebrew, Arabic, Russian, Korean, or Japanese—is essentially "mindless" (for most viewers won't be able to read the words but will perceive them simply as visual patterns), thus reinforcing the relationship to mystical method. On the other hand, the choice of term that is endlessly repeated may often be politically charged. Thus, for example, "coexistence" written repeatedly on one side of the canvas in Hebrew and on the other in Arabic combines the mystical meditative aspect of *kavanah* and senseless repetition with a political question that offers as little simplicity and clarity regarding an answer within the *profanus* as does the question of God's hiddenness within the *sacer*.

Marilyn Banner's work also touches on Hebrew letters but in a very differently "calligraphic" mode. She creates encaustic on wood panels dominated by the large shapes of kabbalistically significant letters—like *aleph*, first letter of the Hebrew alphabet, its form offering two elements that point up toward heaven and two pointing down toward earth (like the two upstretched arms and down-pushing legs of a person), or *shin*, with its three fingers extending heavenward, which is the first letter of God's power-protective "name," *Shaddai*. Or she puts the two letters together, creating in combination, *AySH*, meaning "fire" and recalling both the desire of and the danger to the Enoch-emulating mystic to be transformed in ascending to contact with the *mysterion*—and also recalling the first of the "mother letters" and the element to which it corresponds in the *Sepher Yetzirah* (figure 11.3).

But Banner's letters are often also disguised as birds (as if she is synthesizing the shared Jewish-Christian-Muslim mystical and/or visual symbolic vocabulary that offers birds as symbols of the soul—and which, in 'Attar's long mystical poem *The Conference of the Birds*, is carried to an elaborate allegorical extreme)[40] or other creatures forming part of the God-shaped world. Differently, her expansive installations of *Soul Ladders* offer a connection between worlds, suspended from gallery ceilings and hovering just above the floor level, alluding on the one hand to the vision of a ladder between heaven and earth dreamed in the *sacer* time of night by the Hebrew patriarch, Jacob, as he fled into the *sacer* space of the wilderness from the anger of his brother, Esau. On the other hand, the ladders also refer to the ladder of the *sephirot* delineated in the *Zohar*. In this second, more emphatically mystical context, the ladders suggest (as the *sephirot* do) aspects of the aspectless Creator, aspects of the creative process, and aspects of the creation itself. The artist personalizes this (well aware of her role as an artist-creator) with the images of her own ancestors—including several who perished during the Holocaust—that she often embeds within the flotsam and jetsam hanging from her *Soul Ladders'* rungs.

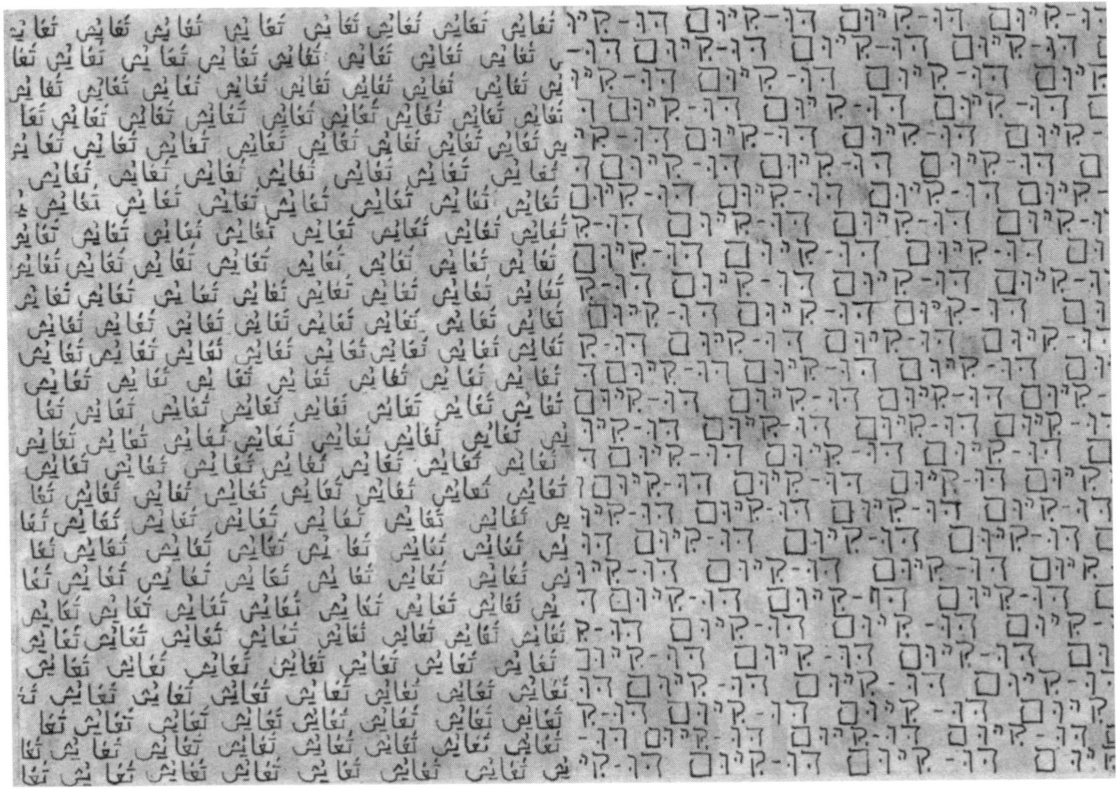

Figure 11.2. Jane Logemann, Co-Existence.

Source: Jane Logemann, reprinted by permission.

Figure 11.3.   Marilyn Banner, *The Letter* Shin.
Source: Marilyn Banner, reprinted by permission.

Anselm Kiefer's work adds another twist to this last, Holocaust turn: He is a non-Jewish German born in 1945, the year when World War II ended, who intermingles the issue of artistic creativity with the trauma (for him, as a Christian German) of destruction that defines the Holocaust. He grew up in a country in which, for the entirety of his youth, the subject of the Holocaust was never discussed, as if it hadn't happened, or when some inkling that it had happened was allowed, it was characterized as a minor event, distant in time, space, and conception from the Germany that authored it. An artist choosing to enter into that territory would find himself confronted with one of the banal sides of the question dogging the steps of Jewish artists for two millennia (particularly as they sought to express themselves within the larger contexts of Christian art and its consistent figurative and symbolic references to God): how to represent that which is not representable.

The question of visually expressing what faith insists is there, in spite of its invisibility, is transmuted by Kiefer into visually expressing what history insists is there, when everybody involved asserts, I saw nothing; I heard nothing; I smelled nothing. It must not be as *they* claim it was. Representing the unrepresentable actually occupies several further levels of reality reflected in work like Kiefer's. One is the problem that assails every visual or verbal artist addressing the Holocaust: How can one possibly convey in words or images the full power of the horror? A second connects Kiefer to Jewish and non-Jewish theologians and questioners regarding God: not the generic Jewish question of visually representing the invisible but the post-Holocaust question of whether there *is* a God or what *kind* of God there is who failed to intervene to save (among others) a million and a half children incinerated by the Nazis.

Among Kiefer's large-scale works—installations and canvasses overrun not only with oil paint but also with emulsion, shellac, sand, and woodcut— are several from the 1990s that turn to these questions by way of specific references to Jewish mysticism. The enormous (12.5 feet high) construction *Breaking of the Vessels* (1990) alludes simultaneously to that central doctrine in late Lurianic Kabbalah and to *Kristallnacht*, the "Night of Broken Glass" of November 9–10, 1938, which marked the beginning of systematic physical violence against German (and, shortly, other) Jews.[41] The Lurianic doctrine speaks of the unified goodness—understood as that primordial light with which the ordering of the physical universe began, according to Genesis 1:2—of the initial creation, which, in the aftermath of the act of disobedience enacted by Adam and Eve, exploded into an infinite array of sparks (*n'tzotzot*). In turn, those sparks are trapped throughout the universe in shells or vessels (*kleepot*; see chapter 9, pp. 202, 211–12), which must ultimately be smashed to liberate the sparks. This will happen in the messianic era, when, like those sparks, the exiled will be ingathered.

Kiefer's piece offers three (as in the triune God of Christianity) shelves with large sheets of lead that offer the appearance of Talmudic tomes in the ashen library of a destroyed synagogue. Over that structure hovers an acrylic (aquatec) arch on which the culminating phrase delineating the endlessness of the God beyond the uppermost of the *sephirot* resides: *ain soph*("endless").[42] Balanced by the scattering of large shards of glass in a far-flung configuration on the floor below the "bookshelf" structure, that arch cannot fail to be seen as a pun on the cynical arch above the gateway to Auschwitz, inscribed with its dictum, *Arbeit Macht Frei* ("Work Makes One Free")—as if work or any other measure could free the victims of the Nazis. The entire installation puns on the ugly problematic of Nazi pretense with regard to saving the world through destroying select parts of it—with Jews as the primary part among those parts to be destroyed—and the Jewish mystical quest to understand how and when God will take concerted action by means of a messianic presence toward the perfection that humans seem incapable of achieving for the universe.

Among the works that most interestingly address the God question—by asking another—is Kiefer's *Zimzum* (1990).[43] That word, we may recall, means "shrinkage" or "withdrawal" and is used in Lurianic Kabbalah to refer to the process according to which God made room for the universe: for how, the Lurianic kabbalists asked, if God is the absolute Absolute, could there be room for the universe *unless* God ceded room by shrinking Itself into a corner of reality? By an analogous process, God ceded Its all-powerfulness in granting humans free will and thus the power to be and do as we choose—to obey or disobey, to create or destroy. Kiefer's enormous canvas, inscribed with the word *Zimzum*, is dark and tumultuously textural. A series of orthogonals leads from below, where the observer stands, into the recesses of the upper part of the canvas. The lines converge at a horizon line where Albertian thought would have located the "vanishing point."[44]

But at that point in Kiefer's painting, we can discern a series of verticals that one might interpret as a tower—such as the tower that marks the terminus of the train tracks at Auschwitz, to be precise, so familiar by the 1990s from repeated imagery as to be a virtual icon, one of the preeminent visual symbols of the Holocaust. In this case, the orthogonals become the multiplying lines of railroad tracks; the vanishing point is not merely Albertian and not merely a reference to the Lurianic concept of God's shrinkage but a reference to the vanishing of six million Jews toward that tower (and the vanishing of the Jews of Germany: Hundreds of thousands left before the Holocaust, but how many left as Kiefer was growing up?) and to the question of God's presence or absence while that process was being furthered.

Moreover, rather than driving simply toward their vanishing point, the orthogonal lines leave open a vast, dark chasm just before they arrive at the horizon line, where they disappear: It is like a black hole—and literally a black hole on the image—in the otherwise untrammeled pattern of diagonal lines. In modern physics, black holes have been understood as massive presences throughout the universe so powerful that they suck the very light from beyond them into their depths. Like the Nazis, they are virtuosi with regard to causing everything around them—even light itself (which is why they are black)—to disappear. The God of the Holocaust is a powerful presence—in spite of the Nazis, is an impotent or even nonexistent presence in the face of the Nazis, and is the bringer of light to those who survived thanks to God and the absorber into itself of all light, leaving only darkness behind, to those whose multiple losses led to the loss of their faith in a God who couldn't save those who were destroyed.

The question of the invisible God is subsumed into that of the nonexistent or impotent or uncaring God; is subsumed into that of the absent Jews in postwar Germany; is subsumed into that of the absent Holocaust in postwar German discourse; is subsumed into the impossibility of words to convey God (just as Jewish mysticism seeks to transcend words, turning sense into nonsense, as the mystic seeking God must transcend the realm of the sensible if he or she would accede to the God beyond sense) and the impossibility of words to convey the Holocaust; is subsumed into the impossibility of visual art to convey God or to convey the Holocaust—all this is conveyed by references to kabbalistic discourse.

Kiefer, then, is a Christian artist making explicit and, in a distinct sense, politicized use of Jewish mystical ideas. Among other recent Christian artists who have been drawn to Jewish mystical themes (but with no political agenda), as well as to themes that undergird the Jewish mystical tradition, is Chicago painter Victoria Martin. Her work often engages *merkavah* mysticism, interweaves its ideas with those drawn from other spiritual traditions, West and East, or with contemporary scientific ideas, or seeks beneath the foundations of the *merkavah* tradition along earlier textual paths.

One of Martin's paintings that focuses on cosmogony/cosmography offers a series of conceptual and visual imbalanced balances. A series of rectilinear forms dominates the left-hand third of the image, ascending in a color sequence that moves from greens to blues to purples. These forms contrast with a curved form, dominated by blues, that fills out the right-hand two-thirds. If the left-hand image draws the eye from bottom to top, the right-hand image, in a nautilus-shell-like-form, draws the eye from outside inward toward its center, so that together these two primary elements in the painting struggle to push the viewer's perspective from two to three dimensions.

The left-hand image is a sevenfold ascent: These are the seven "camps" of the angels and their assessments of offerings and petitions of the *Sepher HaRazim*; at the same time, conceived as a series of temples or altars, they are the seven lower heavens through which Enoch ascended and the seven lower chambers (*heikhalot*) of *merkavah* mysticism. On the one hand, the lower six structures or chambers and their accompanying symbols suggest the realms of petition and reward within the *Sepher*, from the lowest, where anyone can petition, to the second, where only the purest of heart may hope for success, to the realm whose guardian has eyes like the sun, to that of crowns like flame and that of incandescent clouds, to that wherein honeycombs are offered to the righteous. On the other hand, the seventh structure is intended as an image of the throne of God: The horizontal "beam" connecting its two inner pillars complete the shape of an "H," one of the letters whose Hebrew equivalent stands for God's unpronounceable name. It explodes with ten emanating sparks of light, and the entirety is surmounted by the *aleph*, the first letter of the Hebrew alphabet (beginning of beginnings) and of the word "light" (*'or*).

The right-hand swirl is centered around an explosion of light—the big bang of contemporary astrophysics; the bang begins with a hydrogen atom from the cataclysmic expansion of which the universe is said to have emanated at the beginning of time and from which it continues to extend.[45] Swirling within the painting's emanational nautilus form are quasars and galaxies and a disclike extrusion that is our solar system. The artist has sought to cast into visual terms the paradoxical and unimageable notions that define the cosmogonic and cosmographic landscapes of both premystical and mystical texts and contemporary scientific theories alike (see figure 11.4).

Figure 11.4.   Victoria Martin, The Sefer Ha-Razim's Seven Heavens and the Big Bang.
Source: Victoria Martin, reprinted by permission.

Still differently, Makoto Fujimura offers a doorway into the issue of accessing the *mysterion* through visual art as a Christian artist whose cultural (as opposed to religious) background is double sourced. He is a Japanese American painter who lives and works in New York City, the heartland of abstract expressionism, but went to Japan to study *Nihonga*, an old Japanese painting technique, in part as a search for his own roots.[46] His textless, abstract, chromaticist cycle of paintings that focus on the months of the year is inspired both by European figurative cycles on that subject (the most famous are those done by the Limbourg brothers for the Duc de Berry in early fifteenth-century Burgundy) and by Japanese screens. That is, he is thinking across visual cultures, and to this he has added an intensely meditative quality that recalls Newman and Rothko: His panels are intended to become abstract, purely colored windows into the *mysterion* for the meditative, tightly focused viewer.

This is all the more so with his large (162" × 70") triptych *The Trinity* in which gold leaf and red and blue pigments reflect traditional Western coloristic symbolism in painting—gold as all-valuable truth, blue as true faith, red as sacrifice and love—while the *shoji* screen[47] on which he has painted also reflects the Eastern tradition. Each panel is actually a double panel, even more obviously suggesting Japanese screens. They also suggest doors that lead to the *sacer* realm and, in the meditative depths engendered by the manner in which the inner colors seep through the outer colors, draw the eye into them, as doorways into the *mysterion* within the *sacer*.

New York–born Amy Beth Swartz (b. 1936) offers yet another angled instance of cross-cultural mystical visual thought. She combines her profound interest in Kabbalah with focus on the chakra system of Yoga, as well as on Taoism, Qi Gong, Buddhism, and Native American spirituality. The influence on her of literature that explores the kabbalistic notions of the ten *sephirot* and the four worlds, as well as the concept of the *shekhinah*, has been consistent since the mid-1970s, and by the early 1980s, this influence crisscrossed her study of healing processes derived from Native American traditions and her focus on the chakras. One obvious example of this is her *States of Change* series, done between 1999 and 2001. In *Sephirot #1* (1999), for instance, on a circular canvas (its shape a symbol of perfection, completion, of the God who is without beginning and end), she superimposes the absolute order of a grid system over the shadowy image of a figure seated in a basic cross-legged Yoga position, with the lowest chakra (which may be seen to correspond to *malkhut*, the lowest *sephirah*) emphasized and the entirety overrun with a delicate and chaotic gold leaf pattern: Order and chaos meet in this image, which offers a doorway into connecting *profanus* and *sacer* by means of a Yogic meditation image that is labeled in kabbalistic terms.

Swartz uses the combination of ordered grid and gold-leafed chaos in her *Shen Qi* series—named for a Chinese meditation practice that is ultimately based on musical tones and the controlling of breath in a manner analogous to the tonal control exerted to create different pitches in music (and discussed in Abulafian Kabbalah)—which includes at its heart a group of *Cabbalistic Scheme of the Four Worlds* paintings.[48] Kabbalah's emphasis on the Hebrew letters, inherited all the way from the pre-*merkavah Sepher Yetzirah*, is central to her *Visible Reminders* series painted in 2001 and 2002. Within twenty-two paintings (the number of letters in the Hebrew alphabet), she "hides" letters, words, and phrases in order to push the viewer to see what is beyond the visible in order to uncover the invisible. Thus, for example, the seventh painting, *There Is a Time* (2002), focuses on the seventh letter, *zayin* (which is the first letter in the Hebrew word for "time," *zman*) and offers the passage from the biblical book of Ecclesiastes (a by-definition divinely inspired text), "To everything there is a time and a season under heaven." She obscures the phrase, written and rewritten across the canvas in a meditative repetition (whereby ultimately the mind conscious of the *profanus* sense of the words will be emptied of that sense to allow space for God) by overlaying the words with horizontal bands of dripping black, gray, and white paint.

How different, in medium, style, and apparent subject from all of this is the work of Eleanor Dickinson! Dickinson's work documents Pentecostal Christians in the American South, in both documentary videography and the drawings that she bases on stills from those documentaries. Her focus turns the

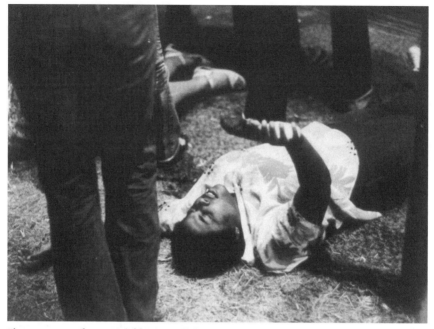

Figure 11.5.   Eleanor Dickinson, Still from Video Revival, 1980. © Dickenson.
Source: Eleanor Dickenson, reprinted by permission.

long abstract narrative regarding mysticism and mystics through which we have come, by way of verbal prescriptions *toward* mystical experiences and descriptions *of* mystical experiences, into concrete visual records of ecstatic believers in the throes of merging with the *mysterion*. Everyday individuals, *in-spirited* with God and having given themselves up to God, are shown thrown to the ground, their eyes closed, their arms and hands thrown up in an *orans* position, their expressions variously of absolute calm stillness or explosive in expressing God's innermost presence within them (figure 11.5).[49]

THE UNFINISHED, ENDLESS STORY

This last part of our discussion leads me to two final notes with regard to the address of mysticism by means of modernist media. One is that, just as throughout this entire narrative, its vast territory has forced me to cherry-pick what and whom to focus on and with how much depth and detail to engage each subterritory, so in the matter of twentieth-century literature and art—particularly visual art—I have explored only the tip of the iceberg of interest and exploration by diverse artists expressing an obvious interest in diverse aspects of the history and experience of mysticism within the Abrahamic traditions. Particularly since the 1990s, the general explosion of interest in spiritual matters has been reflected in an extraordinary range of attention to spirituality on the part of visual artists, including, but not limited to, what may be labeled mystical thought. Some of the further material that one might pursue will be found in the bibliography.

The second note is that one might also include, as I have *not* done in my discussion—yet another drawing of a line in the interests of the space available for this volume—still other media. Thus, variously, music, for example; I have already alluded to classical music such as that by Phillip Glass (who, I also noted, is, incidentally, one of those who would be labeled a "Jubu"), whose mesmerizing sequences of rhythmic patterns with their graduated shifts of tonal and harmonic nuance derive in part from a mystical sensibility. So, too, there has been a distinct growth in popular music that draws not merely from the Christian, Jewish, or Muslim religious tradition but from the mystical vocabulary of all three—and also often emphasizes strongly repetitive motifs reminiscent of the strong repetitions that are part of the verbal and visual mystical tradition—or combines aspects of traditional mystical thought with modes of music far outside the usual Abrahamic ambit. Certainly, the music of Matisyahu,[50] referred to as "Hassidic Reggae," falls into that category, to offer one obvious example.

So, too, film has been a medium, almost since its inception as a technology, that has occasionally turned to aspects of the mystical tradition—from Paul Wegner's 1920 German expressionist film *Der Golem und Wie Er in der Welt Kam* (*The Golem and How He Came into the World*) based on Gustav Meyrink's novelized account of Rabbi Loew and his creation, to the 2005 Leonardo Defilippis film, *Therese: The Story of Saint Therese of Lisieux*, both of which focus directly on aspects of the mystical tradition. On the other hand, a work like the 1999 Rupert Wainwright film, *Stigmata*, leads from the tradition in its own direction. *Stigmata* is the story of a Catholic girl in Pittsburgh, upon whose hands and feet the stigmata miraculously appear. They turn out to be the consequence of a sort of *dybbuk*-like possession: They derive from the spirit of a deeply religious priest who had been excommunicated for heresy due to his discovery of an early text that was deemed to undermine the foundations of Roman Catholicism.[51]

The 1998 film *Pi: Faith in Chaos*, written and directed by Darren Aronofsky, encompasses Kabbalah in its focus on numerology to address the question of how inherently ordered or chaotic the universe ultimately *is*. Working across disciplines, the story, which begins as a narrative about mathematical sequences that may or may not be able to guide one into an understanding of the stock market, moves toward the quest for an understanding of the Torah by means of kabbalistic numerological thinking—which is, ultimately, the quest to understand the universe. The mathematical genius protagonist, Max, shifts again and again between reality and hallucination—it is not always clear to the viewer as to which side of that condition we are ourselves seeing. In the end, one might say that he survives absolute madness by killing the part of himself that has been pushing him into such a dangerous array of territories, both mental and physical. Or perhaps he survives by apostatizing: abandoning his genius in exchange for mental peace. There are many other films that could be noted, but limited space prevents further exploration here.[52]

cᲢᲢᲢ

Where all of this leads in the end is toward the realization that the quest for the endless is endless. We cannot fail to recognize not only the enduring human sense of something beyond our *profanus* realm concerning which we hunger and thirst for an emotional and spiritual connection but also the sense possessed by many humans that there is something still deeper and potentially more meaningful than normative spiritual engagement offers, hidden within the *sacer*, but also more difficult and potentially dangerous to access. That *mysterion* is felt to be at the center of all of reality—and yet beyond all of reality, in some unique, singular, unifying place that is no place at all, with no center at all, as "place" and "center" are understood in that most liberating and limiting of human instruments, language.

That centerless center within a placeless place, a spaceless space within timeless time, is embedded within a singularity defined by paradox, to which access is possible only through the suspension of all that sense and language and their concomitants offer, all that might be understood as rational and understandable. There is something about our species that, from its inception to our own day, causes many of us to seek access to, to yearn for union with, that singularity that leads not only beyond earth but also beyond whatever "garden variety" sense of heaven others of us believe exists. Such devotees of what is beyond the beyond seek along diverse, parallel paths governed by diverse, parallel systems of conviction and belief—particularly parallel where the Abrahamic traditions are concerned—for some kind of ineffable oneness with that One.

NOTES

1. In a nutshell, Buber distinguishes between "I-Thou" relationships, in which each side of the party recognizes the "I" of others—the full presence-in-the-world of

others—and "I-It" experiences, in which the "I" sees only its own fullness and reduces the other to something less. In his three-part, book-length essay, Buber first discusses this in human-human terms (in which spoken language is a primary instrument), then in human-animal and other terms (where spoken human language is not the primary instrument, yet I can develop an "I-Thou" relationship with a dog, a cat, a tree, a stone), and finally in human-divine terms (where, again, language cannot reach, and yet I can also, he asserts, develop an "I-Thou" relationship with the God whose very existence I doubt by willing myself to a momentary suspension of that doubt).

2. Erhard Training Seminars, founded by Werner Erhard in 1971, offer a methodology for transforming one's self by learning to recognize the paradoxes of not being able to explain why each of us is what we are for each other—that Buber-like interface (which Erhardians term "mystical") is ineffable; yet, language is the instrument with which we also engage our difficulty in understanding and engage each other—of letting go of the need to explain *relationship* and yielding to *trust*, of then recognizing that we are together even when we are not in the same space, which is why we don't need each other (because we can be apart and fully free of each other, and because "even when I am not with you, I am with you. That's the *mystical*," writes Erhardian Laurence Platt in 2006 in his essay "Mystical Connection" (in *Conversations for Transformation*, www.laurenceplatt.home.att.net/wernererhard/. 2006.—"and yet we do need each other, like we need oxygen. It's the inquiry into all of this that leads to serenity—that transforms us." Scientology, created in 1958 by L. Ron Hubbard as a further development of his earlier self-help system, Dianetics, claims to be an "applied religious philosophy" and the basis, as such, for a new religion. It asserts that we are all immortal spiritual beings whose issues and problems stem from forgotten decisions from previous "lives" and the stored negative mental energy that derives from them. Scientology training and counseling has as its goal to aid the devotee to regain his or her native spiritual abilities lost over the course of many lifetimes: One might say that it seeks *en-stasis*, a digging deep into one's self to locate the immortal center in its original, pure form, a secularized mode of seeking the God within us. Its critics view it as an unscrupulous commercial enterprise analogous to the way in which the Kabbalah Center is viewed by its critics (see above, pp. 287ff). "Bo" and "Beep"—they also called themselves "Do" and "Ti" (as in the musical scale)—were Marshall Herff Applewhite and Bonnie Lou Nettles. They believed themselves to be incarnations of individuals with a higher *sacer* consciousness—at one point they saw themselves as incarnations of the two witnesses in the New Testament book of Revelation—and when Nettles died of liver cancer in 1985, Applewhite became convinced that she had returned to that higher state from which they had both come and that she would return to claim him and their followers. He and his dwindling group of thirty-eight followers mass-suicided on March 23, 1997, with the arrival of the Hale-Bopp Comet, for "Bo" had asserted to his flock that "Peep" would be returning to take them "from the Human Level to the Next Level"(quoted, among other places, in the article by Bob Waldrep, "The Lost Sheep of Bo and Peep: Reaching for Heaven," on the Watchman Fellowship website www.wfial.org/index.cfm?fuseaction=artNewAge. article_16.—to a rendezvous (putting it in our terms) with the *sacer mysterion*—by

means of a spaceship waiting behind the comet. Jim Jones was a preacher who claimed to be an incarnation of Jesus, Akhenaten, Buddha, Lenin, and Father Divine. His Peoples' Temple, which claimed to offer a salvational path for humanity, in part because of its genuine interracial and multiethnic sensibilities, became notorious for the mass suicide-murder, through drinking cyanide-laced Flavor-Aid, of most of its nearly one thousand members in its commune in the Guyanan jungle in 1978.

3. Rabbi Schneerson is the fifth in a line beginning with his own namesake, Menachem Mendel Schneerson (known as the *Tzemach Tsedek*), who was the third in the ChaBaD line of leadership, making Menachem Mendel the seventh *tzadik* in the ChaBaD line.

4. *Rebbe*—or in direct address, *Reb*, followed by a name (thus, for example, "Reb Schneerson")—is an honorific, a Yiddish word derived from the Hebrew *rav* (which yields "rabbi" in English), essentially meaning "teacher."

5. She is his niece, according to some sources.

6. Having heard Yehuda speak publicly in 2005—a rambling presentation that offered a perfect wedding of structureless form and gobbledeegook content—I am more than comfortable with my conviction that he, at least, is a charlatan whose spiritual guidance can only serve those who possess a solid combination of strong spiritual yearning and spiritual and intellectual blindness and deafness.

7. David Klinghoffer, "How Kabbalah Is Like Brain Surgery," Beliefnet, 2004, www.beliefnet.com.

8. Philip S. Berg, *The Essential Zohar* (New York: Bell Tower, 2002), 5. The reader might notice that I have not included this work in my suggestions for further reading.

9. See chapter 5, p. 4.

10. Moustafa Gadalla, *Egyptian Mystics: Seekers of the Way* (Greensboro, NC: Tehuti Foundation, 2003).

11. A soon-to-be-published volume (that did not appear in time for a fuller discussion of it) by Gerald Epstein, MD, called *Living Kabbalah: Awaken to Spirit to Create Balance in Daily Life through Imagery* (New York: ACMI Press, 2008) offers an original and insightful synthesis of Practical and Esoteric kabbalistic thinking. The reader is directed toward producing self-generated images to effect general well-being and spiritual and physical healing (aspects of practical Kabbalah) as he or she transcends words (as esoteric Kabbalah does). Epstein's book suggests a means of connecting to the Other by more effectively connecting to the innermost self—thereby offering a quiet *en-stasis* as an effective *ek-stasis*—while treating Kabbalah both as part of its own history and as sharing specific common ground with other spiritual and even secular systems, East and West. I might also call to the reader's attention Mark Verman's *The History and Varieties of Jewish Meditation* (Northvale, NJ, and London: Jason Aronson, Inc., 1996), which combines a historical discussion with experiential offerings in translating aspects of the Jewish mystical tradition into contemporary terms.

12. I am leaving to the side somewhat earlier literary works that are directly based on and/or completely built around elements in the Abrahamic mystical traditions, such as Gustav Meyrink's novel *The Golem* or S. Ansky's play *The Dybbuk*. The first is simply a novelized rendering of the story of Rabbi Loew and his Golem; the sec-

ond is constructed around the Lurianic notion of how the immortal human soul functions—in this case, with unfinished business in the *profanus*, not only can it not finalize its journey into the *sacer* but also it inhabits someone else's body until that business is complete (see above, chapter 9, note 12). *Dybbuk* comes from the Hebrew "root meaning" to stick to something (as glue, *devek*, does; see chapter 9, p. 219). I am also by and large leaving aside contemporary novelizations and dramatizations of traditional mystical texts. But one certainly cannot fail to mention Peter Brook's marvelous rendering of Farid Ud-Din 'Attar's *Conference of the Birds*, trans. Akkham Darbandi and Dick Davis (New York: Penguin Books, 1986), as a performance work or Howard Schwartz's *The Four Who Entered Paradise* (Northvale, NJ, and London: Jason Aronson, Inc., 1995), a novella that offers a mind-stretching and poetic meditation—a modern midrash—on the journey into the *pardes* undertaken by Rabbis Ben Azzai, Ben Zoma, Elisha ben Abuyah, and Akiva, from which only Rabbi Akiva returned intact.

13. Jorge Luis Borges, *The Aleph and Other Stories, 1933–1969*, trans. Norman Thomas di Giovanni (New York: Bantam Books, 1971), 10–11.

14. Borges, *The Aleph*, 12–13.

15. Borges, *The Aleph*, 13–14.

16. Borges, *The Aleph*, 13.

17. Andre Schwarz-Bart, *The Last of the Just*, trans. Stephen Becker (New York: Bantam Books, 1961), 5.

18. Schwarz-Bart, *The Last of the Just*, 22.

19. Schwarz-Bart, *The Last of the Just*, 421–22.

20. Schwarz-Bart, *The Last of the Just*, 422. The last line, then, of Schwarz-Bart's novel might be said to pun on the ultimate theological question raised by an event such as the Holocaust: Is there in fact—and, if so, where?—an all-powerful and all-good God in a world in which 1.5 million children are incinerated? For many, the answer is both yes and no: "somewhere, I don't know where."

21. Cynthia Ozick, *The Pagan Rabbi and Other Stories* (New York: Schocken Books, 1976), 3.

22. Ozick, *The Pagan Rabbi*, 22–23.

23. Ozick, *The Pagan Rabbi*, 28.

24. Ozick, *The Pagan Rabbi*, 29.

25. Ozick, *The Pagan Rabbi*, 31.

26. Ozick, *The Pagan Rabbi*, 36.

27. See chapter 6, pp. 24–28.

28. See chapter 3, p. 33, and note 12 above.

29. For a fuller discussion of this and of the ways in which visual art functions on a symbolic as well as a straightforward level, see Ori Z. Soltes, *Our Sacred Signs: How Jewish, Christian and Muslim Art Draw from the Same Source* (New York: Westview Press, 2005).

30. They were intensely discussing this in each others' studios in the late 1940s and early 1950s. Their interest in the question of Jewish art and in Jewish mystical thought, especially that of Isaac Luria, was first presented in my 1984–1990 video course, *Tradition and Transformation: A History of Jewish Art* (Cleveland: Electric

Shadows Productions, 1990. In the late 1990s, the subject began to emerge for other art historians, notably Donald Kuspit. Please note that in this discussion, I have only been able to include a handful of artists and even fewer illustrations, due to the double complication of space considerations and image permissions.

31. See chapter 9, p. 200, and the discussion of Anselm Kiefer above.

32. And even that "name" is a circumlocution for the ineffable name of God known only to the high priest in the Temple in Jerusalem when it stood in the past and to the messiah who will arrive in the future.

33. I am thinking most obviously of the so-called Rothko Chapel next to the de Menil Museum in Houston, Texas, whose space comprises simply white walls adorned with large Rothko paintings.

34. Stuart Preston, "Sculpture and Paint," *New York Times*, April 26, 1959, X17; Martica Sawin, "In the Galleries: Morris Louis," *Arts* 33 (May 1959): 59.

35. For more detailed discussions of this, however, see Soltes, *Tradition and Transformation*, segment 9B; Soltes, "Jewish Art? Judaic Content? Representational? Abstract?" (1996 catalogue of the exhibition of the same name at the B'nai B'rith Klutznick National Jewish Museum); and Soltes, *Fixing the World: American Jewish Artists in the Twentieth Century*, (Hanover, NH: University Press of New England, 2003), Part II. In both of these last two volumes, one of the artists discussed at some length, David Einstein, not only refers distinctly to the influence of Louis's veil paintings on his work but also recognizes the Jewish mystical quality in both Louis's and his own painting. I have not included Einstein here due to space considerations.

36. Ellen H. Johnson, ed., *American Artists on Art from 1940 to 1980* (New York: Harper and Row, 1982), 31.

37. This idea is ultimately borrowed from Islamic art, in which the hand, known as the *hamsa* (the Arabic word for "five") serves as a protective amulet both because of its "fiveness" as a symbol of the Five Pillars of Islam and because of its "four-and-oneness" as a symbol of God's relationship to us (see pp. 300–1). Ultimately, we can in turn trace the upraised hand as a religious symbol—as a symbol of the connection between *profanus* and *sacer*—to traditions that predate all three Abrahamic faiths (see Soltes, *Our Sacred Signs*, 148).

38. In normative Hebrew letter numerology, *mem* = 40, *taf* = 400, and *resh* = 200, but she is following the Abulafian lead, of course, of eliminating all zeros, in which case both *mem* and *taf* = 4 and *resh* = 2. In *'or*, the letter used for the vowel "o" is the same as that for the consonant "v," for reasons beyond this discussion.

39. I am thinking of Sol Lewitt's wall drawings on the one hand and of the music of Phillip Glass (who happens, perhaps not incidentally, to be a "Jubu") on the other (see above chapter 10, pp. 276–77 and p. 311).

40. See chapter 8, pp. 168ff.

41. *Kristallnacht*, on the one hand, marked the first pan-German act of physical violence against the Jews of Germany, yielding scores of deaths and hundreds of injuries and countless damages to and destructions of synagogues, as well as to Jewish homes and shops. The Jews were required by the German government to pay the "replacement costs" for the damage inflicted on them. Ironically, though, Nazi ideology changed thereafter: A Jew on the street was safer from random hooligan violence than

before. Of course, that was simply because a more systematic and final solution to the Jewish problem was being worked out.

42. I am using Kiefer's spelling here. We recall that the ten *sephirot*, from *malkhut* to *keter*, are viewed in classic Kabbalah simultaneously as ten "aspects" of God and as a bridge between humanity and divinity. In the latter sense, they are viewed simultaneously as encompassed by humanity, so that it is only after one has ascended to and through the tenth *sephirah* that one approaches the endlessness of God—and (since they are also thought of as ten "aspects" of God), when one has "entered" the first *sephirah*, one is already ascending through the Other Realm toward pure Godness.

43. Kiefer's spelling is consistent with the German pronunciation of "z" as what in English would be "Ts" or "Tz," thus this is the same Hebrew word that I have been transliterating as "tzimtzum."

44. In a mid-fifteenth-century treatise, Leon Battista Alberti discussed how a painter can create the illusion that his flat surface is volumetric, thus that his two-dimensional image has three dimensions, by graphing out a series of diagonal—orthogonal—lines from the lower corners toward a meeting point in the middle of the horizon line that he termed the "vanishing point."

45. We must not understand that expansion in three-dimensional terms, as if there is a center and a periphery like that of a balloon in the Euclidean world. Rather, the expansion must be understood in four-dimensional terms (or more than four), in which every point in the universe may be understood to be the center, and the periphery is defined as a movement at an incalculable distance at the speed of light away from whatever point is the "central" point of view.

46. *Nihonga* (*ni-hon* is Japanese for "Japan[ese]" and *ga* means "painting") uses finely ground vegetable and mineral pigments suspended in washes, glazes, and emulsions. This yields a delicate and clear quality more reminiscent of illuminated manuscripts than of large paintings (at least until the advent of the chromaticists) in the Western tradition.

47. In Japanese architectural design, *shoji* refers to a screen that functions as a room divider, whether freestanding or as a sliding door, typically made of a wooden frame with transparent *washi* paper (paper made using fibers from the bark of one of several kinds of plant or tree) stretched over it. Fujimura has had to layer his pigments very delicately over such a material.

48. I am using the alternative transliteration for "kabbalistic" that the artist uses.

49. The *orans* (in Latin, "praying") position is one in which the arms are raised and the hands are held wide open with the palms out to receive the spirit of God (as opposed to what has evolved as a traditional mode of Christian and sometimes Jewish prayer, with the hands clasped together in toward the chest). The position has its origins in pre-Abrahamic religions, as evidenced in Phoenician/Canaanite visual imagery, for example, where the upraised arms of the priestess are directed toward Ba'al.

50. This is the Hebrew stage name of Matthew Paul Miller (b. 1979), a Jewish American musician who, after becoming a member of ChaBaD Lubavitch in around 2001, began to incorporate Hassidic themes into music composed in rock and reggae style.

51. The story's loosely based inspiration was the "discovery" of the so-called *Gospel According to St. Thomas* some time earlier and the controversy caused by that discovery with respect to early church doctrines and the very question of what constitutes divinely inspired writ and of who *decides* what constitutes divinely inspired writ.

52. An interesting discussion of part of this, specifically of the discussion of Catholic saints in film, will be found in Theresa Sanders' lively and insightful *Celluloid Saints: Images of Sanctity in Film* (Macon, GA: Mercer University Press, 2002).

Suggestions for Further Reading

Al-Qushayri. *Principles of Sufism [The Risala]*. Translated by B. R. von Shlegell. Oneonta, NY: Mizan Press, 1990.

Ansky, S. *The Dybbuk and Other Writings*. Edited with an introduction by David Roskies. New Haven, CT: Yale University Press, 2002.

Arberry, A. J. *The Koran Interpreted*. London: Allen and Unwin, 1955.

———. *Sufism: An Account of the Mystics of Islam*. New York: Harper Torchbooks, 1970.

Ariel, David S. *The Mystic Quest: An Introduction to Jewish Mysticism*. Northvale, NJ, and London: Jason Aronson, Inc., 1988.

———. *Kabbalah: The Mystic Quest in Judaism*. Lanham, MD: Rowman & Littlefield, 2005.

Attar, Farid ud-Din. *The Conference of the Birds*. Translated by Afkham Darbandi and Dick Davis. New York: Penguin Books, 1986.

Band, Arnold J., trans. and commentator. *Nahman of Bratslav: The Tales*. New York: Paulist Press, 1978.

Barks, Coleman, et al., trans. *The Essential Rumi*. San Francisco: HarperSanFrancisco, 1995.

Bell, Gertrude. *The Teachings of Hafiz*. London: Octagon Press, 1985.

Berg, Philip S. *The Essential Zohar*. New York: Bell Tower, 2002.

Bloch, Chayim. *The Golem: Legends of the Ghetto of Prague*. Vienna: Author, 1925.

Blumenthal, David R. *Understanding Jewish Mysticism: A Source Reader: The Merkabah Tradition and the Zoharic Tradition*. New York: Ktav Publishing House, 1978.

Borges, Jorge Luis. *The Aleph and Other Stories, 1933–1969*. Translated by Norman Thomas di Giovanni. New York: Bantam Books, 1971.

Bronstein, Leo. *Kabbalah and Art*. Hanover, NH: Brandeis University Press, 1980.

Buber, Martin. *Hassidism and Modern Man*. New York: Harper Torchbooks, 1958.

———. *The Origins and Meaning of Hassidism*. New York: Harper Torchbooks, 1960.

———. *Tales of the Hassidim: The Early Masters*. New York: Schocken, 1947.

——. *Tales of the Hassidim: The Later Masters.* New York: Schocken, 1948.

——. *Tales of Rabbi Nachman.* Translated by Maurice Freedman. Bloomington: Indiana University Press, 1956.

Burkert, Walter. *Ancient Mystery Cults.* Cambridge, MA: Harvard University Press, 1987.

Charles, R. H., ed., and W. F. Morfill, trans. *The Book of the Secrets of Enoch.* Oxford: Clarendon Press, 1896.

Chittick, William C. "Jami on Divine Love and the Image of Wine." *Studies in Mystical Literature* 1, no. 3 (1981): 193–209.

——. *The Sufi Path of Knowledge: Ibn al-'Arabi's Metaphysics of Imagination.* Albany: State University of New York Press, 1989.

Clark, J. M. *The Great German Mystics.* Oxford: Oxford University Press, 1949.

Clissold, Stephen. *St. Teresa of Avila.* London: Sheldon Press, 1979.

Cohn-Sherbok, Dan, and Lavinia Cohn-Sherbok. *Jewish and Christian Mysticism: An Introduction.* New York: Continuum Press, 1994.

Coleman, James W. *The New Buddhism.* Oxford: Oxford University Press, 2001.

Conze, Edward. *Buddhism: Its Essence and Development.* New York: Harper Colophon, 1975.

Corbin, Henry. *Creative Imagination in the Sufism of Ibn 'Arabi.* Princeton, NJ: Princeton University Press, 1969.

Cordovero, Rabbi Moses. *The Palm Tree of Deborah.* Translated by Louis Jacobs. New York: Hermon Press, 1974.

Cutsinger, James S. *Paths of the Heart: Sufism and the Christian East.* Bloomington, IN: World Wisdom Publications, 2002.

Dan, Joseph. *Gershom Scholem and the Mystical Dimension of Jewish History.* New York: New York University Press, 1987.

——. *The Heart and the Fountain: An Anthology of Jewish Mystical Experiences.* Oxford: Oxford University Press, 2002.

Dasgupta, S. N. *Hindu Mysticism.* New York: Frederick Ungar Publishers, 1967.

Dole, N. H., and Belle M. Walker, eds. *The Persian Poets.* New York: Thomas Y. Crowell and Co., 1901.

Dov Baer. *On Ecstasy.* Translated and introduced by Louis Jacobs. Chappaqua, NY: Rossel Books, 1963.

Dresner, Samuel H. *The Zaddik: The Doctrine of the Zaddik According to the Writings of Rabbi Yaakov Yosef of Polnoye.* London, New York, and Toronto: Abelard-Schuman Press, 1960.

Eck, Diana L. *Darshan: Seeing the Divine Image in India.* Chambersburg, PA: Anima Books, 1981.

Egan, Harvey. *An Anthology of Christian Mysticism.* Collegeville, MN: Liturgical Press, 1971.

Eliade, Mircea. *The Sacred and the Profane: The Nature of Religion.* New York: Harcourt Press, 1987.

Epstein, Gerald. *Living Kabbalah: Awaken to Spirit to Create Balance in Daily Life through Imagery.* New York: ACMI Press, 2008.

Epstein, Perle. *Kabbalah: The Way of the Jewish Mystic*. Garden City, NY: Doubleday and Co., 1978.

Fadiman, James, and Robert Frager, eds. *Essential Sufism*. New York: HarperCollins, 1997.

Firestone, Reuven. *Journeys in Holy Lands: The Evolution of the Abraham-Ishmael Legends in Islamic Exegesis*. Albany: State University of New York Press, 1990.

Flanagan, Sabina. *Hildegard of Bingen: A Visionary Life*. London: Routledge Press, 1989.

Franck, Adolphe. *The Kabbalah: The Religious Philosophy of the Hebrews*. New York: Bell Publishing Co., 1940 (a translation from French of the 1843 classic).

Furlong, Monica. *Therese of Lisieux*. New York: Pantheon Books, 1987.

Gadalla, Moustafa. *Egyptian Mystics: Seekers of the Way*. Greensboro, NC: Tehuti Foundation, 2003.

Gager, John. *Moses in Greco-Roman Paganism*. Nashville: Abingdon Press, 1972.

Gairdner, W. H. T. *"The Way" of a Mohammeddan Mystic*. Leipzig, Author, 1912.

Gibb, E. J. W. *History of Turkish Poetry*. Vol. 1. London, 1900–1909. Reprinted by Gibb Memorial Trust, London, 2002.

Gibb, H. A. R. *Mohammedanism*. Oxford: Oxford University Press, 1949.

Glotzner, Leonard R. *The Fundamentals of Jewish Mysticism: The Book of Creation and Its Commentaries*. Northvale, NJ, and London: Jason Aronson, Inc., 1992.

Goddard, Dwight, ed. *A Buddhist Bible*. Boston: Beacon Press, 1970.

Goldberg, Myla. *Bee Season*. New York: Anchor Books, 2001.

Green, Arthur. *Tormented Master: The Life and Spiritual Quest of Rabbi Nahman of Bratslav*. New York: Shocken Books, 1981.

Greenstone, Julius H. *The Messiah Idea in Jewish History*. Philadelphia: Jewish Publication Society of America, 1906.

Hafiz. *Fifty Poems*. Translated by A. J. Arberry. Cambridge: Cambridge University Press, 1947.

Halevi, Z'ev ben Shimon. *An Introduction to the Cabala: Tree of Life*. New York: Samuel Weiser, Inc., 1972.

Halperin, David J. *The Merkabah in Rabbinic Literature*. New Haven, CT: American Oriental Society, 1980.

Heschel, Abraham Joshua. *God in Search of Man: A Philosophy of Judaism*. New York: Farrar, Strauss, and Giroux, 1955.

———. *Man Is Not Alone: A Philosophy of Religion*. New York: Farrar, Strauss, and Giroux, 1951.

Hildegard of Bingen. *Scivias*. Translated by Mother Columba Hart and Jane Bishop. Mahwah, NJ: Paulist Press, 1990.

———. *Symphonia armoniae celestium revelationum*. Translated and with commentary by Barbara Newman. Ithaca, NY: Cornell University Press, 1988.

Hoffman, Edward. *The Way of Splendor: Jewish Mysticism and Modern Psychology*. Boston and London: Shambhala Publications, 1981.

Horodetsky, Samuel. *Shivhei HaBesht*. Tel Aviv: Dvir Publishers, 1947.

Ibn Al'Arabi. *The Bezels of Wisdom*. Mahwah, NJ: Paulist Press, 1980.

————. *The Treatise on Being*, T. H. Weir, transl. London: Beshara Publications, 1975.

Idel, Moshe. *The Mystical Experience in Abraham Abulafia*. Albany: State University of New York Press, 1988.

————. *Studies in Ecstatic Kabbalah*. Albany: State University of New York Press, 1988.

Idel, Moshe, and Bernard McGinn, eds. *Mystical Union in Judaism, Christianity and Islam: An Ecumenical Dialogue*. New York: Continuum Press, 1996.

Inge, W. R. *Christian Mysticism*. New York, 1899.

Iqbal, Shaikh Muhammad. *The Development of Metaphysics in Persia*. London: Luzac & Co., 1908.

James, William. *The Varieties of Religious Experience*. London: Fontana Library, 1960.

Jami, Hakim. *Lawa'ih*. With English translation by E. H. Whinfield and Mirza Muhamad Kasvini. London: Royal Asiatic Socitey, , 1906.

————. *Yusuf and Zulaika: An Allegorical Romance*. Translated by David Pendlebury. London: Octagon Press, 1980.

Johnson, Ellen H., ed. *American Artists on Art from 1940 to 1980*. New York: Harper and Row, 1982.

Jonas, Hans. *The Gnostic Religion*. Boston: Beacon Press, 1963.

Kamenetz, Rodger. *The Jew in the Lotus: A Poet's Discovery of Jewish Identity in Buddhist India*. New York: HarperCollins, 1994.

Kaplan, Aryeh. *The Bahir: A Translation and Commentary*. Northvale, NJ, and London: Jason Aronson, Inc., 1995.

————. trans. and commentator. *Sefer Yetzirah: The Book of Creation*. Northvale, NJ, and London: Jason Aronson, Inc., 1995.

Kapleau, Philip, comp. and ed. *The Three Pillars of Zen*. Boston: Beacon Press, 1971.

Kaufman, William E. *Journeys: An Introductory Guide to Jewish Mysticism*. New York: Bloch Publishing Co., 1980.

Khan, Hazrat Inayat. *The Complete Sayings*. New Lebanon, NY: Sufi Order Publications, 1978.

————. *The Heart of Sufism*. Boston and London: Shambhala Publications, 1999.

————. *The Inner Life*. London: Shambhala Publications, 1997.

Khan, Pir Vilayat Inayat. *Awakening: A Sufi Experience*. New York: Putnam Books, 2000.

————. *The Message in Our Time: The Life and Teaching of the Sufi Master Pir-O-Murshid Inayat Khan*. San Francisco: Harper and Row, 1979.

Klinghoffer, David. "How *Kabbalah* Is Like Brain Surgery." *Beliefnet*, 2004, www.beliefnet.com.

Lachman, Gary. *Rudolf Steiner: An Introduction to His Life and Work*. New York: Tarcher/Penguin Books, 2007.

Lane, E. W. *Manners and Customs of the Modern Egyptians*. London: John Murray, 1836.

Langer, Jiri. *Nine Gates to the Chassidic Mysteries*. New York: Behrman House, Inc., 1976.

Levin, Meyer. *The Golden Mountain: Marvelous Tales of Israel Baal Shem and of his Great-Grandson, Rabbi Nachman, Retold from Hebrew, Yiddish and German Sources*. New York: Behrman House, Inc., 1951.

Lings, Martin. *What Is Sufism?* London: Allen and Unwin, 1975.

Loewenthal, Naftali. *Communicating the Infinite: The Emergence of the Habad School*. Chicago and London: University of Chicago Press, 1990.

Lossky, Vladimir. *The Mystical Theology of the Eastern Church*. London: James Clark and Co., 1957.

Maimonides. *The Guide for the Perplexed*. Translated by Max Friedlaender. New York: Dover Publications, 1956.

McDermott, Robert. *The Essential [Rudolf] Steiner*. San Francisco: Harper Books, 1984.

Merton, Thomas. *The Climate of Monastic Prayer*. Kalamazoo, MI: Cistercian Publications, 1969.

———. *Contemplation in a World of Action*. New York: New Directions Publishing, 1971.

Meyrink, Gustav. *The Golem*. New York: Dover Publications, 1976 (published in one volume with Paul Busson's *The Man Who Was Born Again*).

Minkin, Jacob S. *The Romance of Hassidism*. North Hollywood, CA: Wilshire Book Co., 1971.

Mueller, Ernst. *A History of Jewish Mysticism*. Oxford: East and West Library, 1946.

Nathan of Nemirov. *Hayyei MoHaRaN (The Life of Rabbi Nahman of Bratslav)*. New York: Maznaim Publishing Group, 1965.]

Newman, Louis I. *The Hassidic Anthology*. Northvale, NJ, and London: Jason Aronson, Inc., 1987.

Nicholson, Reynold A. *The Mystics of Islam*. Bloomington, IN: World Wisdom Publications, 2002 (a reprint of the 1914 classic).

Olender, Maurice. *The Languages of Paradise: Race, Religion and Philology in the Nineteenth Century*. Cambridge, MA: Harvard University Press, 1992.

Otto, Rudolph. *The Idea of the Holy*. London: Oxford University Press, 1923.

Ozick, Cynthia. *The Pagan Rabbi and Other Stories*. New York: Schocken Books, 1976.

Padeh, Zwe, and Donald Wilder Menzi, trans. and intro. *The Tree of Life: Chayyim Vital's Introduction of the Kabbalah of Isaac Luria*. Northvale, NJ, and London: Jason Aronson, Inc., 1999.

Padwick, Constance C. *Muslim Devotions*. London: SPCK, 1961.

Pagels, Elaine. *The Gnostic Gospels*. New York: Vintage Books, 1981.

Parrinder, Geoffrey. *Mysticism in the World's Religions*. London: Oxford University Press, 1976.

Philo Judaeus. "On Curses," sec. XI, and "On Rewards and Punishments," sec. XV–XX. Loeb Library bilingual edition.Cambridge, MA: Harvard University Press, 1949.

Pickthall, Mohammed Marmaduke. *The Meaning of the Glorious Koran*. London: Allen and Unwin, 1930.

Platt, Laurence. *Conversations for Transformation*, www.laurenceplatt.home.att.net/ wernererhard/. 2006.

Prescott, Theodore L. et al. *Like a Prayer: A Jewish and Christian Presence in Contemporary Art* (Exhibition Catalogue). Charlotte, NC: Tryon Center for Visual Art, 2001.

Rabinowicz, Harry M. *Hasidism: The Movement and Its Masters*. Northvale, NJ, and London: Jason Aronson, Inc., 1988.

Rabinowitsch, Wolf Zeev. *Lithuanian Hassidism*. New York: Schocken Books, 1971.

Regardie, Israel. *A Garden of Pomegranates: An Outline of the Qabalah*. St. Paul, MN: Llewellyn Publications, 1978.

Rudolph, Kurt. *Gnosis: The Nature and History of Gnosticism*. San Francisco: Harper Books, 1987.

Rumi, Jalaluddin. *Masnavi*. Translated by E. H. Whinfield. 2nd abriged ed. London: Mevlevi Order, 1898.

Russell, D. H. *The Method and Message of Jewish Apocalyptic*. Philadelphia: Westminster Press, 1964.

St. Augustine. *The Enchiridion on Faith, Hope, and Love*. Edited by Henry Paolucci and translated by J. F. Shaw. New York: Henry Regner Co. (Gateway Edition), 1966).

St. John of the Cross. *Dark Night of the Soul*. New York: Dover Publications, 2003.

St. Teresa of Avila. *The Collected Works*. Translated by Otilio Rodriguez, O. C. D., and Kieran Kavanaugh, O. C. D. Washington, DC: Institute of Carmelite Studies, 1980.

Sanders, Theresa. *Celluloid Saints: Images of Sanctity in Film*. Macon, GA: Mercer University Press, 2002.

Schaya, Leo. *The Universal Meaning of the Kabbalah*. Baltimore: Penguin Books, Inc., 1974.

Schimmel, Annemarie. *Mystical Dimensions of Islam*. Chapel Hill: University of North Carolina Press, 1975.

Schneur Zalman of Liadi. *Likutei Amarim Tanya*. Bilingual ed. Brooklyn, NY: Kehot Publication Society, 1984.

Scholem, Gershom. *Kabbalah*. New York: Dorset Press, 1987.

———. *Major Trends in Jewish Mysticism*. New York: Schocken Books, 1969.

———. *The Messianic Idea in Judaism and Other Essays on Jewish Spirituality*. New York: Schocken Books, 1971.

———. *On the Kabbalah and Its Symbolism*. New York: Schocken Press, 1965.

———. *Origins of the Kabbalah*, Princeton, NJ: Princeton University Press, 1987.

———. *Sabbatai Zevi: The Mystical Messiah*. Bollingen Series XCII. Princeton, NJ: Princeton University Press, 1973.

Schwartz, Howard. *The Four Who Entered Paradise*. Northvale, NJ, and London: Jason Aronson, Inc., 1995.

Schwarz-Bart, Andre. *The Last of the Just*. Translated by Stephen Becker. New York: Bantam Books, 1961.

Sells, Michael Anthony. *Early Islamic Mysticism*. Mahwah, NJ: Paulist Press, 1995.

Shah, Idries. *The Sufis*. Garden City, NY: Doubleday, 1964.

Sherwin, Byron. *Mystical Theology and Social Dissent: The Life and Works of Judah Loew of Prague.* London and Toronto: Associated University Presses, Inc., 1982.

Smith, Margaret. *Early Mysticism in the Near and Middle East.* London: Sheldon Press, 1931.

———. *Rabi'a the Mystic.* Cambridge: Cambridge University Press, 1928.

Sobhani, Ayatollah Ja'far. *Doctrines of Shi'i Islam: A Compendium of Imami Beliefs and Practices.* Translated by Reza Shah-Kazemi. London and New York: I. B. Tauris Publishers, 2001.

Soltes, Ori Z. "Jewish Art? Judaic Content? Representational? Abstract?" Catalogue essay for exhibition of the same name. Washington, DC: B'nai B'rith Klutznick National Jewish Museum, 1996.

———. *Mysticism in Jewish Art* (Exhibition Catalogue). Washington, DC: B'nai B'rith Klutznick National Jewish Museum, 1996.

———. *Fixing the World: American Jewish Painters in the Twentieth Century.* Hanover, NH: Brandeis University Press, 2003.

———. "Spirituality into a New Millennium: Mysticism in Jewish Art." In *Spiritual Dimensions of Judaism: Studies in Jewish Civilization.* vol. 13. Edited by Leonard J. Greenspoon and Ronald A. Simkins. Omaha, NE: Creighton University Press, 2003.

———. *Our Sacred Signs: How Jewish, Christian and Muslim Art Draw from the Same Source.* New York: Westview Press, 2005.

———. *The Ashen Rainbow: Essays on the Arts and the Holocaust.* Washington, DC, and Baltimore: Eshel Books, 2007. See chapter 5, "Later Visual Art and the Holocaust."

Sperling, Harry, and Maurice Simon, trans. *The Zohar.* 5 vols. London and New York: Soncino Press, 1984.

Stace, Walter T., ed. and commentator. *The Teachings of the Mystics.* New York: Mentor Books, 1960.

Steiner, Rudolf. *Anthroposophical Leading Thoughts.* London: Rudolf Steiner Press, 1999 (translation of the 1924 classic).

———. *Mysticism at the Dawn of the Modern Age.* London: Rudolf Steiner Press, 1999 (translation of the 1925 classic).

Subhan, Bishop John A. *Sufism: Its Saints and Shrines.* Lucknow, India: Lucknow Publishing House, 1960.

Swedenborg, Emanuel. *Divine Love and Wisdom.* West Chester, PA: Swedenborg Foundation, 2003 (translation of the 1763 work).

———. *The True Christian Religion Containing the Universal Theology of the New Church.* New York: Swedenborg Foundation, 1946 (translation of the 1771 work).

Szarmach, Paul E. *An Introduction to the Medieval Mystics of Europe.* Albany: University of New York Press, 1984.

Tagore, Rabindranath, trans. *Songs of Kabir.* New York: MacMillan Co., 1916.

Teilhard de Chardin, Pierre. *Hymn of the Universe.* New York: Harper and Row, 1965.

———. *The Phenomenon of Man.* New York: Harper and Row, 1959.

———. *Eurythmy as Visible Speech*. London: Rudolf Steiner Press, 1984.

Therese of Lisieux. *Autobiography of a Saint: The Story of a Soul*. Translated by Ronald Knox. London: Fontana Press, 1960.

Thomas à Kempis. *The Imitation of Christ*. New York: Vintage Books, 1998.

Trachtenberg, Joshua. *Jewish Magic and Superstition: A Study in Folk Religion*. New York: Athenaeum, 1979.

Tuchman, Barbara. *A Distant Mirror: The Calamitous 14th Century*. New York: Random House, 1978.

Ugolino, di Monte Santa Maria. *The Little Flowers of St. Francis*. New York: Vintage Books, 1998.

Underhill, Evelyn. *The Mystic Way: A Psychological Study in Christian Origins*. London: Lighting Source, Inc., 1913.

———. *Mysticism*. Oxford: OneWorld Press, 1999.

———. *Mystics of the Church*. Harrisburg, PA: Morehouse Publishing, 1988.

Verman, Mark. *The History and Varieties of Jewish Meditation*. Northvale, NJ, and London: Jason Aronson, Inc., 1996.

Waddell, Helen, trans. and intro. *The Desert Fathers*. New York: Vintage Books, 1998.

Waite, A. E. *The Holy Kabbalah: A Study of the Secret Tradition in Israel as Unfolded by Sons of the Doctrine for the Benefit and Consolation of the Elect Dispersed through the Lands and Ages of the Greater Exile*. Secaucus, NJ: University Books, Inc., 1975.

Ware, Timothy. *The Orthodox Church*. New York: Penguin Books, 1981.

Weiss, Joseph. *Studies in Eastern European Jewish Mysticism*. Oxford: Oxford University Press, 1985.

Wiesel, Elie. *Four Hasidic Masters and Their Struggle against Melancholy*. Notre Dame, IN, and London: University of Notre Dame Press, 1978.

Williams, John Alden, ed. *The Word of Islam*. Austin: University of Texas Press, 1994.

Wirszubski, Chaim. *Pico della Mirandola's Encounter with Jewish Mysticism*. Cambridge, MA: Harvard University Press, 1989.

Wolters, Clifton, trans. *The Cloud of Unknowing*. Baltimore: Penguin Books, 1973.

Zaehner, R. C. *Hindu and Muslim Mysticism*. New York: Schocken Books, 1969.

———. *Mysticism, Sacred and Profane*. Oxford: Clarendon Press, 1957.

Index

Please note that names are listed as they are most commonly used or likely to be sought. Thus for example, "Meister Eckardt," not "Eckardt, Meister," but Abulafia, Abraham." All titles, unless commonly treated as if they are part of a name, follow the name. Thus "Ishmael, Rabbi," and Gregory XI, Pope," and Augustine, Saint." Words in Arabic, Hebrew, Greek, Latin, Persian and Sanskrit are italicized unless they are so commonly used as to be treated virtually as if they were English. Thus "Torah," but "*acedia*." Works discussed at some length, anonymously authored or best known by their own name are listed on their own (e.g., *Zohar*); works briefly mentioned and/or better known through their author are listed only under the author's entry.

About the Author

Ori Z. Soltes teaches in the theology and fine arts departments at Georgetown University, as well as lecturing in the National Associate Program of the Smithsonian Institution. He is former director and curator of the B'nai B'rith Klutznick National Jewish Museum in Washington, D.C. He was educated in classics and philosophy at Haverford College, in classics at Princeton University and The Johns Hopkins University, and interdisciplinary studies at Union University. He is the author of over 140 articles, exhibition catalogues, essays, and books on a range of topics, including *Our Sacred Signs: How Jewish, Christian and Muslim Art Draw from the Same Source*, and *The Ashen Rainbow: Essays on the Arts and the Holocaust*.

BREVARD COMMUNITY COLLEGE
MELBOURNE CAMPUS LIBRARY
3865 N. WICKHAM ROAD
MELBOURNE, FL 32935